MW01042791

# HIV AIDS
# Care &
# Counselling
## A MULTIDISCIPLINARY APPROACH

## SECOND EDITION

Alta van Dyk

Pearson
Education
South Africa

Part of the Maskew Miller Longman group

*I dedicate this book to everyone
who is infected and affected by HIV and AIDS.*

*Your courage, determination, compassion and hope
inspire us all.*

Pearson Education South Africa
Part of the Maskew Miller Longman Group
Forest Drive, Pinelands, Cape Town

*HIV/AIDS Care and Counselling:
A Multidisciplinary Approach*

ISBN 1 868 91078 4

© Pearson Education South Africa 2001

All rights reserved. No part of this publication may be reproduced, stored in a retrieval system, or transmitted in any form or by any means, electronic, mechanical, photocopying, recording, or otherwise, without the prior written permission of the copyright holder.

First published 1999
Second Edition 2001

Publisher: Hanli Venter
Editor: Roger Loveday

Artwork: Karlie Hadingham and Gawie du Toit
Book design and typesetting: Zebra Publications
Cover design: designworx


Printed by CTP Book Printers

# Preface

*The best time to plant a tree is twenty years ago. . . . The next best time is now.*
(An African proverb)

HIV/AIDS arrived on the world scene without warning. A mere two decades ago it was unknown — lurking somewhere, waiting for the right moment to ambush the human race. Today HIV/AIDS covers Africa in dark clouds of fear, uncertainty and suffering. The virus has destroyed the innocent hopes, desires and plans of countless numbers of people whose lives have been cut short by an unseen enemy. For those of us who live in Africa, it is a human catastrophe from which no single one of us in the region will be exempt because HIV/AIDS affects us all. This truism about the HIV/AIDS pandemic will become ever more evident and obvious as each month and year passes.

Never before in the history of the human race has one disease presented so many challenges and brought about so many unanticipated changes. Being HIV positive makes a tremendous impact both on the medical, psychological, social, spiritual, educational and economic life of the infected person, his or her affected others and the community as a whole. All this places a tremendous burden on the shoulders of health care professionals who need to offer HIV-infected individuals and their significant others complete and dedicated services which exceed the customary bounds of conventional medical care and treatment.

Each health care professional working in the field of HIV/AIDS needs to become a comprehensive caregiver, adviser, educator and counsellor in diverse cultural and social contexts. The term 'health care professional' — as used in this book — therefore includes everyone who cares for the physical, psychological, social, financial, educational and spiritual health of HIV-infected and -affected people. The purpose of this book is to make a small contribution towards the empowerment of people from various professions and backgrounds so that they can make a difference — and plant a tree of hope and health right now.

The book provides counsellors, nurses, social workers, doctors, caregivers, volunteers, educators and religious workers with the necessary knowledge and skills for counselling people about every aspect of life and practice that is relevant to HIV/AIDS. It goes into some detail about how to care for HIV/AIDS patients and how to create a safe and reassuring environment for HIV-infected and -affected people.

Because the book is multidisciplinary in its approach, it also deals with important issues such as behaviour change, HIV/AIDS education and lifeskills training for children, the traditional African worldview and AIDS, community home-based care, orphan care, bereavement, and the spiritual and emotional guidance of people living closely with the HIV/AIDS phenomenon. The last section deals with legal and policy issues. These will assist personnel managers to deal with and implement appropriate HIV/AIDS policies in the workplace. I trust that this book will not only help to prevent the spread of HIV, but that it will also help everyone concerned to become more caring and compassionate about those who have not been able to escape the consequences of being infected by the HI virus.

Each chapter of this book is prefaced by a short quotation from the poetic drama *Raka*, written in 1941 by the Afrikaans poet N.P. van Wyk Louw (1906–1970). I have used Raka as a metaphor for HIV/AIDS and the destruction and havoc it inflicts on individuals and the community.

Raka, half-human and half-ape, appears without warning near the village of Koki and his people. Raka uses primitive cunning, guile and brute strength to undermine the culture and very existence of the community. Everybody except Koki is afraid to resist Raka, and some of the villagers are even attracted and drawn to the beast's insidious primitive sensuality and power. The hero Koki, aware of the deadly challenge posed by Raka, ventures into the dark forest to confront him.

The quotes from *Raka* are translations of freely selected (and sometimes slightly adapted) passages from the poem. *Raka* has a tragic ending, and the work warns that beasts of unknown origin may at any time attack and destroy our culture, our integrity, our hopes, our community and our very lives. That is why I think *Raka* is an appropriate metaphor for the threats and challenges of the HIV/AIDS pandemic.

This book could not have been written without the support of my family, friends and colleagues. I extend my sincere gratitude to the following of my colleagues for their critical reading and other contributions: Letitia King and Gisela van Rensburg (Department of Advanced Nursing Sciences, Unisa), Matshepo Nefale (Department of Psychology, Unisa), Ida van Dyk (Department of Social Work, Unisa), Joan Orr (Department of Primary School Education, Unisa), Peet van Dyk (Department of Old Testament, Unisa), Nthabiseng Seepamore (Gauteng Department of Social Services and Population Development), Thomas Kekana (Educational Psychologist), and Mina Kekana (Remedial Therapist). My special thanks go to Hanli Venter from Pearson Education and my editor Roger Loveday, who — through their excitement and belief in what the book is trying to achieve — became good friends. To my soul mate, Peet — thank you for your unconditional love and support and for your patience with your workaholic companion. And to my children Jaco, Marlene and Ewald — yes, the book is finally finished . . . there will be time to go to the movies again.

Alta van Dyk

# Contents

*Please note that a detailed contents list is given at the beginning of each chapter.*

# Fundamental Facts about HIV/AIDS

**After completing Part 1 you should be able to:**

develop and present an HIV/AIDS awareness programme which conveys the following information to a target group (a target group may consist of people from widely differing backgrounds, interests, concerns and levels of education, such as, for example, schoolchildren, caregivers in community home-based care programmes, social workers, nurses, specialist interest groups, ordinary members of the community, and so on):

- the normal functioning of the immune system
- the effects of HIV on the immune system
- the way in which HIV is transmitted
- the clinical symptoms of HIV infection and AIDS
- the diagnosis of HIV infection from symptoms and from HIV test results
- the management and treatment of HIV-infected people

## INTRODUCTION TO PART 1

It is vital for AIDS counsellors to be very well informed about all aspects of HIV infection and AIDS, and to have the resources and motivation to keep abreast of the latest developments in this rapidly developing (and often controversial) field. One has to accept the fact that people will *always* ask AIDS counsellors very basic questions about HIV/AIDS — regardless of whether they function as psychological, spiritual, medical, marriage guidance, educational or social counsellors. Most of the care and counselling needs of HIV-infected clients directly or indirectly involve the effect of the virus on their lives. Part 1 of this book will answer most of the questions that you or your clients might have about HIV and AIDS.

**Chapter 1** offers a definition of HIV and AIDS and surveys the historical background to the contemporary HIV/AIDS pandemic. This chapter explains the unique characteristics of the HI virus and how it affects the human immune system.

**Chapter 2** examines how the virus is transmitted via sexual intercourse and contaminated blood and how it may be transmitted from mother to baby. It also explores important issues such as the problems disempowered women have in avoiding HIV infection, and the contribution of socioeconomic deprivation and various other social ills to the spread of HIV. The chapter surveys some of the latest developments in the continuing breastfeeding versus formula-feeding debate in Africa.

**Chapter 3** catalogues and describes the symptoms of HIV infection, AIDS and AIDS-related illnesses in adults as well as children. Because tuberculosis (TB) is the most serious and most commonly occurring opportunistic infection found in HIV-infected individuals in Africa, this chapter devotes special attention to the diagnosis and treatment of TB. Chapter 3 also emphasises how important it is for health care professionals who work in Africa to be able to recognise the symptoms of various other sexually transmitted diseases (STDs).

**Chapter 4** describes the diagnosis of HIV. Methods of testing for HIV are discussed in some detail in this chapter, and additional material is provided for health care professionals who have no access to HIV antibody tests. Suggestions are made as to how they might diagnose HIV infection and AIDS in adults and children by recognising the symptoms specific to this disease in Africa. This chapter also describes the different HIV tests (such as the ELISA antibody test, rapid tests, and P24 antigen and PCR tests) and basic concepts such as the 'window period'.

The management of HIV infection and AIDS is discussed in **Chapter 5**. Ways of determining the relative health of the immune system (such as procedures used to establish the CD4 cell count and the viral load in the bloodstream), along with methods of treatment such as anti-retroviral therapy, are also discussed. The use of anti-retroviral drugs for the prophylactic treatment of rape survivors, the prevention of mother-to-child transmission, and the management of hazardous occupational exposure to HIV (by needlesticks, for example) are also addressed in this chapter.

# 1 HIV/AIDS: Origins and Effects

. . . . . . . . . . . . . . . . . . . . . . . . . . . . . . . . . . . . . . . . . . . . . . . . . . . . . . . . . . . . . . . . . . .

*The coming of Raka*

*From across the water he stepped out, among the broken reeds . . .*
*and he laughed silently with white teeth showing — crouching, waiting . . .*
*and the great beast emerged suddenly and quietly from the warm slime.*
*And finally Koki's heart recognised that he had come to a boundary —*
*that he was enclosed by something dark and dull and strong.*

. . . . . . . . . . . . . . . . . . . . . . . . . . . . . . . . . . . . . . . . . . . . . . . . . . . . . . . . . . . . . . . . . . .

A few decades ago, a terrible disease, previously unknown to the human race, began to kill people in the most alarming and terrifying circumstances. It was as though some primeval beast had surfaced in the collective bloodstream of the human race. Wherever this microscopic beast appeared, it produced panic, fear, guilt, hysteria, accusations, excruciating suffering and always, in the end, death.

Now the beast has a name: HIV/AIDS. It is known to be a virus unlike any virus previously encountered by the human race. Its devastating effects are being felt all over the world, but nowhere more tragically than in sub-Saharan Africa, where by far the majority of all infections in the world occur. Today HIV/AIDS has become one of the most destructive plagues in the history of the human race. It is a monster which threatens to destroy human society as we know it because it has changed all the rules by which we live. Although we, as concerned human beings, often seem defenceless against this scourge, we should not despair because it is not yet too late to take decisive and practical steps to defend ourselves against the ravages of HIV/AIDS. But there is no room for complacency. Time is running out. The statistics look more and more frightening.

## 1.1   THE DEFINITION OF AIDS

AIDS is the acronym for Acquired Immune Deficiency Syndrome. We say that this disease is *acquired* because it is not a disease that is inherited. It is caused by a virus (the human immunodeficiency virus or HIV) which enters the body from outside. *Immunity* refers to the body's natural inherent ability to defend itself against infection and disease. *Deficiency* refers to the fact that the body's immune system has been weakened so that it can no longer defend itself against passing infections. A *syndrome* is a medical term which refers to a set or collection of specific signs and symptoms that occur together and that are characteristic of a particular pathological condition.

Although we use the term 'disease' when we talk about AIDS, AIDS, strictly speaking, is *not a specific illness*. It is really a *collection of many different conditions* that manifest in the body (or specific parts of the body) because the HI virus has so weakened the body's immune system that it can no longer fight the pathogen (or disease-causing agent) that invades the body. It is therefore more accurate to define AIDS as a *syndrome* of opportunistic diseases, infections and certain cancers — each or all of which has the ability to kill the infected person in the final stages of the disease.

## 1.2 HISTORICAL BACKGROUND TO AIDS

The first recognised cases of the Acquired Immune Deficiency Syndrome occurred in America in the summer of 1981 when a very rare form of pneumonia, caused by the micro-organism *Pneumocystis carinii*, and Kaposi's sarcoma (a rare form of skin cancer), suddenly appeared simultaneously in several patients. These patients had a number of characteristics in common: they were all young homosexual men with compromised (damaged) immune systems (Adler, 1988). Soon afterwards, a new disease, which undermined the immune system and caused diarrhoea and weight loss, was identified in central Africa in heterosexual people.

Initially, scientists and doctors were baffled because the causes and the modes of transmission of this new disease (called 'slimming disease' in Africa) could not immediately be identified. It was only in 1983 that it was discovered that the disease was caused by a virus which at that stage was known as LAV (lymphadenopathy-associated virus) and HTLV-III (human T cell lymphotropic virus Type III). In May 1986 the virus causing this condition was renamed HIV (human immunodeficiency virus).

At present there are two viruses associated with AIDS, namely HIV-1 and HIV-2. HIV-1 is associated with infections in Central, East and southern Africa, North and South America, Europe and the rest of the world. HIV-2 was discovered in West Africa (Cape Verde Islands, Guinea-Bissau and Senegal) in 1986 and it is mostly restricted to West Africa. All current indications are that while HIV-2 is as dangerous a virus as HIV-1, it acts more slowly. This only means that it takes longer for the symptoms of infection to develop in an HIV-2 infected person.

The history of the discovery of the HI virus is both interesting and controversial. Dr Luc Montagnier of the Louis Pasteur Institute in Paris, France, discovered HIV-1 in 1983. A year later Dr Robert Gallo of the United States claimed that *he* had been the first to discover the virus. What followed was a protracted court case about the alleged 'theft' by Gallo of Montagnier's virus, which had been sent to Gallo in good faith for research purposes. The bi-partisan feelings aroused by this court case were so intense that they threatened to undermine the 1987 bilateral talks between the French prime minister, Jacques Chirac, and the American president, Ronald Reagan. The issue was eventually resolved by a last-minute compromise which permitted both Montagnier and Gallo to be officially recognised as co-discoverers of the virus (Connor & Kingman, 1988).

## 1.3  THEORIES OF THE ORIGINS OF HIV/AIDS

There are many far-fetched theories about the origin of AIDS. These range from a belief that the virus was developed as an instrument of biological warfare to a view that the virus is being used by aliens from outer space to kill the people of Planet Earth!

A more sober view now generally accepted by scientists is that HIV crossed the species barrier from primates to humans at some time during the twentieth century (Korber, 2000). HIV is related to a virus called SIV (simian immunodeficiency virus), which is found in primates such as chimpanzees, and Macaque and African green monkeys. The virus probably crossed from primates to humans when contaminated animal blood entered open lesions or cuts on the hands of humans who were butchering SIV-infected animals for food. While the initial spread of HIV was probably limited to isolated communities who had little contact with the outside world, various factors, such as migration, improved transportation networks, socioeconomic instability, multiple sexual partners, injecting drug use and an exchange of blood products, ultimately caused the virus to spread all over the world.

**Enrichment**

### The HIV/AIDS epidemic — a grim picture

A decade ago, HIV/AIDS was regarded as a serious health crisis. Estimates from 1991 predicted that 9 million people in sub-Saharan Africa would be infected with HIV and that 5 million would die by the end of the decade. We can now see that the actual rate of infection at the present moment is three times higher than the projection made at that time. As the 21st century dawned, 71 % (24.5 million) of all the people in the world with HIV lived in sub-Saharan Africa. Africa's 12.1 million AIDS orphans represented 95 % of the AIDS orphans in the world. Of the 5.6 million new HIV infections worldwide in 1999, 3.8 million (about 68 %) occurred in sub-Saharan Africa — the region with the fastest growing epidemic (Joint United Nations Programme on HIV/AIDS [UNAIDS] Report, June 2000c). HIV/AIDS is now much more serious than a health crisis in Africa: it has assumed all the proportions of a total human catastrophe from which no person living in the region will be exempt.

If you want to obtain the most up-to-date information about HIV/AIDS in Africa as well as in the rest of the world, visit the UNAIDS website: http:/www.unaids.org. If you don't have access to the Internet, read your local papers, visit your local HIV/AIDS prevention centres, and get information from your government's health department.

## 1.4  THE HI VIRUS

AIDS is caused by the HIV or human immunodeficiency virus (see figure 1.1). The HI virus has a circular shape and it consists of an inner matrix of protein called the core, in which the genetic material (viral RNA) is housed. The core is surrounded by an outer layer of protein with numerous small glycoprotein projections on its surface.

Like other viruses, HIV can only reproduce itself inside a living cell which it parasitises for purposes of reproduction. HIV can therefore only live and multiply in human cells. But since *all* viruses possess this very same characteristic, what makes HIV so dangerous? The answer is that the HI virus does something that no other virus known to humankind has ever done: it directly attacks and hijacks the most important defensive cells of the human immune system, the CD4 or the T helper cells. As it does this, it slowly diminishes the total number of healthy CD4 cells in the body — thereby undermining the ability of the human immune system to defend itself against attack from exterior pathogens.

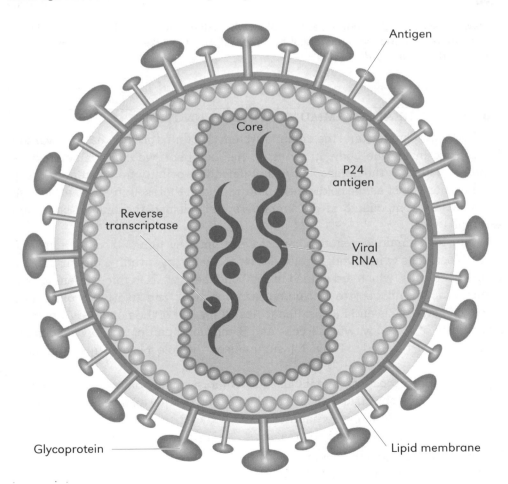

**Figure 1.1**
*A model of the structure of the HI virus*

The feature that makes HIV so effective in destroying human lives is the fact that *the defensive components of the human immune system (the CD4 or T helper cells) have no known way of defending themselves against the HI virus.*

We will now look briefly at how the immune system successfully defends the body against attack by *other* bacteria or viruses — viruses such as the well-known influenza or 'flu' virus (Evian, 2000; Gayton, 1971; Jaret, 1986; Selwyn, 1986; Weber & Weiss, 1988). When we understand the differences between how an HIV and an ordinary virus (such as the flu virus) function, we will understand (1) exactly how HIV is different from other viruses and (2) why the human body is ultimately defenceless against HIV invasion.

**Activity**

> Devise a series of transparencies to explain what AIDS is, what the HI virus looks like, and where it comes from (historical background). Try to make use of descriptive pictures rather than words.

## 1.5   HOW A HEALTHY IMMUNE SYSTEM FUNCTIONS

The best way to understand the immune system is in terms of a microscopic *war* that takes place inside the body. In terms of this metaphor, we can characterise the immune system as the *defence force* that defends a country from external threats and invasions. Just as the soldiers of an army defend their country from attack and invasion, the components of the immune system defend the human body from external attack.

The body's immune system comprises a complex system of blood proteins and white blood cells which work together to repel attacks by invading organisms. The white blood cells (which are formed in the bone marrow) form three different 'regiments', namely *phagocytes* (including macrophages), and two types of *lymphocytes*, namely T cells and B cells. Phagocytes form part of the *non-specific* defence mechanism of the body, while T cells and B cells form part of the *specific* defence mechanism of the body. Table 1.1 summarises the role players in the immune system.

While each of these 'regiments' has its own mission and defence strategy, they all have the same objective, which is to identify and destroy all invasive substances or organisms which might be harmful to the body. There are four phases in each immune response which the body makes:

Phase I:    Recognising the enemy
Phase II:   Strengthening the body's defence
Phase III:  Attacking the invader
Phase IV:  Halting the attack once the battle has been won

## Table 1.1
### 'Regiments' of white blood cells (leucocytes) defending the body

| First regiment | Second regiment (T lymphocytes) | Third regiment (B lymphocytes) |
| --- | --- | --- |
| • Phagocytes (spies)<br>• Macrophages (messengers) | • CD4 cells (T helper/general)<br>• Killer T cells (killers)<br>• Suppressor T cells (peacemakers)<br>• Memory T cells (record keepers) | • Plasma B cells (manufacturers of antibodies)<br>• Memory B cells (record keepers) |

The function of each 'regiment' (phagocytes, T cells and B cells) during the four phases of immune response is illustrated graphically in figure 1.2 on page 10. (In the explanation that follows, the numbers refer to the numbers in the illustration.)

## Phase I: The battle begins

**Phagocytes**, which may be called the 'spies' of the immune system, constantly 'patrol' the whole body (the bloodstream, tissue and lymphatic system). Their purpose is to identify any substance, object or organism that is foreign (and potentially dangerous) to the body. Phagocytes are also called the 'scavengers' of the immune system. When the phagocytes detect an enemy, they immediately try to engulf and destroy it. While phagocytes are usually effective in destroying chemical poisons and environmental pollutants such as dust, smoke and asbestos particles, they cannot destroy organic invaders such as viruses, bacteria, protozoa and fungi. Thus, when *organic* invaders (such as flu viruses) invade the body, the phagocytes send for the **macrophages** to help them to repel the invaders (these 'macrophages' are special types of phagocytes).

An important function of the **macrophages** is to mobilise the specific defence system which consists of the **lymphocytes** (i.e. the T and B cells). The macrophage achieves this defensive mobilisation by surrounding the virus and capturing a specific particle, called an **antigen**, from the invading virus. The macrophage then displays this antigen on its own cell surface as a 'captured banner or flag of war' (Jaret, 1986). This flag (the antigen) plays a critical role in the immune system's response: it alerts the next 'regiment', namely the **T cells**, to attack the invaders. (See encircled part in Phase I in figure 1.2.)

**T cells** are pre-programmed in the thymus to recognise the antigen (the 'flag' carried by the macrophage) by its shape. The antigens on the surface of the virus fit exactly into the receptors of T cells (like pieces of a puzzle). In the thymus, the T cells

## The definition of an antigen

An antigen is any foreign (or invading) substance which, when introduced into the body, elicits an immune response such as, for example, the production of antibodies that react specifically with these antigens. Antigens are almost always composed of proteins, and they are usually present on the surface of viruses or bacteria. When antibodies react to antigens, they can either destroy or de-activate the antigens.

'learn' to recognise all the antigens (puzzle pieces) that nature may create — and these occur in millions of different forms. Thus, for example, one T cell may learn to recognise (or fit) the antigen of the hepatitis virus, while another may recognise a certain type of flu antigen. There are even T cells which can recognise artificial antigens which have been manufactured in laboratories — antigens which the body has never encountered in millions of years of evolution.

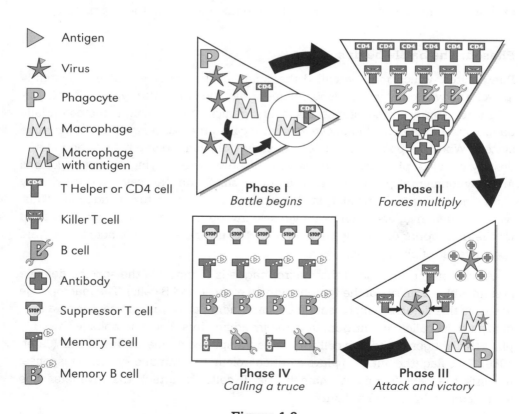

**Figure 1.2**
*How the immune system functions*
(Source: Adapted from Jaret, 1986, pp.708–709)

The type of T cell which recognises the antigen (or the 'banner' displayed by the macrophage) is known as **CD4** cells (these are also called **T helper cells**, or CD4 lymphocytes). The CD4 cells are the most important cells in the immune system, and can metaphorically be understood as the 'generals' or 'commanders' of the body's defensive army. These CD4 cells combine forces with the macrophages and so the next phase of the war begins.

**Enrichment**

**The role of CD4 cells in the body's immune response**

CD4 cells play a crucial role in the body's immune response. CD4 cells protect the body from invasion by certain bacteria, viruses, fungi and parasites; they destroy some cancer cells; they are involved in the production of substances necessary for the body's defence, such as interferon and interleukins; and they influence the development and function of macrophages and monocytes. Opportunistic infections can only overwhelm the body once the number of CD4 cells has become radically depleted (Evian, 2000).

## Phase II: The forces multiply

Once the CD4 cells have combined with the macrophages, they activate the remaining components of the defence system in order to mobilise its full capacity. Thus, as the CD4 cells begin to multiply, they activate more phagocytes and send chemical messages ('orders') to the **B cells** and **killer T cells** (T8 cells) — which are sensitive to the invading virus — to multiply. (See Phase II in figure 1.2.)

These **B cells** (or the third 'regiment') are located in the lymph nodes, and we may compare them to small munitions factories. The B cells then multiply and divide into two groups: **plasma B cells** and **memory B cells**. The plasma B cells manufacture antibodies which render invading organisms harmless by neutralising them or by clinging to their surfaces (thus preventing them from performing their function).

## Phase III: The attack and victory

While the immune system prepares its forces, the viruses penetrate some of the body cells (the only place where they can multiply). When they are ready, the **killer T cells** (with the aid of certain CD4 cells) destroy these infected cells by chemically piercing their membranes so that the contents spill out. This 'spilling out' interrupts the multiplication cycle of the virus (see Phase III in figure 1.2). Once the contents of an infected cell have spilled out, **antibodies** neutralise the viruses by attaching themselves to the viruses' surfaces, thereby preventing them from attacking other cells. This slows the progress of the invading organisms and makes them easy victims for

**Enrichment**

## The immune system explained to children

Let's imagine that the body is a very important mining company that has to be protected from nasty invaders who want to harm the company. Meet the security guys working for this very important company, which is called 'The Body'.

Mr **Phagocyte** (a type of white blood cell) is the company's spy. While he is busy chucking out dust and smoke particles, he spots a real nasty customer — the flu virus. Mr Phagocyte immediately calls the company's liaison officer, Mr **Macrophage**, to come and check out the situation. Mr Macrophage (another white blood cell) confiscates the invader's identity document (an **antigen**) and takes it directly to the most important person in the company — the director or the general, Mr **CD4**. Mr CD4 is a type of T cell (also referred to as Mr **T Helper Cell** because he helps to protect the body against dangerous outside forces).

Mr CD4 takes one look at the invading virus's ID document and immediately recognises the flu virus. He realises that his company is in trouble, and that he should immediately give the command to attack. Mr CD4 joins forces with Mr Macrophage and together they activate the body's defence system. They call more CD4 cells and phagocytes to the scene, and they send messages to the **B cells** and **Killer T cells** to join them.

In the meantime, the flu virus is hiding in the body's cells where it tries to multiply its own forces as quickly as it can. The killer T cells, with the help of some of the CD4 cells, drive the flu viruses out of their hiding places by destroying these hiding places (the cells). While this is happening, the B cells are working very hard to manufacture **antibodies**. These antibodies now grab the exposed flu viruses, cling to them, slow them down and make them easy targets for the phagocytes to attack and destroy. When all the invaders have been killed, the company can slowly begin to return to normal once again.

The last stage is in the hands of Mr **Suppressor T cell**, who is The Body's peacemaker. When he sees that the situation is under control, he orders the B cells to stop making antibodies and he simultaneously orders the killer T cells to stop their attack. The phagocytes clean up the litter of dead cells and other substances, and the body begins to heal.

But this incident will not be forgotten: **Memory T** and **Memory B cells** will always remember Mr Flu virus and any of his relatives if they ever again try to invade the company. These memory cells will recognise them immediately and stop them in their tracks. The company is therefore now immune to attacks by Mr Flu and indeed any kind of Mr Flu who has the same identity.

the **phagocytes** or the macrophages, which then come to 'digest' them. Antibodies also produce chemical reactions which can kill infected cells. When all the invaders have been destroyed, the war is won and all that remains to be done is 'demobilisation'.

### Phase IV: The cessation of hostility

Once the attackers have been vanquished, a third member of the T cell family takes control: the **'suppressor T'** or the peacemaker (see Phase IV in figure 1.2). Suppressor T cells release a substance which stops B cells from doing their work (namely the manufacture of antibodies). They also 'order' the killer T cells to stop attacking and the CD4 cells to stop their work. **Memory T** and **B cells** 'remember' the specific invader (antigen) and they remain in the blood and lymphatic system — ready to act defensively should the same virus once again invade the body. At this point, the 'war' has been won and the person will in future be immune to this particular virus.

It usually takes from a week to a few months to develop effective immunity against invading agents. While a person may therefore become very ill when he or she is first exposed to a disease to which he/she has not yet developed immunity, subsequent exposures to the same invading agent will quickly be countered before any damage can be done. Thus, for example, if the human body is exposed to minute (but non-fatal) doses of some types of dangerous invading agents such as tetanus toxin, the body will develop such an intense immunity against the toxin that the person will be able subsequently to withstand 100 000 times the normally lethal dose of the toxin without any ill effects. This example illustrates how extremely efficient the body can be in developing the kind of immunity it needs to protect itself against foreign invasive agents (Gayton, 1971, p. 118).

## 1.6   THE EFFECT OF HIV ON THE IMMUNE SYSTEM

When HIV invades the body, the macrophages attempt to do their usual job by capturing a particle (an antigen) from HIV. *But it is when the macrophages attempt to make contact with the CD4 cells to warn them about the invasion, that the real problem begins: the viruses attack the CD4 cells directly — a unique response that makes HIV so dangerous (and ultimately fatal) to human beings.* Figure 1.3 illustrates the life cycle of the HI virus and shows how HIV 'hijacks' the CD4 cell and 'forces' it to channel its activities into manufacturing more viruses. (Have a look at figure 1.3 to see how the HI virus invades a CD4 cell.)

The glycoprotein projections on the virus's outer layer attach themselves firmly to the outer layer of the CD4 cell (onto a CD4 receptor on the host cell wall) (see Step 1 in figure 1.3). The CD4 cell and the virus now join membranes (see Step 2 in figure 1.3). The virus then sheds its outer layer and enters the CD4 cell with its own genetic material (viral RNA) (Step 3).

In order to use the cell to manufacture more viruses, the HIV's viral RNA must be changed (or 'reverse transcribed') to DNA. The HIV itself carries with it an enzyme called *reverse transcriptase* (see Step 3) which it then uses to transform its viral RNA into double-strand viral DNA (Step 4).

The viral DNA then fuses with the host cell's own DNA or genetic material in the nucleus of the cell (Step 5), and makes numerous copies or replicas of viral RNA and viral proteins (Step 6). The protease enzyme enables this new viral RNA and the viral

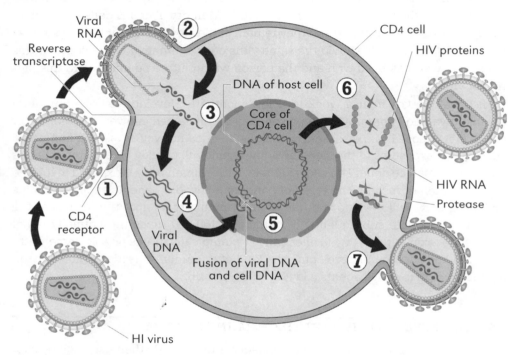

Step 1:  The HI virus attaches to the CD4 cell's receptors.

Step 2:  The CD4 cell and HI virus join membranes.

Step 3:  The HI virus injects its RNA (as well as reverse transcriptase) into the CD4 cell.

Step 4:  Viral RNA is changed into viral DNA through a process called reverse transcription.

Step 5:  The viral DNA joins with the cell's DNA in the core of the cell, causing it to produce more viral RNA.

Step 6:  The viral RNA produces more HI viruses.

Step 7:  The new viruses break free from the cell, killing it and infecting more cells.

**Figure 1.3**

*How the HI virus invades a CD4 cell*

proteins to merge and bud from the cell membrane as fully functional HI viruses — perfect replicas of the original HI virus that entered the cell in the first place (Step 7). As the new HI viruses bud from the cell, they kill the hijacked cell in the process. They then move out into the bloodstream or surrounding tissue to infect more cells — and repeat the whole process over again.

Although all viruses live and multiply solely in cells, HIV hijacks the most important defensive cell in the immune system (the CD4 cell) and turns it into an efficient virus factory to manufacture perfect replicas of itself. When this happens, the CD4 cells are unable to do what they would normally do when confronted by an alien virus, i.e. orchestrate and coordinate the body's defences *against* the HI viruses. Instead, they themselves are captured and forcibly turned into small factories to manufacture the very carriers of death against which they are supposed to defend the body (HI viruses).

Although several antibodies are formed during this process, they are completely powerless against HIV because HI viruses hide (completely undetectable) inside the CD4 cells while they subvert the cell for their purpose (to manufacture copies of themselves). The body is then left defenceless because the soldiers of the body's army (the antibodies) will certainly not attack and kill their *own* generals (i.e. the CD4 cells). One can also not expect them to function effectively without any orders from their generals.

**Enrichment**

**HIV is a retrovirus. What is a retrovirus?**

'Retro' indicates that HIV does the 'reverse' of what other viruses do. The normal transcription of genetic information in cells is **from DNA to RNA to proteins**. But the genetic information of HIV (and other retroviruses) is contained in RNA (rather than in the DNA — as in ordinary viruses). HIV uses an enzyme (reverse transcriptase) to transform its viral RNA into DNA in order to produce more viruses.

*Does HIV infect only CD4 cells?*

It is not only CD4 cells that HIV infects. The glycoprotein projections on the virus's outer layer attach themselves to CD4 receptors, which are present on various types of cells such as monocytes (a large phagocytic white blood cell), macrophages, tissue cells in mucous membranes (mucous membranes are found, for example, in the genital tract and anal-rectal area), and certain brain cells. Scientists were initially astonished by the presence of the virus in the brain because the blood-brain barrier usually prevents *all* foreign substances such as viruses from entering the brain. Because macrophages are among the few cells that move through the blood–brain barrier, researchers quickly deduced that HIV enters the brain by hiding in these very cells (Levy, 1990).

### *What do we mean when we say that HIV mutates very rapidly?*

Although HIV is a perfectly adapted killer virus, it has yet another extraordinary property which makes it virtually untraceable by the immune system. *HIV is able to mutate or change very rapidly.* The body's immune system relies heavily on its ability to recognise micro-organisms from their outer protein layer. Because HIV mutates or changes its outer layer so rapidly, it is extremely difficult to detect any similarity between the outer layer of one HI virus and the outer layer of another HI virus. Because of this rapid mutation, the body cannot defend itself against its enemy because its enemy is constantly changing its identity. (We may compare the virus to a thief who leaves different fingerprints every time he or she commits a crime.) This peculiarity of HIV (the fact that it rapidly changes its 'identity') is one of the reasons why it is so difficult to develop an HIV vaccine.

**Activity**

Explain the effect of HIV on the immune system to children. Expand on the story in the enrichment box on page 12 about the flu virus's attack on the company called 'The Body'. Explain to children what will happen to this company when it is attacked by an HI virus instead of a flu virus.

## 1.7   THE BODY'S RESPONSE TO HIV INFECTION

Different people (for reasons as yet not fully understood) respond differently to HIV infection. Some people remain healthy and active for as long as 10 to 20 years with little or no signs of immune depression, while other people deteriorate rapidly and develop full-blown AIDS within 5 to 7 years, or even sooner. There are many known reasons why HIV infection may progress more rapidly in some individuals than in others. Some of the reasons why people respond differently are: there are different strains of HIV (some are more virulent or active); when people are infected, they receive different dosages of the virus (larger or smaller dosages); different human bodies respond differently to the virus, and the general health status of the person concerned affects the course of the disease. People who are already chronically ill with illnesses such as malaria or tuberculosis (TB), and whose health status is poor because of malnutrition, poverty, recurrent infections, repeated pregnancies or anaemia, will experience a much more rapid deterioration than relatively healthy individuals who become infected with HIV (Evian, 2000).

## 1.8   CONCLUSION

Although scientists currently have a clear and precise understanding of how HIV destroys the body's immune system, all attempts to eliminate the virus completely from the body, or to make the human body immune to the virus, have hitherto failed. *At this stage therefore the only way to stop AIDS is to prevent transmission of the virus.* This is only possible when one has a proper understanding of exactly how the virus is transmitted from one person to another. The transmission of HIV from one person to another is the theme of the next chapter.

**This chapter at a glance**

· · · · · · · · · · · · · · · · · · · · · · · · · · · · · · · · · · · · · · · · · · · · · · · · · · · · ·

*Raka wants to enter*

*But now Raka kept close to the homestead, like a dog.*
*Around the kraal he sneaked with a sound like the rustling*
  *of small night animals.*
*A woman would sometimes turn in her sleep — restlessly,*
*and then suddenly cry out from lust and fear.*
*Because only half awake,*
*she knew that the beast was naked and prowling around in the dark.*

· · · · · · · · · · · · · · · · · · · · · · · · · · · · · · · · · · · · · · · · · · · · · · · · · · · · ·

HIV infection is transmitted primarily through sexual intercourse, when HIV-infected blood is passed directly into the body of another person, or when a mother infects her baby during pregnancy, childbirth, or as a result of breastfeeding. HIV has been identified in various body fluids but it is especially highly concentrated in blood, semen and vaginal fluids. Although HIV is present in saliva, tears, sweat and urine, the concentration of the virus in these fluids is very low.

## 2.1 HOW HIV IS TRANSMITTED THROUGH SEXUAL INTERCOURSE WITH AN HIV-INFECTED PERSON

HIV infection is sexually transmitted primarily through *unprotected* vaginal or anal intercourse (i.e. sexual intercourse without a condom), and (possibly) through oral sexual contact under certain conditions. HIV is transmitted when the virus enters a person's bloodstream via the body fluids of an infected individual. In order to gain entry into the body, the HI virus needs to connect to CD4 receptors, which are found on various types of cells such as macrophages and CD4 cells. Because many of the cells in the linings of the genital and anal tract have just such receptors, HIV can easily gain entrance into these cells (Evian, 2000).

Because the membrane linings of body cavities — especially in the anal-rectal area, and, to a lesser extent, in the vagina — are very delicate, they can be torn as a result of friction generated during sexual intercourse. Such (often microscopic) tears make it easy for the virus to enter the sex partner's bloodstream — either through the tears or by mixing with blood from larger tears.

Women are more likely than men to become infected with HIV during unprotected vaginal intercourse. HIV-positive women in particular are highly contagious during menstruation because of the presence of HIV-infected blood. The recipient of semen in anal sex (the passive partner) runs a greater risk of infection than the active partner because of the inflexibility of the mucous membrane in the anus. The mucous membrane that lines the anal-rectal area is easily torn during anal intercourse.

Individuals who have other sexually transmitted diseases (STDs) such as syphilis, gonorrhoea, chancroid and chlamydia are particularly prone to HIV infection. Research has shown that an untreated STD in either partner increases the risk of HIV transmission during unprotected intercourse ten-fold (World Health Organisation [WHO], 2000a). Individuals with genital herpes or genital ulcers or sores are especially susceptible to HIV infection because these conditions create openings in the mucous membranes through which HIV can move.

As we noted in chapter 1, HIV is attracted to the *immune cells* of the body. STDs cause genital inflammation and the inflammation attracts numerous immune cells with CD4 receptors to the site of infection. This of course creates ideal conditions for the HI virus to latch onto the CD4 receptors in and around the genital tract. Because of this relationship between genital infections and immune cells, it is five to ten times easier for HIV to enter the body cells of people with STDs — especially through genital ulcers or sores (Evian, 2000). The discharges produced by many STDs contain a very high concentration of HIV if that person is also HIV positive.

 *Why are women more easily infected by HIV than men?*

The risk of becoming infected with HIV during unprotected vaginal intercourse is two to four times higher for women than it is for men (WHO, 2000a). One of the reasons why women are more susceptible to HIV infection than men is that women, as the recipients of semen, are exposed to semen for a longer time. While semen remains in the body of a woman for a few hours, a man is exposed to the body fluids of a woman for only a short time. Because there may also be a higher concentration of HIV present in semen than in vaginal fluids, transmission to a woman is more likely. Woman also possess a larger surface area of mucosa (the thin lining of the vagina and cervix) which is exposed to their partner's secretions during sexual intercourse.

In addition, many women have cervical or vaginal conditions, such as STDs, erosions, open sores and infections, that facilitate the transmission of HIV. Apart from STDs, infection or damage to the vaginal walls is often caused by the use of herbal and other substances for the practice of 'dry sex' (see 'The dangerous practice of "dry sex"' on page 144). Spermicidal (i.e. sperm-killing) preparations may also cause allergies, irritation and inflammation of the vaginal walls. It was, for instance, reported at the XIIIth International AIDS Conference in Durban that spermicidal creams containing nonoxynol-9 are no longer considered safe for use.

Transmission of HIV is also more likely to occur just before, during or immediately after menstruation because of the large, raw area of the inner uterine lining that is exposed (Evian, 2000). Younger women are especially vulnerable to HIV infection because their genital tracts are not yet fully mature, their vaginal secretions are not so copious, and because they are more prone to vaginal mucosa laceraions (UNAIDS, 2000c). There is also evidence to suggest that women once again become more vulnerable to HIV infection *after* menopause (WHO, 2000a). Rape, rough sex, previous genital mutilation (female circumcision) and anal sex (which is often practised to preserve virginity and to prevent pregnancy) can cause tearing and bleeding and this further increases the risk of HIV transmission.

Apart from their biological vulnerability, women can also be vulnerable in societies which accord women a lower status than men. This lower status makes women dangerously vulnerable in sexual relationships because their low status means that they do not have the authority to express or enforce their needs. Thus, most women from poor (socioeconomically depressed) communities have little or no control over their sex lives. They are not in a position to negotiate safer sex practices because they fear violence and abandonment should they try to do so. The husbands of women from poor communities often have casual sex when they have to leave their families behind to find work in the big cities. Sometimes dire poverty and need drives women from such communities to prostitution because (ironically) this is often the only way they feel they can 'survive'. Their low self-image and lack of personal authority also make such women particularly vulnerable to rape. Young girls especially are often coerced, raped or enticed into sex by someone older, stronger or richer than themselves. It is well known that older 'sugar daddies' often offer schoolgirls gifts or money in return for sex.

A shocking report by the Medical Research Council of South Africa indicated that the majority of women in their study who reported that they had been raped, were raped between the ages of 10 and 14 years of age, and that schoolteachers were the perpetrators in 33 % of these cases. In many cases, the teachers threatened to fail the girls in their examinations if they did not have sex with them ('Verkragters is in ons skole', 2000).

 *Can lesbians get AIDS?*

Lesbians who have sex with women as well as with men, can contract HIV infection if they have sex with infected men. The risk of women who have sex only with women being infected is small — provided they do not have bisexual relationships. One of the ways in which lesbian women can contract HIV infection is by *sharing* contaminated sex toys (vibrators, for instance) for vaginal or anal penetration. Because sex toys can cause bleeding or irritation of the vaginal or anal lining, it is easier for the HI virus to enter the body if people use them or share them. When sex toys are used, they should be thoroughly cleaned and preferably not shared.

**Enrichment**

### Empower women with vaginal microbicides*

A major factor in controlling the spread of HIV would be a microbicide in the form of a vaginal cream. Many women are simply not in a position to insist that their partners use condoms because they fear rejection or a violent reaction from their partners if they do. What women ideally therefore need is a non-barrier method which they themselves can apply and control without their partner's knowledge. Researchers are currently developing an HIV microbicide that will directly target the virus and interfere with its ability to infect cells. The World Bank has recently announced that it will pay for and help to distribute a successful microbicide to developing countries once it has been developed (Wainberg, 2000).

*A *microbicide* is a substance that kills microscopic organisms such as viruses.

**Activity**

Develop a government programme that will educate women to make themselves less vulnerable to HIV infection. Start by listing the reasons why women are particularly vulnerable to HIV infection, then suggest how each of these factors can be neutralised.

*How many sexual contacts with an HIV-positive person are necessary before one becomes infected oneself?*

It is impossible to say how many sexual contacts with an infected partner/s are necessary before an HIV-negative person becomes HIV positive. Research on married couples, where the one partner was HIV positive, has shown that there is no correlation at all between the number of sexual contacts and the infection rate. While some partners may became infected after one sexual contact, others may remain uninfected after several hundred contacts. Several factors may contribute to the chances of contracting HIV infection after a single sexual act. Some of these factors are multiple sex partners, the presence of other sexually transmitted diseases (STDs), the viral concentration (or 'load') in the semen or vaginal fluids of the infected individual, trauma (or bleeding) during sex, and menstruation. In spite of all this, one should always keep in mind that *one single unprotected sexual contact* with an HIV-positive partner may in some cases become a date with death.

*Can one be infected with HIV through having oral sex?*

Oral sex (stimulation of the penis with the mouth, or stimulation of female genitals with the lips and tongue) may cause a person to become infected with HIV if the lining of the partner's mouth is exposed to infected seminal fluid or vaginal and rectal mucus — especially if the person providing the oral stimulation has sores, bleeding gums or inflammation in his or her mouth. (See 'General safer sex rules' on page 142 for methods of making oral sex safe.)

Enrichment

**Male circumcision and HIV infection**

Several studies have indicated that circumcised men are less likely to become infected with HIV than uncircumcised men (we are talking now only about men who never use condoms, i.e. men who have unprotected sex). One of the reasons for this may be that the skin of the glans penis usually thickens after circumcision. A study in Kenya among the Luo group, found that while 25 % of uncircumcised men were infected with HIV, just under 10 % of circumcised men were infected. A study of over 6 800 men in rural Uganda has suggested that the timing of circumcision is an important factor affecting rates of infection: HIV infection was found in 16 % of men who were circumcised after the age of 21 and in only 7 % of those circumcised before puberty.

A recent review of 27 published studies on the association between HIV and male circumcision in Africa found that, on average, circumcised men were half as likely to be infected with HIV as uncircumcised men. Although it seems as if circumcision (especially if it is done before boys become sexually active) does provide some degree of protection against HIV infection, the practical implications for AIDS prevention are not obvious or straightforward. Circumcision in Africa is part of various ethnic, religious and adult initiation traditions, and if the same blade is used without sterilisation between circumcisions on a number of boys, HIV-infected blood could pass from one boy to another.

Circumcision should definitely **NOT** be promoted as a way of preventing HIV infection because it is **NOT** a way of preventing infection. In addition, the belief that it is a way of preventing infection may cause ignorant people to abandon safer sex practices such as using condoms. Rumours already exist in many African countries that circumcision acts as a 'natural condom'. While circumcision may slightly reduce the probability of HIV infection, it certainly does not eliminate it. In one South African study, it was found that two out of five circumcised men were infected with HIV, compared with three out of five uncircumcised men. Relying on circumcision for protection against HIV would, under such circumstances, be a bit like 'playing Russian roulette with two bullets in the gun rather than three' (UNAIDS, 2000c, pp. 70–71).

*When is an HIV-infected person most infectious to other people?*

Although it is possible for HIV to be transmitted at any time during the course of the disease, HIV-infected people are considered most infectious soon after becoming infected with the virus (i.e. in the first 4 to 8 weeks during sero-conversion) *and* during the AIDS phase when the symptoms of full-blown AIDS appear. HIV-infected people are more infectious during these phases because the viral load in the infected person's blood is very high at these times.

. . . . . . . . . . . . . . . . . . . . . . . . . . . . . . . . . . . . . . . . . . . . . . . . . . . . . . . .

## 2.2 TRANSMITTING HIV THROUGH CONTAMINATED BLOOD

The HI virus can be transmitted from one person to another when a person receives HIV-contaminated blood in a blood transfusion, when he or she uses needles that are contaminated with HIV-infected blood to inject drugs, or when he or she is injured with blood-contaminated needles, syringes, razor blades or other sharp instruments.

### Blood transfusions and blood products

According to the World Health Organisation (WHO, 2000a), there is a 90–95 % chance that someone receiving blood from an HIV-infected donor will become infected with HIV themselves. All donated blood should therefore be screened for HIV antibodies, and blood that is found to be infected should be destroyed. The WHO states that all blood transfusion services throughout the world should observe the following three essential guidelines so as to ensure a safe blood supply: (1) All national blood transfusion services should be organised on a non-profit basis; (2) While there should be a policy of excluding all paid or professional donors, voluntary (non-paid) donors who fall into the category of *low risk* as far as infection is concerned, should be encouraged to come back regularly; (3) All donated blood must be screened for HIV, as well as for hepatitis B and syphilis (and, if possible, also for hepatitis C).

Blood products, such as Factor VIII (which is used for haemophiliacs), are heated to 60 °C and this heating process destroys the virus. It is unfortunately not possible to render whole blood safe by means of heating because red blood cells disintegrate at high temperatures.

Although blood is currently far safer than it was in the past, the 'window period' (the period *after* infection but *before* antibodies are formed) still creates problems for blood transfusion services. Because infected blood which is donated during the window period does not show up as HIV positive, it slips through the net and is therefore not destroyed. Although the risk of HIV infection via a blood transfusion is very low, there is, unfortunately, no such thing as 'no-risk blood'. It is therefore the moral and ethical responsibility of people who engage in high-risk sexual activities and high-risk drug-using activities not to donate blood. Blood transfusions should only be administered to patients when it is necessary to do so to save their lives. Under certain circumstances, it is possible for patients to donate their *own* blood for storage and later use during and after a scheduled operation.

The HI virus is also present in the organs, tissue or semen of infected donors. All donor products are therefore tested for HIV antibodies. HIV-positive people should be encouraged not to carry donor cards.

## Injecting drug users

People who share syringes and needles to inject drugs run a very high risk of being infected with HIV. In many countries outside Africa, drug injection is called the 'second epidemic' that drives the virus. In some countries (such as Georgia, Italy, Portugal, Spain and Yugoslavia) over half of all AIDS cases have been attributed to the use of contaminated needles when injecting drugs (UNAIDS, 2000c, p. 74).

HIV is easily transmitted when needles are shared because drug users usually inject drugs directly into their bloodstreams. In order to ensure that the needle has struck a vein, drug users first draw blood into the syringe before they inject the drug. A drop or two of blood always remains in the needle and it is this drop that is injected directly into the bloodstream of the next user. Because the virus is highly concentrated in blood, these tiny 'blood transfusions' of HIV-infected blood between drug users using the same infected needle constitute an ideal method for passing on the virus.

People who inject drugs not only put themselves at risk; they also put their sex partners at risk. It is estimated that nine out of ten cases of transmission of HIV among heterosexuals in New York City can be traced back to having sex with a drug user who receives drugs intravenously (UNAIDS, 2000c, p. 75). The problem of HIV transmission is aggravated by the fact that many people who inject drugs resort to prostitution to obtain the money they need to support their drug habit.

Although Africa (relatively speaking) does not yet have a very large number of people who use syringes for the self-administration of drugs, the authorities should not wait until it is too late before educating people about how easy it is to transmit HIV by sharing infected needles. Some African countries with less stringent border and harbour regulations than South Africa are very popular as points of entry for drug traffickers. South Africa itself is increasingly becoming a destination and transit point for drug traffickers, and so one may expect that intravenously injected drugs will sooner rather than later become a very serious problem in this country.

## Blood-contaminated needles, syringes and other sharp instruments

HIV can be transmitted though contaminated needles and sharp instruments in hospitals or in clinics where standards of medical hygiene are low. It can also be transmitted through tattooing, ear piercing and contact with infected blood at the scene of an accident. When indigenous tribal rituals require incisions to be performed on a person (as, for example, in circumcision or scarification), the people performing these operations sometimes use HIV-contaminated razor blades or other sharp instruments. This is an obvious way to transmit HIV. Traditional healers and their clients should be educated about the importance of using clean instruments to save lives.

### How great is the risk of HIV transmission when one person has been accidentally exposed to the blood of an infected person?

Nurses and other people who care for HIV-infected people are often concerned about the risk of contracting HIV. All known cases of HIV transmission in health care settings have occurred in the context of **accidents**, i.e. occasions when a health care professional has been accidentally exposed to infected blood and/or other body fluids in a way that permits transmission of the virus. Examples of such accidents are occasions:

- when a person is accidentally pierced with a needle containing blood from an infected patient (a needlestick injury)
- when a person is cut by a scalpel, glass or other sharp instrument that is contaminated with infected blood
- when a person makes prolonged contact with an infected person's blood without the use of gloves
- when a person whose skin is chapped, has abrasions, or is affected by dermatitis is exposed to large amounts of HIV-infected blood
- when HIV-infected blood accidentally splashes into the eyes or mouth of the caregiver (Centers for Disease Control [CDC], 1989; Lusby, 1988)

The average risk of HIV infection following a percutaneous ('through the skin') exposure to HIV-infected blood is 0,3 % (or approximately one chance out of 300). The risk of HIV infection after a needlestick injury with an HIV-contaminated *hollow-bore* needle is approximately 0,37 %. There is a lower risk of being infected after a needlestick from a solid needle (such as a suture needle) or after being cut by scalpel blades than after a needlestick from a hollow-bore needle. Splashes of blood or body fluids contaminated with blood, semen, or vaginal fluids in the eyes or mouth of the caregiver, carry a considerably lower risk, i.e. about 0,1 % or less (Schoub, 1997a; 'Update', 1996). While the above statistics show that accidental exposure to HIV-infected blood does not necessarily lead to infection, it is understandable that such statistics are not reassuring to people who have been exposed to the virus in any of these ways.

The risk of HIV transmission may however be higher if an injury involves large volumes of blood (as would be the case with a deeply penetrating wound), if the needle has been in the vein or artery of the HIV-infected person, or if the viral load in the blood is high (as is the case in pre-terminal AIDS patients or during acute sero-conversion illness). (See 'Management of occupational exposure to HIV' on page 73.)

Health care personnel should note that any serous fluid (the yellowish protein-rich liquid which separates from coagulated blood), amniotic (pregnancy) fluid, cerebro-spinal fluid (CSF), pleural (chest) fluid, as well as fluid from the abdomen, heart and joints are all as infectious as HIV-infected blood when a person is HIV positive.

**Enrichment**

**Hepatitis B and HIV: which is more infectious?**

While all health care professionals are (quite rightly) afraid of HIV infection, some may be unaware of the risks posed by hepatitis B. Hepatitis B is a blood-borne viral infection of the liver which is caused by the hepatitis B virus (HBV). HBV is transmitted in the same way as HIV, namely through sexual contact, needle-sharing, the infection of a baby by its mother, and through contaminated blood or blood products. As with HIV, HBV is not transmitted by casual contact (like shaking hands, sharing eating utensils, etc.).

The occupational risk of both HIV and HBV infection is directly proportional to the degree of contact that a health care professional has had with infected blood or blood products. While this is true for both diseases, the fact remains that the risk of transmission is much greater for hepatitis B than it is for HIV when a person is exposed to the same volume of blood infected with both diseases. While the chances of becoming infected by a single exposure to HIV-infected blood after a needlestick injury with an HIV-infected needle is 0,37 %, the danger of HBV transmission under similar circumstances ranges between 20 % and 40 %.

Although most people recover from hepatitis B in about six months, others may continue to suffer from chronic infections, severe liver problems, cirrhosis, cancer or even acute fatal liver failure. Health care professionals should therefore be extremely cautious when they handle body fluids if they wish to prevent themselves from being infected by both HIV and HBV. One of the important differences between HIV infection and hepatitis B is that hepatitis B is preventable through vaccination. Health care professionals who work in situations in which they are exposed to blood and body fluids, should insist on being vaccinated against hepatitis B. (Three doses of Engerix-B confer a protection that lasts for about 3 to 5 years. This vaccine is readily available at most pharmacies.)

*What quantity of infected blood needs to be present before HIV is transmitted?*

It is impossible to say exactly how much blood is required to transmit HIV. Obviously, the risk of infection is directly proportionate to the concentration of HIV (the viral load) in the blood. Recently infected individuals with acute sero-conversion illness as well as patients in the final stage of infection (AIDS) usually have very high viral levels in their blood. It stands to reason that the higher the concentration of HIV in the blood, the lower the quantity of blood that is needed to transmit the virus. Because it is impossible to tell just by looking at a person how high the concentration of HIV is in his or her blood, or indeed even whether a person is infected or not, one should always follow the golden rule: **Always take proper precautions when handling blood and any other body fluids.**

 *For how long can the virus survive outside the body?*

We should distinguish between the lifespan of HIV when (1) it is outside the body *and* outside body fluids, and (2) when it is outside the body but still present in body fluids like blood. As soon as the HI virus is no longer in the context of a body fluid, it becomes extremely fragile — especially when it is exposed to oxygen, heat and dryness in the atmosphere. While HIV cannot survive outside body fluids for very long, it can probably live outside the body for many hours so long as it remains in some or other body fluid like blood. Body fluid spills should always be handled with extreme care. One should always take proper precautions when handling blood or body fluids that contain visible blood. (See 'Cleaning up blood and other body fluid spills' on page 355 for methods of cleaning up body fluid spills.)

## 2.3   MOTHER-TO-CHILD TRANSMISSION OF HIV (MTCT)

Mother-to-child transmission (MTCT) of HIV is one of the major causes of HIV infection in children. It is estimated that about 600 000 children are infected in this way each year (this figure accounts for 90 % of HIV infection in children) (WHO, 2000a). Unless preventative measures are taken, up to 40 % of children born to HIV-positive women are infected. HIV can be transmitted from an infected mother to her baby either via the placenta during pregnancy, through blood contamination during childbirth, or through breastfeeding.

### Pregnancy and childbirth

More than 60 % of the cases of transmission of HIV infection in pregnancy occur during labour and delivery. A woman is more likely to transmit the virus to her foetus during pregnancy if she becomes infected just before or during pregnancy, or if she has an HIV-related illness or full-blown AIDS (the last phase of the infection). The reason why the mother is more infectious at these times is because the HIV viral load is usually very high and the CD4 cell count is low during sero-conversion and when an individual is ill with AIDS.

Mother-to-child transmission during labour can be reduced:

1. by using anti-retroviral therapy for mother and baby (see 'The use of anti-retroviral therapy in the prevention of maternal-foetal transmission' on page 73);
2. by vaginal cleansing (disinfection of the birth channel with an antiseptic solution such as 0,25 % chlorhexidine during vaginal examinations);
3. by avoiding unnecessary rupture of the membranes;
4. by avoiding an episiotomy when it is not absolutely necessary;
5. by minimising trauma to the foetus (e.g. by avoiding procedures such as foetal scalp monitoring, forceps delivery, vacuum extraction — each of which may cause minor skin lacerations); and
6. by carrying out a Caesarian section if possible (Evian, 2000).

**Enrichment**

**Re-infection with HIV should be avoided**

HIV-infected individuals often think that they do not have to protect themselves against re-infections with HIV. It is, however, very important for an HIV-infected person to protect himself or herself against re-infections with HIV. While each new infection can cause an increase in the viral load in the blood, the person infected for a second or subsequent time may even become infected with a new strain of the virus. HIV-infected pregnant women should always use condoms to prevent re-infection. Any new HIV infection during pregnancy or breastfeeding is likely to result in an increase in the viral load, and this will increase the likelihood of MTCT. Re-infection may also cause the mother's disease to progress more rapidly.

## Breastfeeding

About 30 % of the babies who are infected through MTCT contracted the virus through breastfeeding (WHO, 2000a). The baby might be at greater risk from breastfeeding if the mother was infected with HIV late in her pregnancy or in the months following birth because of the higher virus count during the sero-conversion phase of infection. Women are also more infective when they show symptoms of AIDS (Visagie, 1999). MTCT from breastfeeding can, however, occur at any time during feeding. What increases this risk even more is the fact that between 80 % and 90 % of women in rural and remote areas in Africa, breastfeed their babies for as long as two years. Some African studies have shown that breastfeeding increases the risk of infection by between 12 % and 43 %.

Factors that may also affect MTCT during breastfeeding are a vitamin A deficiency in the mother or child, breast diseases such as mastitis, cracked nipples, and diseases such as thrush and gastroenteritis in the infant.

The breastfeeding versus formula (bottle) feeding debate in Africa revolves around very complex issues. These issues are based on the following facts: formula milk may not be readily available in poor communities; mothers may not have access to clean and safe water supplies wherewith to prepare the feed; mothers may not know how to sterilise bottles; mothers may not know how to prepare the formula milk (i.e. what the correct powder-to-water ratio should be); mothers may be ignorant of the fact that they should use clean, boiled and cooled water for formula feeding. Some mothers may also not know that they will compromise the baby's health if they add more water (increase the water in the water-powder ratio) in an attempt to save money.

**Enrichment**

### Breast milk research

**The exclusive breastfeeding versus the mixed breastfeeding debate:** The dilemma of whether mothers should exclusively breastfeed their babies or combine breast-feeding with giving the baby other fluids and foods was extensively debated at the XIIIth International AIDS conference in Durban (2000). Some researchers recommended that mothers who cannot afford formula milk should exclusively breastfeed their babies for six months. This means in effect that the baby will not receive any other fluids or food to supplement the mother's breast milk. Studies have shown that HIV infection was significantly lower in babies who were exclusively breastfed than in babies who received mixed feeds.

It is hypothesised that babies who are mixed-fed are more vulnerable to the HI virus because feeds other than breast milk may disturb the lining of the gastro-intestinal tract (or gut), and a disturbed gastro-intestinal tract facilitates the entry of the HI virus into the baby's system. The studies recommend that breastfeeding be abruptly and totally terminated after six months (without any weaning period) because the positive effects of exclusive breastfeeding are reversed after six months, making infection once more a danger.

The debate, however, is far from closed, and health care professionals should keep themselves abreast of the latest research developments. The personal circumstances of each individual mother should also always be taken into account before any advice about what she might do is given to her.

**Expression and pasteurisation of breast milk:** Mother-to-child transmission of HIV may also be prevented if breast milk is expressed and 'pasteurised'. Researchers at the Kalafong Hospital in South Africa are investigating methods of pasteurising infected breast milk, which would render the HI virus inactive. Pasteurisation usually occurs at temperatures of between 56 °C and 62 °C. The HI virus is inactivated at these temperatures because its protein structure is broken down.

The following method is one of the methods that researchers from Kalafong Hospital propose for sterilising HIV-infected mother's milk. The mother boils 500 ml of water in an aluminium pot. After the water has reached boiling point, the mother takes the pot off the stove and places a glass container (such as, for example, a clean peanut butter bottle) containing her expressed milk into the pot. As soon as the glass container is placed into the water, the temperature of the water begins to cool down while the temperature of the milk begins to rise to about 60 °C — the ideal temperature for pasteurisation to take place (Jeffery, Webber & Mokhondo, 2000).

The World Health Organisation still recommends breastfeeding in poor countries to prevent babies from dying from gastroenteritis and malnutrition. The health care professional should take all the circumstances of each mother into account before she makes a decision about whether to advise a mother to breastfeed or feed from a bottle. She should also consider the health status of the other children in the area where the mother lives. If other children in the community are at risk, or are already dying, from infections (such as respiratory infections or diarrhoea) and if they are suffering from poor nutrition, it is probably safer for the mother to breastfeed her baby.

The whole question of bottle feeding should be handled very sensitively in Africa. Since mothers usually breastfeed in public, they are often stigmatised as being HIV positive when they do not breastfeed their babies.

> The decision to breastfeed her baby or feed her baby with formula milk from a bottle should always (in the last analysis) be the mother's own decision. Health care professionals should give mothers all the information and advice they need to make their own informed choice. Never decide for other people what they should do: inform them as best you can and then trust them to make the right decision for their circumstances.

### Birth control for HIV-infected women

Condoms are an ideal form of contraception because they also prevent HIV transmission during sexual intercourse. Women who use other contraceptives (such as the pill) must understand that these contraceptives do not prevent HIV infection and that they may infect their sexual partners if they do not use condoms as well. Intra-uterine contraceptive devices (IUCDs) are not recommended for HIV-infected women because they sometimes cause pelvic inflammations. The string of the IUCD may also cause minor abrasions to her partner's penis and this may facilitate HIV transmission to the partner. IUCDs may also increase menstrual blood flow and the chance of HIV transmission (Evian, 2000, p. 208). Mothers who breastfeed should be encouraged to use condoms to prevent re-infection and MTCT through breast milk.

**Activity**

- Design a wall poster for a rural clinic to illustrate how HIV is transmitted. Take into account the fact that because 85 % of the population who are served by this clinic are illiterate, they cannot read.
- Advise an HIV-infected mother, who lives in an informal settlement many kilometres from the nearest clinic, on the best way to feed her newborn baby.

## 2.4   THE TRANSMISSION OF HIV INFECTION TO CHILDREN

Apart from being infected with HIV in the uterus, during labour or after birth through breast milk, infants and children may also be infected by the following practices or procedures that transmit HIV (WHO, 2000a, p. 5-1):

- transfusion with HIV-contaminated blood or blood products
- the use of non-sterile equipment in health care facilities
- the use of non-sterile equipment by traditional healers (e.g. in surgeries, or during the processes of male and female circumcisions or scarification)
- sexual abuse
- needle-sharing between drug addicts
- sexual initiation practices involving sex workers
- child prostitution

## 2.5   MYTHS ABOUT THE TRANSMISSION OF HIV

More than two decades of practical experience and research into the epidemic have shown that HIV is NOT transmitted through:

- airborne routes such as coughing and sneezing (with the precaution that, in the case of tuberculosis, a mask should be worn when the sputum contains blood)
- casual skin contact such as handshaking, hugging and touching
- sharing food, water, plates, cups, spoons, toilet seats, showers or baths with an HIV-infected individual
- sharing clothing, towels and bed linen with an infected individual — provided that the linen is clean
- public swimming pools. (Chlorine destroys and water dilutes the virus.)
- pets or insects such as mosquitoes, bedbugs and moths. (Distribution patterns of AIDS in Africa show that young children who are bitten by mosquitoes do *not* contract HIV infection. A mosquito furthermore usually obtains its entire meal from a single person. If a mosquito is disturbed and flies to another person, it will suck blood *out* rather than inject it.)
- playing team sports — provided that there is no contact with blood
- restaurants and cafeterias. (Exposure to heat, air, salad dressings and gastric juices destroys the HI virus.)
- sharing telephones, drinking fountains and public transport with HIV-infected people
- physical contact such as hugging and comforting an HIV-infected person
- living with an AIDS patient and sharing household equipment. Research shows that the people living with an AIDS patient do not contract the disease if they take the necessary precautions, such as adhering to the rules of basic hygiene,

abstaining from sharing razors and toothbrushes (a person may have bleeding gums) and avoiding contact with body fluids

- social contact between schoolchildren and sharing school facilities (provided that practices such as the mingling of blood by gang members are avoided)

- normal (dry) kissing. (The virus occurs in very low concentrations in saliva and a dry kiss or a kiss in greeting appears to be safe. People should be warned to avoid French or deep kissing if there are sores or punctures in the oral cavity that occur, for example, when a person has bleeding gums.)

- donating blood. Although HIV can be transmitted through blood transfusions or through receiving infected blood, there is no way that a person can become infected through the process of *donating* or *giving* blood — provided that the instruments used during the process are clean.

There are some truly horrifying myths that are circulating in some communities about how to avoid HIV infection and AIDS. These myths are extremely dangerous and should be counteracted in our society by means of intensive public education. Some people (for example) erroneously believe that they will not get AIDS (or that AIDS can actually be cured) if they have sex (1) with very fat women (they evidently don't have the 'slimming disease'), (2) with virgins, (3) with girls younger than 12 years of age, or (4) with very young boys. Beliefs like these can be the cause of abhorrent criminal behaviour and can also cause HIV infection to spread like wildfire.

It is unnecessarily stressful to live with all types of unfounded fears about AIDS. We should once again remember that the virus is transmitted ONLY when body fluids are exchanged in sexual intercourse or when a person is exposed to contact with HIV-contaminated blood.

**Enrichment**

**Depressed socioeconomic conditions and poverty as contributory factors to the spread of HIV infection**

HIV/AIDS and other sexually transmitted diseases are often more common in socioeconomically depressed communities where high levels of unemployment force men to migrate to the cities, where the traditionally low status of women does not give women the authority to negotiate safe sex practices, where extreme poverty often forces women to sell their bodies for sexual purposes in order to obtain money to survive, where living conditions are calamitous and access to health services is either intermittent or non-existent, where ignorance, illiteracy and poor education are widespread, where alcohol abuse (which lowers thresholds of inhibition and so compromises sensible decision making) is rife, and where the old traditions that created cohesion and mutual help in communities have either been undermined or have disappeared altogether.

**Activity**

Organise a discussion group at work or in your community to discuss the following topics:
- The psychological function of myths and urban legends. Why do we share myths and urban legends with each other? How do they make us feel?
- Share a few generally believed myths or urban legends with each other. These myths may concern AIDS or any burning issue in your community.
- Discuss each myth or urban legend objectively and discuss the reasons why the myth is not true.

## 2.6  CONCLUSION

AIDS is a very serious disease that devastates both individuals and societies alike. Fortunately we now know exactly how the virus is spread and what we can do to prevent and manage HIV infection. We can help to prevent the spread of HIV by caring properly for infected people and by diagnosing the disease as soon as possible after infection. The disease will however never be properly controlled or managed if infected people are stigmatised, persecuted or expelled from their communities. Effective management should take place within the community in which infected people live. Effective management therefore depends on being able to recognise the symptoms of HIV/AIDS and AIDS-related diseases (see chapter 3), and on the earliest possible accurate diagnosis of HIV infection (see chapter 4).

# 3 Symptoms and Diseases Associated with HIV/AIDS

*Hints that Raka is around*

*At first he was not aware of the frightened wild animals*
*milling around in herds, and the small animals*
*gathering before his feet with anxious eyes.*

Because of the unique way in which HIV attacks and disarms the immune system, all the body's defence mechanisms are disarmed. This means in effect that the body is no longer able to protect itself against other diseases. As a result, all kinds of bacteria, fungi, protozoa and viruses are able successfully to invade the body because they encounter no resistance. Even various kinds of cancers may take root and spread in the now-defenceless HIV-infected body. Metaphorically speaking, the HI virus throws open the body's protective gates (i.e. its immune system). This allows all kinds of infections and diseases to take possession of a body no longer protected by its immune system.

The health of an HIV-infected individual therefore depends on the condition of his or her immune system at any particular time. As we noted in chapter 1, the HI virus mainly attacks and kills the CD4 cells. If we therefore measure the actual number of CD4 cells (or lymphocytes) in the body, we have a very accurate indicator of the current status of the HIV-infected person's immune system. This count, called a CD4 cell count, is also the best predictor of how easily opportunistic infections will be able to take root in an HIV-infected person. It is, however, not always possible to measure CD4 counts (because it is an expensive and complex test), and so health care professionals often have to rely on an analysis of visible HIV-related symptoms to make an approximate diagnosis of the health status of an HIV-infected person.

## 3.1 THE DIFFERENT PHASES OF HIV INFECTION

Although HIV infection cannot in practice be precisely demarcated into separate and distinct phases with easily identifiable boundaries, it can nevertheless be theoretically divided into the following phases:

- the primary HIV infection phase (or acute sero-conversion illness)

- the asymptomatic latent phase

- the minor symptomatic phase

- the major symptomatic phase and opportunistic diseases

- AIDS-defining conditions: the severe symptomatic phase

## The primary HIV infection phase (or acute sero-conversion illness)

The acute phase of HIV infection (also called acute sero-conversion illness) begins as soon as sero-conversion has taken place. Sero-conversion means the point at which a person's HIV status *converts* or *changes* from being HIV negative to HIV positive. This usually coincides with the time when an HIV antibody test will show that a person is HIV positive.

Sero-conversion usually occurs 4 to 8 weeks after an individual has been infected with the HI virus. Approximately 30 % to 60 % of people infected with HIV will develop a glandular fever-like illness at the time of sero-conversion, and the symptoms of this fever will usually last from between one and two weeks. This sero-conversion illness is often mistaken for a 'flu-like' viral infection, and it is characterised by symptoms such as a sore throat, headache, mild fever, fatigue, muscle and joint pains, swelling of the lymph nodes, rash, and (occasionally) oral ulcers (Schoub, 1997b).

Because of the rapid replication of the virus, the HIV viral load is usually very high during the acute phase. Immediate and aggressive treatment with anti-retroviral therapy (ART) at this stage may be effective in reducing the viral load to undetectable levels, or even in eradicating the virus (Evian, 2000; Schoub, 1997b).

## The asymptomatic latent phase

The second phase of HIV infection is the asymptomatic latent or silent phase. In this stage an infected person displays no symptoms. Infected individuals are often not even *aware* that they are carrying the HI virus in this stage, and may therefore unwittingly infect new sex partners. Even though the infected person may be ignorant of its presence, the virus nevertheless remains active in the body during this stage and it continues to damage and undermine its victim's immune system. A positive HIV antibody test is often the only indication of HIV infection during this latent phase.

HIV-infected people can remain healthy for a long time, show no symptoms and carry on with their work in a normal way. Some people remain HIV positive for many years without any manifestation of clinical disease while others may deteriorate rapidly, develop AIDS and die within months. In some cases the only symptom during this phase is persistent generalised lymphadenopathy, or swollen glands.

The asymptomatic phase is usually associated with a CD4 cell count of between 500 and 800 cells/mm$^3$. (The normal CD4 cell count in healthy (non-infected) individuals is approximately 800–1 200 cells/mm$^3$.)

## The minor symptomatic phase of HIV disease

In the third phase of infection, minor and early symptoms of HIV disease usually begin to manifest. The minor symptomatic stage commences when people with HIV antibodies begin to present with one or more of the following symptoms:

- mild to moderate swelling of the lymph nodes in the neck, armpits and groin (persistent generalised lymphadenopathy)
- occasional fevers
- herpes zoster or shingles
- skin rashes, dermatitis, chronic itchy skin, fungal nail infections
- recurrent oral ulcerations
- recurrent upper respiratory tract infections
- weight loss up to 10 % of the person's usual body weight
- malaise, fatigue and lethargy

> The minor symptomatic phase is usually associated with a CD4 cell count of between 350 and 500 cells/mm$^3$.

The individual in the minor symptomatic phase of HIV infection is usually able to carry on with his or her normal activities, despite being symptomatic.

 *What is shingles?*

Shingles (or herpes zoster) is a viral infection that is caused by the same virus that causes chicken pox. In the days before the HIV/AIDS pandemic, shingles used to be seen only in older people or in those who had weakened immune systems. Nowadays shingles is very common in people with HIV infection and AIDS, and it is even often seen in young people. Shingles is often one of the first symptoms of HIV infection. Shingles affects nerve cells, and it is characterised by an extremely painful skin rash or tiny blisters on the face, limbs or body. It can also affect the eyes, causing pain and blurred vision. Shingles can be very severe in people with depressed immune systems.

## The major symptomatic phase of HIV infection and opportunistic diseases

Major symptoms and opportunistic diseases begin to appear as the immune system continues to deteriorate. At this point, the CD4 cell count becomes very low while the viral load becomes very high. The following symptoms are usually an indication of advanced immune deficiency:

- persistent and recurrent oral and vaginal candida infections (or thrush): candida or thrush in the mouth is a common sign of immune deficiency and it does not usually occur unless the CD4 cell count is decreased — usually to < 350 cells/mm$^3$)
- recurrent herpes infections such as herpes simplex (cold sores)
- recurrent herpes zoster (or shingles)
- bacterial skin infections and skin rashes
- intermittent or constant unexplained fever that lasts for more than a month
- night sweats
- persistent and intractable chronic diarrhoea that lasts for more than a month
- significant and unexplained weight loss (more than 10 % of the usual body weight)
- generalised lymphadenopathy (or, in some cases, the shrinking of previously enlarged lymph nodes)
- abdominal discomfort, headaches
- oral hairy leucoplakia (thickened white patches on the side of the tongue)
- persistent cough and reactivation of tuberculosis
- opportunistic diseases of various kinds

> The major symptomatic phase is usually associated with a CD4 cell count of between 150 and 350 cells/mm$^3$.

The person in the major symptomatic phase of HIV infection is usually bedridden for up to 50 % of the day during the last month.

**Enrichment**

**HIV and malaria**

A continuous eight-year study in Uganda has confirmed that HIV-infected individuals are more prone to malaria than non-infected individuals. It has also been demonstrated that malaria causes a seven-fold increase in the HIV viral load of people with HIV infection. People with HIV infection should therefore take extra precautions when visiting malarial areas.

## AIDS-defining conditions: the severe symptomatic phase

Only when patients enter the last phase of HIV infection can they be said to have full-blown AIDS. It usually takes about 18 months for the major symptomatic phase to develop into AIDS.

> AIDS patients usually have a very high viral load, and a CD4 cell count of below 200 cells/mm$^3$.

In the final stage of AIDS, the symptoms of HIV disease become more acute, patients become infected by relatively rare and unusual organisms that do not respond to antibiotics, the immune system deteriorates exponentially, and more persistent and untreatable opportunistic conditions and cancers begin to manifest. The AIDS patient in this stage is usually bedridden for more than 50 % of the day during the last month. While people with AIDS (the last phase of HIV disease) usually die within two years, anti-retroviral therapy and the prevention and treatment of opportunistic infections may prolong this period.

Enrichment

**A definition of opportunistic diseases**

Opportunistic infections or diseases are caused by micro-organisms which do not normally become pathogenic in the presence of a healthy immune system (because a healthy immune system will kill them or render them inert). But when an immune system is unable to defend the body because it is being destroyed by HIV, opportunistic infections will 'take any opportunity' (hence the name) to attack the body successfully.

Any of the following symptoms, conditions or opportunistic infections can occur in the AIDS patient:

● Because of continuous diarrhoea, nausea and vomiting (which may last for weeks or even for months), an AIDS patient is usually thin and emaciated. Continuous diarrhoea is often caused by infections of the bowel.
● The patient is plagued by oral manifestations of HIV infection such as oral candidiasis, oral hairy leukoplakia, herpes simplex (cold sores), varicella zoster and bacterial periodontol conditions. Thrush in the mouth may become so painful that the patient is no longer able to eat.
● Persistent, recurrent vaginal candidiasis (yeast infection or thrush) is often the first sign of HIV infection in women. An increased incidence and severity of cervical cancer has also been reported in women with HIV infection. Studies indicate that amenorrhoea in women of reproductive age, and severe pelvic

infections with abscess formation can also be associated with HIV infection in women (Friesen et al., 1997; Smeltzer & Bare, 1992).

- Persistent generalised lymphadenopathy (PGL) may be said to be present when lymph nodes are larger than one centimetre in diameter, in two or more sites other than the groin area, for a period of at least three months.

- Severe and recurrent skin infections such as warts, ringworm and folliculitis (inflammation of the central nervous system) occur in some AIDS patients. These conditions usually cause blisters and ulcerations.

- Respiratory infections may cause the patient to present with a persistent cough, chest pain and fever.

- Pneumonia, especially pneumocystis carinii pneumonia (PCP), is often seen in patients with AIDS. PCP is a parasitic infection of the lungs caused by a protozoa. PCP is characterised by a continual dry, non-productive cough, laboured and sometimes painful breathing, weight loss and fever. The disease is less common in black Africans.

- A wasting of the body's tissues and marked weight loss are often observable in patients with AIDS.

- Severe herpes zoster (or shingles) often occurs in people with depressed immune systems.

- The AIDS patient is usually fatigued and exhausted and this can promote multiple infections such as shingles, herpes, dermatitis or skin infections and ulcerative herpes simplex and persistent generalised lymphadenopathy.

- Peripheral neuropathy, which is characterised by pains, numbness or 'pins and needles' in the hands and feet, often occurs in AIDS patients.

- AIDS patients sometimes suffer from neurological abnormalities such as HIV encephalopathy which is characterised by symptoms such as memory loss, poor concentration, tremor, headache, confusion, loss of vision and seizures.

- AIDS patients may develop cryptococcal meningitis (a fungal infection in the central nervous system) which presents with fever, headache, malaise, nausea, vomiting, neck stiffness, mental status changes, and seizures. Toxoplasma encephalitis (a protozoal infection of the brain which causes damage to the brain itself) can also occur.

- Cytomegalovirus retinitis, an inflammation of the retina of the eye, often occurs in AIDS patients. It may lead to blindness. The disease is caused by the cytomegalovirus (CMV), which is often excreted in the urine, saliva, semen, cervical secretions, faeces or breast milk of immune-depressed patients. CMV infections usually occur in the late stages of AIDS when the CD4 levels fall below 50 cells/mm$^3$.

- Kaposi's sarcoma, a rare form of skin cancer, is characterised by a painless reddish-brown or bluish-purple swelling on the skin and mucous membranes (such as in the mouth). Kaposi's sarcoma can also occur in the gastro-intestinal tract and lungs. Kaposi's sarcoma reacts well to chemotherapy or to alpha-interferon, but it can develop into invasive open lesions and cause death if not promptly treated. Kaposi's sarcoma is less common in black Africans.

- Lymphoma or cancer of the lymph nodes may present with enlargement of lymph nodes, the spleen or liver.
- Tuberculosis is a very serious opportunistic infection which affects people with AIDS. According to a UNAIDS Report (2000c), up to 50 % of HIV-infected individuals in Africa have active tuberculosis. (Tuberculosis is such a critical health problem in Africa that it will be dealt with in more detail in section 3.3.)
- Other sexually transmitted diseases (see section 3.4).

Enrichment

**The importance of regular PAP smears**

Because HIV infection may increase the risk of cervical cancer, it is important to do a PAP smear of the cervix on all HIV-infected women every one to two years. Encourage the women to come back for the results of their PAP smear, and refer them for gynaecological evaluation if their results are abnormal (Evian, 2000).

## 3.2  SYMPTOMS OF HIV INFECTION IN CHILDREN

Children with HIV infection often present with non-specific conditions which are commonly found in general paediatrics. The most common symptoms and conditions associated with HIV infection and AIDS in children are:

- failure to thrive and weight loss
- prolonged fever
- recurrent oral thrush (candidiasis)
- chronic diarrhoea and gastroenteritis
- tuberculosis
- recurrent bacterial infections (causing upper respiratory tract infections, otitis media or ear infections, pneumonia, urinary tract infections and meningitis)
- lymphoid interstitial pneumonitis or LIP (an otherwise rare respiratory or lung disease found in HIV-infected children; it is characterised by a continuous cough and mild wheezing)
- anaemia, pallor, nose bleeds
- persistent generalised lymphadenopathy (swelling of the lymph nodes in the neck, armpit and groin)
- hepatomegaly (enlargement of the liver)
- splenomegaly (enlargement of the spleen)

- skin conditions such as herpes zoster, herpes simplex and seborrhoeic dermatitis
- enlargement of the parotid gland and parotitis (inflammation of the parotid gland)
- delays in attaining developmental milestones or the loss of those already attained
- neurological abnormalities such as seizures and reduced head growth
- severe herpes simplex infection
- complicated chickenpox or measles
- any other AIDS-defining condition such as pneumocystis carinii pneumonia, Kaposi's sarcoma, toxoplasmosis, cytomegalovirus, etc.

(Sources: Evian, 2000; Paediatric HIV Working Group, 1997; WHO, 2000a)

Symptoms that are common to many treatable conditions in children, such as diarrhoea, recurrent fever, and dermatitis, tend to be more persistent and severe in HIV-infected children. HIV-infected children also do not respond as well as non-infected children to treatment and are more likely to suffer life-threatening complications.

The clinical course of HIV infection in children differs significantly from that of adults. The time lapse between infection and the onset of full-blown AIDS is usually much shorter in children than it is in adults, and the majority of infected infants develop disease during the first year of life. Children who acquired HIV infection during pregnancy, birth or breastfeeding can be divided into two main groups: *rapid progressors* and *slow progressors* (Evian, 2000). Rapid progressors usually develop symptoms of HIV/AIDS between 6 and 12 months of age. They are usually sickly from birth, have constant diarrhoea, never thrive and usually die within the first two years of life. Children who are slow progressors usually develop mild symptoms some time after the first year of life. They often survive to older childhood years and even into the early teenage years.

The progress of AIDS in children may be accelerated by poor nutrition and illnesses such as gastroenteritis, tuberculosis, respiratory infections, malaria and measles.

It is often difficult to diagnose HIV infection in a child under 18 months of age because an HIV antibody test may react to the antibodies transferred from the mother to the child during pregnancy.

## 3.3   TB AND HIV: THE SCOURGE OF AFRICA

Tuberculosis is the most serious and most common opportunistic infection that attacks HIV-infected people, especially in Africa. It is estimated that approximately 50 % or more of the HIV-infected people in Africa are co-infected with tuberculosis (Coker & Miller, 1997; UNAIDS, 2000c). Tuberculosis is the most common cause of death in AIDS patients because it is reactivated by the failing immune system.

- Make a sketch of the adult human body. Label the different parts of the body: the head, eyes, mouth, throat, lymph nodes, lungs, abdomen (stomach), skin, genital and anal area, and feet. Use each of these body parts as a heading. Also make one heading for 'general problems'. Arrange all the symptoms and conditions usually associated with advanced HIV disease or AIDS under these labels. The symptoms and diseases usually associated with AIDS should be clear after one glance at your sketch of the human body.
- Make a sketch of a young child and indicate the symptoms usually associated with AIDS in children (as you did in the activity above, but adapted for children).

Tuberculosis accelerates HIV disease and is responsible for 32 % of all HIV-related deaths in Africa.

Researchers are deeply concerned about the high incidence of TB in HIV-infected people in South Africa. In 1996 the World Health Organisation declared the TB epidemic in South Africa to be the worst in the world. In Hlabisa, a community of 205 000 people in KwaZulu-Natal, adult TB patients increased from 8,7 % in 1991 to 70 % in 1997. Most of these TB patients are also co-infected with HIV ('True terror,' 1997).

But why is this dual infection with TB and HIV so dangerous?

### The dangers of the TB-HIV combination

The combination of TB and HIV is, for the following reasons, a disastrous combination (Evian, 2000; Van Dyk, 1999; WHO, 2000a):

- The risk of an HIV-infected patient with a deficient immune system developing tuberculosis (or of having his/her old infection reactivated) is ten times higher than it would be if the patient were not infected with HIV.
- HIV shortens the time between exposure to the TB bacillus (the causative agent of TB) and the development of active tuberculosis.
- The mortality (death) rate from TB is much higher in people who are infected with HIV. A four-fold (or higher) increase in mortality rates because of tuberculosis has been described for HIV-positive patients.
- TB can shorten the time it takes for HIV to become full-blown AIDS, and it can also worsen the condition of someone suffering from AIDS.
- HIV-infected people have a much greater chance of developing extra-pulmonary TB (i.e. TB *outside* the lungs). These forms of TB include TB of the lymph glands, brain, bone, spine, joints, heart, kidney, liver, genital tract and so on.
- TB can diminish the number of CD4 cells in the body while correspondingly increasing the HIV viral load.

● The presence of HIV reduces the accuracy of the methods that are used to detect TB infection. HIV-positive people with a low CD4 cell count may not be able to mount an immune response to a tuberculin skin test. The skin test will therefore give a false negative result in such circumstances. Sputum smears may also be negative — and even chest X-rays may be unreliable. Such false results lead to non-diagnosis. This gives the TB an opportunity to spread even more widely in the community.

● The *recurrence* of TB is more common in HIV-infected individuals.

● The development of multiple-drug-resistance in infected people is a cause for great concern. HIV-positive patients with TB might find it much more difficult to comply conscientiously with the treatment regimen because the side effects which they experience from taking traditional TB medicines may be much more severe than the side effects that people not infected with HIV would experience. HIV-infected patients may therefore be tempted to skip doses or stop taking the medication altogether. This kind of cessation of treatment facilitates the development of TB bacilli which are increasingly resistant to medication.

Because HIV and TB frequently occur together in Africa, it is vitally important for health care professionals to be well informed about tuberculosis and to recognise the symptoms of TB when they see it.

## The cause of tuberculosis

Tuberculosis is an infectious disease that is caused by the bacillus *Mycobacterium tuberculosis*. While it usually affects the lungs, it may also spread to almost any part of the body, including the kidneys, the meninges (of the brain), the lymph nodes and bones. While TB in these sites may cause serious illness in an affected person, such patients are not likely to transmit the disease unless they *also* have tuberculosis of the lungs.

In contrast with most infectious agents, the bacillus of tuberculosis usually remains dormant in the body for a number of years after the infection has taken place and after the immune system has managed to bring the original infection under control. If, during this dormant period, the immunity of the host is suddenly weakened or compromised (as happens when a person suffers from continuous malnutrition or when the immune system is suppressed by HIV), the TB organisms begin immediately to multiply. This multiplication may cause any one of several tuberculous diseases. If the patient's body is able to recover from this illness, the tubercle bacilli once again revert to becoming dormant.

## The spread of tuberculosis

A person with tuberculosis can spread the disease while merely talking, coughing or sneezing. If a susceptible person inhales the droplets thus emitted, he or she may become infected. Health care professionals should protect themselves by wearing tightly fitting masks and by teaching patients to cover the mouth and nose when coughing or sneezing.

Enrichment

**Tuberculosis — a risk for all**

The growing wave of tuberculosis is not only a menace for those infected with HIV. Tuberculosis can spread through the air to HIV-negative people. It is the only major AIDS-related opportunistic infection that threatens HIV-negative people in this way (UNAIDS, 1997).

## The symptoms of tuberculosis

The symptoms of pulmonary (lung) tuberculosis are:

- fever with chills
- night sweats
- loss of strength
- a persistent productive cough with purulent sputum
- weight loss
- anaemia
- the coughing of blood
- the presence of large numbers of TB bacilli in the sputum

Health care professionals working with HIV-infected people should always be alert to the possibility of TB — especially in patients who present with persistent coughs, night sweats and weight loss. Such patients should attend their nearest TB treatment clinics as quickly as possible.

## The diagnosis of tuberculosis

Tuberculosis can be diagnosed in three ways: (1) by means of a tuberculin skin test (Mantoux test), (2) by examining a sputum sample (smear and culture), and (3) by chest radiography.

A sputum examination is the most important test for diagnosing TB. But because sputum tests are sometimes negative in HIV-infected people, chest X-rays should immediately be done in cases where TB is strongly suspected. One should note however that the tuberculin skin test is not a good diagnostic indicator in Africa because most Africans have been exposed to TB and will therefore test positive on tuberculin skin tests. In the South African mines, for instance, 97 % of mineworkers test positive on tuberculin skin tests because of previous exposure to the TB bacilli.

Because of the high prevalence of HIV infection in Africa, tuberculosis clinics should be encouraged to offer TB patients voluntary counselling and HIV testing.

## The treatment of tuberculosis

TB can be completely cured in almost every case of infection if the patient *completes* a course of antibiotic treatment (the emphasis here is on 'completes'). Active tuberculosis is usually treated with the simultaneous administration of a combination of drugs which destroy the infective organisms, such as Isoniazid (INH) or Rifadin (Rifampicin). (HIV-positive individuals receive exactly the same treatment for TB as do HIV-negative patients.) This therapy is continued for at least six months (up to eight months for recurrent tuberculosis) or until the disease is brought under control.

To combat the development of drug-resistant organisms, health care professionals should pay close attention to any side-effects that arise from taking TB medication (effects such as peripheral neuropathy, jaundice, fever and rash, renal failure, visual disturbances, hearing loss, bleeding tendency and shock) — and patients should be helped to understand how important it is not to skip doses or to stop taking the medication (until the courses are complete).

Weight loss should stabilise and cough and night sweat symptoms should show definite signs of alleviation within 4 to 6 weeks after the commencement of treatment. Sputum samples should be negative after 3 to 5 months (Evian, 2000).

Prophylactic (preventative) treatment with INH may reduce the incidence of tuberculosis in HIV-infected individuals and it should (in any case) be offered to all HIV-infected individuals with a CD4 cell count of under 350 cells/mm$^3$ provided that (1) they make a commitment to adhere to therapy and (2) they show no signs of active TB (see the enrichment box 'Prevention of TB in HIV-infected individuals' on page 48).

Compliance with TB treatment can be enhanced by implementing the DOTS (or Directly Observed Treatment Short course) strategy in communities. The DOTS strategy uses 'patients' observers' to watch TB patients swallow each dose of medicine for the complete treatment period of six months. Trained health care workers, responsible members of the community (such as traditional and religious leaders, teachers and employers), as well as volunteers (such as shopkeepers, family members, friends and former TB patients themselves), are appointed in the community to ensure that patients stick to their daily regimen and take their medication as often as they need to for the prescribed time.

**Enrichment**

**Prevention of TB in HIV-infected individuals**

'Prophylaxis' (noun) = preventative treatment against disease (The Concise Oxford Dictionary, Ninth Edition)

One should never use INH to attempt TB prophylaxis (i.e. prevention before it begins) in HIV-infected individuals unless the infected person makes a serious commitment to adhering to the requirements of the therapy. Neither should one use INH to attempt TB prophylaxis in patients who already show symptoms of active TB infection (i.e. weight loss, cough, chest pain, abnormal chest X-ray). Patients with active TB are never treated with only one drug (INH), but always with a combination of drugs. This is done in an attempt to prevent the development of drug resistance to INH. INH alone is only given as prophylaxis to prevent TB in non-TB-infected individuals. If INH is accidentally given to a patient who already has active TB, the TB bacilli may become resistant to the effects of the drug.

**Activity for nurses**

Make an appointment with your nearest TB clinic, hospital or private practitioner, and learn how to 'read' and interpret an X-ray of a patient with tuberculosis. When you have done this, ask yourself whether you are now able to diagnose TB in a patient by looking at the X-rays.

## 3.4 STDs AND HIV: THE DEADLY ALLIANCE

Sexually transmitted diseases (STDs) constitute a major public health problem in southern Africa. It has been estimated that more than 1 million patients seek treatment for STDs every year at municipal clinics and in private practice alone. Many more are seen at hospitals and primary health care clinics. It is, however, believed that most STD cases in Africa are not presented at Western health facilities, but that they are treated by traditional healers (Green, 1994).

For the following reasons, patients who have sexually transmitted diseases are particularly prone to HIV infection:

● Patients with genital ulcers (sores) are especially susceptible to HIV infection because the sores create openings in the mucous membranes — openings through which the HI virus can easily move.

● Statistical evidence suggests that STD infections, which do not cause ulcers, can also facilitate the transmission of HIV (Green, 1994). Genital inflammation causes the migration of millions of lymphocytes (such as CD4 cells) to the site of the infection (in and around the genital tract). As we noted earlier, these cells have special receptors on their surfaces, receptors to which HI viruses attach themselves in preparation for easy entry into the body (Evian, 2000). STDs (especially genital ulcers) thus make it five to ten times easier for the HI virus to enter the body.

- The concentration (number) of HI viruses is very high in genital discharges and secretions. An HIV-infected person who also suffers from an STD is obviously therefore extremely infectious.
- People with STDs are also more vulnerable to HIV because the likelihood is much greater that they are having sex with many different partners. This increases their risk of coming into contact with sexually transmitted infections and HIV.
- Because an HIV infection may delay the healing and cure of STDs, HIV infection often makes STDs more acute and difficult to treat.

Special attention should therefore be paid to patients who frequently visit STD clinics, and health care professionals should always be on the lookout for HIV infection. Most non-viral STDs are curable and preventable. It is therefore of the utmost importance for health care professionals to identify people with STDs as soon as possible, to treat them, and to refer them for HIV testing after pre-test counselling. *It is the belief of many AIDS researchers in Africa that the control of STDs may be the key to combating HIV.* In South African mines, for example, health care professionals attempt to combat AIDS by preventing and treating STDs.

Although a complete discussion of STDs is beyond the scope of this book, it is extremely important for health care professionals to be able to recognise the main symptoms of all STDs. The most important STDs associated with HIV infection can be divided into five categories. These categories are distinguished in terms of the main symptoms that each STD causes (Evian, 2000; National Department of Health, 1997; Van Dyk, 1999). Home-based care of patients with STDs will be discussed in 'Genital problems' on page 388.

### Symptom category I: Discharge from the penis or from female urethra or cervix (not vagina)

The common causes of discharges from the penis or from the female urethra or cervix are *gonorrhoea* and *chlamydia* (or non-gonococcal urethritis). The discharge is usually an abnormal, white, yellow or greenish colour and it is often profuse and purulent. Men often complain of severe pain in the testes accompanied by scrotal swelling and tenderness. Rectal gonococcal infection is common in homosexual men and it may present with a rectal discharge and a burning pain in the rectum. Gonococcal pharyngitis (throat infection) often occurs in both sexes after oral-genital contact (or oral sex).

Although *candidiasis* usually occurs in women, it is also found in men, especially among uncircumcised men. It often occurs in men with AIDS. The symptoms are that the foreskin and the area underneath it become very sore and red. There may be a yellow discharge under the foreskin. The skin of the penis, scrotum and around the anus sometimes also becomes red, sore and itchy.

Discharge from the penis or from the female urethra or cervix is often treated with antibiotics such as *ciprofloxacin* **and** *doxycycline* together. (Alternative medication is also available.)

Enrichment

**Diagnostic versus symptomatic treatment of STDs**

In the past, STDs (such as syphilis or gonorrhoea) were treated after they had been diagnosed in a laboratory where medical technicians were able to identify the causative agent with special equipment. While this is certainly the most scientific method of diagnosing an STD prior to treatment, it is both an expensive and time-consuming method — especially in rural areas where there are no laboratories and where clients often do not (or can't) come back for follow-up treatment.

The diagnosis of STDs (prior to treatment) is now based on symptoms. Health care professionals use a symptom 'check list' before deciding what medication to prescribe. For example: While patient A has a discharge, but no ulcers or abdominal pain, patient B has a discharge as well as genital ulcers. On the basis of these symptoms, patient A's treatment will differ from that of patient B. One of the disadvantages associated with the 'symptom category' approach is that a patient may be given more medication than is necessary.

## Symptom category II: Discharge from the vagina

Abnormal vaginal discharge is usually caused by STDs such as *trichomoniasis, genital candidiasis*, and *bacterial vaginosis*.

Trichomoniasis infection in women produces vaginitis and to a lesser extent cystitis (bladder infection). If the infection is mild, only a slight discharge may be noticed. If it is extremely severe or acute, patients may complain of a copious, thin, offensive-smelling, white, yellow or yellow-green discharge which may be 'frothy' in appearance. On examination, acute inflammation of the vulva and inner thighs are often visible. The vaginal walls and cervix may be covered in a thin discharge. The mucous surfaces may be observed to be extremely red after the discharge has been removed.

Genital candidiasis (thrush) usually occurs in women and manifests as infections of the vagina and vulva. Genital candidiasis is often found in association with HIV infection. While the symptoms in women are vulva irritation and vaginal discharge, it should be noted that many women may be symptom-free. The discharge is usually scant and watery, but it can be profuse, thick and white ('like cottage cheese') in severe cases. The vulva may be red and oedematous and fissures may be present.

Bacterial vaginosis, or 'non-specific vaginitis', is one of the most important causes of vaginal discharge. It is characterised by a grey, homogeneous, adherent vaginal discharge which is usually malodorous (bad smelling). Bacterial vaginosis is, unlike other causes of vaginal discharge, not associated with pruritis (itchiness), dysuria (painful urination) or dyspareunia (painful sexual intercourse). The main complaint is the discharge itself, which may be profuse and is usually described as having a 'fishy' odour.

Abnormal vaginal discharge is often treated by administering *ciprofloxacin* and *doxycycline* and *metronidazole* simultaneously. Women with discharge from the vagina sometimes also show symptoms of pelvic inflammatory disease or PID (see symptom category V).

## Symptom category III: Genital ulcer/sores disease

A thorough and proper understanding of genital ulcer disease is vital for our fight against HIV infection because (as we noted earlier) open lesions and ulcers contribute to the spread of HIV infection by facilitating the transmission of HI viruses across non-intact and inflamed mucosal and skin surfaces. Most genital ulcers or sores are caused by *syphilis*, *genital herpes* and *chancroid*. Open lesions and ulcers are most commonly found on the glans penis and the penile shaft in men, and on the labia, vulva, vaginal walls or cervix in women. Anal and rectal syphilis ulcers are also frequently seen in homosexual men.

Genital ulcers are usually associated with enlarged lymph nodes in the groin area. These enlarged nodes can become very painful and precipitate pustule formation in some cases of chancroid. Chancroid is the most common cause of genital ulcerations in black people in Africa, followed by syphilis. Chancroid has also been found to be a major co-factor in the heterosexual transmission of HIV in developing countries. It is therefore extremely important to be able to diagnose and treat chancroid as accurately and as quickly as possible.

Genital ulcers are usually treated with *benzathine penicillin* **and** *erythromycin* together.

### Genital herpes

Herpes simplex (genital herpes) is very common indeed, especially in individuals with HIV infection. It is usually a recurrent infection and it recurs most frequently when a person is ill or is suffering from stress or around the time of menstruation. Herpes simplex presents with small blister-like sores which often blend to form larger sores. While genital herpes is very painful, it usually settles after about 2 weeks. In patients with HIV infection, herpes may occur more frequently, be more severe and painful, and often remain active for longer than it would in non-HIV-infected people (Evian, 2000). While herpes simplex (which is caused by a virus) can unfortunately not be treated with antibiotics, genital ulcers can be suppressed with *valaciclovir* or *acyclovir* in severe cases. Because these medications are very expensive, their widespread use in poor countries is not possible. The only practical solution is to prevent herpes infections.

Enrichment

**Preventing HIV infection by eliminating STDs**

HIV/AIDS forces us to think holistically. Health care professionals can no longer afford to focus on only one aspect of illness: somehow the possibility of HIV/AIDS will always be hovering somewhere in the background. Thus, for example, when clients present with an STD, treatment of the STD should only be one part of the total health care package delivered. The client should also be counselled about safer sex practices and HIV testing. Condoms should be provided and partners should be referred for treatment. Holistic and comprehensive care and counselling is unfortunately not always delivered. Analysis of data from Carletonville miners in South Africa shows just how great the potential impact of prevention might have been among clients with sexually transmitted diseases — had it been offered. The Carletonville studies found that fewer than 25 % of miners presenting at the clinic for the first time with an STD were infected with HIV. Of those who had further bouts of sexually transmitted infections and who came back for treatment a second, third or fourth time, the rate of HIV infection rose to over 40 %. By the time the same men had been treated for their tenth episode or more, 80 % of them were HIV positive. (These figures tell their own story.) Most of the men who were interviewed said that they **never used condoms** in their primary relationships. This means that many of these infections were acquired or were passed on through sex with a spouse or regular partner. If effective prevention measures had been directed at these men when they presented with their first episode of sexually transmitted infection, many would have been able to avoid being infected with HIV (UNAIDS, 2000c, pp. 72–73).

### Symptom category IV: Genital discharge as well as a genital ulcer or sore

Individuals often present with STDs which cause both genital discharge *as well as* genital ulcerations or sores. Such cases should be treated with a **combination** of medication. Thus one might prescribe *benzathine penicillin* (for example) to cure the ulcers **together with** *ciprofloxacin* (for example) to cure the discharge.

### Symptom category V: Lower abdominal pain (Acute Pelvic Inflammatory Disease)

Acute Pelvic Inflammatory Disease (PID) is caused by the spread of micro-organisms from the vagina and the cervix to the uterus, fallopian tubes and pelvic organs. PID is often caused by gonorrhoea, and it is characterised by severe lower abdominal pain and a typical PID gait, which includes slow walking and grasping of the lower abdomen. A vaginal discharge which is often offensive is frequently noted and the women present with a high temperature (or fever). PID is usually treated with *ceftriaxone* or *cefotaxime*.

## 3.5 CONCLUSION

As the immune system becomes more and more compromised, many different kinds of diseases and symptoms may present themselves in the HIV-infected person. Whenever possible, HIV infection should be confirmed with a blood test. In many poor and rural areas such blood tests are, however, not a viable option. In such cases, a specific combination of clinical symptoms may often serve fairly accurately to diagnose HIV infection. The diagnosis of HIV infection and AIDS will be discussed in more detail in the next chapter.

**Activity**

> A colleague of yours doesn't feel well and she looks feverish to you. She complains of painful urination, itchiness and she also presents with a yellow bad-smelling discharge. Her husband works on a mine and she usually sees him only at weekends. What advice will you offer her?

# 4 Diagnosis of HIV Infection and AIDS

. . . . . . . . . . . . . . . . . . . . . . . . . . . . . . . . . . . . . . . . . . . . . . . . . . . . . . . . . . . . .

*Definite signs of Raka's presence*

*The men saw the signs of his strength in the bush:*
*it must have been the work of his hands,*
*the carcass of a buffalo lying in a footpath,*
*with its knees buckled beneath its dead body.*

. . . . . . . . . . . . . . . . . . . . . . . . . . . . . . . . . . . . . . . . . . . . . . . . . . . . . . . . . . . . .

HIV infection can be diagnosed by means of an assessment of the clinical history, an identification of risk factors, a clinical assessment of signs and symptoms, and blood tests. The diagnosis of HIV infection is usually based on both a clinical assessment and subsequent confirmation by means of an HIV antibody test. It is, however, not always possible to do tests in places like, for example, remote rural areas or for babies under 18 months of age, and many health care professionals therefore have to rely on a clinical diagnosis of HIV infection.

## 4.1   CLINICAL DIAGNOSIS OF HIV INFECTION: SIGNS AND SYMPTOMS

In order to make a clinical diagnosis of HIV infection, the first important step is to take a detailed case history of the client. Ask the person how long he or she has been ill and inquire about any other symptoms he or she has experienced in the past. Ask the client about his or her sexual practices and about the health of his or her sexual partner/s and children.

The World Health Organisation has developed criteria for the diagnosis of HIV infection in situations where access to HIV antibody tests is limited. These criteria are based on the recognition of certain major and minor criteria.

### Clinical criteria for diagnosing HIV infection in adults

The following clinical criteria (Table 4.1) for diagnosing symptomatic HIV infection in adults were developed by the World Health Organisation for health care professionals who do not have access to HIV antibody tests (Friesen et al., 1997, p. 102).

The WHO criteria should be adapted to the illness pattern in Africa. Researchers in Botswana found that the most common symptoms among those individuals who tested HIV positive on the ELISA test were weight loss (47 %), persistent cough (30 %), prolonged fever (23 %), chronic diarrhoea (21 %), tuberculosis (16 %), herpes zoster (13 %) and oral candidiasis (11 %). Bacterial pneumonia was evident in only 8 % of the cases, failure to thrive was visible in 7 %, and the least common symptom was generalised lymphadenopathy (6 %) (Edhonu-Elyetu, 1997). It was also found that chronic diarrhoea, weight loss, herpes zoster (or shingles) and non-healing

## Table 4.1
*Criteria for diagnosing HIV in adults*

The presence of opportunistic conditions such as Kaposi's sarcoma or cryptococcal meningitis is sufficient for the diagnosis of AIDS. HIV infection (or AIDS) is also diagnosed if at least **two major** criteria and **one minor** criterion are present in the patient in the absence of other known causes of immune suppression such as malnutrition.

| Major criteria | Minor criteria |
|---|---|
| • Fever that has lasted for more than one month<br>• A weight loss of more than 10 % of the usual body weight<br>• Chronic diarrhoea for more than one month | • Cough that has lasted for more than one month (often associated with tuberculosis in Africa)<br>• Generalised pruritic dermatitis<br>• Oral candidiasis or thrush<br>• Chronic or aggressive ulcerative herpes simplex<br>• Herpes zoster (or shingles)<br>• Persistent generalised lymphadeno-pathy |

## Table 4.2
*Criteria for diagnosing HIV in children*

A child is considered to have AIDS if **two major** and **two minor** criteria are present in the absence of any other known cause of immune deficiency.

| Major criteria | Minor criteria |
|---|---|
| • Weight loss, abnormally slow growth or a failure to thrive<br>• Prolonged fever that has lasted for more than one month<br>• Chronic diarrhoea for more than one month | • Chronic cough that has lasted for more than one month<br>• Generalised lymph node enlargement<br>• Recurrent common infections (such as those of the ear and throat)<br>• Chronic dermatitis (skin infections or rash)<br>• Fungal infections of the mouth and/or throat (oral candidiasis or thrush)<br>• The mother has been proved to be HIV positive |

genital ulcers, *if found together*, predicted a positive ELISA result in 95,5 % of the cases. It is recommended that, in the absence of an ELISA test, these symptoms could be used to diagnose HIV infection for intervention purposes. It is also suggested that shingles should be given the status of a *major* diagnostic symptom in the WHO clinical case definition for HIV/AIDS — at least for use in African countries that cannot afford HIV antibody tests. It should be noted that the occurrence of shingles in young people in Africa is *almost always* associated with HIV infection.

## Clinical criteria for diagnosing HIV infection in children

Table 4.2 lists clinical criteria for diagnosing HIV infection in children. These criteria were developed by the World Health Organisation to help health care professionals make symptom-based diagnoses when HIV antibody tests are unavailable (Evian, 2000, p. 161).

## 4.2   HIV TESTING AS DIAGNOSTIC TOOL

There are three main reasons why HIV antibody testing is carried out. It is carried out for purposes of screening donated blood, the epidemiological surveillance and mapping of HIV prevalence, and the diagnosis of HIV infection in individuals. While HIV testing was previously mainly used to confirm or to diagnose suspected HIV infection, people are now encouraged to make use of voluntary counselling and testing (VCT) services to find out their HIV status. It is hoped that if people know their HIV status and are sero-negative, they will be motivated to adopt preventative measures to prevent future infection. The hope is also that if people are sero-positive, they will learn to live positively, take the trouble to access care and support at an earlier stage, learn to prevent transmission to sexual partners, and plan for their own and their families' futures (WHO, 2000a, p. 1-4).

> Pre- and post-HIV test counselling must always be done before and after testing a client for HIV infection. The reason for testing, the nature of the test, the implications of a positive or a negative test result, and the client's prospects (in either case) should be discussed with every client before testing. Informed consent and confidentiality are mandatory. Pre- and post-HIV test counselling is discussed in chapter 11.

The diagnosis of HIV infection is based mainly on the laboratory testing of blood samples. Two broad classes of tests may be distinguished. These are (1) *HIV antibody tests,* which react to *antibodies* which have formed in reaction to the virus, and (2) tests which detect the *actual virus* (HIV) in the blood.

## HIV antibody tests

Two of the best-known HIV antibody tests are the ELISA (enzyme-linked immuno-sorbent assay) and the Western Blot tests. Although these tests cannot trace the actual virus itself in the blood, they react to the HIV *antibodies* that are formed by the immune system in an unsuccessful attempt to protect the body against the virus. Such antibodies can usually be detected in the blood 4 to 6 weeks after infection. The antibody tests will therefore only become positive approximately 6 weeks after infection. (In some cases it may take much longer — from between 3 and 12 months — before a person tests HIV antibody positive.)

### The ELISA antibody test

The ELISA HIV antibody test is the most popular and commonly used test. It is widely available and reasonably cheap. The test is very sensitive and reliable, and produces very few false negative results. Because false positive results (where a test result is positive, while the person is actually HIV negative) can occasionally occur, an HIV-positive test result should *always* be confirmed by means of a second test. A positive ELISA test is usually confirmed by means of another subsequent ELISA test. In special circumstances, a Western Blot test or a PCR test (see 'The PCR technique' on page 60) can be used for confirmation.

Rapid HIV antibody tests can also be used to confirm a positive ELISA test, especially in remote or rural areas where resources are limited. Rapid tests are as accurate as the ELISA, and many doctors believe that the use of rapid tests in conjunction with the ELISA test is as reliable (or even more reliable) than the combination of the ELISA and Western Blot tests (Schoub, 1997b).

### Rapid HIV antibody tests

Rapid HIV antibody tests can be performed outside a laboratory (in places such as clinics or even at the bedside of a patient), and the results are usually available within 10 to 30 minutes. Rapid HIV tests are relatively easy to use (they involve a prick of the finger with a lancet), they are relatively cheap and they demonstrate a high rate of reliability if they are correctly used. Rapid tests are very useful for the diagnosis of HIV infection in rural or isolated areas which are far removed from diagnostic laboratories and where clients often cannot afford to come back for test results. All positive rapid HIV results should, however, *always* be confirmed with a laboratory-based ELISA antibody test. In rural areas where this may be a problem (for the reasons mentioned above), confirmation of the first rapid test can be carried out by conducting a second but *different* rapid test (Evian, 2000). A second confirmatory test will, however, not be necessary if a person presents with clear symptoms of immune depression.

Rapid HIV diagnostic home-kit tests are also available, but these tests should be used with extreme care. It is not advisable to do the home test without proper pre-test and post-test counselling. The results can also be incorrect if the testing instructions are not followed exactly, if the test has not been stored at the required temperature, if the expiry date of the test has been exceeded, or if poor-quality test kits are used. A positive result obtained from a home test should *always* be confirmed by a subsequent laboratory test.

**Enrichment**

**The sensitivity and specificity of tests**

The two factors which determine the accuracy of a serological (blood) test are sensitivity and specificity. The sensitivity of a test is its ability to pick up very low levels of antibodies (its ability to detect HIV positivity), and the specificity of a test is its ability to distinguish specific antibodies from other cross-reacting non-specific antibodies (i.e. its ability to demonstrate HIV negativity and not give false positive results) (Evian, 2000; Schoub, 1997b).

If the health care professional has the slightest suspicion that the test results are giving a false negative result (for instance, a positive ELISA and a negative Western Blot, for a person who is known to practise high-risk behaviour), he or she should advise that person to be tested again after 3 weeks. If the person concerned is in the 'window period', complete sero-conversion should have taken place after 3 weeks. The test will then produce more accurate results.

**The window period**

The window period is the period between the onset of HIV infection and the appearance of detectable antibodies to the virus. In the case of the most sensitive HIV antibody tests currently recommended, the window period is about 3 to 4 weeks. This period can sometimes be longer (approximately 6 weeks) if one uses less sensitive tests. In some cases, the window period can be up to 12 weeks, or (in rare cases) up to between 6 and 12 months before HIV antibody tests give positive results. In the latter cases, any blood tests (such as the ELISA, rapid tests and the Western Blot) conducted during this window period may give false negative results. This means that although the virus is present in the person's blood there are, as yet, no (detectable) antibodies in the blood. In such cases the tests erroneously show that the person has not been infected. During this window period the individual is already infectious and may unknowingly infect other people. People who are exposed to or who practise high-risk behaviour are well advised to arrange for a repeat test after 3 to 6 months — and to use safer sex practices like condoms while waiting for their results.

**HI virus tests**

HIV P24 antigen and HIV PCR tests do not have to rely on the development of *anti-bodies* before they yield a positive test result. Because these tests detect the actual HI virus (or HIV antigens) in the blood, they yield a positive HIV test result much sooner after infection than do the ELISA, the Western Blot or the rapid tests. HIV P24 antigen and HIV PCR tests usually produce positive results within 10 to 14 days after infection. (The window period is thus much shorter than with HIV antibody tests.) These tests are unfortunately extremely expensive and are not always available in remote areas of the country.

**The HIV P24 antigen test**

The HIV P24 antigen test detects the predominant HIV antigen (P24), which is usually detectable in the blood shortly after initial HIV infection and again in the late stages of infection. Although the P24 antigen test is useful in certain clinical situations (e.g. for newborn babies), it lacks sensitivity (Evian, 2000).

**The PCR technique**

The *PCR* or the Polymerase Chain Reaction technique can be used for diagnostic as well as post-diagnostic purposes. A *qualitative* PCR is used for diagnostic purposes (to diagnose an individual as HIV positive or HIV negative). The qualitative PCR test is especially useful in cases where early diagnosis is required (e.g. for post-exposure prophylaxis purposes), for diagnosing babies born to HIV-infected mothers (see enrichment) and for use as a post-rape test before beginning anti-retroviral therapy. A *quantitative* PCR test is mainly used post-diagnostically for treatment purposes (see 'The viral load' on page 66). It is possible, by using the quantitative PCR test, to establish the number of viral RNA particles in the blood. This is also called the *HIV viral load test*. The viral load is usually a reliable indicator of the infected individual's prognosis (outlook), and it is also used to measure an individual's response to anti-retroviral therapy.

 · · · · · · · · · · · · · · · · · · · · · · · · · · · · · · · · · · · · · · · · · · · · · · ·

*What is meant by a 'positive HIV antibody test'?*

A *positive HIV antibody test* means that the individual has been infected with HIV and therefore, as a carrier of the virus for life, he or she is in a position to infect other people. A positive HIV antibody test does *not* reveal when or for how long the person has been infected. The test also gives no indication of the stage of infection, nor of the time it may take to develop AIDS. It is important to keep in mind that a positive HIV antibody test does not necessarily mean that the person has already developed AIDS (the last stage of HIV infection).

· · · · · · · · · · · · · · · · · · · · · · · · · · · · · · · · · · · · · · · · · · · · · · · · · · · · ·

**When a baby can be tested for HIV infection**

It is only possible to use HIV antibody tests, such as ELISA, Western Blot or rapid tests, when a baby is about 15 to 18 months old to establish whether or not a baby born to an HIV-infected mother is infected with HIV. Prior to this age, it is impossible to ascertain if the antibodies in the baby's blood belong to the baby or to the mother. In HIV-infected women, the maternal HIV antibodies are passively transmitted across the placenta to the foetus during pregnancy. These maternal antibodies can persist in the baby for as long as 18 months. It is however possible to establish the HIV status of the baby within approximately 30 days after birth with the HIV P24 antigen and the HIV PCR tests. These tests detect the HI virus itself in the blood and do not depend on the existence of antibodies for a positive result. The P24 antigen and the PCR tests are too expensive and sophisticated for general use, but they are often used for abandoned children who are up for adoption, or for children requiring major surgery.

- A young HIV-positive mother in your community is very worried about the HIV status of her baby of three months old. She says to you: 'They refuse to test my baby at the clinic. They keep saying that my baby is too young to be tested. What do they mean — too young?' How would you go about counselling this young mother?
- The same young woman has another question for you. She asks: 'The clinic also tested my husband, but he is HIV negative. They told him to come back for another test in three months' time. They said something about a "window". What did they mean? Is he infected or not?' What would you tell her?

Write a brief summary of your answers with all your main points clearly indicated. Use metaphors to explain the concepts.

*What is meant by a 'negative HIV antibody test'?*

A *negative HIV antibody test* means that no antibodies against HIV have been found in the blood. A negative test outcome may mean one of two things: either the person has not been infected, or the person may have been infected but the antibodies have not yet formed (the person may be in the window period). A very small percentage of HIV-infected people (usually people in the last stage of infection) do not have any HIV antibodies in their blood (their tests therefore repeatedly produce false negative test results). This usually happens when a person's immune system is so depressed that it does not have the ability to form any antibodies.

**?** *What is an 'indeterminate' test result?*

An indeterminate test result means that the test is not clear either way and it is therefore not possible to tell if the person is HIV antibody positive or negative. The test should be repeated after a few weeks or an HIV antigen test or PCR test should be done.

**?** *Are people immune to AIDS when they have HIV antibodies in the blood?*

The antibodies formed against HIV do *not* protect the individual from the devastating effects of the virus. These antibodies, unlike the antibodies in other infections, do not provide immunity against HIV or AIDS. They are formed as the body *unsuccessfully* attempts to defend itself against the virus.

> HIV testing is only a tool. That tool is blunted to the degree that it is used to harm other people (Coates, 1990, p. 1).

## 4.3 CONCLUSION

The early diagnosis of HIV infection is important because the management of HIV infection through medication and by adapting to a more healthy lifestyle can in many cases drastically delay the onset of AIDS.

# 5 Management of HIV Infection

*Delaying Raka*

*Behind him he heard the angry grunt of the beast. . . .*
*He swung around.*
*In its tracks the big thing came to a halt.*
*With a grin, it retreated a few steps,*
*angered, but afraid, half ashamed of itself.*

There are no absolute hard-and-fast rules about caring for people with HIV/AIDS, and there is therefore no one specific management protocol. The management and care of HIV infection should always focus on the specific needs of a patient at any particular moment. The care and treatment offered will therefore depend on many and varied factors such as (1) how far the disease has progressed in a specific patient, (2) the symptoms experienced by the patient at any given time, (3) the kind of opportunistic infections that are attacking the individual, and (4) the kind of medical care (whether hospital, clinic, home-based or hospice) that is available to the patient in practice. The assessment of the immune system and the use and function of anti-retroviral drugs will be discussed in this chapter. The management and care of specific symptoms and HIV-related conditions in the hospital, the clinic and in home-based care will be discussed in chapter 16.

## 5.1 CLINICAL ASSESSMENT

Once a patient has been diagnosed as being HIV positive, it is important to do a full clinical assessment of the patient's health. Regular check-ups (at least every 6 months if the person is healthy, but more frequently if the patient has symptoms) should be done to monitor changes (if any) in the person's health. Regular check-ups can help health care professionals to identify and treat physical as well as psychological problems at an early stage and to promote the general health of the patient. Attention should be given to each of the following points in the initial as well as in each follow-up visit:

- the weight of the patient
- examination of the skin, mouth and teeth, eyes, lymph nodes, genitals, respiratory system, abdomen
- blood tests (e.g. full blood count), CD4 cell count, viral load test
- neurological assessment
- chest X-rays (if necessary)

Regular medical and growth checks (at least once every 3 months) are very important for monitoring the health of HIV-infected children. The child's weight, developmental progress, head size, immunisation status, nourishment and feeding should all be closely monitored. The clinician should take careful note of any symptoms which may be an indication of opportunistic diseases.

## 5.2 ASSESSMENT OF IMMUNE STATUS AND VIRAL LOAD

In order to manage HIV infection, opportunistic infections and AIDS, it is important to monitor the individual's CD4 lymphocyte count as well as the viral load in the blood on an ongoing basis.

CD4 cell counts are important to:

- evaluate the status of the immune system
- prevent or treat opportunistic diseases

A viral load test is important to:

- assess the severity of the infection (or the prognosis)
- prescribe relevant medication
- measure the patient's response to therapy (medication)

### Immune status and the CD4 cells

The single most important test for determining an individual's immune status is the CD4 lymphocyte count. CD4 cell counts are the best predictors of the risk of opportunistic infections in HIV-infected people. CD4 values below 500 cells/mm$^3$ are usually an indication of immune suppression and vulnerability to opportunistic infections (see enrichment box below). It is recommended that preventative treatment against specific infections, such as tuberculosis and pneumocystis carinii pneumonia, be based on CD4 cell counts. This is preferable to waiting for symptoms to occur and *then* treating these very serious conditions (see 'The prevention of opportunistic infections' on page 72).

**Enrichment**

**Normal CD4 cell counts**

It is very important to take a baseline CD4 cell count as soon as possible. This initial CD4 count can then be used as the baseline against which any changes can be measured. Although the normal CD4 cell count is approximately 1 000 cells/mm$^3$, variations are found among human beings, and some healthy (HIV-negative) people may have CD4 cell counts as low as 600 cells/mm$^3$.

It is unfortunately not always possible to do CD4 cell counts because of the high cost of these procedures and the absence of sophisticated laboratory facilities in rural areas. Health care professionals in such situations have to rely on their observation of the general clinical condition of the patient and symptoms of opportunistic diseases in particular.

### The viral load

It is important to know the actual number of HI viruses in the blood in order to manage HIV infection effectively. An increasing viral load is usually an indication of active HIV disease and the rapid development of immune deficiency. It is therefore an indicator of a poor health prognosis (or future) for the patient. An increasing viral load is usually accompanied by a decreasing CD4 count. It is also important to monitor the viral load of individuals who are receiving anti-retroviral therapy (ART). *If the viral load of a person on ART begins to rise, this is an indication that the treatment is not working.*

### The relationship between the viral load and CD4 cell count

There is a very special relationship between the viral load and the CD4 cell count, and, if considered together, they can predict whether a person's journey towards full-blown AIDS will be rapid or slow. The following metaphor can be used to describe this relationship between viral load and CD4 cell count (Schoub, 1997b): the viral load value can be compared to the *speed* of a train on its journey towards AIDS, while the CD4 cell count represents the distance markers on the way to the destination (i.e. AIDS). The higher the viral load in the blood, the faster the train will move towards its destination. The journey to AIDS, however, will take much longer if the *distance* to the destination is longer (i.e., if the CD4 cell count is higher). To prolong an HIV-infected person's journey, it is imperative to keep the viral load (or the speed of the train) as low as possible, and to keep the CD4 cell count (the distance) as high as possible.

**Activity**

> Draw a picture to explain to a client the relationship between the viral load and the CD4 cell count. (Use the example of the train on its journey towards AIDS if you cannot think of anything else.)

Figure 5.1 shows the relationship between a person's CD4 cell count, his or her viral load and the phases of HIV infection.

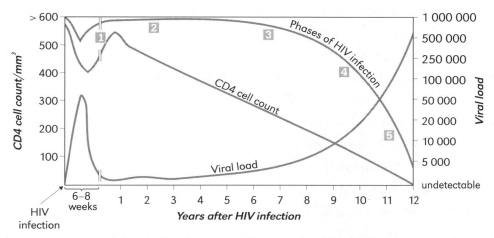

1 The primary HIV infection phase (or acute sero-conversion illness)
2 The asymptomatic latent phase
3 The minor symptomatic phase
4 The major symptomatic phase and opportunistic diseases
5 AIDS-defining conditions: the severe symptomatic phase

Note: This pattern may differ from individual to individual. Viral load values, for instance, may differ considerably from person to person.

**Figure 5.1**

*The relationship between a person's CD4 cell count, viral load and phases of HIV infection*

(Source: Adapted from Evian, 2000, p. 76)

## 5.3 MANAGEMENT OF HIV INFECTION: THE USE OF ANTI-RETROVIRAL THERAPY (ART)

The ultimate purpose of anti-retroviral therapy (ART) is to reduce the HIV viral load as much as possible — preferably to undetectable levels — for as long as possible. Because this in turn means that less damage will be inflicted on the immune system, the patient will experience an improvement in his/her immune functioning and the onset of AIDS will be delayed. A combination of two or three different anti-retroviral drugs has been shown to produce the best effects and to reduce the possibility of viral resistance.

**Anti-retroviral therapy**

There are currently three main categories of anti-retroviral drugs:

● Nucleoside reverse transcriptase inhibitors (NRTIs) such as:
  o zidovudine (Retrovir) (AZT)
  o didanosine (Videx) (ddI)

- o   zalcitabine (Hivid) (ddC)
- o   lamivudine (Epivir) (3TC)
- o   stavudine (Zerit) (d4T)
- ● Non-nucleoside reverse transcriptase inhibitors (NNRTIs) such as:
  - o   nevirapine (Viramune) (NVP)
- ● Protease inhibitors (PIs) such as:
  - o   saquinavir (Invirase) (SQV)
  - o   ritonavir (Norvir) (RTV)
  - o   indinavir (Crixivan) (IDV)
  - o   nelfinavir (Viracept) (NFV)

For optimum viral suppression, triple-therapy is recommended. Combination treatment with two nucleoside reverse transcriptase inhibitors (NRTIs) and one protease inhibitor (PI) is recommended for optimum effect (e.g. AZT, 3TC and Crixivan). The majority of patients on this triple-therapy treatment programme will reach the desired target of undetectable HIV-RNA levels in the blood. The NRTI-PI triple-therapy regime is however very expensive and the alternative recommendation is a combination of two nucleoside reverse transcriptase inhibitors (NRTIs) plus a non-nucleoside reverse transcriptase inhibitor (NNRTI) (e.g. ddI, d4T plus Nevirapine).

Mono-therapy (treatment with only one agent such as AZT) is no longer recommended for HIV therapy because it only produces a temporary reduction in viral load and the patient develops a resistance to the drug within a few weeks or months. Mono-therapy (AZT) is only used in some cases as a short-term limited course treatment of HIV infection in pregnant mothers so as to prevent vertical transmission to the baby. Bi-therapy (with two NRTI drugs such as d4T and ddI) is still used when resources are limited. Drug resistance may also develop in bi-therapy, but it takes longer to develop than with mono-therapy.

Children are treated with the same anti-retroviral drugs that are given to adults, but the dosages are adjusted to suit the age or weight of the child. The use of anti-retroviral therapy in children promotes or restores normal growth and development, improves the quality of life, prevents complicating infections and malignancies, and prolongs the child's life.

It is an ongoing research challenge to find new drugs, new categories of drugs and the most suitable combination of drugs for categories of patients with different needs. It is also a challenge to eliminate treatment failure and determine how to measure the possibility that a patient will develop resistance to anti-retroviral drugs. Health care professionals should therefore make every attempt to remain abreast of new developments in this ever-changing field.

## The effect of anti-retroviral drugs on the HI virus

Anti-retroviral drugs act by blocking the action of *enzymes* that are important for the replication and functioning of HIV. Figure 5.2 illustrates the effect of anti-retroviral drugs on the HI virus.

The *reverse transcriptase inhibitors* disturb the life cycle of the HI virus by interfering with the reverse transcriptase enzyme in the replication of the virus (see figure 5.2, step A). By interfering with the reverse transcriptase enzyme, the virus is no longer able to change its RNA into viral DNA. The *protease inhibitors* interfere with the formation of new viruses by 'paralysing' the protease enzyme and so preventing the assembly and release of newly replicated HI viruses from the infected cells (see figure 5.2, step B).

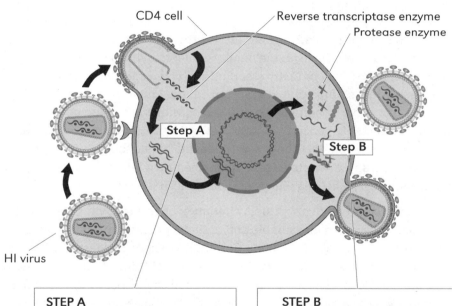

| STEP A | STEP B |
| --- | --- |
| **Drugs that work here:** | **Drugs that work here:** |
| • Non-nucleoside reverse transcriptase inhibitors (NNRTI) | • Protease inhibitors (PI) |
| • Nucleoside reverse transcriptase inhibitors (NRTI) | (Drugs interfere with the protease enzyme and prevent the formation of new viruses.) |
| (Drugs interfere with the reverse transcriptase enzyme.) | |

**Figure 5.2**

*The effect of anti-retroviral drugs on the HI virus*

Make (or ask the children in your class to make) a model from different coloured clays or plasticine to demonstrate the interaction between the HI virus and a CD4 cell. Use the model to explain to the children what anti-retroviral drugs do to the virus.

## When to initiate drug therapy

Earlier hopes that HIV could be eradicated from infected individuals were based on the erroneous assumption that a complete and definitive suppression of viral replication could be achieved by the use of anti-retroviral drugs. It is now known that HIV cannot be completely eradicated from the body and that replication of HIV still occurs — although at concentrations that are too low to be measured by viral tests. There are also growing concerns and unease about the long-term adverse effects of early therapy. Apart from adherence problems (i.e. the difficulty of getting patients to take their medication regularly), there are legitimate worries about the impact that long-term therapy will have on the quality of life, individual and state budgets (these medications are — by ordinary standards — very expensive), adverse interactions between various drugs that are prescribed, the build-up of viral resistance, the creation of metabolic abnormalities and the possibility of inducing premature cardiovascular disease (Carpenter et al., 2000). Doctors and patients should together carefully weigh the risks against the possible benefits before they begin any course of anti-retroviral therapy. Patients have to make their own informed decisions, and take responsibility for the consequences of their choices.

There is an increased tendency to delay initiation of anti-retroviral therapy until immune deficiency becomes measurable and until the probability that diseases will develop has become high (WHO, 2000b). Current guidelines suggest that therapy should be initiated in (1) all patients with *symptomatic* HIV infection, regardless of CD4 counts and viral load, (2) all patients with CD4 cell counts below 350 cells/mm$^3$, and (3) all patients with a high viral load (above 30 000 copies/ml) — irrespective of CD4 cell count (Carpenter et al., 2000). Some sources recommend that treatment should be *considered* for patients with HIV-RNA viral load levels of greater than 10 000 to 30 000 copies/ml and/or CD4 cell counts between 350 cells/mm$^3$ and 500 cells/mm$^3$ (Evian, 2000).

Viral load counts should be done at 3 to 4 monthly intervals in order to monitor the effectiveness of anti-retroviral therapy. If the medication is effective, the viral load count should eventually stabilise at acceptably low levels. If the viral load increases, it is an indication that the treatment is not working. The patient's drug therapy then needs to be re-evaluated and changed.

**Anti-retroviral therapy? Not an easy choice for a patient to make**

Anti-retroviral therapy will cause irreversible changes in a patient's life, and the health care professional should consider every advantage and disadvantage inherent in therapy before recommending or prescribing it to any patient. One should take careful cognisance of each of the following factors when one is considering anti-retroviral therapy (based on Evian, 2000, p. 80):

- A patient who wants to take anti-retroviral therapy should obviously be committed and well informed and should be in a position to adhere to a strict medication regime. This means that they should be able to take 2 to 3 tablets two to three times a day (taking some dosages with food and some on an empty stomach).
- Some patients may experience side effects such as nausea, vomiting, abdominal discomfort, diarrhoea, skin rashes, fatigue, headache, anaemia, liver toxicity, fever, peripheral neuropathy and kidney stones.
- Current treatments are permanent and life-long and it is absolutely essential for the patient to adhere strictly to the therapy. Patients often stop treatment because of side effects and this may lead to the development of viral resistance to the drugs.
- Drug therapy should be monitored on a regular basis by measuring the viral load. This monitoring enables one to know whether the viruses are being successfully suppressed.
- Because anti-retroviral therapy is expensive, it is beyond the reach of most people who are HIV positive.

 *Can HIV be eliminated completely?*

HIV can unfortunately not be eliminated completely from the body. Because the virus remains latent or dormant throughout the body, it can easily become reactivated in the right conditions. When the virus is reactivated, it continues to ravage the infected person's immune system and puts him or her on the 'train' heading towards full-blown AIDS. When the viral load becomes 'undetectable' in the blood, it simply means that the viral load is so low that it cannot be detected with the kind of blood tests available to us. *It does not mean that there are no more viruses in the body.* Research has also shown that once anti-retroviral therapy is discontinued, viral replication usually resumes and viral loads begin to rise again (Evian, 2000).

*Can the anti-retroviral medication 'cure' AIDS?*

Although HIV infection can be treated so that the viral load is kept low and the immune system is kept as healthy as possible, *there is still no cure for AIDS or HIV infection.* The current emphasis in the treatment of HIV-infected individuals is therefore on strengthening the immune system so that infected people can be kept as healthy as possible. The current emphasis is also on keeping the viral count as low as possible and on treating opportunistic infections (see chapter 16).

**Enrichment**

**An AIDS vaccine for all by 2007: myth or reality?**

Researchers all over the world are currently working around the clock to find a vaccine against HIV. HIV is a very complex virus and the development of an effective and safe vaccine is enormously hampered by the genetic diversity of HIV, the different strains of HIV, and the fact that HI viruses mutate and recombine. Some researchers believe that although they might not be able to develop a vaccine that actually prevents HIV infection, they might be able to develop a vaccine that will be able to prevent the clinical manifestations of the virus and one that ensures a lower transmission rate (i.e. makes the virus less infectious). We will only know in the future if President Clinton's stated hope that American research scientists would have produced an effective vaccine for all by 2007 will be realised.

## 5.4  THE PREVENTION OF OPPORTUNISTIC INFECTIONS

Because their depleted immune systems make HIV-infected people vulnerable to opportunistic infections, they can only maintain a reasonable quality of life if they can prevent themselves from being infected by such opportunistic infections. Prophylactic (preventative) treatment for opportunistic diseases is generally based on CD4 cell counts. Prophylactic treatment usually works very well in preventing infections such as oral and vaginal thrush (candida albicans), pneumocystis carinii pneumonia, tuberculosis, toxoplasmosis and herpes infections.

Tuberculosis is the commonest opportunistic infection in Africa, and TB prophylaxis therapy should routinely be given to patients whose CD4 cell counts drop below 350 cells/mm$^3$ (this prevents the re-activation of latent TB bacilli). If CD4 cell counts are not available, TB prophylaxis should be considered in a patient who shows signs of immune deficiency. (Isoniazid (INH) is the drug of choice for TB prophylaxis.) To avoid drug resistance, it is important to make sure that the patient does not have active TB, and that he or she will be able to take the medication as prescribed. (See 'TB and HIV: the scourge of Africa' on page 43.)

Prophylaxis therapy for pneumocystis carinii pneumonia (PCP) should be started when the CD4 cell count drops to lower than 200 cells/mm$^3$ (PCP is usually treated with co-trimoxazole, e.g. Bactrim or Septran).

It is important to prevent opportunistic infections in children with HIV infection. Prophylactic treatment should be considered for infections such as tuberculosis, pneumocystis carinii pneumonia, candida and recurrent bacterial infections. It is recommended that prophylaxis against TB and PCP in children should start as soon as the child shows clinical signs of HIV infection or as soon as they have a positive HIV PCR test (Paediatric HIV Working Group, 1997).

## 5.5 THE USE OF ANTI-RETROVIRAL THERAPY IN THE PREVENTION OF MATERNAL-FOETAL TRANSMISSION

The use of anti-retroviral therapy (such as AZT or nevirapine) should be considered for use in HIV-positive pregnant women and their newborn infants as it has been shown to reduce the rate of maternal-foetal transmission of HIV. Studies have shown that the administration of zidovudine (AZT) could reduce the risk of transmission from mother to baby by 51 % to 67,5 % — depending on the duration of the treatment (WHO, 2000a). Pregnant women who are considering the use of anti-retroviral therapy during pregnancy should however be counselled that transmission may still occur in some cases despite therapy.

Nevirapine is a cheap, easy-to-administer, one-dosage oral drug which is usually given to the mother at the onset of labour, as well as to the newborn baby within 72 hours of birth. Nevirapine is found to be as effective as AZT (Evian, 2000), and it offers a more optimistic and realistic alternative for anti-retroviral therapy for developing countries. Nevirapine is also very helpful in rural areas where a mother may not necessarily attend ante-natal clinics, and where she is often only seen during labour. Although anti-retroviral therapy may be effective in reducing HIV transmission to the baby, it does unfortunately not prolong the life of the mother. (Health care professionals should stay informed about new developments in anti-retroviral therapy for HIV-infected pregnant mothers.)

## 5.6 MANAGEMENT OF OCCUPATIONAL EXPOSURE TO HIV

Although the risk of contracting HIV after occupational exposure to the virus is very low (0,3 %), everything possible should be done to protect health care professionals against HIV infection. Research has shown that anti-retroviral drugs such as AZT, 3TC and protease inhibitors can significantly reduce the risk of HIV infection after percutaneous ('through the skin') exposure. Post-exposure prophylaxis with anti-retroviral therapy must start as soon as possible (within 1 to 24 hours after the injury) to reduce the chances of viral reproduction as much as possible. Some authorities feel that even if there has been a delay of up to 2 weeks after exposure, it is still advisable to offer post-exposure anti-retroviral prophylaxis.

### Post-exposure prophylactic treatment

A combination of AZT and 3TC is usually recommended for a 4-week treatment period. IIf virus resistance to AZT is a distinct possibility (e.g. if the source patient has been on AZT treatment for longer than 6 months), or in those rare cases of massive exposure following a blood transfusion with contaminated blood or an injection with a substantial volume of blood, a protease inhibitor (such as Crixivan) should also be added to the prophylaxis regimen for 4 weeks.

Any fluid contaminated with blood, semen, vaginal fluid, cerebrospinal fluid (CSF), pleural or other serous fluid should be considered to be potentially infectious. These body fluids pose the same risk of transmitting HIV as does infected blood. Non-infectious body fluids are urine and faeces (unless they are contaminated with blood). Post-exposure prophylaxis is not recommended if exposure has been to urine and faeces alone.

Post-exposure prophylaxis is unfortunately not always successful. Treatment may fail if the health care professional has been exposed to an HIV viral strain that is resistant to the anti-retroviral drugs that he or she takes for prophylactic purposes, if the viral load in the source patient is very high, or if the post-exposure prophylaxis is given too late or for too short a duration (Evian, 2000).

While the side effects of the anti-retroviral medication are usually uncommon in healthy health care professionals, they may include symptoms such as fatigue, headache, nausea and vomiting.

- While working in a hospital as a volunteer, you notice that a nurse is pricked with a needle while working with a very confused AIDS patient. What advice would you give to the nurse?
- Make a wall poster indicating all the steps that health care professionals should take after accidental exposure to HIV-infected blood in the health care situation. (See 'Management of accidental exposure to blood and other infectious body fluids' on page 418.)

## 5.7 MANAGEMENT OF RAPE SURVIVORS

Because of the high incidence of violent crime in South Africa, health care professionals are often called upon to treat the trauma that accompanies rape or sexual assault on adults as well as children. The risk of HIV infection after rape depends on factors such as the HIV status of the rapist, the viral load in the blood of the rapist and the coexistence of STDs — especially ulcerations. The risk of HIV infection may also be higher in cases of violent rape and the rape of children because of the considerable physical trauma that is inflicted by the rapist.

It is very important to begin prophylactic treatment with anti-retroviral therapy as soon as possible (within 1 to 24 hours) after the assault. A combination of AZT and 3TC is usually recommended for a 4-week treatment period. In high risk situations such as when, for example, the assailant *is known* to be infected with HIV, and where considerable trauma and bleeding are evident, a protease inhibitor, such as Crixivan, is also administered for 4 weeks.

The rape survivor is not only at risk of infection by HIV, he or she is also at risk of being infected by other sexually transmitted diseases such as hepatitis B. It is therefore important for victims (1) to be tested and treated prophylactically for STDs and (2) to be vaccinated with hepatitis B vaccine.

**Enrichment**

**'Starter packs' for rape survivors**

Rape often takes place 'after hours' or over weekends when it is difficult to get anti-retroviral medication. 'Starter packs' consisting of a two- to three-day supply of anti-retroviral drugs are available to rape survivors (or to health care professionals after accidental exposure to HIV-infected blood). Starter packs should be available at all health care services for the immediate initiation of post-exposure prophylactic treatment. It should be noted that the starter pack is designed to provide medication for only the first two to three days because it is designed as a stop-gap emergency measure. Anti-retroviral prophylaxis should, however, be taken for 4 weeks after the assault or accident. The client should therefore be advised to visit the doctor or clinic for follow-up medication.

## 5.8 IMMUNISATION OF CHILDREN AND ADULTS WITH HIV INFECTION

Children with HIV infection should be fully immunised. No vaccines are contraindicated in HIV-infected children, with the exception of BCG (the TB vaccine).

The following guidelines apply to BCG:

- BCG should be given to **ALL** HIV-infected babies, who show **NO SYMPTOMS** of HIV/AIDS at birth.
- BCG should **NOT** be given to HIV-infected children who **SHOW SYMPTOMS** of advanced HIV infection or AIDS.
- BCG should also not be given to HIV-infected adults under any circumstances.

Because tuberculosis is so common in HIV-infected individuals, the siblings of HIV-infected children (or the children of HIV-infected parents) should all be immunised with BCG.

**Why should BCG not be given to symptomatic HIV-infected children (or adults)?**

Vaccines are usually prepared from a weak form of the infecting agent (the virus or micro-organism). BCG, for instance, is prepared from a weak form of the tuberculosis bacilli (*Mycobacterium tuberculosis*). If this weakened form of the TB bacillus is injected into a person with an already weakened immune system (as is the case in symptomatic HIV infection), it may actually *cause* active tuberculosis. Instead, therefore, of *preventing* tuberculosis with BCG, one can actually *cause* the disease in the patient with a depleted immune system if one immunises him or her with BCG.

The WHO recommends that babies and children with HIV infection (healthy as well as symptomatic children) should be immunised with the following vaccines:

● oral polio (OPV) at birth, 6 weeks, 10 weeks, 14 weeks and again at between 4 and 5 years of age
● diphtheria, tetanus, pertussis (DTP) at 6 weeks, 10 weeks, 14 weeks and again at 18 months
● diphtheria and tetanus at between 4 and 5 years
● mumps, measles, rubella (MMR) at 9 months and measles at 18 months
● HBV (hepatitis B) at 6 weeks, 10 weeks and again at 14 weeks
● haemophilus influenza type B (Hib) at 6 weeks, 10 weeks and again at 14 weeks
● Yearly immunisation against influenza ('flu') is also strongly recommended. (It should be administered during March to April in the southern hemisphere to provide adequate protection before the commencement of winter.)
● A single dose of polyvalent pneumococcal vaccine should be administered to children with HIV infection. It is however only recommended for children over 2 years of age.

If a child is very ill, immunisation with live vaccines should be delayed until the child is better. Annual immunisation against influenza ('flu') is also strongly recommended for HIV-infected adults.

## 5.9 CONCLUSION

In Part 1, we were concerned largely with the physical aspects of HIV and AIDS — how the virus is transmitted and what effect it has on the body. Although all this information is vitally important in the fight against HIV/AIDS, *behaviour change* remains the most important measure for preventing the spread of this disease while no real cure or effective vaccine is available for HIV. Part 2 will deal specifically with how to prevent HIV/AIDS by changing behaviour patterns that increase the risk of infection and will explain how ordinary people may acquire whatever lifeskills are necessary to prevent infection.

# Prevention and Empowerment in the HIV/AIDS Context

**Learning outcomes**

- develop an HIV/AIDS education and prevention programme for the working place that is based on sound theoretical principles of behaviour change and appropriate methods of learning
- explain the traditional African perceptions of illness, sexuality, condom use and community life to a friend and develop an education and prevention programme which incorporates these beliefs
- demonstrate the correct use of a male as well as a female condom to somebody
- develop an HIV/AIDS education and lifeskills training programme for school children that takes the age and the developmental characteristics of the children concerned into account

## INTRODUCTION TO PART 2

Because there is no cure or vaccine for HIV and AIDS, our only defence against infection is prevention. Prevention however entails much more than a set of rules of what to do and what to avoid. Effective prevention requires an accurate knowledge of how human beings behave in different contexts. It is important to know *when* or *under what conditions* people will be prepared to change their sexual behaviour. To be successful, HIV/AIDS prevention programmes should also take cultural differences, beliefs and customs into account. Because changing learned sexual behaviour is extremely difficult, our best hope for success in preventing the spread of HIV infection lies in empowering our children with the necessary knowledge, attitudes, values and lifeskills, not only to prevent infection, but also so that they can care for those who are less fortunate.

The building blocks of a successful HIV/AIDS education and prevention programme are discussed in **Chapter 6**. This chapter reviews various theories that describe the conditions that have to obtain before people will be prepared to change their behaviour. This chapter also discusses the basic principles of adult education, the methods and strategies that promote learning, and the facilitation skills that we need to help people to learn new skills and attitudes.

HIV/AIDS prevention programmes will never succeed in Africa if we do not take the traditional African worldview into account. **Chapter 7** gives an overview of traditional African perceptions of illness, sexuality, children, community life and condom use. The chapter examines the implications of traditional African beliefs and customs for HIV/AIDS prevention programmes in Africa.

**Chapter 8** gives practical advice on how to prevent HIV infection. *Safe*, *safer*, as well as *unsafe* sexual practices are all discussed, and numerous ideas and tips are given on how to practise safer sex. The prevention of HIV in injecting drug users is also addressed in this chapter.

HIV/AIDS education and lifeskills training for children are discussed in **Chapter 9**. Children's developmental characteristics, their perceptions of illness in general, as well as their understanding of HIV and AIDS in their different developmental phases, are all discussed. This chapter provides guidelines for educators about the kind of content they can include in HIV/AIDS education and lifeskills programmes for children in the primary as well as the secondary phase of schooling.

# 6 Principles and Strategies for Prevention

*How Raka can be kept at bay*

*This swift beast must die,*
*or he will reign over us*
*and he will bring a great and prolonged pain with him.*

AIDS is different from any other epidemic disease that has ever plagued the world. It is not only incurable, it is like the beast Raka from N.P. van Wyk Louw's epic poem because it challenges our deepest secrets and taboos about sex and death — whether as individuals or as a community. People vainly try to defend themselves against this *Raka* of destruction and fear by building defensive walls of myth, stigma, prejudice, and blame around themselves. Although one may understand the psychological processes that compel people to try to distance themselves from all manifestations of HIV and AIDS, their denial (in so doing) unfortunately makes us all more vulnerable to the effects of HIV/AIDS. Health care professionals are therefore faced with the tremendous task of trying to break down the walls of ignorance and prejudice so that they can convince every member of the community that HIV/AIDS touches the core of every person's life and that we should all work together to prevent the great and prolonged pain that this disease brings with it.

In 1990, Osborne said that 'the Achilles heel of HIV is its dependence on behaviour that is voluntary. Our best attack is that which enlists the community [member] in his or her own defence' (p. 3). To enlist and train a whole community in its own defence, is no small task. In this chapter we will examine the most important compounds of any successful HIV/AIDS prevention programme.

## 6.1 THEORETICAL PRINCIPLES: WHEN WILL PEOPLE CHANGE THEIR BEHAVIOUR?

The initial reaction of the public health authorities in many countries as they tried to cope with the AIDS epidemic was to try to persuade individuals and targeted groups to change their behaviour by providing them with relevant information about HIV/AIDS. We now know that if we hope to change behaviour, we need to do more than supply correct information to vulnerable groups. According to Fishbein and Middlestadt (1989, p. 109):

> There are certain types of information that are necessary for developing effective educational communications or other types of interventions. The AIDS epidemic is much too serious to allow interventions to be based upon some educator's untested and all too often incorrect intuitions about the factors that will influence the performance or nonperformance of a given behaviour in a given population.

If health care professionals want to be successful in changing people's sexual behaviour, they first need to understand the various theories about how behaviour change can be effected. Although a detailed discussion of the different theoretical models is beyond the scope of this book, we will nevertheless review the most important principles of behaviour change, which form the basis of all these theories. These principles are based on the theory of reasoned action (Fishbein & Ajzen, 1975), the theory of planned behaviour (Ajzen, 1991), the Health Belief Model (Becker & Maiman, 1975; Rosenstock, 1974), the AIDS Risk Reduction Model (ARRM) of Catania, Kegeles and Coates (1990), the social-cognitive learning theory of Bandura (1977), and the learning theory of Rotter (1966).

According to the theories of *reasoned action* and *planned behaviour*, people are defined as *reasonable* beings who systematically process and use all information available to them when they *plan* their *behaviour* (Ajzen, 1991; Fishbein & Ajzen, 1975). To change people's behaviour, it is therefore necessary (in terms of this theory) to understand and change the cognitive structures that govern specific behaviour. Health care professionals can, for example, not begin to understand and change a person's behaviour if they do not have an appreciation or understanding of that individual's intentions, beliefs, attitudes, subjective norms and his or her self-efficacy. Figure 6.1 gives an overview of the cognitive, emotional and social components that should be included in any programme that is designed to bring about sexual behaviour change.

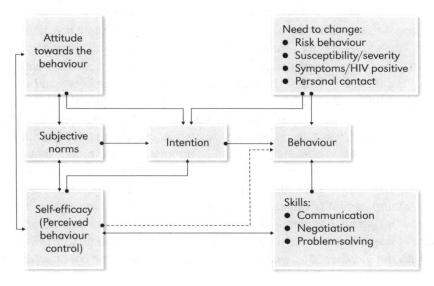

**Figure 6.1**
*Cognitive, emotional and social factors influencing behaviour change*
(Source: Adapted from Ajzen, 1991, p. 182)

## Recognition of the need to change

Before people can change any particular behaviour, they first need to recognise the *need* to change that behaviour. The factors that often contribute to the realisation that high-risk sexual behaviour should change are: (1) the individual's self-description of being at risk; (2) the perception of an individual's own susceptibility or vulnerability to HIV infection; (3) the perception that the disease will have serious consequences and that it will affect the person's whole life; (4) the belief that performing a specific behaviour will reduce susceptibility to (or the severity of) the illness; (5) a concern about good health in general; (6) experiencing the symptoms of illness; (7) personal contact with somebody who is HIV-infected or who has AIDS, and (8) an HIV-positive diagnosis (Becker & Maiman, 1975; Fishbein & Middlestadt, 1989).

## Be specific about the behaviour you want to change

The health care professional should be absolutely specific about the behaviour that needs to be changed. Talking to people about 'safer sex practices' in general will rarely have any effect on their behaviour because the concept 'safer sex practices' is vague and refers to a whole category of behaviours instead of to one specific behaviour. A specific behaviour that one would like to change in an individual should therefore be identified (in cooperation with the individual concerned). Thus, for example, one might (together with the client) construct the following definite statements: 'I must always use a condom', 'I should have only one sex partner', or 'I must always use sterile needles for injecting drug use'. (See 'The male condom' on page 134 and 'The female condom' on page 138 on how to be specific about condom use.)

Identify the *action*, *target*, *context* and *time* of the behaviour that you want to change. One should recognise the vital conceptual differences between *buying* and *using* a condom (**action**), *latex* versus *non-latex* condoms (**target**), a *primary long-term relationship* and *casual sex* (**context**), and casual sex *once a week* or casual sex *once a year* (**time**). Prevention strategies will vary according to the particular aspect of behaviour that one is considering. It is also important to remember that a prevention programme which was developed to *change* sexual behaviour (e.g. a strategy to increase or to decrease a specific type of behaviour) will not necessarily be effective for *maintaining* sexual behaviour (e.g. a strategy for continuing to use a condom every time the person has sexual intercourse). Cognitive factors associated with the *initiation* of specific behaviour may be totally different from the factors that are associated with the *increase*, *decrease* or *maintenance* of that same behaviour (Fishbein & Middlestadt, 1989).

If one wants to develop sexual behaviour change programmes that are successful, one must focus on behaviour that is under the *control* of the individual — rather than behaviour which is dependent on external factors. If a (disempowered) woman has no power to negotiate the use of male condoms with her unwilling partner, a counsellor should rather concentrate on convincing her to use the female condom (this might at least be an action that she is able to control).

## Intentions to perform a specific behaviour

If individuals want to change their behaviour, they must first develop the *intention* of changing that behaviour. According to *the theory of reasoned action*, a person's behaviour can be predicted if one can determine whether he or she has an *intention* to carry out that specific behaviour. Intentions reflect all the motivational factors that influence specific behaviour. Intentions are indications of how hard people are willing to try, or how much effort they are planning to put into the performance of a behaviour (Ajzen, 1991, p. 181). As a general rule, we can say that the stronger the intention or the commitment to do something, the greater is the probability that a person will perform that behaviour.

AIDS educators should therefore also concentrate on people's behavioural intentions in their HIV prevention programmes. The same principles that apply to behaviour change (in terms of specificity, action, target, context, and time) should also be taken into account when one is trying to change or reinforce intentions. In order to change behaviour, it is necessary to reinforce the intention that directly corresponds to the specific behaviour. If the desired behaviour is 'to use a latex condom every time the person has sexual intercourse', the intention to be reinforced will be the intention 'to use a latex condom every time the person has sexual intercourse' and not the intention 'to practise safer sex' or merely 'to use a condom' (both of the latter are too vague to be of any use).

It is obvious however that intentions do not always predict behaviour. When people do not have control over their own behaviour (as in the case of disempowered women who cannot negotiate condom use with their sex partners), the best intentions in the world may not necessarily translate into behaviour. Good intentions are also often hampered by the *unavailability* of opportunities and resources such as time, money, condoms and the necessary skills.

## Attitudes towards the specific behaviour

The intention to change sexual behaviour (by using condoms, for instance) depends on a person's *attitudes* towards that particular behaviour (e.g. condom use). If people truly believe that condom use will have a positive outcome for them, then the probability that they will actually use condoms will be much greater. If however they feel negative towards the use of condoms (or find the use of condoms problematic, for whatever reason), then a great deal of explanation, negotiation and persuasion may be required before such people will actually use condoms (the desired behaviour). It is therefore of the utmost importance for the counsellor to establish a person's attitude towards *the specific behaviour* that needs to be changed before one can expect the change to occur (Fishbein & Ajzen, 1975).

Strongly positive attitudes, attitudes which are the end product of a lot of thinking, and attitudes which have great personal relevance and have been formed in the crucible of direct and personal experience, are far stronger predictors of behaviour than vague, generalised attitudes that have been formed as a result of exposure to impersonal second-hand and indirect information (Petty, 1995). The prediction of behaviour change can be made more accurate when one considers attitudes towards alternative courses of action. Thus, for example, you can more accurately predict whether or not a person will use condoms if you measure both the person's attitude towards condom use, as well as his or her attitude towards *not* using condoms (Petty, 1995). If our prediction of attitudes is to be successful, we need to know what a person's attitude is to all alternative forms of behaviour.

### The influence of subjective norms on behaviour

The intention to change behaviour also depends on the *subjective norms* of the individual. Subjective norms are influenced by

● the beliefs of important reference groups, or individuals, in a person's life, as well as by

● the desire to please these reference groups or individuals. If condom use is *not* acceptable to friends or lovers, and if it is important for the person to impress his or her friends, it will be very difficult for that person to change his or her behaviour and start using condoms. In such cases it may be necessary to counsel peer groups or partners before individuals will consent to use condoms (Fishbein & Ajzen, 1975).

Before a person's behaviour can be changed, it is important to establish if this specific behaviour is under *attitudinal* or *normative* control. If a teenage boy's decision not to use condoms is under attitudinal control (i.e. he has a negative attitude towards condom use because it inhibits his sexual pleasure), the counsellor's attempt to change his behaviour by using normative or peer pressure will fail dismally because his behaviour (in this case) does not depend on what his friends think (normative control).

### Self-efficacy or perceived behaviour control as a predictor of behaviour change

To have an intention to change behaviour is not enough: people should also *believe* that they have the *ability* to perform the desired behaviour. Bandura (1977) refers to a person's *belief* in his or her *ability* to control behaviour, or to carry out specific behaviour successfully, as *self-efficacy*. According to Bandura (1991, p. 257), self-efficacy is central to any person's ability to function:

> People's beliefs in their efficacy influence the choices they make, their aspirations, how much effort they mobilise in a given activity, how long they persevere in the face of difficulties and setbacks, whether their thought patterns are self-hindering or self-aiding, the amount of stress they experience in coping with difficult environmental demands, and their vulnerability to depression.

Ajzen (1991) uses the term 'perceived behaviour control' to refer to people's perception of the ease or difficulty of performing a specific task. People with high self-efficacy (or a high perception of behaviour control) are better motivated to master new situations and behaviour, and they are more persistent in their attempts to reach specific goals than people with low self-efficacy.

Low self-efficacy has been identified by many researchers as an obstacle to sexual behaviour change. Low self-efficacy has been found to correlate positively with high-risk sexual practices, with an unwillingness to change behaviour, and with relapses from low- to high-risk behaviour (recidivism) (Montgomery et al., 1989). On the other hand, subjects who were categorised as being in the lowest category of risk for HIV infection generated the highest self-efficacy scores.

AIDS educators must not underestimate the importance of self-efficacy in their programmes. They should increase or reinforce people's self-efficacy by making sure that people possess the required communication, negotiation and problem-solving skills to carry out the desired actions and that they know exactly how to apply their newly acquired behaviour (e.g. how to use a condom). The person's belief in his or her ability to use a condom and to discuss condom use with partners should also be reinforced. Researchers found that both intentions to change behaviour, as well as perceptions that the behaviour can be controlled (high self-efficacy), significantly increased the probability that behaviour could be changed for the better.

The chances that a person will change his or her behaviour (e.g. by using condoms) are much better if that person (1) forms a strong intention (in this case, to use condoms), (2) demonstrates a favourable attitude (in this case, towards condom use), (3) possesses positive subjective norms and (4) also possesses a high level of self-efficacy and the perception that he or she *can* control his or her behaviour. Intentions, attitudes, subjective norms and perception of behaviour control may all however become undermined if a person becomes discouraged and disheartened by (perceived) obstacles or difficulties that seem to block his or her progress towards behaviour change.

## Obstacles and rewards that impede or encourage behaviour change

People will only change their behaviour if they perceive the new behaviour as potentially effective, beneficial and as practically feasible (Rosenstock, 1966). The probability of a person changing his or her behaviour therefore depends on that person's perceptions of the *benefits* or *rewards* that will accrue from the new behaviour, as well as that person's perceptions of the *disadvantages* or *obstacles* that will result from changed behaviour. Researchers have found that people are prepared to change their sexual behaviour in various ways if they believe that this behaviour is beneficial (in the sense of decreasing their risk of infection), and if they know that they have social support (i.e. support from friends and the community) (Montgomery et al., 1989).

One of the main reasons why people do not change their behaviour is that they perceive the existence of obstacles that (in their *perception*) hinder and obstruct the possibility of behaviour change (Janz & Becker, 1984). Research into the prevention of HIV infection identified the following factors as obstacles that hindered sexual behaviour change (Montgomery et al., 1989; Schurink & Schurink, 1990; Van Dyk, 1991):

- People abandon all attempts to use condoms if they find it *stressful* to initiate or to maintain the behaviour.
- *Society's intolerance* towards certain sex practices and safer sex makes it more difficult for people to change their behaviour.
- *Unsupportive sex partners and peers* lead to abandonment of all attempts at safer sex. Research found that people often do not use condoms because they do not want to offend their sex partners, because sex partners don't 'like' condoms or because they are afraid that the partner will leave them. Partners often refuse to use condoms because it 'feels different' and because of the stigma attached to the use of condoms (in some circles). Condoms are often associated with syphilis, filth, uncleanliness, unfaithfulness and family planning.
- The lack of *communication skills* is one of the greatest obstacles that stands in the way of behaviour change. People find it difficult to ask partners to use condoms — especially if they do not know the partner well. They are also often afraid that the partner may think that they have AIDS. Women, in many cases, do not have the power to negotiate condom use with their husbands or partners.
- People find it difficult to handle a partner's *refusal* to use condoms.
- It is very difficult for people to change their sexual behaviour if they are not offered *alternative sex practices* which can replace risky behaviour. (See 'General safer sex rules' on page 142 for examples of alternative sex practices.)
- A *fatalistic attitude to life* hinders sexual behaviour change. Many young South Africans, for example, currently believe that they are at much greater risk from the possibility of violence than from the possibility of infection by HIV. As one

student puts it: 'With AIDS I still have a chance to live for many years. My neighbourhood is so dangerous, I am not sure that I will still be alive tomorrow morning.'

- In a Zimbabwean study, students listed the following obstacles to condom use: the necessity for advance planning, inaccessibility (i.e. difficulties in obtaining condoms), a lack of privacy (problems about storing condoms or being found with condoms in one's possession), and an inability to *communicate* with their partners (Sherman & Bassett, 1999).

- The use of *alcohol* and *recreational drugs* diminishes the power of individuals to make responsible decisions. Even subjects who possessed a firm intention always to use condoms and who had often used condoms in the past, reported that they often had sex without condoms when they had been under the influence of alcohol or drugs (their responsibility threshold was drastically lowered).

- Condoms are often not *available* and *accessible*. People, especially young people, do not use condoms if they are not readily available. They are either ashamed to ask for condoms over the counter, or else they don't have the money to buy them.

- *Cultural norms* and *religious beliefs* are often not conducive to condom use (see 'Traditional African perceptions of condoms' on page 121).

It is up to health care professionals to try to identify the obstacles that stand in the way of safer sex practices and to help people to surmount these obstacles. People are more likely to change their behaviour if the rewards inherent in changed behaviour (rewards such as peace of mind) are made obvious. Encourage individuals to make lists of rewards as well as obstacles.

This will enable you to discuss each individual's concerns and (if at all possible) find suitable solutions. Some solutions are quite easy to put into practice. Many people are simply unaware of their existence.

## Perception of health control: The internal versus external locus of control debate

It is important for the prevention of illness as well as the promotion of health to know to what extent people believe that they have control over their own health status. According to health locus of control theory, people who believe that they have no control over their own health (external locus of control) will be less inclined to get involved in preventative and promotive behaviour than people who believe that they can do something to improve their health (internal locus of control) (Rotter, 1966; Wallston, Wallston & De Vellis, 1978). People with an internal locus of control believe that they can influence and control their own health through personal behaviour. People with an external locus of control, on the other hand, believe that they don't have much control over their own health because their health depends on external factors such as luck, chance, fate, other people, or uncontrolled forces from 'outside' of themselves. The assumption is therefore that people with an external locus of control will often not do much to prevent illness or to improve their health.

Research on locus of control and sexual behaviour change has generally found that people with an internal locus of control will be more inclined to change high-risk sexual behaviour than people with an external locus of control. The implications of these findings for educational programmes to change high-risk sexual behaviour are complex. To simply say that 'educators should change people's locus of control from external to internal' is a demonstration of arrogance and ignorance.

Locus of control is not only a personal issue, it is also a cultural issue. Many cultures (such as, for example, many indigenous African cultures) have a collectivistic worldview (i.e. a worldview that emphasises the primacy of group over personal interests). People from such cultures are acculturated to operate on the assumption of an external locus of control. According to Mbiti (1969, p. 106), the identity of the traditional African is totally embedded in his or her collective existence and all decisions (including decisions about health) are taken with the group's knowledge and approval. It is obvious that it would be almost impossible (as well as impractical) to imagine that human agents would be able to change the underlying cultural and philosophical assumptions of an entire group of people.

Health care professionals who work in Africa should therefore accept the fact that Africans have an external locus of control as an incontrovertible given — and learn to work *with it* rather than against it when they devise means to change high-risk sexual behaviour. In collectivist cultural contexts of this kind, it is the family, the community and peer counsellors who should rather be involved in prevention programmes because they possess the authority and prestige to dictate sexual mores and customs (see 'Community involvement in AIDS education, prevention and counselling' on page 124).

**Skills to convert intentions into actions**

Intention or a strong commitment to change behaviour can only be translated into action if people possess the kind of skills and help that will allow them to do so. For an individual to change his or her sexual behaviour may require complex negotiations with sexual partners who may not have the same degree of commitment towards change. Verbal communication skills, negotiation skills and problem-solving skills are all needed before one can get one's partner successfully to commit to safer sex behaviour (such as, for example, condom use). Health care professionals should assist people to practise their communication and negotiation skills through experiential activities such as modelling and role play.

## Theories of behaviour change: a summary

The theories of behaviour change provide a tremendous amount of information that is extremely useful for understanding behaviour and for implementing interventions that will be effective in changing behaviour (Ajzen, 1991, p. 206). These theoretical principles underlying behaviour change should be kept in mind by health care professionals when they develop programmes to prevent HIV infection in the community. Table 6.1 summarises the principles that underlie behaviour change.

### Table 6.1

*A summary of the theoretical principles of behaviour change*

A person will be more likely to change his or her sexual behaviour if he or she:

- realises the need for behaviour change (e.g. feels vulnerable to HIV infection if he or she has sex with multiple sex partners)
- knows exactly what specific behaviour needs to be changed and how to go about changing it (e.g. he/she knows that a new condom should be used for every act of intercourse)
- has the intention or commitment to perform the behaviour (e.g. the intention to use a condom every time he or she has sex)
- has positive attitudes towards the behaviour (e.g. he or she believes that condom use will prevent HIV infection, and that condoms are quite comfortable to use)
- has the support of friends in changing the behaviour (e.g. his/her peer group totally accept and approve of condom use)
- has a strong belief (high self-efficacy) in his or her ability to perform the specific required behaviour (e.g. he or she knows exactly how to use a condom effectively and easily, or is able to insist — without fear of retribution — that a condom be used every time he or she has sex)
- knows exactly how to perform the behaviour effectively (e.g. how to use the condom in such a way that the condom will not break or leak)
- perceives that many more benefits and rewards will accrue from the new behaviour (e.g. condom use) than obstacles
- has the necessary skills to perform and maintain the behaviour (e.g. the communication, negotiation and problem-solving skills to make condom use an acceptable behaviour)

## The stages of behaviour change

According to the transtheoretical approach of Prochaska and DiClemente (1984, pp. 24–29), behaviour change involves movement through four different stages of change. In the first stage of precontemplation, people are unaware of having any problem at all, and so they can logically have no intention of changing their behaviour (e.g. they will not even be considering the use of condoms). Contemplation is the stage in which people become aware that a personal problem exists (e.g. they are aware of the dangers of unsafe sex and they are seriously thinking about using condoms, but they have not yet made a commitment to change). Action is the stage in which people change their overt behaviour and the environmental conditions that affect their behaviour. In this stage people are acting on their beliefs in personal self-efficacy (e.g. people start using condoms and they believe in their ability to maintain this behaviour). The last stage of behaviour change is the stage of maintenance. This is the stage in which people work to maintain their newly acquired behaviour and to prevent relapses to the kind of behaviour from which they made the change. Maintenance is not an absence of change; it is a continuance of change (e.g. people use condoms, but they still have to work very hard to maintain the behaviour and to prevent relapses into unsafe sex practices). Cessation of a problem only occurs when people no longer experience any temptation to return to the problem behaviour, and if they no longer have to make any efforts to prevent themselves from relapsing.

Activity

Why do you think is it important to be able to identify the exact stage of behaviour change in which a person currently finds himself or herself? How would it, for example, influence your HIV/AIDS prevention message if you knew that a person is in the precontemplation phase? Or if you knew that a person was in the action phase?

## 6.2   HIV/AIDS PREVENTION PROGRAMMES

The purpose of HIV/AIDS education is not only to disseminate information, but also to change attitudes and behaviour, to equip people with the necessary lifeskills, to empower them to prevent the spread of HIV infection and to care for people who are already infected. The following principles and strategies should be kept in mind as one develops HIV/AIDS prevention programmes (based on UNAIDS, 2000c; Van Dyk, 1999; WHO, 2000a):

### National support

HIV/AIDS prevention programmes can only be successful if they are backed by political will and leadership. No prevention programme can be successful without the support, commitment and high-profile advocacy of a country's leaders. A single, comprehensive, powerful national AIDS plan involving a wide range of role players ranging from government to the private sector is necessary. Successful programmes should impart knowledge, counter stigma and discrimination, create social consensus on safer behaviour, and boost HIV prevention and care skills. These can be cost-effectively accomplished through mass media campaigns, through peer or outreach education, through lifeskills programmes in schools and workplaces, and by ensuring that voluntary counselling and HIV testing are available.

## Peer support

Behaviour change is most likely to occur if peers educate and support each other. Youth programmes that are run by the youth, by groups that comprise street children, injecting drug users and refugees, are all extremely effective in promoting practices and behaviour leading to reduction of HIV transmission. Sexual practices, drug-taking and other risk behaviours are much more likely to be openly discussed, explored and understood within such safe group environments.

Peer education programmes both empower and educate people. According to Harrison, Smit and Myer (2000, p. 287), a successful peer education programme transfers the control of knowledge from the hands of experts to lay members of the community, thereby making the educational process more accessible and less intimidating. Peer education also allows group debate and the negotiation of messages and behaviours that lead to the development of new collective norms of behaviour rather than to attempts to convince individuals to change their own behaviour on a basis of rational decision making.

Powerful examples exist throughout the world of the success of peer involvement in prevention strategies. Peer counselling has, for example, been very successfully applied by the South African mining companies. Willing and enthusiastic people should be identified and then trained to work as peer counsellors in their own communities. Health care professionals, teachers and religious leaders can play an important role in facilitating the formation of these groups and providing expert knowledge where necessary.

## Involving people living with HIV/AIDS

People living with HIV/AIDS are often the best advocates and activists for social and behaviour change and they should be included in the developmental and implementation stages of HIV/AIDS prevention programmes. The personal story of someone living with HIV presents a powerful message. These messages can mobilise people and resources and thus initiate successful prevention programmes. Involving people living with HIV/AIDS in prevention programmes in their own communities helps to ensure that the programmes are relevant and meaningful to the specific community or population group in question.

## Cultural, religious and social sensitivity

There is no standard programme that will be meaningful, relevant and effective for *all* people in *all* times and places. Prevention programmes must be contextualised so that they are sensitive to local customs, cultural practices, religious beliefs and values, as well as to other traditional norms and practices. Traditional African beliefs and customs, which should be taken into account when developing HIV prevention programmes in Africa, are discussed in chapter 7.

## Facilitating empowerment

Empowerment can be facilitated by involving and encouraging individuals, groups and communities to address their own health concerns and to find solutions to their own problems. People who are empowered to come up with their own plans and solutions are more likely to implement effective HIV prevention programmes.

Individuals (especially women in disadvantaged positions, and young people) should be empowered by being taught communication skills, negotiation skills, assertiveness, decision-making strategies, self-esteem, self-efficacy, lifeskills, and the fundamentals of competent sexual behaviour, problem solving and conflict resolution.

Although the personal and social disempowerment of women in Africa is often emphasised (and is indeed sometimes a serious problem), the inherent strength and autonomy of African women, especially in women's groups (where such qualities are more than evident), should not be overlooked by health care professionals working in Africa. Ulin (1992) commented that rural African women have always been able to mobilise and organise themselves informally to meet the needs of their communities by making the best use of the advantages and opportunities for solidarity inherent in family ties, neighbours and other informal networks. Ulin believes that the solidarity of women in rural African communities may be their greatest source of strength for coping with the AIDS epidemic.

## Condom distribution

Condom distribution should be an important component of any HIV prevention programme. Condoms should be easily accessible to both men and women. They should be available and distributed in places where a sense of privacy is increased and embarrassment is reduced — through self-service (i.e. where people can simply help themselves to however many they need) in clinics, hospitals, factories and mines. Condoms should also be distributed free of charge if possible. Health care professionals need to know where free condom distribution centres are and if possible they should keep a supply themselves.

## Combating stigma, isolation, stereotypes and discrimination

By showing their own support and responsibility to care for all people, regardless of their health or social status, health care professionals can act as role models for others in helping to combat stigma, discrimination and the isolation of people living with HIV/AIDS. Prevention strategies will become far more successful if and when HIV is treated like any other disease, and when people feel safe to be open about their HIV status.

Health care professionals have to become aware of their own stereotypes and attitudes before they can educate people on HIV/AIDS prevention. They should think about and listen to the 'language' they use when they speak: prejudiced language may alienate them from their target group. While saying 'He caught AIDS' as opposed to 'He has AIDS' may mean the same thing, the first sentence is loaded with negative meanings that betray the implicit attitudes of the speaker. (Such a negative meaning may be that AIDS is something over which we (the innocent) have no control, something that we 'catch' from 'them' — the contaminated out-group.) People often say 'He is HIV' instead of 'He is HIV positive' or 'He is infected with the HI virus'. A sentence that is constructed like this implies an identity with the virus, i.e. the person *is* the virus, instead of the person *has* the virus.

AIDS educators should also be careful not to use sexist language. To always refer to *he* and *him* in the context of HIV/AIDS may imply that men are always the guilty party. Victimising language should also be avoided. Instead of saying 'She suffers from AIDS' one should rather say 'She lives with AIDS' or 'She is HIV positive'. Instead of referring to 'rape victims', one should rather use positive language and refer instead to 'rape survivors'. Be careful not to fall into the trap of using prejudiced or discriminatory language. If you refer to people with HIV infection as 'those people', you are clearly dividing the world into two groups: the innocent, healthy *us*, and the guilty, diseased *them*.

While we all unfortunately sometimes think in terms of stereotypes, we should make every effort to handle our own stereotypes so that we can root them out and thus avoid offending others and hurting feelings. If we interact with members of a 'stereotyped' group, we will quickly learn to recognise our own prejudices and eliminate them.

## Stereotypes, prejudice and discrimination

Stereotypes are cognitive frames of reference or patterns of expectations that strongly influence the processing of incoming social information. A stereotype is usually an over-simplified, one-sided and relatively fixed generalisation or rigid view of a group, an individual or of certain activities or roles. Stereotypes are, for instance, beliefs that all members of specific social groups share certain traits or characteristics. Prejudice is a negative attitude toward the members of a social group that is based solely on their membership of that group. Discrimination refers to negative behaviours or actions that are directed towards members of social groups who are the objects of prejudice. Discrimination is prejudice in action (Baron & Byrne, 1994, pp. 218–219).

**Activity**

Devise an exercise to make people aware of their stereotypes, negative attitudes or prejudices. Or use the following riddle in a group:

A man and his son were involved in a serious car accident. Emergency vehicles sped to the gruesome scene. On arrival, paramedics applied CPR to both victims. Once stabilised, the patients were rushed by ambulance to the hospital. Unfortunately, the man died during transit as a result of his fatal injuries. The boy was rushed into the emergency theatre. Medical personnel were waiting with scalpels gleaming underneath the bright theatre lights. Just before the operation commenced, the surgeon cried out: 'I can't operate. This is my son!'

Who is the surgeon?

Ask the participants to write the answer down, and to raise their hands if they believe they have the answer. Do you know the answer? The surgeon, of course, is the boy's mother. If you could not figure the riddle out, is it because you are strongly imprinted with the stereotype that only men can be surgeons?
(Credit to Ms Hanli van der Westhuizen for the riddle.)

## Volunteer Counselling and Testing (VCT) as a new HIV-prevention strategy

Volunteer Counselling and Testing (VCT) has emerged as a major strategy for the prevention of HIV infection and AIDS in Africa. Apart from raising awareness about HIV/AIDS, many studies show that knowing one's HIV status is instrumental in effecting behaviour change and the adoption of safer sex practices (Mkaya-Mwamburi et al., 2000; Serima & Manyenna, 2000).

Availability of accessible and affordable VCT services is a problem that should be addressed by governments. It is also preferable to use rapid HIV antibody tests (see 'Rapid HIV antibody tests' on page 58) because distances from the clinic and a lack of transport often make it difficult for people to come back to the clinic for their test results. If VCT services do exist, the community should be well informed about such services. It should be widely advertised and health care professionals and community workers should be sensitised and trained in pre- and post-HIV test counselling.

## Respect of human rights and the improvement of social structures

HIV/AIDS is also a developmental challenge. Society as a whole would be made less vulnerable to HIV in the long run if governments were to make a serious attempt to grapple with social problems such as poverty, unemployment, migratory labour, the subordinate status of women, and child abuse. Social goals such as education, the empowerment of women and human rights should therefore be promoted.

## A holistic approach

Counselling, education, support and care services and resources should be combined to provide a holistic continuum of HIV prevention and care. A comprehensive prevention programme that addresses the various aspects of HIV/AIDS in different contexts (churches, schools, hospitals and tertiary institutions) will prevent the stigma and discrimination often associated with HIV specific programmes.

## 6.3   TEACHING AND LEARNING ABOUT HIV/AIDS

Health care professionals are increasingly required to act as HIV/AIDS educators. The general public (including youth, pregnant women, school children, parent groups, sex workers, and drug users) all urgently need information about HIV/AIDS. In addition, traditional healers, trained birth attendants, other health care workers, social workers, teachers, volunteers, family members, caregivers, friends, counsellors, religious and civic leaders and community health workers all require continuing education on issues related to the prevention and care of HIV/AIDS. It is very important to identify and train peer counsellors so they can be equipped with the necessary skills to counsel their peers. There is also a great need for training-the-trainer courses so that trainers can go back to their departments, companies or communities to educate people about HIV/AIDS. Teaching does not always have to be formal. It can take place anywhere and at any time. Whenever you obtain any valuable information, share it with whomever you can. By doing that, you may save someone's life.

Basic principles on *how* to teach HIV prevention will be discussed in this section. *What* we teach (content) will depend on the needs of the target group. The information given in this section is based on the WHO Fact Sheets on HIV/AIDS (WHO, 2000a, pp. 9-2 to 9-6).

## Basic principles of adult education

It is important, before commencing any educational programme, to assess the learning needs of the group and to be familiar with the cultural environment from which the participants have come. Use a questionnaire to establish the group's needs. Find out what they already know, what they don't know, and what misconceptions they entertain. Ask the participants what their needs and expectations are and what they expect to gain or learn from the course. This information will make it possible for you to plan relevant educational sessions and materials and deliver information that is meaningful and useful to the participants.

Evaluation of the educational strategies used and the learning outcomes of the participants is also critically important. Most adults learn best if they are actively involved in the learning process. It is also important to realise that different people learn through the medium of different educational strategies. If we remember this, we will be careful not to use one single learning method in all situations. Thus, for example, it might be important (on one occasion) to provide an opportunity for learners to practise one particular technique, while (on another occasion) it might be more appropriate to lecture, to review a textbook or utilise another kind of document. Learners also need time to reflect on their learning and to revisit what they have learned through the use of techniques such as practice, discussion, critical questioning, research, or active participation in teaching others.

Educational sessions should be conducted in such a way that learners feel safe about admitting their ignorance when they do not understand something. Educational sessions should also empower learners actively to seek additional teaching/learning and support. If students fear ridicule, they will certainly not expose themselves to humiliation by admitting their ignorance. If students do not take the opportunity to obtain whatever information they need in your workshop, they might become inadvertently involved in unsafe and unethical practices in their subsequent careers — simply because they were too embarrassed (or too afraid of being humiliated) to ask pertinent and direct questions.

It is therefore a matter of the *utmost importance* for the facilitator to create an atmosphere in which no student will feel too embarrassed to ask for information about any kind of behaviour and practices whatsoever — for example, the sexual practices of gays or lesbians or the problems that are likely to be encountered by sex workers in their encounters with clients. A workshop facilitator who does not create the right atmosphere for free, frank and full discussion and inquiry, should not be working in the field of HIV/AIDS counselling.

Timing is also important in the teaching/learning process. Learners learn best when they feel they have a need to know. It is the responsibility of the teacher to foster this 'need to know'. In addition, the retention of learning should be assessed periodically and supported over time (WHO, 2000a).

AIDS education involves consideration of sensitive issues such as sexuality, different sexual practices, drug use, and other risk behaviours. Traditionally, health care professionals have not been educated to feel comfortable with openly discussing sensitive, embarrassing, or 'offensive' practices. Practice in discussing these subjects should begin in a safe learning environment. Finally, it is important to teach risk analysis and risk-avoidance strategies.

## Preparing educational sessions

When you are engaged in preparing an HIV/AIDS educational session, you should ask yourself the following questions:

- Who are the people in the audience? Are they male, female, young or older, educated or less well educated? What is their level of knowledge about the subject? It is important to have a very clear idea of who your participants are before you choose or produce educational materials.
- What do you hope to achieve? What outcome do you expect the educational session to produce? What is your main message? Do your expected outcomes match the learning needs of the group?
- How will you access the information you need to conduct the session?
- How long will the educational session take? Will the participants be able and willing to stay for the entire session?
- How much will the educational session cost? Is enough money available to finance the course?
- Have you made provision for tea and lunch breaks?
- What equipment will you need? Is the equipment you need available, or can you adapt your session so that you will be able to use whatever is available?
- Is existing material available to you? If material is available, use this (and adapt it if necessary) rather than start from scratch. Contact the Department of Health and AIDS centres to get posters, pamphlets, etc.
- Is the language appropriate? Are you presenting the information at the educational level of the learner? Is your language too complex or too simple for the participants? What is the literacy level of the group?
- Are the illustrations appropriate and culturally sensitive? Are they clear enough for the participants to understand? Do the illustrations reflect issues and images with which the participants are familiar?

- Is video material appropriate for your specific group? Although it is important to be specific about sex practices and preferences, participants may be offended if they perceive the material to be pornographic.
- Do the educational materials look good and attract people's attention? Are the designs and colours attractive? Are they culturally sensitive? Can the participants identify with the materials?
- Does the educational material avoid discrimination? Does the material use examples of people who are similar in racial origin, age, and sexual orientation to the target group? Do the illustrations foster stigma or fear? Showing a person dying of AIDS might, for example, lead some people to believe that *all* people living with HIV are about to die.
- Does the educational material generate feelings of fear? Messages such as 'AIDS Kills' might scare people away. Such scare tactics rarely help to promote effective behaviour change. Positive messages, on the other hand, often promote changes in attitudes and behaviour. It cannot be denied that some illustrations that catch people's attention, even 'negative illustrations', can frequently be effective in raising people's awareness. The key to success is to know the target group well and to choose your messages accordingly.
- Does the educational material avoid moralising and preaching? People resist listening to someone telling them what they *should* and *should not* do. Such practices often make learners resistant to opening themselves to the message — and therefore far less likely to engage in open and productive discussions. For example, once young people have been told in a session that they should 'never engage in sexual intercourse before marriage', they will probably make no contribution at all to any subsequent discussion about safer sexual practices. The best materials provide information in a clear and respectful way and they empower people to make their *own* decisions.
- Do your educational strategies build on skills that have already been acquired and do they promote confidence? It is important to build on the expertise of the group. What do they already feel confident about doing? How can that confidence be carried over to other circumstances?
- Does it help to build a supportive environment? People learn best when they feel cared for and supported. If people work together towards the same ends, much can be achieved. Does the learning session provide participants with opportunities for supporting one another? Can your group be supported in promoting effective change in other people, in changing health care practices, and even changing legislation?
- What educational materials work best for the participants? Consider using attractive posters, local radio, TV or newspaper announcements, leaflets, fact sheets, and training aids such as flip charts, or flash cards. Open discussions,

interviews with people living with HIV/AIDS and their families, listening to stories from other care providers or patients, and advertisements, all deliver powerful educational messages. It is also important for participants to visit people living with HIV/AIDS in hospital and in the community.

● How will you distribute educational material? Sadly, there are often excellent educational materials that are not used simply because the methods of distribution are ineffectual.

● Do the learners leave with any materials that will reinforce their learning? Learning takes place over a period of time and needs repeated reinforcement. What methods of reinforcing learning have you considered? Do you have fact sheets ready for distribution? Will the posters you select reinforce learning? Do you provide additional educational sessions? Do you test the learners at a later date? Do you require supervised practice after a teaching/learning session? Is there a library available and a list of recommended reading? What other strategies have you considered to reinforce learning?

● Have you considered pre-testing the educational material before it is printed or published? Pre-testing educational material can be a very important step towards ensuring that the message is understood, is well received and has the potential to motivate behaviour change and promote best practice.

● What methods of evaluating the educational sessions have you considered? Evaluation of student learning can be done by using questionnaires before and after the programme. Observation of practice and observation or anecdotal reports of behaviour change are other forms of evidence. Did the participants also evaluate the teacher and the educational sessions? Has behaviour change been observed over time (i.e. has retention of learning taken place)? What other forms of evaluation have you considered? What will you do with the evaluation information? Will you make changes to your educational material and teaching/learning processes if necessary? It is a good idea to ask the participants to evaluate the educational sessions at the end of each day so that you can adapt the next day's sessions if necessary.

**Activity**

Visit your nearest Health Department or AIDS Training, Information and Counselling Centre and collect all the pamphlets, posters, fact sheets and other training material you can get. These materials are usually distributed free of charge. Evaluate the material by using the relevant criteria for the development of effective educational material discussed above. List the strengths and weaknesses of the pamphlets or the other material that you have collected.

## Methods of teaching/learning

There are many teaching methods or strategies that can promote learning. You should take the needs of the learners into account and, in order to obtain maximum benefit from the learning process, you should preferably utilise a combination of methods.

### Lectures and mini lectures

Certain factual information (e.g. technical or medical information) can best be explained by lectures or mini-lectures. The facilitator should make the lecture as interesting as possible by using visual aids such as pictures, drawings, etc. Densely formatted transparencies which consist only of written material will quickly have your learners nodding off.

### Group participation

Evidence shows that people learn best when they participate in learning rather than when they are merely passive observers. In the past, students were placed in rows and then lectured to by the facilitator of the group. Although this method is some-times useful when one wants to communicate a certain body of knowledge quickly, reinforced learning leading to behaviour change is best accomplished through the active participation of the learners. It is often extremely effective to *reverse* the lecture/group participation process by (1) asking the participants to brainstorm a specific problem (e.g. the basic principles of HIV/AIDS counselling), (2) letting them present feedback to the group, and then (3) wrapping up the session with a mini-lecture on 'the basic principles of HIV/AIDS counselling'.

### Group discussion

Group discussions are useful if group members feel comfortable with one another and if individuals are not reluctant to speak. Feelings of group safety can take time to develop and are not always achieved. The group facilitator (the educator) can however use his or her skills to facilitate group discussions and provide encouragement. Group discussions expose members to the beliefs, values, and practices of others, and usually lead to peer support. Topics may either be discussed in a big group, or one can divide the participants into smaller 'buzz' groups which then report back to the big group in plenary feedback sessions.

One of the best ways to encourage group discussion is through problem posing and problem solving. These problems can either be developed by the facilitator or from the experiences of the participants. For example, if the facilitator poses a problem like the one described in the following paragraph, a lively debate is guaranteed:

You are an AIDS counsellor working in a Voluntary Counselling and Testing Centre. One of your clients, Peter, is HIV positive. He refuses to tell his wife of his HIV status and he strictly forbids you to inform his wife. He does, however, not want to start using condoms, because his wife might get suspicious. What do you do? Do you tell his wife? (See chapter 17 for ethical and legal implications.)

## Role play and simulation

Learners often find it beneficial to practise new learning by acting in, or observing, a role play or simulated exercise. This kind of practice makes learners more confident and skilful in expressing in the 'real world' what they have learned through role play. The 'fish bowl' technique is a very effective learning tool. It means that the role players sit in the middle of a circle formed by the rest of the group who observe the interactions in the role play (e.g. a health care professional counselling the family of an HIV-infected individual). After the role play has ended, the group can discuss and analyse the processes that they have observed. Debriefing should always be done after a role play session so that the participants can be made aware that their role playing was only a make-believe situation. People can become very emotionally involved in role play and they often leave the session with feelings of depression and sadness if proper debriefing is not undertaken.

**Enrichment**

### Ice breakers

When people do not know each other well or when they come from varying back-grounds and are expected to participate in a group discussion, it is always wise for a facilitator to introduce an 'ice breaker' at the beginning of the session. An ice breaker is an exercise which helps people to get to know each other and feel comfortable with each other. It also helps to break down some of the barriers that often exist between people (Nel, 2000). Some ideas for ice breakers are: (1) Ask participants to devise their own imaginary T-shirts with their personal motto on the front, a picture of themselves (how they see themselves) underneath the motto, their likes on the one sleeve, their dislikes on the other sleeve, their achievements and their dreams on the back, and so on. (2) Ask each participant to choose an animal that represents him or her, and then ask each person to explain to the group why he or she chose that particular animal. (3) Ask participants to name three things (not people) that they would like to take with them if they had to leave this planet. (Can you think of a few original ice breakers of your own?)

## Building on successes of learners

Find out what your learners have been successful in achieving and use these exper-iences of success to teach other subjects. This strategy provides learners with a sense of confidence and empowerment. Ask the learners to bring ice breakers, exercises and examples that work for them in the communities where they work. Your aim as a facilitator should not only be to teach, but also to learn from your learners.

## Group activities

There is considerable evidence to suggest that people learn best when they are actively engaged in their learning. Often the group develop their own teaching/learning sessions. Evidence shows that young people learn best from their peers and when they are actively engaged in the development of peer group learning. Young people enjoy group activities such as games, the making of collages and jigsaw puzzles.

## Group excursions

If enough time has been allocated to an HIV/AIDS programme (as in, for example, a five-day course), it is always a good idea to organise excursions to facilities that care for people with HIV/AIDS, such as hospices, hospitals and orphanages. Visits to AIDS Training Information and Counselling Centres, and to community projects providing home-based care or AIDS-orphan care, are also very valuable experiences for students.

## Visual and learning aids

Posters, photographs, pictures, overhead projections, slide presentations, videos, and works of art can all be powerful educational tools. Discussion can follow the use of such visual aids. For example, the group can be asked what the visual aid meant to them, what they liked or disliked about it, what was unclear, disturbing, or helpful. Another interesting technique to use is to ask learners to make their own picture collages (from magazines, for example) — collages that represent their feelings about selected issues that have been discussed in the class. One can then ask learners to explain (interpret) to the rest of the group what their collages mean. Discussions provoked by newspaper clippings can also sometimes be very informative and thought-provoking.

Flip charts, fact sheets, a white board, flash cards, wall charts, drawings done by the group or others, diagrams, tables, and graphs also provide clear and easy access to information. These visual aids can also be used to promote group discussion. For example, questions such as 'What does this graph tell you?', 'What is missing from this information?', 'How could you go about getting this information?', 'What does this drawing tell you?', 'How would you have drawn this picture differently?', all promote discussion. Models of anatomy can be used to help learners to understand how HIV and other sexually transmitted diseases are passed from one person to another. Models are also suitable for practising correct condom use. Because models can be used to demonstrate many basic nursing care procedures, they can be helpful for training caregivers who will provide home-based care.

Enrichment

**Learning aids don't have to be expensive**

Nthabiseng Seepamore (2000), a social worker and AIDS educator, uses a glass water jar with a narrow neck, two drinking glasses, water, red food colourant, and a condom to illustrate to her learners why a condom prevents transmission of the virus from one person to another. Seepamore uses the following technique. She fills the water bottle as well as the drinking glasses with tap water. She then adds the red food colourant to the water jar and explains to the learners that the red colour represents the HI virus in the body. The water in the jar is now red, while the water in the drinking glasses is still clear, representing two people without HIV infection. Seepamore now slowly pours the red water from the jar into one of the glasses. The clear water in the glass turns red, showing how the HI virus spreads from the infected to the uninfected person. She now puts a condom over the neck of the water jar with the red fluid and tips the jar over the second glass of clear water to 'pour' the red water into the glass. The red water stays behind in the condom, and the water in the second glass stays clear. Seepamore explains to her learners that this is exactly what happens in the body: the HI virus is trapped in the condom and therefore cannot infect the sex partner.

## Case studies

Ask the learners to draw on their own work experience as AIDS educators to prepare and present a case study. Discuss the case study in the group. Many new and alternative views on handling problems usually come up, and they can be a valuable learning experience for all. Be constantly aware of confidentiality issues and encourage everyone to use fictional names and places in order to protect the identity of infected people.

## Interviews with HIV-infected people

If you can arrange to conduct a public or open interview with an HIV-infected person, it will be a very powerful learning experience for most learners. Not only do they get 'first hand' information, the experience also challenges their stereotypes and prejudices. Afterwards learners will often say things like 'But I thought HIV-positive people look different' or 'She can't be HIV positive because she's not thin and skinny!'

## Guest speakers

Learners usually enjoy listening to guest speakers who are experts in their fields. It also breaks the boredom of always listening to the same presenter.

## Story-telling and sharing one's experiences

Story-telling and the sharing of one's own experiences can often promote effective learning. People like to hear about the experiences of others, and they often find that they can relate to these experiences more easily than when trying to grasp facts that seem to have little relevance to themselves. Fictional stories are also helpful for sharing important messages. Although a story might be about a fictional character, a listener can usually easily relate to and understand the message being conveyed.

In their *AIDS home care handbook*, the WHO (1993) uses an example to illustrate how a story can be a very effective means of explaining sometimes difficult issues to people in such a way that they can really relate to the people in the story. The story tells how HIV came into Yulia and Mukasa's family and what happened to them and their children over several years. Pictures showing different events in their lives (such as their wedding, Musaka's loneliness and casual sex in the city, Yulia's pregnancy, the funeral of their baby, and so on) are used to bring the characters in the story to life. By changing the names, the setting (rural or city), and the background, this story can be adapted to suit any audience.

## Participating in drama

Dramatic events can also be a powerful way of expressing important information. Not only do the participants of the drama learn from this method, but the audience can also be brought into the drama. Young people are particularly open to this form of learning.

## Learning through games and play

Board games, the making of models out of clay or play dough and puppets can all be used to present important messages. Puppets often help to make the subject matter more playful and less intimidating. Puppets can be made by the students and they can also collaborate in the creation of the story which the puppets will present.

## Singing, dancing, drumming and drama

Teaching in the African context should include traditional healing and learning methods to tell the story of AIDS. The African tradition of social sharing, rituals, story-telling, dramatisation, singing, clapping, dancing and drumming should be explored and creatively used by AIDS educators to get the HIV/AIDS message across. Dance, for instance, is and has long been a medium of education in Africa for teaching important cultural values (Pasteur & Toldson, 1982). Metaphors, song and dance are especially useful when a language barrier exists between an AIDS educator and learners, and it can be used very successfully to integrate the message of AIDS with the traditional African concept of sickness. People often express what they have learned best by writing songs and poetry. Many black AIDS counsellors include spiritual aspects, prayer and ancestor consultation in their presentations.

> Health care professionals often work in contexts and cultures which are not familiar to them. Be open-minded and remember that you are there to help. Be yourself and be honest. If you do not feel comfortable with the customs of a specific community, then don't participate in them. If you do something that you do not believe in, you will in any case come over as acting artificially and perhaps even insincerely. It is nevertheless important for you to show respect for whatever community you are working with and for their beliefs and customs. If you come over as a consistent and honest person, people will listen to your message.

## Social marketing and use of the media

Social marketing and the use of the media can be powerful methods of sharing information. Posters can be displayed where people live, work and play. Leaflets and written information can be left for people at health care centres, shopping centres, parks, shebeens, sport stadiums, gyms and other recreational facilities. One can involve the media in getting educational messages across to the larger community. Students can be encouraged to participate in media presentations. Cartoons and comic strips can reach wide audiences and be useful methods for peer support and education.

## Community fairs or meetings

Places where communities come together, such as fairs or meetings, can be used to present important information. Such community gatherings can increase public awareness of the issues and challenges of HIV/AIDS and encourage the wider community to become actively involved in the care and prevention of HIV.

## 6.4  FACILITATION SKILLS

*To facilitate* means to enable people to discover how much knowledge they already have, to enable them to explore their own potential, and to generate their own further learning. Facilitation involves creating an environment that is conducive to learning, experimentation, exploration and growth (Rooth, 1995, p. 9). One needs special skills to be a successful facilitator (the traditional trainer, presenter, educator or counsellor). A facilitator should always bear the following points in mind (Nel, 2000; Van Dyk, 1999):

● Establish a set of agreed-upon ground rules for the group as soon as possible (these ground rules may, for example, include agreed rules about confidentiality, equal participation, honesty, feedback, time management, smoke breaks, leaving the group, taboo subjects, mutual respect and language issues).

● Equal participation of all is important. Encourage silent participants without shaming them and without discouraging those who have a lot to say.

● Remember that people have the right to differ and disagree.

● Try to keep the discussion on track without controlling the process too much.

● Do not force your ideas on the group. Allow learners the freedom to explore — regardless of what you as the facilitator believe is the solution.

● Remember to pose open-ended questions.

● Encourage reflection. Give participants the time and space to reflect on activities and to absorb, consolidate and transform their experiences into lasting meaningful learning.

● Ensure that most participants agree with the conclusions reached or that they have at least had the chance to express their views.

● Be flexible. Assess the group's needs and expectations. Be respectful of their prior knowledge, and try to engage them on the level on which they habitually function.

● Remember that a successful facilitator guides, listens, advises, assists, affirms, manages and probes. A successful facilitator allows people to empower themselves in a safe environment.

● Be sensitive to group dynamics, communication and behaviour dynamics.

● Observe confidentiality at all times.

● Be sensitive to cultural issues. In a traditional African setting it is, for instance, not advisable to mix sexes and different age groups, especially when a sensitive and often 'taboo' subject such as sex is discussed. Out of respect for the men (or elders) in the group, women and young people will often not respond or take part in the discussions. Since wisdom is often associated with old age in some black cultures, adults may be reluctant to pay attention to a younger facilitator. Men are also often not willing to listen to women who, traditionally, are regarded as minors. The nurse's uniform may, however, in some cases imbue a woman with authority. Drawing on the expertise of the older people in the group and learning from them will make sessions more effective. The use of peer educators is probably the most effective means of educating traditional African people in sexual matters.

● Speak the 'language' of the group. Slang words and the use of sub-group terminology may cause a total communication breakdown between facilitators and their learners. It is therefore important for facilitators to become acquainted with the terminology used by the group with which he or she is involved. Don't refer to sexual behaviour and body parts in unfamiliar medical terms. Use the words that are familiar to the group.

- Be aware of the different meanings of certain concepts in different subgroups, and make sure that you are understood correctly. The concept of 'high-risk sexual behaviour' may, for example, mean different things to different people. Within the teenager subgroup, two sexual relationships per year may sometimes be defined as 'safer' sex — as opposed to frequent casual sex. Words such as 'promiscuity' and 'prostitution' also have different connotations in diverse cultures. If it is customary, for example, for a married man to have more than one sex partner, he will not perceive himself as being promiscuous. Women classified by men from a particular culture as prostitutes (sex workers) may simply be considered to be lady friends by men belonging to a different culture. Even when such women are rewarded with presents, such gifts are not necessarily regarded as payment for prostitution (Zazayokwe, 1989). AIDS counselling programmes that warn against 'prostitution' without explaining the concept, might therefore easily fail in communities where men define prostitution differently.
- If you don't know something, say so. If a participant asks you a question that you don't know, just say, 'I don't know but I will find out for you.' Don't give wrong or vague information to 'save face'. Make sure that you do find an answer and tell the person as quickly as possible. In this way you will show respect for the person's question, and he or she will not lose confidence in you or respect for you.
- Remember that the four cornerstones of being a good facilitator are empathy, respect, genuineness and concreteness ('concreteness' means presenting all material in a structured way and using clear, unambiguous terms and concrete explanations).

## 6.5 CONCLUSION

AIDS educators should be creative in exploring and using different methods and materials and transferring information effectively. They should be sensitive to their group's needs and should keep the theories of behaviour change in mind when they devise their programmes.

# 7 **Prevention in Traditional Africa**

*Raka sniffs around the kraal*

*And then Raka came up from his sleeping place*
*and peered at the red streaks and glow of the fire,*
*falling through the wooden pole fence of the kraal.*
*Then they heard his cry, like that of an animal*
*And when the coals of the fire were white and cold —*
*they heard him sniffing loudly at the thin spars of the kraal.*

In the beginning it was called 'Juliana's disease'. It was first noticed in the village of Lukunya, on the Ugandan border sometime in early 1983. A handsome Ugandan trader had come through selling cloth for women's kangas patterned with the name Juliana. A village girl with no money traded the stranger sex for a kanga, as did several other women who coveted the beautiful Juliana cloth. Some months later the first girl became sick: she had no appetite, could hold down no food, and had constant diarrhoea, which filled her with shame. In a few weeks she wasted away, grew weak, and had to be carried everywhere. Before she died, two other women, also adorned in Juliana's cloth, came down with the strange disease. The people of Lukunya decided that the Ugandan was a witch, and that Juliana's cloth had evil powers. To conquer Juliana's disease, traditional healers toiled to lift the stranger's curse. They were, however, unable to lift the powerful curse and the death toll continued to rise. Within a year the curse had spread to the neighbouring villages. Rumours of widespread witchcraft spread throughout the Kagera region, and traditional healers felt compelled to solve the Juliana mystery (Garrett, 1995, pp. 334–335).

If education and prevention programmes are to be successful in Africa, it is important for us to understand and appreciate the traditional African worldview.* The people of Africa experience the world in a unique and very specific way that is different from the way in which Westerners experience the world. This unique African worldview has for far too long been ignored by the Western world. HIV/AIDS education and prevention programmes have mostly been based on Western principles, and no attempt has been made to understand or integrate the diverse cultural and belief systems of Africa into such programmes. One may ask if this is not one of the reasons why HIV/AIDS prevention programmes have tended to fail so dismally

*Despite the differences between Africans from different cultures in terms of geography, language, religion and ways of life, there is a dominant socio-religious philosophy shared by all Africans. It is therefore possible to talk of a common African perspective or African worldview (Gyeke, 1987; Okwu, 1978; Sow, 1980). In Africa, where a constant process of westernisation is taking place, many Africans internalise both traditional African and Western beliefs.

in Africa. It is important for health care professionals who work in Africa to understand what health, sickness and sexuality mean in the traditional African context, and to incorporate these beliefs into their HIV/AIDS prevention programmes. It is also important to appreciate the importance of community life in African societies.

## 7.1  PERCEPTION OF ILLNESS IN TRADITIONAL AFRICA

If something bad happens to a traditional African, he or she will not attribute such an event to bad luck, chance or fate. They believe instead that every illness has been directed by an intention and a specific cause, and in order to fight the illness, it is necessary to identify, uproot, punish, eliminate and neutralise the cause, the intention behind the cause, and the *agent* of the cause and intention. As they attempt to understand an illness, traditional Africans will always ask the questions 'Why?' and 'Who?' (Sow, 1980). Traditional Africans believe that mental as well as physical illness can be caused by disharmony between a person and the ancestors, by a god or spirits, by witches and sorcerers, by natural causes, or by a breakdown in human relationships.

### The ancestors and God as causal agents of illness

In traditional religious systems in Africa, God is seen as a supreme being or creator who has withdrawn himself from human beings, and who is thus perceived as distant and remote from the people. Although traditional Africans believe in God and honour him, they see God as too important to bother with their everyday problems. The living spirits of the deceased ancestors are the 'mediators' between the people and God (Mbiti, 1969; McCall, 1995; Sow, 1980).

Ancestors form a very important and intrinsic part of the daily lives of traditional Africans. Ancestors are seen as benevolent spirits who preserve the honour and traditions of a tribe, and they usually protect their people against evil and destructive forces. Ancestors can, however, punish their people by sending illness and misfortune if people do not listen to their wise counsel, if certain social norms and taboos are violated, and if culturally prescribed practices and rites are neglected or incorrectly performed.

In some cases, it is believed that ancestors do not actually send illness themselves but that they merely allow it to happen by withdrawing their protection. When ancestors express their anger or displeasure by withdrawing their protection, their descendants are left exposed to attacks by witches and sorcerers. The illnesses caused by the ancestors are seldom serious or fatal, and traditional Africans are usually quick to restore their relationship with their ancestors through offerings and sacrifices (Beuster, 1997; Bodibe, 1992; Hammond-Tooke, 1989; Mbiti, 1969).

## God, the ancestors and AIDS

There is no indication in the literature that *traditional* Africans attribute AIDS to the anger of ancestors or to God's punishment. The influence of Christianity can, however, be seen in the beliefs of some black Christians who believe that AIDS is God's punishment for immorality and sins (Van Dyk, 1991).

## Witches and sorcerers as causal agents of illness

The day-to-day fate of traditional Africans is regulated and controlled by the complex relations between humans and the invisible but powerful beings and creatures who inhabit an intermediate otherworldly zone of existence that is the territory of evil spirits, witches and sorcerers. Nearly all forms of illness, suffering, misfortunes, conflict, as well as accidents and death, are ascribed to beings who operate from this zone (Sow, 1980).

Most Africans recognise both an *immediate cause* as well as an *ultimate cause* for disease or misfortune. A person with AIDS may, for instance, fully understand that the *immediate cause* of her illness is a virus, but she will nevertheless still ask: 'Why me and not my neighbour? While I sleep only with my husband, my neighbour is running around with many men.' The only answer that will really satisfy this woman is that *someone*, by means of magical manipulation, has 'caused' or 'sent' the virus to make her (rather than her neighbour) ill (this is the *personal or ultimate cause* of the illness).

Many black people, therefore, consult both traditional healers as well as Western health care professionals for the same condition: while the traditional healer is consulted to diagnose the *personal cause* of the condition (e.g. bewitchment) or to *prevent* a recurrence of the illness (e.g. by performing a ritual), a Western doctor is consulted for medication to *treat* the condition *symptomatically* (Hammond-Tooke, 1989; Herselman, 1997; Mbiti, 1969). If health care professionals do not understand this belief in immediate and ultimate causes of illness, they may feel threatened by the erroneous idea that black people do not 'trust white medicine'.

Witches or sorcerers are usually blamed for illness and misfortune in traditional African societies (Felhaber, 1997). Because people in Africa often use the services of witches and sorcerers to send illness, misfortune, bad luck and suffering to their enemies, they also believe that whatever bad luck or illness befalls them is sent by witches or sorcerers. Hammond-Tooke (1989) compared the perceived causes of illness in a conservative Ciskeian rural area in South Africa with the causes of illness in an urban area, and he found a strong belief in witchcraft in *both* the rural and urban areas. Table 7.1 reflects the causes of illness and misfortune as divined by traditional healers in Ciskei.

**Table 7.1**

*Perceptions of the causes of illness in an African context*
(Source: Hammond-Tooke, 1989, p. 123)

|  | Ancestors | Witchcraft or sorcery | Non-mystical factors (accidents and alcohol) |
|---|---|---|---|
| Rural | 8 % | 72 % | 17 % |
| Urban | 7 % | 45 % | 48 % |

Enrichment

**The difference between witches and sorcerers**

Although many traditional Africans do not distinguish between witches and sorcerers, witches are believed to have supernatural abilities and to commit evil deeds and cast spells with the help of mythical animals and supernatural creatures (or 'familiars'). One of the most widely known mythical monsters used by witches is the uthikoloshe or the tokoloshe. Witches also use small animals such as wildcats, owls, snakes or polecats to do their evil bidding.

Sorcerers, on the other hand, do not have mystical powers, but they act anti-socially to cause harm to people. Sorcerers usually misuse their natural ability or knowledge of medicine or herbs for non-healing purposes. They often put poison in food or place objects charged with malevolent force on a path or in a place where they will be 'picked up' or accidentally touched by the passer-by (the targeted victim). Sorcerers can also use the victim's urine, hair or nails to harm him or her. Traditional Africans often refuse to use bedpans or urine bottles in hospitals because they are afraid that the contents may fall into the hands of sorcerers (Hammond-Tooke, 1989).

## Witchcraft and HIV/AIDS

Witchcraft is believed to be the causal agent in HIV transmission, AIDS and death in many African countries, especially among the rural poor or people with the least education (Boahene, 1996; Bond, 1993; Yamba, 1997). More than 25 % of Zambian subjects in Yamba's study ascribed STDs to witchcraft. 'Why else,' they argued, 'will one man become infected and the other remain uninfected when *both* men have had sexual contact with the same woman?'

## The psychological function of witchcraft beliefs

Accusations of witchcraft and sorcery are usually levelled against others when the harmony of a group is threatened or disturbed because conflict, jealousy, tension and unhealthy competition have become too prominent and are threatening to over-whelm the stability of relationships in African community life (Beuster, 1997; Hammond-Tooke, 1989). The harmony of Africa has been disastrously disrupted by the advent of AIDS because it has occasioned the untimely death of innumerable young people and has given rise to an unprecedented lowering of life expectancy among all groups and classes of people. In African societies, death is only accepted as natural when old people die. In most other cases (where 'the queue of dying is jumped'), death is seen as a punishment or as the work of evil spirits and witches (Okwu, 1978; Yamba, 1997). The psychological rationale of blaming witchcraft for the breakdown of African societies is therefore understandable. The traditional African belief in malevolent witchcraft helps to make sense of the horrors and dis-ruptions caused by HIV/AIDS (Yamba, 1997). If one blames external factors such as witches and sorcerers for AIDS, this projection of responsibility serves to console both family, victims and society as a whole. It also serves as an explanatory hypoth-esis that is comprehensible in terms of the traditional African worldview, and so it helps to alleviate feelings of guilt and anxiety.

The belief in witches also helps people to attribute meaning to the things that happen to them. Such beliefs provide answers that science cannot provide — such as an explanation of the personal or the ultimate causes of illness. According to Seeley et al. (1991), witchcraft beliefs are both an expression and a resolution of a community's need to explain why some people who are 'at risk' do not contract AIDS and why some people die much more quickly than others.

Attributing HIV infection to witchcraft may also help the bereaved family to avoid feeling stigmatised by their community (Campbell & Kelly, 1995). Ironically, Boahene (1996) found that people who believe that AIDS is caused by witches are more likely to be supportive of HIV/AIDS patients because their understanding is that the patients have became infected with the virus through the agency of sources that are 'beyond their control'.

Witchcraft beliefs nevertheless also have very negative implications for AIDS counselling and education in Africa. The belief that *everything* that happens to a person can be attributed to external, supernatural beings or powers (an external locus of control) implies that individuals cannot be held responsible or accountable for their own behaviour. This outlook tends to prevent people from exercising their personal initiative in searching for solutions (Viljoen, 1997). Boahene (1996) found that many people in Africa do not consider their own behaviour to be a possible reason for HIV infection, Because of this misconception, they cannot appreciate the need for using HIV-preventative methods.

Witch-blaming may be a 'healthy' psychological move for the victim, but the personal cost for perceived witches in African society can be very great indeed since it may result in their death. There are many cases in which witches are still hunted down and killed in Africa. And it is often feared that accusations of witchcraft may follow the disclosure of a positive HIV test result if confidentiality is broken (Seeley et al., 1991).

Enrichment

**Witchcraft in Western Europe**

The motives behind the witch myth lie deep in the human psyche and are not confined to traditional Africa. The last English witch was burnt in 1722. Witchcraft in Western Europe can also be explained in terms of social tensions and antagonism. Waves of witch hysteria coincided with the rise of Protestantism and the breakdown of the feudal system in Europe (Hammond-Tooke, 1989, p. 49). Scapegoating, stereotyping, prejudice and discrimination can clearly be seen in beliefs about witches when the routine tensions of social life are projected onto a marginalised person or group of people.

## Implications of the belief in witches for HIV/AIDS education in Africa

Experience has taught AIDS educators working in Africa that to ignore and ridicule traditional witchcraft beliefs has adverse effects on their HIV/AIDS prevention programmes. These beliefs should rather be taken into account and integrated into HIV/AIDS prevention programmes. Programmes should, for example, recognise the belief that the *personal* or *ultimate cause* of an illness may be witchcraft, but the fact should be stressed that the *immediate cause* is a 'germ' which is sexually transmitted. In her counselling of traditional Africans in South Africa, Zazayokwe (1989) dealt successfully with the problem of causality by telling people that *they* may know where the HIV infection originated, but that *she* knows what the disease does inside the body and how they can prevent contracting it. In their research in Uganda, Seeley et al. (1991) found that, as AIDS has become more widespread, an explanation that combines scientific fact and witchcraft theory is more frequently used and is more accessible to people. While the Rakai of Uganda, for example, are aware that HIV is sexually transmitted, they attribute the chance of being infected through a sexual act to the power of witchcraft.

Many traditional Africans believe that witches or sorcerers use sexual intercourse as the contact point for their medicine or spells to infect people with STDs and HIV (Green, Jurg & Dgedge, 1993). And throughout the ages, traditional Africans have had their own forms of prophylaxis against witches and sorcerers. To protect themselves against diseases, misfortune and death, they wear charms or amulets which they believe have preventative and protective powers (Hammond-Tooke, 1989; Okwu, 1978). (Nurses are familiar with babies in hospital wearing protective strings around their necks or waists.) One may therefore ask why — in cases of casual sex — the condom cannot be introduced as a preventative charm to block the sexual contact point against the evil spells of witches. The services of traditional healers should be sought to 'fortify' the condoms with protective power before they are distributed among the community *as protective charms*. This will encourage traditional Africans to take responsibility for the *immediate cause* of HIV infection by obstructing the entry point of evil in the form of HIV. The following African proverb applies in these situations: 'If you know there is a snake in your house, you don't ask where it comes from: you kill it.'

## 'Pollution' as cause of illness

Traditional Africans believe that people sometimes get sick because they neglect to purify themselves from states of impurity or 'pollution' by failing to carry out the appropriate rituals that have been prescribed for everyday life since time immemorial among Africans. The crucial difference between this set of beliefs (pollution) and the others (ancestors and witchery) is that illness caused by neglect to perform routine rituals is not actually *sent* by a person or spirit, but that they are the consequence of neglecting the proper prescribed traditional routines of everyday life. Illness of this latter kind is regarded as originating from an *impersonal causation* (Hammond-Tooke, 1989).

Ritual impurities are usually associated with sexual intercourse (in particular sex with a prohibited person), with the activities of the reproductive system, or with situations in which a person comes into contact with corpses and death. The violation of sexual prohibitions in particular can give rise to a variety of health problems. If a man, for example, has sexual intercourse with a woman during menstruation, it is believed that 'bad blood' rushes to his head and causes delirium. Widows, women who have had an abortion or miscarriage, and people who have handled corpses or twins, are all ritually impure or polluted. In order to cleanse himself or herself from ritual impurity, a person has to perform extensive cleansing rituals that involve washing, vomiting and purging (Beuster, 1997; Bodibe, 1992; Felhaber, 1997; Green, 1994; Hammond-Tooke, 1989).

### Pollution and AIDS

Although AIDS is not ascribed to states of pollution or ritual impurity, some of the sexual prohibitions may be helpful in HIV-prevention programmes. Prohibitions such as the prohibition against sexual intercourse with a woman during menstruation, with a widow before she is cleansed (her husband might have died of AIDS), or with women who have had an abortion or miscarriage, should be encouraged because they can prevent HIV infection.

## Germs as a cause of illness: The STD-AIDS connection

Traditional Africans believe that some diseases (such as colds, influenza, diarrhoea in children, STDs and malaria) are caused by natural causes such as 'germs' (Felhaber, 1997). Although they believe that witches may sometimes *use* germs and sexual intercourse to cause illness, traditional Africans accept that the *immediate* cause of STDs is germ-related, that it is transmitted through sexual intercourse, and that it can be prevented by behaviour change (Green, 1994).

Unfortunately, the connection between STDs, AIDS and sexual behaviour change is often not made in Africa. Traditional Africans often cannot understand why they have to change their sexual practices to prevent HIV infection since HIV attacks everything except their sexual organs. They believe that the place where a germ or disease *enters* the body is the body part which becomes ill (the genitalia are usually affected in the case of syphilis, but not in the case of HIV infection).

The AIDS message should therefore be strongly linked to STD prevention in Africa. The knowledge and help of traditional healers should be actively used in the control and prevention of AIDS (Green et al., 1993). Most African patients consult traditional healers for STD treatment, and these healers are particularly competent in handling STDs. They often give sound biomedical advice to their STD patients, advice which is also conducive to AIDS prevention. Among other things, they advise patients (1) to abstain from sex while undergoing STD treatment, (2) to choose healthy sex partners who are unlikely to have STDs, (3) not to have sex with sex workers (or prostitutes) and soldiers, and (4) to locate and advise all recent sex partners to be treated (Green, 1994).

Green (1994) believes that the spread of HIV in Africa can only be curtailed if STDs are more effectively treated and prevented. He feels that more financial and other resources should be devoted to STD control programmes instead of being allocated only to condom promotion and distribution.

## 7.2  TRADITIONAL AFRICAN PERCEPTIONS OF SEXUALITY

Sex not only serves a biological function in African societies. For the traditional African, sex also conquers death and symbolises immortality.

### Personal immortality through children

It is extremely important for traditional Africans to acquire personal immortality through their children. According to Mbiti (1969), history does not move forward into the future in traditional African thought, but backwards in time toward the *Zamani* — the Swahili word for the past. As a person grows older, he or she moves gradually from the *Sasa* (the now-period that represents a person's present experiences) to the *Zamani*. After physical death, people continue to exist in the *Sasa* period as the

**Enrichment**

**Identify and correct misconceptions**

AIDS educators should be very sensitive to cultural beliefs, not only to accommodate them where possible, but also to identify misconceptions that may have adverse implications for responses to AIDS. For example, the Shona people in south-eastern Zimbabwe believe a man who has sex with another man's wife will get a fatal disease called runyoka. A married man places this permanent curse on his wife so that he can punish any other man who has an illicit sexual relationship with her. This disease will only strike the guilty man who has sex with the wife and not the 'guilty' wife or her husband. Scott and Mercer (1994) found that 22 % of the Zimbabwean respondents in their study (25 % in rural areas) believed that AIDS and runyoka are the same disease. The implication of such misconceptions is obvious. Men may think that they are safe from HIV if they do not have sex with married women or if they adhere to sexual taboos (runyoka is also believed to strike a man who breaks sexual taboos by having sex with a woman who is menstruating or has miscarried). Once such misconceptions are identified, AIDS educators can make adjustments such as, for example, teaching people how AIDS differs from runyoka and emphasising that all kinds of unprotected sexual practices expose one to the danger of HIV infection.

'living-dead' for as long as they are personally remembered by name by relatives and the friends who knew them during their life and who have survived them. So long as they are alive in the memories of those who knew them, they are in a state of *personal immortality*. Mbiti explains this in the following way:

> Unless a person has close relatives to remember him when he has physically died, then he is nobody and simply vanishes out of human existence like a flame when it is extinguished. Therefore it is a duty, religious and ontological, for everyone to get married; and if a man has no children or only daughters, he finds another wife so that through her, children (or sons) may be born who would survive him and keep him (with the other living-dead of the family) in personal immortality (Mbiti, 1969, pp. 26–27).

To be forgotten after one's death and to be cast out of the *Sasa* period into the spirit world of the *Zamani* is the worst possible punishment for a traditional African.

Procreation is therefore one way of ensuring that a person's personal immortality is not destroyed. According to Mbiti (1969, p. 26), the failure to bear children is for an African woman worse than committing genocide. She has not only become a dead end for the family's genealogical line: she has also failed to perpetuate her own self through her children. When she dies, nobody of her own immediate blood will be there to 'remember' her, to keep her in the state of personal immortality: she will simply be 'forgotten'. The Shona ethnic group in rural Zimbabwe believes that those who die childless cannot be accepted into the spirit world of the ancestors and they are doomed to wander the earth as evil, aggrieved or haunted spirits (Mutambirwa in Scott & Mercer, 1994, p. 86).

## The importance of having children for day-to-day functioning

For the traditional African, children are not only valued for ensuring immortality. They are also very important in the day-to-day existence of traditional Africans because they can only prosper on the land of their ancestors if they have many wives and children to help them work their lands. There are many duties, such as looking after the cattle, babysitting, working in the fields, and fetching firewood and water, which cannot be adequately performed if the family is too small. In Africa, a man's wealth depends upon the growth of his tribe.

## Implications for AIDS education

Once the importance of personal immortality and the value of children in the lives of Africans is understood, Western health care professionals can appreciate why polygamy (the practice or custom by which one man has more than one wife, or one woman has more than one husband, at the same time) is practised in many African cultures. They can then also understand why convincing Africans to use condoms is so difficult, and why African women often insist on having children, even if they are found to be HIV positive.

### Polygamy in Africa

Western health care professionals mostly frown upon polygamy in African societies, but polygamy often helps to prevent or reduce unfaithfulness, prostitution, STDs and HIV. Mbiti (1969) is of the opinion that polygamy is particularly valuable in modern times when African men are often forced to seek work in the cities and towns. If a husband has several wives, he can afford to take one at a time to live with him in the town, while the other wife or wives remain behind to care for the children and family property. Polygamy often provides a healthy alternative or solution to problems inherent in certain cultural customs. In some African societies, for example, sexual intercourse between a husband and his wife is prohibited while she is pregnant and this abstinence is observed until after childbirth or in some cases even until after the child is weaned. In such situations, polygamy prevents husbands from turning to casual sex.

In societies where polygamy is practised, AIDS educators are wasting their time when they try to advocate monogamy. Much more will be achieved by emphasising loyalty and fidelity between a husband and all his wives and by discouraging sex outside that group. Polygamy is, of course, only safe if all the partners in the relationship are HIV negative.

### Protection while planning to have children

Population control remains a sensitive issue in Africa because it negatively impacts on the growth of a tribe, it deprives parents of needed labour and it undermines traditional beliefs and values (Hickson & Mokhobo, 1992). Instead of telling people in Africa to use condoms (and thereby inevitably to prevent pregnancy), it is necessary to tell them how to protect themselves from STDs and HIV while sometimes allowing 'unprotected' sex to make children. They should be advised not to use condoms until the wife conceives, and to start using condoms again while she is pregnant and nursing the baby. Although this solution is imperfect, it is more realistic than advising people to abstain from procreation, and it would at least *reduce* the risk of partner infection and perinatal transmission in stable relationships (Schoepf, 1992). While having many children is still important for Africans, many women in Africa nowadays do accept the idea of birth spacing and maternal protection.

### The devastating effect of HIV on babies

The fact that HIV (and other STDs) can infect newborn infants is of great concern to traditional healers in Africa because they realise that AIDS may jeopardise future generations, and indirectly also the immortality of their tribe. The devastating effect of HIV on unborn babies should therefore be emphasised in AIDS education programmes as an incentive for change (Green, 1994; Schoepf, 1992). Schoepf found that many young women in the Democratic Republic of the Congo (DRC) who are aware of this fact have sought a return to their ancestral traditions which placed a high premium on premarital virginity. Some married women have urged their husbands to join religious groups to support their resolve to remain faithful. Schoepf also found that although many women in the DRC were not in a position to negotiate the conditions of their sexual practices or condom use for their own safety, they had taken steps to change their children's behaviour. Many of the mothers had in fact broken the taboo against discussing sex with unmarried children in order to help them understand the need for condom protection. Although it may now be too late for many mothers, hope for the children of Africa may still exist.

## 7.3   TRADITIONAL AFRICAN PERCEPTIONS OF CONDOMS

Condoms are not very popular in Africa. Green (1994) found that although AIDS awareness was reasonably high in Uganda in 1993, and although millions of condoms had been distributed, the percentage of Ugandan men regularly using condoms was about 3 % at that time. Taylor (1990) similarly found that although the people of Rwanda were well informed about AIDS and had modified their sexual behaviour on the basis of their perceptions, none of the respondents in his study reported the use of condoms during intercourse.

Many Western authors erroneously ascribe this lack of condom use in Africa to promiscuity, permissiveness and to a lack of moral and religious values (Caldwell, Caldwell & Quiggin, 1989). This clearly illustrates a lack of understanding of the African philosophy behind sexuality and a disrespect for African cultural beliefs. Apart from social and political problems, there are deep-rooted cultural beliefs against the use of condoms in some parts of Africa. The challenge is not to condemn Africa, but to make the hidden cultural logic behind the resistance to condoms known and thereafter to find ways to work with or around it (Scott & Mercer, 1994). Some of the cultural reasons for not using condoms, and the implications of these reasons for AIDS education, will now be discussed.

## Condoms block the 'gift of self'

Taylor (1990) found that the resistance to condom use in Rwanda had nothing to do with ignorance, but with a very specific social and cultural dimension of Rwandan sexuality. Rwandans believe that the flow of fluids involved in sexual intercourse and reproduction represents the exchange of 'gifts of self' which they regard as being of the utmost importance in a relationship. Rwandans believe that the use of condoms will block this vital flow between two partners and that such a blockage may prevent fertility and also cause all sorts of illnesses. Many Rwandan women fear that the condom might remain in the vagina after intercourse and that they therefore risk becoming 'blocked beings'. In a culture where health and pathology are conceptualised in terms of 'flow' and 'blockage', it is understandable that women cannot imagine how a 'blocking' device could also be a healthy device.

Zazayokwe's (1989) research found that some black women in South Africa expressed similar fears: they were afraid to use condoms because they believed that the condom might remain behind in the vagina and eventually suffocate them by moving through the body to the throat. Zazayokwe ascribed this misconception to a lack of basic anatomical knowledge and corrected it by explaining the reproduction system to the women with the aid of models. Determining the *reasons* behind certain beliefs is vitally important for AIDS educators because they cannot attempt to rectify what they don't properly understand.

## *Implications for AIDS education*

Because of their cultural beliefs, it may be difficult to convince the majority of Rwandans to use condoms. AIDS educators should therefore rather expend their energy in looking for other ways to prevent the spread of HIV. Existing cultural forms of sexual intercourse should be investigated and encouraged if they seem to be safe — even though Western educators may find them strange. For example, Taylor (1990) described a safe but exotic form of sexual intercourse practised by Rwandans — called *kunyaza* — where the focus is on heightening both partners' sexual pleasure while keeping penetration to a minimum. Safer behaviour like this should be identified and encouraged.

## Condoms prevent the 'ripening of the foetus'

There is a widespread belief in many parts of Africa, such as East Africa, the DRC and among the Zulus in South Africa, that repeated contributions of semen are needed to form or 'ripen' the growing foetus in the womb (Heald, 1995; Ngubane, 1977; Schoepf, 1992). One of the objections often raised by Africans is that condoms are 'not natural' — not only because they inhibit pleasure, but also because they interfere in the process of natural foetal development. It is also believed that semen contains important vitamins which are necessary for the continued physical and mental health, beauty and future fertility of women.

### Implications for AIDS education

In correcting the 'ripening of the foetus' belief, Schoepf (1992) found an ally in the traditional healers of Kinshasa (DRC) who were able and willing to reinterpret traditional beliefs in ways that facilitate condom use. Traditional healers realised that while their ancestors were correct in stressing the health value of frequent sexual intercourse, they were not confronted by an AIDS epidemic which makes infected semen dangerous. The traditional healers of Kinshasa were therefore prepared to tell their clients that semen should be seen as a *metaphor* for repeated intercourse.

Repeated intercourse is necessary to nourish the mutual love and understanding between the parents, which is essential for providing a nurturing environment for foetal growth. A nurse explained this as follows to a group of mothers: 'When the mother knows she is pregnant, the baby is already on its way to growing. The ancient ones meant that the husband should take an interest in his wife and not run around with other women while she awaits the child' (Schoepf, 1992, p. 231). Clients are assured that the actual semen is not needed to 'ripen' the foetus and that condoms can therefore be used after conception to reduce risks of HIV infection to partners.

Although current practices relating to the prevention of HIV/AIDS are alien to traditional African thinking, many traditional healers are prepared to introduce new ideas and practices into their healing repertoire. They even have specific rituals which they use when they ask for the approval of the ancestral spirits before introducing unfamiliar objects or practices among their people. Green, Zokwe and Dupree (1995) found that traditional healers in South Africa preferred to use lifelike dildos to demonstrate the use of condoms to their clients, but that they first sought the approval of their ancestor spirits by ritually presenting the dildos and condoms to their ancestors and explaining their beneficial use. After the ancestors had signified their approval, the healers were prepared to incorporate the dildos and condoms as a useful part of their standard healing instruments.

## 7.4   THE IMPORTANCE OF COMMUNITY LIFE IN TRADITIONAL AFRICA

The community plays a very important role in the life of traditional Africans. Traditional African beliefs are predicated on principles such as the value of the *collective interest* of the group, the *survival of the community* or tribe, and the *union with nature*. The traditional African cannot exist *alone*: his or her identity is totally embedded in his or her collective existence (Sow, 1980). According to Mbiti (1969, p. 108), the cardinal point that one has to understand about the importance of the community in a traditional African's life may be explained in the following way:

> When he suffers, he does not suffer alone but with the corporate group; when he rejoices, he rejoices not alone but with his kinsmen, his neighbour and his relatives whether dead or living. Whatever happens to the individual happens to the whole group, and whatever happens to the whole group happens to the individual. The individual can only say: I am, because we are; and since we are therefore I am.

The collective existence of traditional Africans gives rise to values such as communality, group orientation, cooperation, interdependence and collective responsibility (Viljoen, 1997).

### Community involvement in AIDS education, prevention and counselling

The collective existence of traditional Africans and the unity of the person with his or her community should be kept in mind by AIDS educators when they work in Africa. Education and healing in Africa always take place in a social setting. A sick person is, for instance, always accompanied by members of his or her family who understand, support and accept the patient (Bodibe, 1992; Chipfakacha, 1997). It is therefore recommended strongly that healing ceremonies, which involve relatives and incorporate the guidance and cooperation of the 'living dead' kin, should also be used in the education and treatment of AIDS patients. (See enrichment box 'Confidentiality: A controversial issue in Africa' on page 125.)

Dancing, singing, rituals and ceremonies should be encouraged because these forms of dramatisation enable people to express their emotions, to overcome anxiety, and to accept and integrate into their personal reality what may seem like very threatening parts of themselves. To incorporate the family and community has the additional benefit that their fears and emotions can also be attended to.

**Enrichment**

## Confidentiality: A controversial issue in Africa

Health care professionals working in Africa should be very sensitive to the issue of confidentiality in the areas in which they work. Because community and collectivity are so important to traditional Africans, Westerners often think that the notions of privacy and individualism are alien to Africans, and that they usually share all their experiences with one another. Normative regulations however regulate the kinds of information that can be shared, and the people with whom one may share it. In Tanzania, for example, such regulation of information may be organised in terms of categories such as gender, age groups, specified relationships among relatives, extended family networks, elders, traditional midwives and healers (Lie & Biswalo, 1994). African people are especially concerned about secrecy and confidentiality where AIDS is concerned, because they fear rejection by the community if their HIV status becomes general knowledge. In Lie and Biswalo's study, 98 % of the subjects indicated that secrecy and confidentiality are very important to them. They pointed out that they would prefer to talk to somebody 'who can keep a secret' about their HIV status. Such people (who can keep secrets) are usually trusted relatives, medical personnel, religious leaders and traditional healers.

One of the subjects in this study communicated his trust in his traditional healer as follows: 'He is a wise man with much life-experience. He will help me and show me respect. I trust him. He is used to secrets. He knows more secrets than anyone. He knows our history — our forefathers' (p. 144). The plea for secrecy is understandable when one reads African newspapers. As recently as January 1999, the brutal killing of an HIV-positive woman from KwaMashu (in KwaZulu-Natal) was reported in the South African newspapers: Gugu was beaten to death by her neighbours for disclosing that she was HIV positive ('Brave Gugu,' 1999). The critical issue, according to Lie and Biswalo (1994), is who should be informed and how. This should be done in such a way as to minimise the risk of rejection and to maximise the mobilisation of social support and existing coping resources. It is therefore a major challenge to the HIV/AIDS counsellor to identify, in cooperation with the HIV-infected person, which significant others should be informed, in what sequence and by whom.

AIDS educators should be creative and imaginative in incorporating traditional beliefs and healing methods into AIDS education programmes. The African tradition of social sharing, of rituals, of story telling, of drama, of singing, drumming and of dancing should be used to relate the threat of HIV infection to traditional Africans. The story of AIDS is already told very successfully in many African countries by using these media, and they should be further cultivated.

Community involvement in the planning, implementation and evaluation of AIDS education programmes is also important for the success of such programmes. A community's essential norms and values, cultural images and language can only be appropriately understood and incorporated with the help of the target community

(Airhihenbuwa, 1989; Boahene, 1996; Campbell & Kelly, 1995; Scott & Mercer, 1994; Walters, Canady & Stein, 1994).

The influence of the traditional African's community and significant others should never be underestimated by AIDS educators working in Africa. In a South African study which was done in 1991, it was found that black South Africans' health and sexual behaviour and the decisions they made in this regard were mainly determined by the 'other people' in their lives (i.e. by an external health locus of control), rather than by themselves (an internal health locus of control) or by fate or chance (Van Dyk, 1991). (See 'Perception of health control: The internal versus external locus of control debate' on page 89.) Those community resources such as community elders, traditional healers, community leaders and peer counsellors that are already established should therefore be trained and co-opted in the fight against HIV transmission.

**Traditional healers as vehicles of change**

No AIDS prevention programme can succeed in Africa without the help of traditional healers. Traditional healers are effective agents of change because they have authority in their communities. They function as psychologists, marriage and family counsellors, physicians, priests, tribal historians and legal and political advisers. They are the guardians of traditional codes of morality and values; they are legitimate interpreters of customary rules of conduct, and they have the authority to change or invent new rules and to influence their people in matters relating to sex. Traditional healers have greater credibility in their communities than village health workers, especially with regard to social and spiritual matters (Green et al., 1993; Holdstock, 1979; Schoepf, 1992; UNAIDS, 2000b).

About 80 % of the people in Africa rely on traditional medicine for many of their health care needs. Traditional healers are well known in the communities where they work for their expertise in treating sexually transmitted diseases, and the World Health Organisation has since the early 1990s consequently advocated the inclusion of traditional healers in national AIDS programmes (UNAIDS, 2000b). Collaborative health programmes involving traditional healers are under way in many African countries, and all indications are that traditional healers can effectively be involved in HIV/STD prevention programmes.

The aims of these programmes are to convince traditional healers to promote the use of condoms and safer sex practices and to counsel their clients on the prevention of STDs as well as HIV. Traditional healers are also encouraged to sterilise their instruments whenever they come into contact with bodily fluids so as to prevent practices that might put themselves at risk of HIV infection. They are also encouraged to refer AIDS patients to hospitals. In numerous cases, condoms are accepted by traditional healers, especially if they fit into their belief systems. Research has also shown that traditional healers abstain from dangerous practices when they are educated about the risks. Thus, for example, traditional healers often ask their clients to bring their own sterile razor blades for invasive procedures (Green, 1988, 1994; Green et al., 1993, 1995; UNAIDS, 2000b).

The South African government recently hired a traditional healer who has many years of experience to train fellow healers. She immediately suggested that traditional healers need to be involved in a *participatory* approach to training and that they need to be shown the utmost respect. Her advice was: 'Let them burn their incense in training.' This means that if their customs are respected, the training will be successful. She also emphasised the importance of using fellow-healers to train others because healers are far more receptive to hearing new things from their peers (UNAIDS, 2000b).

According to a UNAIDS report on collaboration with traditional healers in HIV/AIDS prevention and care in sub-Saharan Africa (2000b), most healers had little difficulty in understanding and accepting information about AIDS symptoms, HIV transmission and prevention, condom use, and condom promotion and distribution. The areas in which they experienced problems were home care, death and dying, mother-to-child transmission, and condom use in countries where the people had a strong desire to have more children.

Training of traditional healers should therefore also concentrate on home care and orphan care. Traditional healers will in future have a very important role to play in the care and support of AIDS patients, their families and the AIDS orphans who remain behind after their parents have died. Because national health systems will not be able to cope with the high AIDS toll in Africa, it will in many cases be the responsibility of traditional healers to advise people about proper home care, to treat opportunistic infections, to counsel young people about HIV prevention and to give psychological and spiritual support to those living and dying with AIDS (Green et al., 1993).

## 7.5 HOW TO USE AFRICAN BELIEFS TO THE ADVANTAGE OF AIDS EDUCATION

Health care professionals who work in Africa should resist the temptation to stigmatise all traditional African beliefs and practices as ridiculous, superstitious and harmful. They should rather focus on those beliefs that can promote AIDS education and prevention. Airhihenbuwa (1989) proposed a strategy or model (the PEN model), in terms of which traditional cultural health beliefs and behaviour can be categorised as positive (P), exotic (E) or negative (N) — thereby providing a basis for Western health care professionals to understand and cope with traditional cultural health beliefs and behaviour.

**Positive cultural behaviour should be encouraged and reinforced**

According to the PEN model, positive cultural beliefs and behaviours are values and behaviours which are known to be beneficial and which should therefore be encouraged and reinforced. Examples of positive values and behaviour are those that discourage or forbid sexual intercourse before marriage, immediately after birth, during menstruation, with widows (the husband might have died of AIDS), and with women who have aborted or miscarried. Other helpful beliefs are the belief that intercourse with a person with an STD is dangerous and the belief that encourages traditional 'thigh sex' or other forms of non-penetrative intercourse — which are sometimes practised by the youth and by unmarried people, or by a husband when his wife is menstruating (Airhihenbuwa, 1989; Green et al., 1993, 1995).

**Exotic cultural behaviour should be accepted and respected**

'Exotic' behaviours are traditional African customs and behaviours that are unfamiliar and strange to Westerners, but that are not harmful to health. These 'exotic' behaviours, such as polygamous marriages (where all partners are uninfected and faithful to each other), cultural rituals, ceremonies and herbal remedies, need not be changed and should be respected.

Health care professionals should appreciate the importance of rituals for the corporate existence of people in Africa. If they find that a ritual (such as male circumcision or tribal markings) is harmful to people's health, they should not attempt to *change or put a stop to the ritual* but rather suggest *ways to make it safer* (by, for example, encouraging the use of clean instruments so that HIV will not be transmitted). In many traditional African societies, a child can only become fully integrated into his or her society after going through extensive rites of incorporation (initiation). To prohibit or discourage these rituals would be to make an outcast of the child in those circumstances where rituals are regarded as important (Mbiti, 1969).

Rites, rituals, incisions and tribal marks signify identification, incorporation, membership and the enjoyment of full rights and privileges in the corporate community. They unite the individual with the rest of his or her community, both the living and the dead, and they should be respected by outsiders.

Some people are even currently pleading for Africans to look into their own past and to bring back some of the long-lost customs that advocated 'safe sex' but that were denounced by Western colonialists and missionaries as pagan or evil — without any attempt to understand the reasons or logic for them and without the provision of any healthy alternative. (See enrichment box 'A plea for Africa "Bring back your long-lost customs!"' on page 129.)

**Enrichment**

### A plea for Africa: 'Bring back your long-lost customs!'

Ahlberg (1994) described the very strict sexual customs and mores that existed among the Kikuyu people of East Africa before the Christianisation process in Africa. The Kikuyu people were fairly open about sexuality and there were many occasions when public discourses about sexual activity were held. During initiation and ritual ceremonies related to marriage and childbirth, the community openly addressed sexual matters through songs and dances. Sexual activity was never indiscriminate or casual, and penetration was strictly prohibited among newly initiated adolescents. It was obligatory for members of the tribe to practise strict sexual discipline, and the rules of sexual conduct were strictly observed. But because missionaries found these ritual ceremonies, songs, dances and the collective public discourses offensive (European missionaries of the nineteenth century, and even later, were extremely prim and strait-laced), they prohibited such valuable practices and traditional disciplines. This had the tragic consequence that while customs such as circumcision continued to be performed in secret, the associated discipline of morality was lost and ceased to be remembered.

According to Ahlberg (p. 233), 'sexuality was dramatically transformed from a context where it was open but kept within well defined social control and regulating mechanisms, to being an individual, private matter surrounded largely by silence. The link between community moral values and sexual behaviour was broken.' The Kikuyu people of East Africa should have been encouraged to practise and preserve their sexual rituals, songs and dances because, although they might have seemed 'exotic' to (foreign) outsiders, they were incredibly valuable for regulating and maintaining balanced and healthy sexual and personal relationships within the community. It is one of the great tragedies of African colonialisation and Westernisation that such valuable knowledge and practices have now largely been lost. Ahlberg believes that if AIDS educators expect any success in combating AIDS in Africa, they should begin to encourage and facilitate a discourse from a point in the 'idealised past'. The Kikuyu people should be reminded that they once had an open sexual model which protected adolescents from engaging in sexual activity outside marriage, and they should be urged to re-establish their old traditional ways rather than merely order adolescents to desist from their current permissive sexual behaviour.

## Negative cultural behaviour should be changed

Although AIDS educators should take care not to interfere in cultural beliefs and behaviour, some traditional behaviours are indeed harmful to people's health and attempts should be made to change these. Examples include the following: having multiple sexual partners; cleansing rituals such as those in Zambia and Botswana whereby a widow has to have sexual intercourse with a close relative of her deceased husband to cleanse her of her husband's spirit (Hickson & Mokhobo, 1992); the custom of inheriting the wife of a deceased brother (who might have died of AIDS); the impregnation of an impotent or sterile brother's wife; the use of sex to express hospitality where the host offers his wife or sister to a visiting guest (Mbiti, 1969); female genital mutilation (or female circumcision), and the practice of 'dry sex' by African women to heighten sexual sensation for men, or (more traditionally) to 'clean the temple for creation' from undesirable vaginal secretions (Moses & Plummer, 1994; Runganga & Kasule, 1995). Ways should also be devised to make the practices involved in the preparation and cleansing of bodies for burial safer. In Sudan, for example, undigested food and excreta are removed from corpses by hand — a procedure that was implicated in the 1976 and 1979 Ebola outbreaks in the DRC and Sudan (Garrett, 1995).

It is absolutely essential to obtain the cooperation of community leaders and traditional healers before even attempting to change dangerous cultural behaviour or practices. Success stories do exist. A positive and global community response was seen in Côte d'Ivoire where people living with HIV/AIDS (in cooperation with women selling food) held a conference for 400 young women to reduce their vulnerability to HIV in the face of risky cultural practices. Follow-up sessions a year after the conference have shown that many families have abandoned female genital mutilation, that condom use among adolescents has increased, and that wife inheritance by another male member of the family has diminished (Sidje, Foua & Aguirre, 2000).

## 7.6  CONCLUSION

It is necessary to impress vividly upon health care professionals and other AIDS educators who work in Africa not merely to criticise and condemn African beliefs, but rather to try to understand the philosophical or cultural and historical reasons that underlie their worldview — and to show the utmost respect for their ancient beliefs and practices. AIDS education and prevention programmes in Africa will only succeed if traditional cultural beliefs and customs are recognised and taken into account.

**Activity**

Make it your purpose to make one friend from a culture other than your own this year. Share your own customs and beliefs with this person and take the time and trouble to learn whatever you can about his or her culture.

# 8 Changing Unsafe Behaviour and Practices

*Koki prepares to fight Raka*

*... and then she named the dark creature,*
*who concealed himself in the cover of the night*
*and sheltered in the green slime of the ponds.*
*And she sang about Koki's courage –*
*the play of his weapons and the boldness of his feet*
*as he danced out into the darkness of the forest*
*to fight against something beastly and strong.*

There is only one weapon against HIV infection and AIDS and that is *behaviour change*. It is unfortunately the most difficult and complex weapon to use because people find it extremely difficult to change their sexual behaviour. Connor and Kingman (1988, p. 1) said: 'The disease that spreads with the help of sex is a formidable foe, because it is transmitted during the most intimate and compulsive of human activities — sex.'

One of the main educational functions of health care professionals is to encourage changes in unsafe sexual behaviour. This is very difficult because sex comprises deeply pleasurable and meaningful acts that touch the very core of what it means to be a human being. In addition, sex is also laden with symbolic and other meanings and resonances for human beings. Health care professionals should therefore set themselves realistic goals: although people will never stop having sex, they can be taught to practise safer sex. In this chapter, safer sex practices as well as the prevention of HIV transmission in intravenous (or injecting) drug users (IVDUs) will be discussed. The importance of lifeskills for the implementation and maintenance of safer sex practices (or abstinence) will also be discussed.

## 8.1 LESSONS FROM THE PAST

There is ample evidence from around the world that confirms that well-designed and skilfully executed prevention programmes can reduce the incidence of HIV. Studies from all over the world have shown that behaviour interventions (which include information, education and communication programmes, condom promotion programmes and other behaviour change initiatives) can bring about changes in high-risk sexual behaviour. Programmes encouraging abstinence from sex and freely accepted postponements of the onset of sexual activity by young people (sexual initiation) have also been successful (Harrison, Smit & Myer, 2000; UNAIDS, 2000c).

The San Francisco gay community demonstrated to the world in the nineties that people *can* be persuaded to employ safer sex. Education about safer sex practices and the dangers of unsafe practices such as unprotected anal intercourse caused the rate of infection among gay men in that city to drop from 8 000 infections in both 1982 and 1983 to 1 000 a decade later — and then to less than 400 a year by 1998 (Coates & Collins, 1998). Unfortunately, it now seems that because many men have access to anti-retroviral therapy, many have once again become indifferent to the risk of HIV infection. The incidence of unprotected anal sex and rectal gonorrhoea is on the increase in some of the world's major cities because of this 'new (but false) sense of security' (UNAIDS, 2000c).

Success stories are not limited to the developed world. As a result of rigorous prevention efforts, a similar trend may be observed — even in resource-poor settings. In Rwanda, for example, condom use in 'discordant' heterosexual couples (i.e. a couple where only one partner is HIV positive) increased from 3 % to 57 % after programmes of counselling had communicated the dangers of unprotected sex to sexually active couples. In the Congo, the use of condoms in similar circumstances has increased from 5 % to 77 %. A mass-media campaign that advocated safer sex in the Congo caused condom sales to increase from 800 000 in 1988 to more than 18 million by 1991 (Coates & Collins, 1998). In Uganda, the percentage of teenage girls who had sex with a partner using a condom tripled between 1994 and 1997. More teenage girls reported condom use than any other age group. This indicates that the acceptability of condoms is growing more rapidly among young people than among older people. Condom use among men having sex with younger women has also increased significantly (UNAIDS, 2000c).

Unfortunately, our prevention efforts in many parts of Africa are not yet adequate. A study in western Kenya found that 63 % of unmarried men and women who had sex in the past year never used a condom. The rate of condom use among married people having sex with partners outside their marriages was even lower. Four out of five married women (80 %) reported that condoms were *never* used when they had sex with men who were not their husbands (UNAIDS, 2000c).

## 8.2 PREVENTION OF SEXUALLY TRANSMITTED HIV

The most common means for the transmission of HIV (as well as STDs) is via sexual intercourse or contact with infected blood, semen, or the cervical and vaginal fluids that are transmitted from one infected person to his/her sexual partner — whether the sex involved transmits the virus from man-to-woman, man-to-man, woman-to-man, or, to a lesser extent, woman-to-woman. HIV transmission through sexual contact can occur vaginally, anally, rectally or orally. Man-to-woman transmission is now the most common form of HIV sexual transmission in Africa. Women (and to a lesser extent men) who remain faithful to their partners (and who therefore do not feel that it is necessary to use condoms) run a very high risk of contracting HIV when their partner has had sexual contact with an HIV-infected person outside (or before) their relationship (WHO, 2000a).

People who make the assumption that their partners are faithful, may in some cases put themselves at a risk of HIV infection. While some people are indeed faithful to their marriage partners, others may be engaging in sexual activities without the knowledge of their partners. Because there is no way of knowing whether *anyone* is HIV negative at any given time, it is always best to take precautions if in doubt. Many people have been infected by partners who (knowingly or unknowingly) passed on the HI virus to them.

The only totally reliable way of preventing oneself from being infected by HIV is *total abstinence* from sex (i.e. not having sex at all). Abstaining from sex is the only 100 % effective way to prevent the sexual transmission of HIV. Young people in particular should therefore be encouraged to abstain from sex or at least to delay their commencement of sexual relationships for as long as possible.

Abstinence is in some instances, however, neither realistic nor desirable. A *mutually faithful relationship* with an uninfected partner is therefore the ideal. Sex with one loyal, uninfected partner is one sure way of not getting HIV infection (with the proviso that both partners *are* absolutely faithful and reliable). In cultures where a man has more than one wife (or vice versa), both he and each of his wives should be uninfected and remain faithful to their relationship.

If a person chooses to have more than one sex partner, the risk of contracting HIV is always inevitably higher. It is therefore wiser (if possible) to limit the number of one's sex partners. In addition, one should always ask searching questions about the sexual history of one's current and future sex partners. One should always therefore practise *safer sex*. Note that the term 'safer sex' is used, and not the term 'safe sex' because, in the presence of the HI virus, one can never guarantee absolute safety.

The best way of protecting oneself against HIV is by opting for sexual activities that do not allow semen, fluid from the vagina, or blood to come into contact with the mouth, anus, penis or vagina of the partner. Barrier methods (such as latex condoms) that prevent semen and other bodily fluids from passing from one partner to another are the most effective preventative methods to use if people are having sex with more than one sex partner. Barrier methods also reduce the risk of contracting other STDs.

### The male condom

The *consistent* and *correct* use of latex condoms is one of the most effective ways for combating the spread of HIV. Laboratory tests have shown that the virus cannot pass through latex condoms. This means that the virus stays inside the condom after ejaculation and cannot enter the partner's body. Various researchers have reported a significantly lower incidence of HIV and other sexually transmitted diseases among people who insist on using a condom. Note, however, that condoms are never 100 % safe because they can leak or tear. Condoms tear easily if they are used incorrectly.

It should be noted that some people are allergic to latex and cannot therefore use latex condoms. Male condoms made of polyurethane (a type of plastic also used to make female condoms) are available for use by people who are allergic to latex. Unfortunately however these are not readily available. Condoms made of other sub-stances such as natural membranes (e.g. lambskin) should not be used. While lamb-skin condoms prevent pregnancy because they do not allow sperm to pass through, HIV and other viruses are so small that they can easily pass through the pores of natural-skin condoms. We should emphasise as often as possible that HIV *cannot* pass through intact *latex* condoms. The pores (holes) in latex condoms are so infin-itesimally small that HIV cannot pass through them.

## How to use a male condom

Not all people know how to use condoms. It is therefore important for health care professionals to feel comfortable in demonstrating the use of condoms. Demonstrate the application of a condom on a dildo (an artificial erect penis, usually made of rubber) and give clients the opportunity to practise. Videos and pamphlets are also useful in illustrating the correct use of condoms. If they do not have dildos on which to demonstrate or practise, the WHO (2000a) recommends that objects such as bananas or cucumbers be used. Present the following specific instructions on how to use a condom (see figure 8.1 for a visual representation of condom use):

- Use a new, unused condom every time you have sexual intercourse.
- Always use a condom from start to finish during any type of sex (vaginal, anal or oral).
- Always put the condom on the penis before intercourse begins.
- Put the condom on only after the penis is erect.
- Make sure the condom is the right way around. First unroll it a little bit to ascer-tain the direction in which it unrolls. It should roll down easily when you are doing it correctly.
- If the male is not circumcised, pull the foreskin of the penis back (gently) before putting on the condom.
- In putting on the condom, squeeze the nipple or empty space at the end of the condom to remove the air. Do not put the condom tightly against the tip of the penis; leave the small empty space at the end of the condom to hold the semen (if this isn't done correctly, the condom might break).
- Unroll the condom all the way to the base of the penis, to a point as close as possible to the testicles.
- If the condom tears during sex, withdraw the penis immediately and put on a new condom.

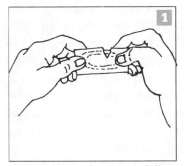

Open the package carefully.

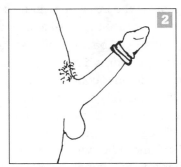

Put the condom on the tip of
the erect penis.

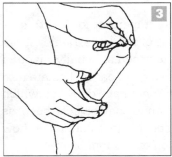

Pinch the tip of the condom to
remove any air from the tip.

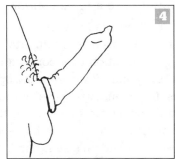

Unroll the condom all the way
to the base of the penis.

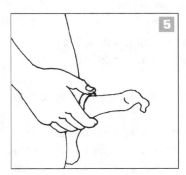

After ejaculating, hold the
base of the condom and withdraw from your partner.

Knot the used condom and dispose of it in a safe container.

**Figure 8.1**

*How to use a male condom*

- After ejaculation, withdraw the penis while it is still erect. Hold the rim of the condom as you withdraw so that the condom does not slip off and spill seminal fluid on your partner.

- Remove the condom carefully before the penis loses its erection so that seminal fluid does not spill out.

- Knot the used condom and wrap it in paper (such as a tissue, toilet paper or newspaper) until you can dispose of it in a safe place such as a toilet, pit latrine, a closed garbage bag, or until you can bury or burn it.

**Activity**

Ask a friend or colleague to play the role of a shy young man who visits your HIV/AIDS prevention clinic. He has recently started his first sexual relationship with a woman and he is concerned about AIDS. Talk to him about HIV and AIDS (he is very uninformed) and show him how to use a condom. Prepare your role play on paper by jotting down the main points of your discussion with the young man.

**Enrichment**

**Man-to-man transmission (Men who have Sex with Men: MSM)**

Unprotected penetrative anal sex creates a very high risk of HIV transmission — especially in the receptive partner. The risk is several times higher than vaginal intercourse because the lining of the rectum is thin and because it tears easily — even small lesions can allow the virus easy access into the partner's bloodstream. According to a WHO report (2000a), a large percentage of men who have sex with men (MSM) are either married or are also having sex with women. Most of these men will not identify themselves as homosexual or 'gay' and because MSM is often stigmatised and criminalised in many countries, it is very difficult to reach these men with health promotion and prevention programmes.

*Lubrication*

Ensure adequate lubrication during intercourse to avoid discomfort and friction. If extra lubrication is needed with latex condoms, use only lubricants with a *water-base* such as KY Jelly (or KY Gel), glycerine or lubricants specially made for use with condoms. Lubricants with an *oil base* should *never* be used because they weaken, dissolve and break latex condoms. *Never* use Vaseline or petroleum jelly, baby oil, massage oil, body lotions with an oil base, cooking or vegetable oil, butter or fats as lubricants with latex condoms. Saliva should also not be used because it is not very effective as a lubricant. KY Jelly or other water-based lubricants can be bought at any pharmacy and at some supermarkets.

Carry out the following exercise in a group as part of a safer sex workshop. It is great fun, and participants will never forget how important it is not to use oil-based lubricants with latex condoms. Give every person in your group a condom and ask them to inflate it like a balloon. Supply them with all kinds of water-based as well as oil-based lubricants such as KY Jelly, Vaseline, cooking oil, massage oil and baby oil. Ask the participants to add their own hand lotions if they have any with them. Ask them to choose any of these lubricants, apply it to the inflated condom and to rub it in. Set your stop watch to see how long it takes for the condom rubbed with Vaseline to burst!

*Tips to prevent condoms from breaking or leaking*

The following tips are helpful for preventing condoms from breaking or leaking:

- Choose pre-lubricated condoms that are specially packed in square wrappers that keep light out.
- Use a brand of condom which shows it has been tested for reliability. Always check the information on the packet before buying condoms.
- Store condoms away from excessive heat, light, and moisture, as these cause them to deteriorate and perhaps break. Store condoms in a cool, dark, dry place if possible. Don't store condoms in the glove department of a car where they will be damaged by excessive heat. Condoms can also easily become damaged in a wallet.
- Check the expiry date on the condom wrapper. Don't use condoms after the expiry date or more than 5 years after the manufacturing date because they may break.
- Do not use condoms that are sticky, brittle, discoloured or otherwise damaged.
- Open the wrapper carefully so that the condom does not tear. Be careful not to tear condoms with long nails, teeth, other sharp objects or jewellery.
- Make sure that the type of condom you use is strong enough for the type of sexual practice you engage in. Use extra strong condoms (e.g. Durex Extra Strong) for anal penetration. Ordinary condoms are generally made for vaginal intercourse, and these may break because of the increased friction and strain placed on the latex by the narrow, less flexible anus.
- Don't ever use two condoms (i.e. one pulled over the other) as the friction will tear the condoms.

## The female condom

The female condom is a strong, soft sheath that is inserted into the vagina before sexual intercourse. It is pouch-shaped and about the same length as the male condom, but wider. The female condom has two plastic rings: a loose ring at the closed end that helps to insert the condom and that keeps it in place during sex, and

**Enrichment**

## Heterosexual anal intercourse

People often assume that only homosexual men have anal intercourse. But research has shown that this is not the case and that between 20 % and 35 % of men and women have heterosexual anal intercourse. Halperin (2000) sees anal intercourse as a neglected risk factor for heterosexual HIV infection: 'We tend to concentrate on classic risk factors (such as condom use, STDs, and multiple partners) in our prevention programmes, while we neglect practices such as heterosexual anal intercourse, "dry sex", and male circumcision.' Various European and US studies indicated that the chances of becoming infected with HIV after one act of unprotected receptive anal sex is approximately 20 times greater than after one act of unprotected vaginal sex. These studies also indicate that anal intercourse may account for up to half of heterosexual transmissions in some countries. Anal intercourse is often practised as a means of avoiding pregnancy, of maintaining 'virginity', or as a preferred pleasure. It is also often practised by commercial sex workers and by men who prefer anal intercourse with women for reasons similar to the reasons why they prefer 'dry sex' (Garcia et al., 2000; Halperin, 2000; Pando et al., 2000). ('Dry sex' will be discussed later on in this chapter.)

a larger ring at the open end, which remains outside the vagina and spreads over the woman's external genitalia.

Because the female condom is made of polyurethane plastic (not latex), it requires no special storage. It can be inserted quite a while before having sex, it does not require immediate withdrawal after ejaculation and it can be used with both oil-based and water-based lubricants. Because the external ring is usually visible during sex, a woman cannot easily use a female condom without her partner knowing about it, but women do have more control over use of this method than they do over the use of a male condom. Because it can be inserted hours before sexual intercourse, it can provide protection in situations where consumption of alcohol or drugs may reduce the chances that a male condom will be used. The female condom also provides protection during menstruation.

The female condom provides extra protection to men and women because it covers both the entrance to the vagina and the base of the penis, both of which are areas where STD sores make it easy for HIV to enter. Although research on the re-use of the female condom (after it has been thoroughly washed) is under way, the current recommendation by the World Health Organisation is that it be used only once before it is discarded. Female condoms are much more expensive than male condoms and they are not as easily acceptable or accessible (UNAIDS, 2000c).

**Activity**

If you do not know what a female condom looks like, try to get one from a clinic or pharmacy. They are unfortunately expensive (if one compares their price to that of the male condom), and they are often not generally available. The female condom is manufactured by: The female health company, and you are welcome to visit them at their website at: *http://www.femalehealth.com*

*How to use the female condom*

Figure 8.2 illustrates how the female condom should be inserted. The following instructions should be presented:

- Before using the female condom, rub it between your fingers in order to spread the lubrication evenly around.
- Twist the inner ring into a figure-8 shape and hold it between your fingers, or just squeeze the inner ring.
- The vagina must be relaxed when you insert the condom. Squat or sit with your knees apart, or stand with one leg raised.
- Push the inner ring into your vagina with your fingers (use the same insertion method you use to insert a tampon), and be careful to ensure that your fingernails or jewellery do not damage the polyurethane.
- Put your index finger in the condom and gently push the inner ring up into the vagina as far as it will go. The condom should fit snugly against the cervix (behind the pubic bone). If it is in the right place, you will not feel it.
- The outer ring should hang outside the vagina, and it should not be twisted.
- During intercourse it is necessary to guide the penis into the condom and to check that the penis has not entered the vagina *outside* the condom wall. Make sure that the condom is not pushed into the vagina by the penis.
- If there is a problem (e.g. if the condom rips or tears, if the outer ring is pushed inside or if the condom bundles up inside the vagina), remove the condom and insert a new one.
- Don't *ever* use a male condom at the same time as the female condom because the friction between them will move both condoms out of their proper positions.
- Remove the condom after male ejaculation by squeezing and twisting the outer ring and gently pulling the condom out of the vagina. Remove the condom before standing up.
- Wrap the condom in tissue paper and dispose of it in a rubbish bin and not in the toilet.

Use more lubrication (e.g. KY Jelly) if the penis does not move freely in and out, if the outer ring is pushed inside, if you feel the condom when it is in place, and if it comes out of the vagina during sex.

(See *http://www.femalehealth.com/insertiondiagrams.html*)

Changing Unsafe Behaviour and Practices

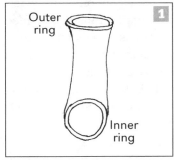

The open end covers the vagina, and the inner ring is used for insertion and to hold the condom in place.

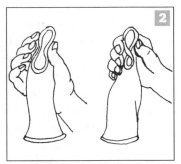

Hold the inner ring between your fingers and squeeze or twist the ring into a figure 8.

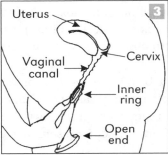

Push the inner ring into the vagina with your fingers (like you would a tampon).

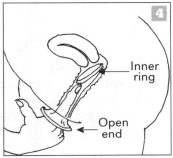

With your index finger, push the inner ring up as far as it can go.

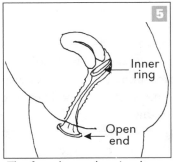

The female condom in place.

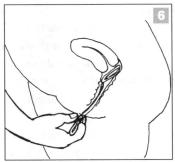

Remove the condom before standing up. Squeeze and twist the outer ring, pull gently, and dispose.

**Figure 8.2**

*How to insert the female condom*

Although the female condom is not meant to replace the male condom, it increases the options available in the fight against HIV and other sexually transmitted infections. According to a Thai study among sex workers in brothels, the women experienced a 34 % decrease in the number of new sexually transmitted infections in cases where a female condom was provided as an extra option to the male condom. The same study also found that sex workers who had access to both the female and the male condom were less likely to have unprotected sex than women who had access only to male condoms (UNAIDS, 2000c).

Research to find effective microbicides in the form of a vaginal cream, which can be controlled by women, is currently under way (see enrichment box 'Empower women with vaginal microbicides' on page 22).

### General safer sex rules

- Avoid all high-risk sex practices such as vaginal, anal and oral sex without a condom. Avoid casual sex, sex with a commercial sex worker (prostitute), sex with a partner who shares needles and syringes with other drug users, and sex with a person whose sexual history is unknown.
- Never allow semen, vaginal fluids, blood or menstrual blood to come into contact with or enter the vagina, anus, penis, mouth or broken skin. Wash your hands with soap and water if they have been in contact with semen or other body fluids. Rinse your mouth with cold (not hot) water if it has had contact with semen and *don't* brush your teeth immediately afterwards.
- Avoid deep, wet or 'French' kissing with an HIV-infected person. Possible trauma to the mouth may occur and bleeding gums or sores may result in an exchange of blood. Kissing is safe when there is no blood involved.
- Avoid sex when either partner has open sores on the genitals or any sexually transmitted diseases (STDs).
- Avoid anal or rough vaginal intercourse. Do not do anything that could tear the skin or the moist lining of the genitals, anus or mouth and cause bleeding.
- Do not perform oral sex when you have a cold, a sore throat, open sores in your mouth or if you have brushed your teeth in the few hours before intended oral sex. Avoid oral sex if there are sores on your partner's genitals.
- It is a good rule not to share dildos, vibrators and other sex toys. But if you must share them, make sure that you use condoms on the dildo and sex toy.
- If you perform oral sex on a man (called fellatio) you should always use a condom. Although the risk of HIV transmission through oral sex is low, it appears that fellatio is the riskiest kind of *oral sex* if the partner performing the fellatio receives semen into his or her mouth. If the taste of latex, particularly of condoms that are prelubricated is repellent to people who want to use condoms during oral sex, they should bear in mind that there are fruit- and mint-flavoured condoms avail-

able for oral sex. You should always however make sure that they are of a good quality before you buy them. (Durex make a variety of high-quality flavoured and coloured condoms.)

- If you want to perform oral sex on a woman (called cunnilingus), a dental dam (or latex sheath placed over the vagina) will make sure you do not get vaginal fluid or menstrual blood into your mouth. Non-porous plastic wraps, such as non-microwavable plastic wrap (e.g. Glad Wrap), can also be placed over the vagina. Or a condom can be cut open for this purpose. Although cunnilingus holds a low risk of HIV transmission (if the skin is intact and if the woman is not menstruating), other sexually transmitted diseases can be transmitted in this way.

- The majority of sexually transmitted diseases occur when infected mucous membranes come into contact with uninfected mucous membranes. When performing oral sex (both fellatio and cunnilingus), the herpes simplex virus and the infective agents that are present if one has gonorrhoea and syphilis infections on the lips, or in the mouth or throat can cause infections of the genitals — and vice versa.

- While oral-anal sex (called anilingus or 'rimming') does not appear to carry a high risk of HIV infection unless there is blood present, the possibility of contracting the hepatitis B virus, the herpes simplex virus, the cytomegalovirus and a number of different parasites from oral-anal sex is very high indeed. A latex sheath (dental dam), Glad Wrap or a spliced-open condom should be used to cover the anal area.

- If you have open wounds on your fingers, you should wear a condom over your finger before inserting it into the vagina or anus of your partner.

- If you practise vaginal and anal fisting (inserting the whole fist into the vagina or anus), you should use latex gloves during the process. You should also take care of your nails because sharp edges can tear gloves and condoms.

- Avoid alcohol and illicit drugs because they can impair your immune system as well as your judgement. If you use drugs, don't share needles, syringes and drug-preparation equipment such as cookers.

- Adopt alternative sexual practices that are less likely to result in infection by HIV, other viruses or infection-causing agents. Safe practices that are still enjoyable include the following:
  o  hugging, cuddling and body-to-body rubbing
  o  erotic massage
  o  petting
  o  thigh rubbing
  o  kissing
  o  bathing or showering together
  o  masturbating alone

- o masturbating together
- o sexual fantasies
- o phone sex
- o using personal sex toys
- o thigh sex (a healthy skin provides a protective barrier against the virus)

(It is not possible to get HIV from direct contact with semen placed *on* the body but not *in* the body.)

Enrichment

**The dangerous practice of 'dry sex'**

'Dry sex' is practised by many women in Africa. Because some men believe that a dry vagina is a sign of faithfulness, or to heighten their sexual pleasure, they insist on 'dry sex' (see 'Negative cultural behaviour should be changed' on page 129 for other reasons). In order to obtain this dry condition, women use herbs, antiseptic solutions (such as Dettol, soap, salt solutions, or Betadine), chemical and other substances (toothpaste, Surf, methylated spirits, vinegar, human urine, baboon's faeces), cotton wool, cotton cloth or newspaper to 'dry out' the vagina (Runganga & Kasule, 1995). This practice is potentially very dangerous because it may promote lacerations (or breaks) in the vaginal walls — a condition that is conducive to the spread of HIV. Proper education (of both women and men), the empowerment of women and assertiveness training for women may be the only way to put a stop to such dangerous practices.

*What is a 'dental dam', and what is it used for?*

A dental dam is a square sheet of latex rubber which is used as a protective barrier during dental work. Because they are made of latex, they can also provide a barrier in those situations where the mouth comes into contact with body fluids that may contain HIV — especially during cunnilingus (oral-vaginal contact) and anilingus (oral-anal contact). Anilingus and cunnilingus are relatively low-risk sexual acts with regard to HIV transmission (in the absence of blood). The placing of a latex barrier between the mouth and the vagina or anus further reduces the chances of contracting HIV through these acts to almost zero.

*Does the female diaphragm prevent HIV infection? And does the contraceptive pill prevent HIV infection?*

In both cases, no. The female diaphragm prevents semen from entering the cervix, but it does *not* protect the vagina or external genitalia from exposure to HIV. Cervical barriers, such as a diaphragm, cap or sponge (used to prevent pregnancy), can however provide extra protection if a condom is also *always* used during penetrative vaginal intercourse. Some teenagers erroneously believe that the contraceptive pill can

protect them against HIV infection. They should be told that although the pill prevents pregnancy, it does not prevent contact with semen (which contains the virus)
in the same way that a condom does. The pill therefore does *not* prevent HIV infection.

 *Is there still a risk of HIV infection if the penis is withdrawn from the
vagina (or anus) before ejaculation?*

Interrupting intercourse by withdrawing the penis from the vagina or (anus) before
ejaculating will result in less exposure to fluids, but withdrawal will not necessarily
prevent a person from getting or transmitting HIV. Vaginal fluids come into contact
with the penis *during* intercourse — regardless of whether the penis is withdrawn
before ejaculation or not. The fluids that come out of the tip of the penis before ejaculation (pre-seminal fluids) contain sufficient amounts of HIV to cause infection.
While withdrawal before ejaculation may therefore reduce the chances of infection,
withdrawal cannot completely protect people from HIV (Kalichman, 1996).

 *Does cleaning (washing) the vagina or anus after sex reduce the risk of HIV
infection?*

There is no evidence to support the belief that vaginal and anal cleansing (douching
or flushing) after sex can prevent HIV infection and other sexually transmitted diseases. In actual fact, cleansing of this kind is *positively not advised* because it is
likely that such cleansing may actually facilitate HIV infection by washing infected
semen *deeper* into the vagina or anus (Kalichman, 1996). Substances (cleansing
agents) used for washing may also cause abrasions in the vagina or anus.

 *Are condoms really safe and effective?*

Yes. Scientific evidence shows that latex condoms are highly effective in preventing
the transmission of HIV and other STDs when they are used *consistently* and *correctly*.
All high-quality condoms are tested by the manufacturers, and according to the Food
and Drug Administration in the USA, condoms are 99.7 % defect-free. The effectiveness of condoms was tested in a 2-year study of 'discordant couples' (couples where
one partner is infected and the other is not) in Europe. It was found that, among the
124 couples who reported consistent use of latex condoms, *none* of the uninfected
partners became infected. However, among the 121 couples who used condoms
inconsistently, 10 % of the uninfected partners became infected. In those cases where
condoms break or slip off, this is almost always caused by user errors such as using a
petroleum-based lubricant, the use of deteriorated or out-of-date condoms, or storing
condoms at a high temperature for a long time in places such as a car glove compart-

ment or a wallet. Only tested, high-quality condoms should ever be used. As people's knowledge about using condoms increases, breakage and slippage decreases. Health care professionals therefore have a big responsibility of making sure that people know how to use condoms correctly (CDC, 2000).

Enrichment

**Problems associated with condom use in Africa**

The use of condoms poses certain problems that are specific to Africa and these should be recognised by health care professionals working in Africa. Apart from cultural and other problems with condoms (see 'Traditional African perceptions of condoms' on page 121), Green (1994) observed that condoms as they are actually used in practice in Africa may only have a 50 % effectiveness rate in reducing most sexually transmitted diseases because of incorrect use and the poor quality of condoms. Condoms are also sometimes inadequately stored and transported under tropical conditions. The high temperatures caused by the African sun can quickly damage the lubrication of condoms and render them brittle and therefore useless. Because of this, Green feels very strongly that AIDS prevention programmes should not rely solely on the use of condoms, but that they should also concentrate on the prevention and treatment of STDs in general.

*Is it still necessary to use condoms if both partners are HIV positive?*

Yes. It is important for HIV-infected individuals to protect themselves against re-infection with other strains of HIV. Any new infection can cause an increase in the viral load of the blood. This may in turn lead to a further decrease in CD4 cells — and an accompanying further weakening of the immune system. In addition to re-infection with HIV, a person can also of course contract *other* sexually transmitted diseases and these may damage the overall health and immune status of the HIV-infected individual.

*Is it safe to use spermicidal creams that contain nonoxynol-9?*

The use of spermicidal creams containing nonoxynol-9 as an ingredient was recommended in the past because the substance was believed to kill HIV. It now seems that nonoxynol-9 may not be as safe as was formerly believed because of the allergies and infections sometimes caused by nonoxynol-9 (we noted earlier in the text that because allergies, infections and skin irritations cause broken or inflamed mucous membranes, they facilitate transmission of the HI virus). Scientists at the XIIIth International AIDS conference (2000) therefore recommended that the use of nonoxynol-9 should be discouraged and discontinued.

## A continuum of sexual practices: From no-risk to high-risk

If we want to determine the extent of risk generated by each different sexual practice, we must first ascertain exactly what *body fluids* are involved in each specific
practice. The highest concentration of the HI virus is found in blood (including menstrual blood), semen, pre-seminal fluids ('pre-cum'), and vaginal secretions. The
concentration of the virus is very low in saliva, tears, urine and sweat.

In the light of this information, we can rate sexual practices on a continuum that
ranges from behaviours that carry no risk of infection (no risk) to those that carry a
high risk (high risk). Table 8.1 gives an indication of the behaviours on the continuum between *no risk* and *high risk*. The risk will, of course, increase with the
number of partners who are involved in unprotected sexual activities.

### Table 8.1
*Continuum of sexual behaviours: From no-risk to high-risk behaviours*

| No risk | Low risk | Some risk | High risk |
|---|---|---|---|
| • Abstinence<br>• Erotic massage<br>• Hugging and body rubbing<br>• Petting<br>• Kissing<br>• Bathing or showering together<br>• Masturbation<br>• Mutual masturbation (if there is no contact between broken skin and semen/vaginal fluids)<br>• Sexual fantasies<br>• Thigh sex<br>• Phone sex<br>• Using personal sex toys | • Oral sex on a man (fellatio) who is wearing a condom<br>• Oral sex on a woman (cunnilingus) with a latex barrier<br>• Anilingus (oral-anal sex) with a latex barrier<br>• Contact with urine ('golden showers' or 'water sports' on unbroken skin) | • Oral sex (on a man or woman without a condom or barrier)<br>• Vaginal penetrative sex with a condom<br>• Anal penetrative sex with a condom (it is safer to withdraw before ejaculation) | • Vaginal penetrative sex without a condom<br>• Anal penetrative sex without a condom (**very high risk**)<br>• Swallowing semen<br>• Sharing uncovered sex toys<br>• Vaginal or anal penetrative sex with a condom if using a petroleum-based lubricant<br>• Unprotected oral-anal contact if blood is present<br>• Unprotected manual-anal intercourse (fisting) without a latex glove<br>• Unprotected manual-vaginal intercourse (fisting) without a latex glove<br>• Contact with menstrual blood |

The owner of a singles bar for women is very concerned about the health of the women who visit her club. She consults you, an HIV/AIDS consultant, to devise a pamphlet to inform the women about women's health issues. What information would you include in your pamphlet?

Refer back to 'How HIV is transmitted through sexual intercourse with an HIV-infected person' on page 19 and re-read the section about the safety of women who have sex with women on page 21. Keep in mind that some of the women who have sex with other women also have sex with men.

## 8.3 PREVENTION OF HIV IN INJECTING DRUG USERS

Sharing needles to inject drugs (or to 'shoot up') is a major factor in the AIDS crisis. Since the AIDS epidemic is fuelled by the sharing of dirty needles in many countries, it is important for governments to plan their actions and laws accordingly. Drug injection poses a threat to drug users as well as to their sexual partners. Many drug users sell sex to pay for their drugs — a means of earning money which fuels the spread of the virus in the general population.

Since we are fortunate in Africa because we do not (as yet) have as great a problem with injecting drug users as do people in other parts of the world, we should use this window of opportunity to get appropriate preventative measures into place. Programmes should focus on the primary prevention of drug use, especially among young people, on the rehabilitation of drug users, and on the prevention of HIV among drug users who do not want to (or cannot) stop the habit.

### Anti-drug campaigns and rehabilitation

Comprehensive anti-drug programmes are needed to prevent drug use, and anti-drug campaigns which deter young people from using drugs should be actively implemented in schools, colleges and universities.

Easy access to rehabilitation programmes should be made available to individuals who want to stop taking drugs, and they should be supported as they complete the substance abuse treatment. Relapse-prevention programmes should also be offered.

### Guidelines on how injecting drug users can reduce the risk of HIV infection

HIV-prevention programmes, including AIDS education, condom promotion, and drug treatment, should all be implemented among injecting drug users who are not interested in rehabilitation programmes. Sustained attempts should however be made to involve drug users in rehabilitation programmes.

The Centres for Disease Control give the following guidelines for drug users who cannot or will not stop injecting drugs:

- Never re-use or share syringes, needles, water, or drug preparation equipment.
- Only use syringes and needles that you obtain from a reliable source (such as pharmacies or needle exchange programmes in countries where these are available to registered drug users).
- Use a new, sterile syringe and needle to prepare and inject drugs.
- If possible, use sterile water to prepare drugs. If you cannot obtain sterile water, at least use clean water from a reliable source (such as fresh tap water).
- Use a new or disinfected container ('cooker') and a new filter ('cotton') to prepare drugs.
- Clean the injection site prior to injection with a new alcohol swab.
- Safely dispose of the syringe and needle after each (one) use.

**Note:** These guidelines should NOT be misconstrued as implying any condoning of drug use. Instead they should rather be regarded as a means of reducing the considerable personal risks that drug users are subjected to as well as the health (and other) risks that drug users pose to the community at large.

### Needle exchange and bleach distribution programmes

Many major cities in Europe and in the USA allow drug users to swap used needles and syringes for sterile equipment. Although needle exchange programmes are successful in preventing the spread of HIV, these programmes are very controversial because many people regard them as condoning drug abuse. In contrast to this view, many research studies in the United States have found that needle exchange programmes (or greater needle availability) reduce HIV transmission *without* increasing the use of illegal drugs (Coates & Collins, 1998).

Some countries have instituted less controversial strategies such as distributing bleach and other supplies for cleaning needles and syringes. Drug users are advised to sterilise their injecting equipment by using a bleach-water solution (one part bleach to ten parts water). They are advised to draw the bleach solution up through the needle to fill the syringe, to flush the solution through the needle twice, to rinse it in clean water twice after cleaning, and not to share rinsing water.

People who continue to inject drugs should have themselves periodically tested for HIV.

## 8.4   THE PROMOTION OF HEALTH AND THE ACQUISITION OF LIFESKILLS

The aims of health education in HIV-prevention programmes should not only be the prevention of illness; they should also focus on the promotion of physical and mental health. HIV/AIDS education should therefore be part of a broader strategy by means of which people are empowered with the necessary lifeskills to make the right health choices and to improve the overall quality of their lives. Health care professionals must help their clients to develop responsible and effective coping skills which will not only enable them to prevent HIV infection but which will also help them to enhance their lives on various levels. Health care professionals should teach the following lifeskills:

- assertiveness
- self-efficacy (a strong belief in your ability to do something)
- a strong self-concept and self-awareness
- a belief in one's right to make choices
- the ability to handle peer pressure
- taking responsibility for one's self and for others in the community
- problem-solving skills
- conflict resolution
- effective communication skills: one of the reasons why condom promotion pro-grammes often fail is because, although people are advised to use condoms, they are not given advice about how to *communicate* with their partners on this issue
- negotiation skills are absolutely necessary if one hopes to persuade 'difficult' partners to practise safer sex and to use condoms.

Lifeskills enable young people who are not yet sexually active to learn safe habits from the start. Lifeskills also enable people who have *already* acquired risky sex patterns to begin to practise safer sex. Women especially should be taught to be more assertive and self-efficient in sexual matters. Women should believe in their ability and right to make their own choices, to insist on condom use, and to say no to sex (when they don't want it).

Various strategies may be used to promote lifeskills. One may use role play to teach individuals new skills which they can then practise, and one can use social modelling which allows individuals to observe (e.g. on video) and understand various models for dealing with interpersonal situations (Bandura, 1989; Franzini et al., 1990). People also need to be taught how to develop their own ability to exercise control over their lives and behaviour. Certain individuals need to be trained to communicate effectively with their sex partners if they are resistant, defensive or manipulative (Sy, Richter & Copello, 1989).

## 8.5 CONCLUSION

Although it is true that a disease that spreads with the help of sex is a formidable foe, *we are not helpless victims*. We have the power to emerge from the war as victors, but only if we are prepared to use the only weapons we have: sexual behaviour change. When promoting safer practices, AIDS counsellors should be specific and not hesitate to give detailed (but sensitive) explanations and demonstrations that enable people to fight the war proactively.

**Activity**

You will often find a lot of giggling, laughing and joking in your safer sex workshops. What do you think is the psychological function of humour in stressful situations like this? How can humour be used as an educational tool? Are you personally comfortable with using humour? When should one be careful or cautious about using humour?

# 9 HIV/AIDS Education and Lifeskills Training

*The children*

*At the edge of the riverbed*
*the children played in the warm clay.*
*But Koki, filled with fear, saw that*
*the game was different this morning.*

*Our future lies with our children.* This saying has never been so resonant with meaning as it is now — in an era when HIV/AIDS is ravishing countless human lives, but none more so than in sub-Saharan Africa. If we cannot stop the current progress of the disease, we can at least try to ensure an AIDS-free future for our children. The role of the school and religious and civic organisations cannot be underestimated in the fight against AIDS. We should empower our children with education and lifeskills — not only so that they can prevent themselves from being infected, but also so that they can have the opportunity to learn to become compassionate, caring members of a society that will be struggling with the aftermath of HIV/AIDS for a long time to come.

## 9.1 LEARNERS, TEACHERS AND HIV/AIDS: A GRIM PICTURE

HIV/AIDS has had a devastating effect on the educational system in many parts of the world where it sows havoc among learners and teachers alike. In their report on the global HIV/AIDS epidemic, UNAIDS (2000c, pp. 29–30) presents the following disturbing facts about the effect of HIV/AIDS on educational systems.

The Central African Republic (where approximately one in every seven adults is infected with HIV) has a 33 % shortage of primary school teachers. During 1996 and 1998, almost as many teachers died as those who retired, and of those who died, 85 % were HIV positive (they all died an average of ten years before reaching the minimum retirement age of 52). Now, because of staff shortages in the Central African Republic, 107 schools have closed and only 66 have been able to remain open. It is estimated that more than 71 000 children between the ages of 6 and 11 will be deprived of a primary education by the year 2005. The impact of AIDS on the Côte d'Ivoire presents the same grim dimensions. In that country confirmed cases of HIV/AIDS account for seven out of ten deaths among teachers. Zambia lost 1 300 teachers in the first ten months of 1998 — the equivalent of around 65 % of all new teachers who are trained annually.

This kind of unimaginable devastation also applies to learners who are either infected or affected by HIV/AIDS. The presence of AIDS in the family often means that children have to drop out of school, temporarily (or permanently) interrupt their schooling because of a shortage of money, or work full time in the home to help sick parents. Research in Zimbabwe showed that 48 % of the orphans of primary school age who were interviewed had dropped out of school — usually when their parents became too ill to look after themselves or when their parents died. Not one orphan of secondary school age was still in school. In a study of orphans in Kenya, boys tended to cite economic reasons for dropping out of primary school (64 % said they could not afford the school fees or that they needed to earn cash from fishing), while 28 % of the girls said that they had become pregnant and 41 % said that they had left to get married (UNAIDS, 2000c, p. 29).

Sexual initiation may occur at a very early age for some children, especially in marginalised communities where sexual abuse and rape are relatively common. A survey of 1 600 children and adolescents in four poor areas of the Zambian capital, Lusaka, found that more than 25 % of children aged 10 said they had already had sex (this figure rose to 60 % among 14-year-olds). In South Africa, 10 % of respondents in a study in six provinces said that they had started having sex at age 11 or younger. The South African Department of Health used the results of this study as the basis for its recommendation that sex education should be introduced to children at around the age of 12 so that it might benefit them before many of them became sexually active (UNAIDS, 2000c). A survey among adolescents in KwaZulu-Natal reported that 76 % of girls and 90 % of boys are sexually experienced by the time they are 15 or 16 years old. In the Free State Province of South Africa, teenagers reported that they were sexually active at around 12 years of age. Relatively few of the teenagers interviewed practised safer sex (Coombe, 2000).

Education and information are fundamental human rights, and children and young people may not be denied the basic information, education and skills that they need to protect themselves against HIV/AIDS. We may not allow religious values, social mores or cultural preferences to prevent children and young people from being empowered with the education and skills that they need to reduce high-risk behaviour.

## 9.2  BASIC REQUIREMENTS FOR SUCCESSFUL HIV/AIDS EDUCATION

HIV/AIDS education should comply with the following requirements and standards if it is to be successful in schools:

- HIV/AIDS education should never be presented in isolation — that is to say, in a special 'AIDS period'. If HIV/AIDS education is presented in isolation, children may acquire an irrational fear of the disease. Such a distorted emphasis may interfere with the child's healthy sexual development because the child may become accustomed to equating sex with disease and death (CDC, 1988; Post, 1988).

- HIV/AIDS education should preferably form part of a lifeskills education programme which includes sexuality education as well as information on HIV and AIDS.
- HIV/AIDS information can also be integrated into the existing school curriculum, either as part of other health-related subjects, or within one or more subject areas such as biology, science, social science, mathematics and religious studies.
- HIV/AIDS education should begin as early as the junior primary school phase (or grade 1). At this early age, the child's behaviour patterns have not yet been established and they are very receptive to the principles that govern healthy behaviour.
- HIV/AIDS education should be an ongoing process. A single lecture or video, or an 'HIV/AIDS information week' in the senior phase, is not sufficient because it is necessary to begin instilling the lifeskills one needs to prevent HIV infection at a young age (these lessons should be continuously reinforced as the child gets older).
- It is important to include parents, community leaders and spiritual leaders so that they make an active contribution (input) to all stages of programme development. If HIV/AIDS programmes are to be successful, they have to have the active support of all stakeholders in the community — and they also need to reflect the whole spectrum of religious, cultural and moral values found in any particular community.
- The CDC (1988) recommends that the class teacher should handle the HIV/AIDS education of children in the lower or primary grades because they are familiar with the children and are probably best equipped to use those teaching strategies that are appropriate to the children's age group. It is preferable for specially trained teachers (such as guidance counsellors) to handle the HIV/AIDS education and lifeskills training of learners in the more senior or secondary grades.
- The educator should feel at ease with the content of the HIV/AIDS curriculum and should be a role model with whom learners can easily identify.
- Information about HIV/AIDS should never be presented in a way that frightens children. Research has shown that anxiety-oriented approaches in HIV/AIDS education are counterproductive because the individual's anxiety levels escalate to a point where they are inclined to evade or deny the truth of the information (Wyatt, 1989).
- HIV/AIDS education that focuses on problems while ignoring sexuality as a normal aspect of all human life may well retard the normal sexual development of the child. The positive and delightful aspects of sexuality should never be

ignored. Children must be made aware that sexual feelings and impulses — which are present from birth — are both pleasant and normal. They must also nevertheless be helped to understand that, although sexual feelings are normal, the active expression of sexuality is not appropriate behaviour for young children (Quackenbush & Villarreal, 1988).

● Sexuality and HIV/AIDS education should always be tailored so that it is appropriate to a child or young person's particular developmental stage. It is therefore important for us to have a clear idea of the degree of cognitive, emotional, social, moral and sexual development in children in specific age groups so that the sexual education we offer to children will be exactly appropriate and suited to the developmental stage through which they are passing. Teachers should (in addition) always remain sensitive to *individual* and *cultural* developmental needs and differences and adjust their education programmes accordingly.

## 9.3   THE BUILDING BLOCKS FOR SUCCESSFUL HIV/AIDS EDUCATION

HIV/AIDS education should never concentrate on the dissemination of information on HIV and AIDS alone. A child can only make responsible decisions if the *knowledge* which he or she obtains is firmly based on healthy *values, norms and attitudes*, and if he or she has the necessary *skills* to implement these decisions. For an HIV/AIDS education programme to be successful, there should be a balance between knowledge, lifeskills, values and attitudes (see figure 9.1).

Basic knowledge, attitudes, values and skills (which are not exclusively HIV/AIDS-related) should be established, promoted and reinforced in all the phases of a child's primary and secondary school career. The content, and the way in which this knowledge and these attitudes and skills are taught, should be adapted to the child's age and developmental phase (Edwards & Louw, 1998; Pilot project on lifeskills, 1999).

### Knowledge

An effective HIV/AIDS education and lifeskills programme should provide the following knowledge in a manner that is appropriate to the age of the child:

● how to conduct relationships with significant others, with friends of the same and opposite sex, and how to cope with strangers
● how to deal effectively with peer group pressure
● what sexual abuse or molestation is, how it can be prevented, and where to find help in case of actual or attempted sexual abuse or molestation (teach young children to distinguish between different kinds of touching)
● how to use leisure time creatively and in a way that brings satisfaction

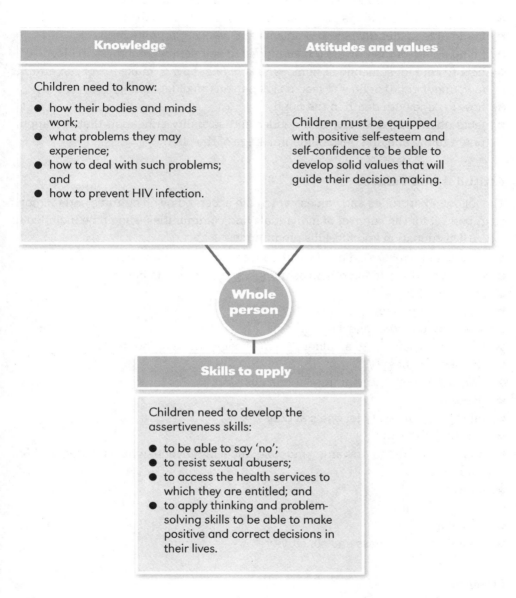

**Figure 9.1**

*The building blocks for successful HIV/AIDS education*

(Source: Adapted from Norton & Dawson, 2000, p. vi)

- how to keep the body safe and healthy and how to avoid harmful behaviour (such as sniffing glue, drinking alcohol or taking various kinds of drugs)
- an adequate knowledge about germs, viruses, HIV and AIDS
- being able to identify health problems and seek appropriate help
- being aware of the universal precautions to be taken when handling blood
- how to care for someone at home who is ill (e.g. how to make tea or run errands (a younger child) or how to feed a sick person (an older child))
- how to cope with death in the family
- facts about sex, sexuality and gender and sexuality education that are appropriate to the age and developmental stage of the child

## Attitudes and values

The following attitudes and values, which are accepted by all cultures and religions as important for the survival of individuals and communities, should be included in HIV/AIDS education and lifeskills programmes:

- building of a realistic, positive self-concept
- respect for the self and others as unique and worthwhile beings
- self-control
- the right to privacy
- the right to protect oneself
- the right to say 'no' to an older person or someone in authority
- the right to chastity
- loyalty and commitment in relationships
- honesty
- taking responsibility for one's actions
- respect for life
- non-discrimination towards and tolerance of anyone who is different from ourselves
- forgiveness
- loving and caring
- social justice
- friendliness, kindness and sensitivity

## Lifeskills

We should help children to develop the following lifeskills because they enable them to implement the knowledge, attitudes, values and decisions they make during the learning process:

- self-awareness
- critical thinking

- responsible decision making
- problem solving
- assertiveness
- negotiation skills (e.g. negotiating abstinence, the postponement of sexual intercourse and safer sex practices such as using condoms)
- communication skills (including listening skills)
- refusal skills (also called 'How-to-say-no' skills)
- planning for the future: goal setting
- conflict resolution
- handling emotions (such as fear, uncertainty, anger, etc.)
- handling failure and coping with related feelings
- tolerance towards others whose values, behaviour, manners or appearance may differ from our own
- a positive self-concept

**Enrichment**

**Sources for lifeskills training in schools**

Excellent materials have been developed on sexuality education, HIV/AIDS education and lifeskills training for primary and secondary schools in South Africa. These programmes are based on outcomes-based principles (which ensure learner participation). Some of this material includes teacher manuals and activity books for learners which contain many practical exercises that assist children to develop necessary values, attitudes and lifeskills. The following references can be recommended for teachers:

- Edwards, D. & Louw, N. (1998). Outcomes-based Sexuality Education. Pretoria: Kagiso.
- Norton, J. & Dawson, C. (written for PPSASA) (2000). Lifeskills and HIV/AIDS Education. A manual and resource guide for intermediate phase school teachers. Johannesburg: Heinemann.
- Rooth, E. (1995). Lifeskills: A resource book for facilitators. Pietermaritzburg: Macmillan.
- Von Mollendorf, J.W., Kekana, M.M., Froneman, T. & Kekana, L.T. (2000). Reach Out Life Orientation. Pietermaritzburg: Reach Out Publishers. (This series includes educator guides as well as learner books.)

For HIV/AIDS education to be successful, it is important to know how children of different ages perceive *illness in general* and *HIV/AIDS in particular*. We know that children's perception of illness depends on their developmental characteristics. In order to arrive at a clearer understanding of what we should include in HIV/AIDS education and lifeskills programmes, we will therefore review (in sections 9.4 and 9.7) the developmental characteristics of children between grade 1 and grade 12.

(Only those developmental characteristics that are relevant to HIV/AIDS education will be discussed.)

## 9.4  THE MIDDLE CHILDHOOD YEARS (ABOUT 6 TO 12 YEARS)

The middle childhood years stretch from about 6 or 7 years to 12 years. What follows below is a discussion of how children develop cognitively, emotionally, socially, morally, sexually and in terms of their self-concept during this phase of their lives.

### Cognitive development

*Cognition* refers to how we acquire information about the world, how we represent and transform such information into knowledge, and how we store, retrieve and use that knowledge to direct our behaviour (Meyer, 1998, p. 10). Egocentric thinking, concrete thinking and the ability to classify are especially relevant to HIV/AIDS education in the middle childhood years.

### *Egocentric thinking*

The young child in the middle childhood years (6 to 7 years old) may still use egocentric and magical thinking. *Egocentrism* is the inability to see situations from any perspective other than one's own, and magical thinking is the belief that one's thoughts alone are powerful enough to effect certain events and changes in the world. (A typical example of magical thinking is when the child wishes that his or her newborn sibling were dead. If then that sibling actually does die, that young child will believe that it was his or her *wish* alone that caused the death.) In older children, this rigid, egocentric outlook is gradually replaced by thought processes that allow children to see things from the point of view of other people in the world. Older children gradually become aware of a variety of points of view, and they become more sensitive to the fact that other people do not always perceive or view events exactly as they do. They also become able to postpone a particular action until they have evaluated alternative responses to situations, and their steady reduction in egocentricity begins to form the foundation on which they will construct an ability to think logically and develop and define concepts of morality as they grow older (Piaget, 1973; Wong et al., 1999, p. 781).

### *Concrete thinking*

Although the child in the middle childhood years is capable of operational thinking, such thinking is still concrete and not abstract. (According to Piaget, children in the middle childhood years are in the period of *concrete operations*.) *Concrete thinking* means that children cannot construct or manipulate abstract ideas or reason in terms of hypotheses or speculate about possibilities. They can only reason in terms of the observable reality or objects in front of them (Meyer & Van Ede, 1998; Piaget & Inhelder, 1969). During this phase (called the *concrete operational phase*) children gradually begin to understand the relationships between *things* and *ideas*. They progress from making judgements based on what they *see* (perceptual thinking) to making judgements based on the consequences of their *reasoning* (conceptual thinking). They are increasingly able to master symbols, to use their memory of past experiences to evaluate and interpret the present, and to classify or group objects together according to the characteristics that they share in common (Wong et al., 1999).

## The ability to classify

The ability to classify develops through three stages. (1) Young children (i.e. younger than 6 years old) classify objects in a very indiscriminate way. They do not have a specific characteristic or criterion in mind when classifying objects, and they often change criteria (for instance, from colour to shape) while classifying objects. (2) Children from about 6 to 9 years old are able to classify objects on the basis of only one characteristic or criterion (such as, for example, colour). (3) Only in the third stage of classification ability, which develops between the ages of 9 and 12 years, does the child begin to understand multiple and hierarchical classification. *Multiple classification* refers to the ability of a child to classify objects on the basis of more than one criterion simultaneously. *Hierarchical classification* implies class inclusion — which means that a person has the ability to understand that a subclass is always smaller than the more general overall class in which the subclass is included (subsumed). The ability of children to classify may vary considerably from one child to another. According to Inhelder and Piaget (1964), who conducted their research on children in Europe, the ability to classify hierarchically usually develops in children between 7 and 11 years of age. Other studies, however, found that children often develop this ability only during mid-adolescence or beyond (Lowell, 1980). A South African study found that 9-year-old children could classify in terms of only one dimension while older children (aged about 12 years) were more frequently able to classify objects in terms of two or three dimensions (Ramkisoon in Louw, Van Ede & Ferns, 1998, p. 327).

## Emotional development

Children in the middle childhood years are relatively independent and self-sufficient and are able to express a variety of emotions. An emotion which is relevant to HIV/AIDS education is the expression of fear.

## Fear

Younger children (about 5 years and younger) are afraid of specific things such as dogs, loud noises, the dark, unfamiliar objects, strangers, 'bad people' and being separated from their parents. Older children (about 6 to 8 years) experience an increase in fear of imaginary and abstract things such as supernatural creatures (witches and ghosts), monsters, darkness, thunder and lightning, burglars, physical injury, death, being alone at home, and media events (such as reports on AIDS, war, violence and child-kidnapping). Older children (9 to 12 years old) are often afraid of tests and examinations at school, school performance, physical injury, thunder and lightning, death and the dark (Botha et al., 1998, p. 271). It has been generally observed by researchers that children's fears correspond to the times in which they live and the events with which they are familiar from the media and from listening to discussions. Today's children are generally afraid of AIDS, pollution and nuclear war.

## Social development

Social developmental abilities that are important for HIV/AIDS education and life-skills programmes are a child's ability to socialise with friends and his or her ability to form prejudice.

### Peer group

The peer group comes to play an increasingly important role in the child's life in middle childhood years. The peer group plays a very important role in the child's social development because it provides children with experiences of comradeship (friendship) and relationships, with opportunities for experimenting with new forms of behaviour, and with opportunities to exercise limited forms of independence. Children also continue to learn to appreciate the numerous and varied points of view that are represented in their peer groups, and this experience serves to diminish the rigidly egocentric outlook that was the characteristic of an earlier developmental stage. The peer group also offers children opportunities for learning positive social skills such as negotiation, assertiveness and competitiveness. Excessive conformity and attachment to a peer group can lead to undesirable activities and behaviour such as experimentation with drugs or sex. Peer group pressure usually becomes a strong motivational factor for the 12-year-old child. (Louw et al., 1998).

### Prejudice

While prejudice (or negative attitudes towards other people) usually develops during the preschool years, children continue to develop their capacity for prejudice during their middle childhood years because of the influence of reinforcement, modelling and imitation. Parents and teachers play a very important role in the development of attitudes in children — not only through the *information* that they convey to the child but also through the *manner* in which they communicate this information. While some teachers may not, for example, express any *explicit* prejudice against homosexuality, their *implicit* prejudice may be revealed very clearly in their whole attitude as well as in their facial expressions, body language and tone of voice when reacting to any kind of manifestation of homosexuality. The influences that cause children to become prejudiced are often therefore very subtle — but nonetheless powerful on that account (Louw et al., 1998). The mass media also obviously play a very influential role in either reinforcing or dismantling the influence of stereotypes and prejudice.

## Moral development

*Moral development* refers to the process by which children learn the principles that enable them to judge behaviour as good or bad and as right or wrong.

### Rules and punishment

According to Piaget, children younger than about 5 years of age are *premoral*. This means that because they do not understand rules, they are unable to judge whether or not a rule has been broken. Between the ages of 5 and 10 (in the phase of *moral realism*), children develop an enormous respect for rules, and they come to believe that rules must be obeyed at all times. They regard rules as absolute, unchangeable, 'holy', and as an extension of the higher authority that they perceive to be invested in authority figures such as their parents, teachers or God. Although these children do not understand the reasoning behind rules, they regard rules as guidelines for acceptable behaviour and they believe that any violation of rules should be punished. Children in this phase also believe in *immanent justice*. This means that they perceive sickness or hurt to be a *punishment* for the breaking of a rule. Children at this stage also believe that what *other* people (especially adults and authority figures) tell them to do is right — and what they themselves think is wrong. (This may become a problem if it leads children to accept criminal behaviour such as sexual molestation as right — or even as a punishment for something that *they* did wrong.) By about the age of 10, children reach the phase of *moral relativism*. In this stage, they display greater moral flexibility. They realise that social rules are arbitrary, less absolute and authoritarian, and that rules can be legitimately questioned and even changed. Older children are able to judge an act by the *intentions* that prompted it rather than merely by its *consequences*. It is however not until adolescence or beyond that children are able to understand morality as an abstract body of concepts constructed from sound reasoning and principled thinking. Older children in middle childhood are also able to understand and accept the concept of treating others as they would like to be treated themselves (Kohlberg, 1985; Louw et al., 1998; Piaget, 1932; Wong et al., 1999).

## Sexual development

By the age of 5 to 7, the sex role identities of children are usually formed and they know that their gender is fixed and that it cannot be changed. They are able to identify with their own bodies and they become increasingly inquisitive about body parts. Older children (grades 4 and 5) are often aware of their own sexual feelings and desires, and they often feel confused and conflicted about these feelings. They explore sex roles and they are usually quite comfortable about discussing human sexuality at this age (Davidson, 1988).

### Curiosity about sex

Because they are curious about sex, children in the middle childhood years often engage in various forms of simple sex play. Sex play in middle childhood is usually experimental and it has nothing to do with love or sexual urges. Because children's attitudes towards sex are formed at an early age, the way in which parents and teachers handle sex play during childhood will have a decisive influence on a child's development. If parents react with anger or disgust to the sexual exploration in which children engage, this will communicate a powerful message (namely that sex is 'bad' and 'dirty'). It will also of course discourage children from ever asking any questions about sex. Such children will then look to others for the information they need to satisfy their curiosity. Their main source of information will usually be their peer group. Information gathered from a peer group often contains considerable misinformation and distortion — a factor that often creates anxiety in children. Negative reactions by parents to their children's questions may also give rise to adverse emotional reactions and guilt feelings in children. The period of middle childhood should be used as an opportunity to teach children the correct terminology for sexual organs and sexual feelings so that they will be empowered to use the correct language when they are older (Wong et al., 1999).

## Self-concept development

One of the most important resources that any child can have as he or she makes life choices is a positive self-concept. All the lifeskills that are necessary to implement knowledge, attitudes and values (lifeskills such as assertiveness, decision making, negotiation, communication, and refusal skills) are based on a healthy, positive self-concept.

*Self-concept* refers to the way in which a person views himself or herself. It is sometimes used interchangeably with 'self-esteem', which refers more specifically to the personal assessment of *value* or *worth* that we attach to ourselves (Gillis,

1994). In addition, the role that significant others play in a child's life is crucial for the development of a robust self-concept. The expectations and esteem that parents and teachers have for a child crucially influence the development of that child's self-concept. It is therefore essential for parents and teachers to make children feel that they are special, likable, worthwhile human beings who are valuable *in themselves* — quite apart from any capacity or ability they might have to make a contribution to the larger world in which they find themselves. Adults must help children to increase their self-confidence by being honest with them, by providing opportunities for creativity, by helping children to succeed in their activities, and by providing positive reinforcement (Wong et al., 1999). Teachers have an especially important role to play in the development of a sound self-concept in the child because children with a poor self-concept are especially vulnerable to criticism and praise in the classroom (Gillis, 1994).

Studies show that a negative self-concept in children is produced by the following factors (Gillis, 1994; Wong et al., 1999):

- insufficient appreciative attention or regard from parents or members of the family
- the conviction that they are constantly ignored and not noticed (this makes children feel invisible and therefore worthless)
- ridicule, excessive and irrational punishments and the insecurity that is caused by harsh and rigid (and inconsistently applied) rules — or (conversely) the insecurity caused by too few or no rules or parental guidelines
- physical violence and threatening or menacing behaviour; psychological neglect; sexual and emotional abuse; negative, cruel and humiliating labels (verbalised abuse) that make children feel worthless, useless and anxious
- inconsistency on the part of parents towards their children (the 'double bind')
- unrealistically high expectations or inconsistent standards applied by parents, teachers or significant others to children
- overprotective attitudes by parents towards their children (this makes children insecure about their own judgement and thus increases their levels of anxiety)
- deprivation of basic necessities such as food, shelter and safety
- a physical disability or a perceived physical disability
- unfavourable or humiliating comparisons based on racial characteristics

Children with positive self-esteem were found to be more independent, creative, energetic, optimistic, self-reliant, sociable, assertive, self-confident, relaxed, extroverted, popular at school and less self-conscious than children with a low self-esteem (Coopersmith, 1967; Norton & Dawson, 2000). Self-concept is also influenced by a child's own achievements and by the degree to which he or she has the ability to regulate his or her own behaviour. It is therefore vitally important for children to develop a high self-efficacy or faith in their ability to meet personal and social requirements.

### General skills

According to Erikson (1968), children in the middle childhood years develop an interest in handling the 'tools' of their culture (whatever they may be) and become keen collaborators in any productive process (Meyer, 1997). Middle childhood is the phase in which children learn to read and write, and during which they also become ready and willing to learn and assume their share of household tasks. These tasks are usually related to the male and female roles that have been defined by their culture, and many children assume responsibilities for tasks inside and outside the home such as baby-sitting, cleaning, and working in the yard (Wong et al., 1999). These skills are all the more relevant in our current HIV/AIDS situation because many households have AIDS patients who need to be cared for. Children can be involved in helping in small ways with such care. *It is however very important not to overload a child with household or caring chores.* (See enrichment box 'The use of children in home-based care — a warning!' on page 331.)

We can divide HIV/AIDS education in the middle childhood years into two categories if we base it on the above-mentioned developmental characteristics:

- The *junior primary school phase* (or foundation phase) for children in grade 1 to grade 3 (approximately 7 to 9 years old). HIV/AIDS education in this phase is discussed in section 9.5.
- The *senior primary school phase* (or intermediate phase) for children in grade 4 to grade 6 (approximately 10 to 12 years old). HIV/AIDS education in this phase is discussed in section 9.6.

### 9.5 HIV/AIDS EDUCATION AND LIFESKILLS TRAINING IN THE JUNIOR PRIMARY SCHOOL PHASE (GRADE 1 TO GRADE 3)

The grade 1 to grade 3 child (about 7 to 9 years old) is in the early stage of the *middle childhood* years. While the child in the junior primary school phase may still show some of the characteristics of the preschool child, the middle childhood years are usually characterised by rapidly increasing levels of cognitive development.

### Children in the junior primary school phase's perception of illness, HIV and AIDS

Young children in the junior primary school phase do not really understand what illness is — mainly because they are unable to think operationally (Piaget, 1973; Piaget & Inhelder, 1969). Because the thought processes of young children are *con-*

*crete,* they form abstract, mental images out of what they observe. They tend to focus on external, observable, perceptual events, and they make no spontaneous references to internal, invisible ideas or concepts. Young children's perception of illness is therefore also concrete. They define illness in terms of the external, observable features that are associated with the disease, and they make no references to what might be happening inside of the body or to the processes of illness. To young children, people merely 'look' ill, and they cannot understand the reality of what it means for people also to 'feel' ill and the fact that their internal organs are also affected by the illness (Walsh & Bibace, 1990).

### Perception of cause, effect and prevention of disease

Children in the junior primary school phase have no concept of the causes, symptoms or consequences of illness. They cannot distinguish between 'cause' and 'effect' because of their limited ability to *classify* and to distinguish between different objects. Children in this phase tend to classify only in terms of one dimension. They therefore tend to group together different ideas or facts that have no logical connection with each other — and they group these ideas or facts into a confused (and confusing) class of their own. While children often group entirely disconnected and unrelated facts together on the grounds of their own subjective and 'egocentric' reasoning processes, they remain unable to *see* the correlation between facts that actually *are* connected (Piaget, 1970).

Because they are unable to conceptualise the *inside* of the body, young children do not understand how causes function and they therefore have no understanding of the meaning of prevention (Walsh & Bibace, 1990). Because of their *concrete thinking* processes, young children understand the consequences of HIV/AIDS only in concrete terms, namely *immediate* death. They are unable to grasp the significance of intermediary factors such as time, medication or the process of dying.

Children in grade 1 to grade 3 are therefore not interested in the causes, symptoms, consequences or prevention of AIDS or any other illness. If young children are asked what causes AIDS, they usually give an answer based on one or other *observable* aspect of AIDS that has nothing to do with its actual causes (as understood by adults). For example, when asked why he thinks people contract AIDS, a young boy answered: 'AIDS is throwing up a real lot' (Walsh & Bibace, 1990, p. 257). While young children will often ascribe illness to germs, they don't usually know what a germ really is, what it looks like, and where it 'hides' (Quackenbush, 1988; Quackenbush & Villarreal,1988). (They may have heard adults talk about 'germs'.)

While older children in the junior primary school phase often begin to distinguish between *illness* and *cause,* they can still not describe how the *cause* leads to the *illness.* Their explanations are often based on associations or *magical thinking* instead of on a description of the mechanisms of transmission (Walsh & Bibace,

1990). Children in the junior primary school phase who mention sex or drugs as causes of AIDS usually do not really understand how such factors cause AIDS. Their answers are generally based on what they have seen on TV or heard from adults.

### Perceptions of people who have AIDS

*Egocentric* perspectives and an inability to think logically dominate the young child's perception of AIDS. They associate AIDS with people in their environment who (in their perception) seem likely 'AIDS candidates'. Their perception of AIDS as a 'fearful disease' also leads them to infer that all people who are seriously *ill* (such as cancer patients) have AIDS. If someone in their immediate community actually *has* AIDS, they often come to the conclusion that everyone who is similar to that person also has AIDS. (They may therefore arrive at the ludicrous conclusion that, for example, 'All thin men with long hair have AIDS'.)

### Fear of AIDS

In spite of their lack of understanding of what AIDS really is, one of the main characteristics of the young child's perception of AIDS is an overwhelming fear of the disease (Quackenbush & Villarreal, 1988; Walsh & Bibace, 1990). This fear of AIDS may be ascribed to their emotional developmental characteristics (see 'Emotional development' on page 161). A child's fear of diseases is rather vague, supernatural and imaginative — and this in itself contributes to feelings of helplessness and being unable to exercise control over contracting diseases. These feelings of helplessness may lead to endless irrational fears and feelings of vulnerability in children. Exposure to television, pictures in magazines and frightening stories from parents and friends also serve to increase a child's fear of AIDS.

### Influence of friends and mass media on perceptions of AIDS

Children in the junior primary school phase develop a sense of autonomy and independence from their parents, and friends play increasingly important roles in their lives. Children are also exposed to information about sex, violence and death by television programmes, videos, films and the Internet. The misconception often exists that young children are not aware of HIV and AIDS. What in fact happens is that as their social contacts broaden and as they are increasingly exposed to mass media, they hear more and more about AIDS. Because of their limited cognitive abilities, children do not always understand what they see and hear and they therefore often have many questions about HIV and AIDS.

### Perception of AIDS as punishment for sin

Because the child in the junior primary school phase tends to evaluate behaviour only in terms of the consequences of that behaviour (reward or punishment), children often believe that people get AIDS because they are 'bad' or because such people are being punished for something they did wrong (Quackenbush & Villarreal, 1988). This view is related to a young child's fears and doubts about his or her own 'goodness' or 'badness' and the consequent fear of punishment. Misconceptions like these contribute to irrational fears about AIDS and can also provide a powerful impetus to the development of prejudice in the minds of children.

## Sexual transmission of HIV

Because children in grade 1 to grade 3 do not understand how sexual intercourse can be a means of transmission for the HI virus, it should not be discussed with children when they are this young. When teachers do present sexual information to children, they should treat sex as a normal part of development.

**Enrichment**

### How to answer a young child's questions about sex and AIDS

Parents and teachers often find it difficult to answer young children's questions about sex and AIDS. The following points should be borne in mind when answering a young child's questions (Wong et al., 1999, pp. 710–711):

- Answer the question honestly and matter-of-factly. This will encourage the child to continue to search for answers.
- Don't answer a question with a 'tall tale' or with anxiety. This will teach children to keep questions about sex to themselves, to create their own (sometimes harmful) fantasies and formulate their own (wrong) theories.
- Find out what children know and think first. You may then be in a position to correct the child's (often wrong) explanation before you present the correct information. Using this method helps to prevent parents or teachers from giving answers to unasked questions.
- Be honest and use the correct anatomical words. Although the child may forget most of the information or words, your sincerity, openness and honesty will set the scene for further sexuality education at a later stage.
- Honesty certainly does not imply imparting to children every fact of life or catering for excessive prurience. When children ask one question, they are looking for one answer. They will ask the next question when they are ready.
- When children do not ask questions, take advantage of natural opportunities to discuss reproduction (e.g. a pregnant family member or a TV programme).
- Neither condone nor condemn the sexual curiosity that is expressed in sex play (e.g. playing 'doctor-doctor'). Rather express the view that if children have questions, they should preferably ask their parents or teachers for answers.
- If children ask questions about condoms, teachers can say that condoms are things grown-ups use to prevent infection with HIV. Children don't need them (because they do not make love like grown-ups do.)

*Summary*

Children in the junior primary school phase do not really understand what HIV/AIDS is and they have no cognitive understanding or interest in the causes, symptoms, consequences or prevention of AIDS. They are, however, afraid of AIDS because it is something vague and menacing over which they have no control. Friends and the mass media and parents often contribute (unwittingly) to this fear. Children are also inclined to regard AIDS as a punishment for sin and they are often very afraid that *they* may contract the disease as a result of misbehaviour. In spite of the cognitive limitations that prevent them from understanding HIV/AIDS, children often have many questions about the disease.

**Implications for HIV/AIDS education and lifeskills training in the junior primary school phase**

The main aim of HIV/AIDS education in the junior primary school phase should be the reassurance of children and the eradication of irrational fears. In view of their cognitive limitations at this age, the HIV/AIDS education of children should not include specific information such as causes, symptoms and prevention. They should instead be equipped with the necessary knowledge, attitudes and lifeskills to help them to avoid HIV infection *in the future* and to better understand those facts to which they will be exposed at a later stage in their education.

The following knowledge, attitudes, values and lifeskills should be included in HIV/AIDS education and lifeskills programmes for children in the junior primary school phase (CDC, 1988; Davidson, 1988; Pilot Project on Lifeskills, 1999; Walsh & Bibace, 1990):

- Children's fears of the epidemic and their anxiety about their own susceptibility to the disease must be addressed. AIDS should simply be defined as a serious illness *which children of their age don't usually contract*. Discretion should be exercised and information should be adapted in those cases when there are children in the school, in the family or in the community who are in fact already infected with HIV.
- Assure children that it is not easy to contract HIV/AIDS. Tell them that they need not fear playing with children who have AIDS or children whose parents have AIDS. Tell them that they will not contract the disease by sitting next to a child who has AIDS or by sharing their lunch or colddrink with such children, or by holding hands, or by giving someone with AIDS a friendly kiss or a hug.
- We should make young children aware of the dangers of HIV infection in a very concrete manner — but without making them afraid. An excellent method that is very successful with young children is to teach them that germs have various 'homes' — and then to illustrate this concept visually by using pictures and games. One could tell them that the cold or flu germ lives everywhere (on places

such as teacups and glasses), and that this is why one catches a cold so easily. One could then go on to say that some dangerous germs (like HIV) live in the blood and one should be very careful to avoid those germs by never touching anyone else's blood with one's bare hands. Tell them that if a friend has a nose bleed or gets hurt on the playground, they should call a teacher or any other adult immediately and that they will put on gloves before they touch the blood. Universal precautions should be explained to young children in ways like this — ways that they will understand and be able to apply.

- Warn children never to play with syringes, injection needles or anything sharp that they may find on the playground, in the street or on rubbish dumps.

- Teach children how to keep their bodies safe and healthy and how to avoid anything that could harm the body. Educational material should focus on personal hygiene and health in general. Research has shown that people who care about their health in general are also less likely to become involved in high-risk sexual activity (Feldman, 1985; Van Dyk, 1991).

- Explain the dangers of drug abuse to children. Discuss drugs or behaviour in ways that can be comprehended by children who can only understand concrete experiences. Thus, for example, one will make far more of an impression on younger children if one warns them not to take too much cough mixture, too many pain pills or to sniff glue rather than if one discusses (in a general way) the evils of smoking dagga.

- Although formal sexuality education is not offered to children in the junior primary school phase, it is extremely important to equip children with the necessary lifeskills to cope with sex and HIV when needed. From an early age, children should be encouraged to feel positive about their bodies and to know the body parts by the correct names. Sex and intimacy should never be presented in a negative light, and children should never be made to feel bad about themselves. If the question should arise, children must be assured that it is natural and healthy to feel curious about sex. Sexuality education for the younger child should focus on dispelling misinformation, on emphasising equality between the two sexes and on having respect for one's own and for everyone else's body.

- Teach children what sexual abuse is, how to try and prevent it and where to find help. Start by teaching young children that there are different types of physical touching — good and bad touches. A mother's caress or hug, or holding hands with a friend, are examples of good touches, while any kinds of touch (e.g. genitalia) that make the child feel uncomfortable are examples of bad touches. Teach children never to stay in situations where they feel uncomfortable. Teach children to shout for help, run away and ask an adult they trust for help. Let children practise this in school (shouting and running; saying 'No!' very clearly and assertively). Let them act out their reactions to different situations in role play.

- Although children are taught to respect older people, they should also be taught that such respect does not mean that they must do everything older people tell them to do — especially if it is wrong and makes the child feel uncomfortable.

- Teach children never to go to the home of a stranger, or walk in the street or fields with a stranger, or get into the car of a stranger. They should also not do any of these things with someone they know (a family member, teacher or good family friend) if that person makes them feel uncomfortable or if the person is behaving strangely or abnormally.

- Teach children about the importance of family life.

- Teach children how to care for someone who is ill. They can be taught to do small things to make a sick friend feel better (e.g. make a card or take food) and to do simple things in the home, such as making tea.

- Help children to cope with death in the family. (See 'Children and bereavement' on page 308 for children's perceptions of death and how to help them to deal with bereavement.)

- The fear of AIDS can be addressed by helping the young child to modify his or her absolute thinking about HIV/AIDS. Explain, for example, that people do not immediately die of AIDS, but that there is quite a lengthy period between the time that they fall ill and the time when they actually die. Because young children are unable to assimilate *reasons*, it is not necessary to provide explanations for these facts.

- Reassure children that the 'germ' that causes AIDS 'does not know if people are good or bad'. People with AIDS are not bad people. Explain to them that contracting AIDS is also not a punishment for wrongdoing.

- Research indicates that people who have learned to be safety-conscious in general, tend to be more careful in other areas of their lives as well (such areas also include their sex lives) (Baldwin & Baldwin, 1988; Williams, 1972). It is thus to the child's advantage (in more than one way) to emphasise safety-consciousness. Children should, for example, be taught to be careful with electricity, fire and swimming pools and always to wear safety belts.

- One of the greatest gifts a parent or teacher can give a child is to help him or her to develop a healthy, strong and positive self-concept. A positive self-concept and accompanying psychological strengths, such as self-efficacy and assertiveness, may help children to avoid child abuse, drugs, premature or unwanted sex and HIV infection.

**Enrichment**

## Enhancing the self-concept of the child

Gillis (1994, pp. 80–81) suggests that parents and teachers can enhance a child's self-concept in the following ways:
- Establish a caring, personal relationship, and create an environment of acceptance and optimism. The child needs to feel that he or she is considered sufficiently worthwhile to merit your special attention, respect and appreciation.
- Emphasise whatever is worthy and good about the child, and boost his or her morale by focusing on existing strengths rather than by trying to improve inadequacies or defects.
- Provide the child with opportunities for experiencing success and set goals that are relatively easy for the child to attain.
- Reward the child's achievements with approval. The child should perceive the approval to be genuine (and he or she will experience it as genuine if it is sincerely given).
- Encourage children to change negative self-thinking attitudes (I can't) to positive self-thinking (I can).
- Use modelling, role play and assertiveness training to help the child to reinforce his or her feelings of confidence in his or her ability to perform a behaviour.
- Teach problem-solving skills.
- Encourage children to assist other children in some activity (helping others is morale-building).
- When friends are present, arrange activities in which you already know that the child will succeed. Praise from friends (or praise given in front of peers) is very effective in enhancing self-concept.
- Initiate pride in mutual projects (e.g. with friends). It boosts the child's self-concept to be part of a team.
- Give the child more responsibility at home or at school (e.g. allow him or her to care for a plant or a pet).

## 9.6 HIV/AIDS EDUCATION AND LIFESKILLS TRAINING IN THE SENIOR PRIMARY SCHOOL PHASE (GRADES 4 TO 6)

### Children in the senior primary school phase's perception of illness, HIV and AIDS

Although children in the senior primary school phase (approximately 10 to 12 years old) are capable of operational thinking, their thinking is still mostly concrete and not abstract and children in this stage still find it difficult to think in terms of abstract hypotheses (Piaget & Inhelder, 1969). Their capacity for logical reasoning has however developed to some extent. This gives them the ability to consider different aspects of one issue simultaneously.

*Perception of the causes, effect and prevention of disease*

Children in the senior primary phase have developed the ability to distinguish between objects and to observe differences between things. They can distinguish between the physical and the psychological as well as between internal and external bodily experiences (Piaget, 1971). Children in this phase are able to distinguish between the causes and effects (or symptoms) of disease. They define illness in terms of specific symptoms experienced by the body. While they describe the symptoms of AIDS as externally observable when they are younger, older children are able to realise that symptoms can also be internal (i.e. that they do also affect the 'inside' of the body) (Walsh & Bibace, 1990).

When they are younger, children ascribe the causes of illness to external factors such as concrete, superficial transmission (physical contact or touch). But as they grow older, they begin to realise that there are processes that permit the illness to get inside the body. Children will initially describe these processes in concrete and global terms (e.g. 'You swallow it' or 'It gets in your blood'). Children in this phase are also unable to think in terms of classes or categories of causes; they can only think in terms of discrete causes which do not have any necessary connection with each other. When they are asked to explain what causes AIDS, children in this age group will often offer a long list of causes from what they have heard in the media, from what other people have said, or from what they imagine to be the causes of AIDS (Walsh & Bibace, 1990).

By the time they reach the senior primary school phase, children are able to see a simple, linear relationship between cause and effect (symptoms). Although their understanding is still largely concrete and non-specific, children in this phase know that HIV can be transmitted through sex, blood, from mother-to-baby, and by 'using drugs' (Montauk & Scoggin, 1989). They are also able to make basic distinctions such as that 'not all kinds of sex' or 'not all drugs' lead to AIDS (Walsh & Bibace, 1990).

Montauk and Scoggin (1989) found that the questions grade 4 and grade 5 children ask are mainly dominated by their own everyday frame of reference. For example, when they asked about the safety of blood, their questions were about blood from their own or their friends' wounds. They also wanted to know if HIV can be transmitted through 'blood-rituals' between friends, and by using pins as 'pea-shooters'. Children at this age also had a lot of questions about the 'French kiss' — not really because they were practising it, but because of curiosity.

Because their thinking processes are still concrete, children in the senior primary school phase still find it difficult to conceptualise prevention (Walsh & Bibace, 1990). In a study undertaken by Montauk and Scoggin (1989), only 4 % of the questions asked by children dealt with the prevention of HIV/AIDS; most of their questions were about condoms (no doubt out of curiosity).

The children in this study were however very interested in the clinical aspects of HIV/AIDS. This is an indication of how preoccupied in general children of this age group are with the question: 'How does it work?' Most of the questions they asked concerned the difference between people having HIV and people having AIDS, what the virus does to the body, and how the body works. Because their thinking processes are less absolute, the older child in the senior primary phase can also better understand that there is a time lapse between HIV infection, the final stage of AIDS and death.

In answering the questions of children in the senior primary school phase, it is important to remember that their capacity for abstract thinking is still limited and that these children feel more comfortable with concrete answers to their questions and problems.

## Acquisition of myths

Children between the ages of 10 and 12 years are very prone to the acquisition of myths. They get confused between fact and fantasy and between hypotheses and reality (Davidson, 1988). One of the reasons for this may be the fact that children at this age are not yet fully capable of hierarchical classification. They are therefore not able to classify things in subcategories of 'cause' and 'non-cause'. They are only able to form the overarching or super-class of 'causes' where they combine real causes and myths.

Although older children often have a good general knowledge about HIV/AIDS, they also nevertheless entertain many myths. Most of the questions asked by children in grades 5 and 6 in Montauk and Scoggin's (1989) study suggested the existence of myths. They asked questions about the transmission of HIV through toilet seats, swimming pools, food, coughing, playing with friends, and through animals, mosquitoes, rats and flies. Brown, Nassau and Barone (1990) found that 54 % of the grade 5 children in their study believed that one can get HIV by using a friend's hair comb, yet 84 % of them did know that HIV cannot be transmitted by touch. This finding illustrates the child's inability to classify and their tendency to generalise. Because they learn in school that lice can be spread by using a friend's comb, they generalise from this correct information to the false hypothesis that HIV can also be spread through sharing a comb — although they know very well indeed that HIV cannot be spread by touch (the super class). Concrete thinking is neatly illustrated by the following question of a young boy: 'If a man has AIDS and gives it to a lady, does he still have it?' (Montauk & Scoggin, 1989, p. 293).

It is extremely important to eradicate myths and misconceptions because they may lead to severe anxiety in children. People who believe in myths also tend to have more prejudices or negative attitudes towards people with HIV/AIDS. For instance, Siegel et al. (1991) found that children with misconceptions about the transmission of HIV believed that children with HIV should not be allowed to attend school.

### Perceptions of people who have HIV/AIDS

A decrease in egocentrism in senior primary school phase children can be seen in their description of people who have HIV/AIDS. They describe people with AIDS in more general terms and they do not see it in specific, personal terms (e.g. a specific person in their neighbourhood) as they might have done when they were younger. The older child usually associates HIV/AIDS with *specific* groups of people such as 'drug users', 'adults' or 'naughty teenagers'. Children in this phase tend to dissociate themselves from groups that they identify as vulnerable to HIV/AIDS. This is, of course, a defence mechanism because it helps them to cope with their own fear of HIV/AIDS.

Because of their decreased egocentrism, children at this stage generally have the ability to see things from another person's point of view and to understand that the points of view of various people differ. They are also able to change their own understandings and adapt them if necessary (Piaget, 1932). They are often deeply moved by stories or by personal contact with people with HIV/AIDS (especially children). This kind of contact helps them to acquire a greater understanding and compassion for people with HIV/AIDS. Children are also more tolerant of uncertainties and ambiguities at this stage and they no longer insist on black and white solutions (Quackenbush & Villarreal, 1988).

### Concrete fears about the transmission of HIV

The fears of children in the senior primary school phase are more concrete. They are no longer afraid of vague, supernatural or imaginary things. Older children's fears about the potential transmission of HIV are therefore also more concrete. But because they have difficulty in distinguishing between myth and fact, causes and non-causes, children in this phase often entertain irrational fears about HIV/AIDS.

### The influence of friends on children's perceptions of AIDS

Because the child in the senior primary school phase is less egocentric and more sensitive towards others, the peer group begins to play a bigger role in the child's social development. The child becomes increasingly sensitive to peer group pressure and they want to please their friends (Davidson, 1988). Friends usually influence the child in two ways in this stage: (1) they often are the source of misinformation, myths and half-truths about sex, HIV and AIDS, and (2) they often coerce the child into experimentation with harmful behaviour.

## The development of prejudices

Social development includes not only the formation of friendships, it also includes the development of prejudices and negative attitudes towards other people. Since prejudice usually develops in the preschool and primary school phases, special attention should be devoted to the eradication of prejudice. Children also tend to use a 'reversed' form of prejudice in the HIV/AIDS context. This means that they will label other children who have characteristics that they don't like as having AIDS. A child may therefore say something like: 'Susan is so fat, if you touch her you will get AIDS' (Quackenbush & Villarreal, 1988, p. 80). Children often tease and label others as having AIDS in order to conceal their own fears and uncertainties about the disease. The unconscious belief is that if they ascribe AIDS to other children with certain characteristics, they will magically 'protect' themselves from contracting the disease. 'I won't get AIDS because I am not like that.'

## Perception of rules about safety, health and HIV/AIDS

Children in the senior primary school phase are able to follow health rules, safety rules and rules to prevent HIV infection. Older children are also able to internalise rules and know what is right or wrong in terms of these rules. They no longer blindly follow rules to avoid punishment; they now follow rules because they perceive the rules to be rational and useful (Davidson, 1988; Piaget, 1932). If children in the senior primary phase are told not to touch blood with their bare hands, they will comply — not to avoid punishment — but because they know that touching blood might be dangerous if the blood is infected.

## Perception of sexuality and the sexual transmission of HIV

Children in the senior primary school phase are in different stages of pre-puberty and early puberty and they are very interested in learning about sexuality, gender roles and human relationships. They are aware of their own sexual feelings and needs, and they often feel very confused by them. Children in this phase are able to understand the sexual transmission of HIV.

## Summary

Because the social world of children in the senior primary school phase is in the process of expanding so rapidly, and because they are able to read well, they are very conscious of HIV/AIDS and they usually have many questions about it. Although their thought processes are still concrete, they understand the concepts of cause, effect (symptoms) and transmission of illness (and HIV) well. Children of this age cannot however conceptualise *prevention*. Children in the senior primary phase are prone to the acquisition of myths and prejudice.

**Implications for HIV/AIDS education and lifeskills training in the senior primary school phase**

The main purpose of HIV/AIDS education in the senior primary school phase is to help children to identify concrete causes of HIV/AIDS, to rectify myths and misconceptions about HIV/AIDS and to prevent the formation of prejudice. The establishment and reinforcement of lifeskills are also important in this phase. The following factors should be taken into consideration in HIV/AIDS education programmes in the senior primary school phase:

- HIV/AIDS education can begin by making an inventory of what children know, including what they have heard, what they have seen and what they think they know. The curriculum can then be adjusted so that it is relevant to a specific group of children, and so that it can prove, disprove and expand on what children already know.

- Affirm that people have natural sexual feelings. Provide basic information about human sexuality, and help children to understand the changes that are occurring in their bodies.

- The transmission of HIV is one of the most important concepts to develop in the senior primary school phase. Children in this phase are beginning to experience puberty and they are curious about sexuality and drugs. Information about the transmission of HIV must therefore be clear and straightforward. Give specific, concrete examples by using phrases and words such as: 'If you have sex with an infected person,' or 'Using needles and syringes that have already been used by infected people', 'Blood transfusions with blood that has been infected'. Reassure children that all donated blood is tested and destroyed if it is found to be infected.

- Children at this stage are very interested in the functioning of the body. They find the functioning of the immune system and the effect of the HI virus on the body fascinating, and teachers should use this opportunity to explain both how a healthy immune system functions and how a deficient immune system (ravaged by HIV) functions. One should however make the explanations concrete by using metaphors, stories, video material, etc.

- One of the main problems with HIV/AIDS education for young people is that they do not understand the long 'incubation' period of HIV infection. They do not understand how a person can be infected without also being sick. Use a metaphor to explain this important concept to children. (The story of the Trojan horse is an apt example because it explains how the enemy hid inside a wooden horse until night fell before coming out to slaughter the citizens of Troy.)

- Be sensitive when you discuss symptoms of HIV/AIDS with younger children. Symptoms such as fever, cough, tiredness, night sweat and diarrhoea are so common that emphasising them may increase the child's anxiety levels. Most

children (and their parents) often have symptoms such as these, and (as a consequence) they may begin to fear that they (or their parents) have AIDS (Quackenbush & Villarreal, 1988). It is often more helpful to concentrate on the less
general symptoms or HIV-related diseases such as PCP or Kaposi's sarcoma
when one discusses symptoms with young children.

- The vocabulary of AIDS should be increased extensively in the senior primary
school phase. How well children will understand AIDS issues in the future will
depend on the strength of the children's AIDS vocabulary. Montauk and Scoggin
(1989) found that children in grades 5 and 6 found it very difficult to ask questions
about sex and HIV/AIDS because their vocabulary did not include the necessary
terminology. Post (1988) is of the opinion that a child should have come into
contact with *most major terms* relating to HIV/AIDS by the time the child is in
the sixth grade.

- Explain the difference between HIV (the virus) and AIDS (the final stage of the
disease) in a simple way to children. Because the use of the different terms may
however be confusing to the younger child in this stage, it may be better to use
the term 'AIDS' to refer to *all* cases of HIV infection when discussing HIV/AIDS
with the younger child.

- Because children at this stage do not have a cognitive grasp of the principle of
prevention, and because they are not really interested in prevention, teachers
should concentrate only on those aspects of prevention that are relevant to the
child of that age. A helpful way of introducing the concept of prevention to young
children is by concentrating on general strategies to improve health (and therefore indirectly to prevent illness). Such an approach will focus on the principles
and practice of hygiene and a healthy style of living. Note however that some
children are sexually active *at a very early age*, and it is important for these children to know how to protect themselves by practising safer sex. Teachers must
always have an open-door policy so that they can encourage children to talk to
them when they have problems and questions of a sensitive nature. It may also
be a good idea to display the telephone numbers of the AIDS helpline, or the
nearest HIV/AIDS Training, Information and Counselling Centre, on the school's
notice board for children to use in case they need private and confidential advice.

- Children must however understand very clearly what is dangerous for them. One
should establish a strong connection between dangerous behaviour that they
should avoid and the everyday world of their own experience. Don't tell young
children to avoid 'contact with body fluids'. Rather tell them not to share toothbrushes, not to shoot pins at other children, not to mix blood in 'blood-brother
rituals', not to play with needles, not to ask a friend to make holes in their ears
for earrings, and not to touch the blood of a friend who has been injured. Children
understand rules, and they will usually abide by these rules.

- If we are to prevent the formation of myths, it is important for us to explain to children how they will *not* get AIDS. Use examples from their everyday experience — examples that make reference to matters that worry them. Don't ever tell children half-truths. Children should be reassured that they will not get HIV/AIDS by sharing ice cream, water fountains, taps, toilet seats and toys, and that they will also not get HIV/AIDS from the school nurse's (sterile) needles, or from travelling on a bus with other children. Reassurance on how they will not get HIV/AIDS will help children to feel less anxious about HIV and it will create an atmosphere of greater tolerance towards people with HIV/AIDS.

- Prevent the formation of prejudice. Language is a very powerful tool and it should be used wisely. Don't, for example, refer to 'risk groups'. Rather refer to 'risk behaviour'. Stress the fact that any person of any race or sex or occupation or status can get HIV/AIDS. We don't only avoid prejudice in order to protect HIV-infected individuals; we also avoid it so that we can protect children. A child who is led to believe that 'only prostitutes and bad people' get AIDS is lured into a false — and ultimately dangerous and self-defeating — sense of security. When AIDS is ascribed only to certain groups, it is easy (and wrong) for a person to say 'I won't get it because I don't belong to that group'.

- When certain children in the school are teased about having AIDS, it is important to act immediately. *Make a strict rule forbidding children to tease other children about AIDS*, and find out what the children know about the disease, and why they are teasing a particular child. This cruel behaviour is often attributable to the child's own anxiety and unanswered questions about HIV/AIDS.

- Concentrate on lifeskills training such as general hygiene, a positive self-concept, self-efficacy, assertiveness, handling of peer pressure, decision making and refusal skills. General safety rules, such as avoidance of drugs and alcohol, and the prevention and handling of molestation should also be reinforced.

- Strengthen moral values and the love and security inherent in the family. Teach children to respect their own bodies as well as those of other people. Teach children that all behaviours have consequences, and that they should take responsibility for their own behaviour.

- Students in grades 4 to 6 have a natural interest in 'how to fix things' and they are often interested in what kind of treatment people with AIDS are receiving. They want to reassure themselves that all problems have solutions. According to Post (1988), the fact that there is no vaccine or treatment for HIV/AIDS may be a valuable lesson in itself: the lesson being that we cannot always repair the consequences of our behaviours. (It is however important to explain to children how HIV-infected people can prolong their lives by living healthy lives.)

- Teach children to have compassion for people with HIV/AIDS.

- Teach children how to develop personal learning and research skills by looking for articles dealing with HIV/AIDS in newspapers and periodicals. Teach them how to classify AIDS-related issues into subcategories with headings such as politics, economics, human rights, and statistics (Post, 1988).
- Teachers should be aware that information on HIV/AIDS may upset some children — especially if somebody in their family (or they themselves) is infected with HIV, if they know people who are using drugs, or if they were sexually molested in the past. Children with special problems should be referred to an HIV/AIDS centre or a psychologist for individualised help.

## 9.7   THE ADOLESCENT YEARS (APPROXIMATELY 13 TO 19 YEARS)

The adolescent years range from about 12 or 13 years of age to about 18 or 19 years of age. The developmental characteristics of the adolescent will be discussed below in terms of cognitive, emotional, moral, social, sexual, identity and self-concept development.

### Cognitive development

Abstract thinking, decision-making abilities, scientific thinking, and adolescent egocentricity are all relevant to HIV/AIDS education in adolescence.

### *Abstract thinking*

Piaget (1972) described the shift from childhood to adolescence as a movement from concrete to formal operational thinking. Most adolescents develop *formal operational thinking* between the ages of 12 and 15. This means that adolescents are able to think in abstract terms and to think about possibilities. They also have the capacity to think through and examine hypotheses. Adolescents also factor a future-time perspective into their thinking: they are not tied so much to the kind of here-and-now thinking that characterised their childhood. Hypothetical thinking enables adolescents to plan ahead and identify the possible future consequences of present actions. Health messages are often based on the ability *to think further than the here-and-now*. While health messages for younger children who primarily use concrete thinking should concentrate on the *immediate* risks or benefits of the behaviour, the emphasis of health messages for older adolescents should focus on possible future benefits. It should also demonstrate the very real connections between wrong choices and risky behaviour and the eventual manifestation of negative and undesirable consequences.

### *Decision-making abilities*

As a young person's capacity for cognitive development increases, so also does his or her capacity for decision making increase during adolescence. Young people develop the ability to consider hypothetical risks and the possible benefits of various kinds of behaviour, as well as the potential consequences (whether desirable or undesirable) of such behaviour, and this ability helps them to make good decisions. Frequently however the pressures of time, commitments, personal stress, unhappiness and peer pressure compel young people to abandon their rational thought processes (Thom et al., 1998). Many adolescents are so overwhelmed by negative pressures of various kinds that they never find themselves in a position to make the kind of rational choices that would be in their own best interests. Such young people need special understanding, support and compassion. They should never be abandoned just because they never had the opportunity to make the kind of choices that would have made them happy.

### Scientific thinking

Adolescents gradually develop the ability to think *scientifically*. This means that they are able to see the relationship between *theory* and *evidence*. They are increasingly able objectively to evaluate evidence presented to them and to change their theories in the light of new evidence. Scientific thinking often leads those who think in this way to eliminate stereotypes and myths. When theories that contradict stereotypes and myths are based on sound evidence, older adolescents are often able to change their beliefs. Scientific thinking also makes it possible for adolescents to consider all the aspects of a problem, as well as all possible solutions.

### Adolescent egocentricity

Although adolescents are less egocentric than younger children, they often fail to differentiate between what is important to them and what is of interest to others. Adolescents are often very self-absorbed indeed. Elkind (1978) refers to this as *adolescent egocentricity* and he explains it as the inability of some adolescents to decentre from their own focus. Adolescent egocentricity manifests in two ways that may have implications for their health-related beliefs and decisions. Firstly, they are so self-conscious that they believe that they are the focus of everyone else's attention *(imaginary audience)*. Secondly, they also believe that they are *unique* and that their personal experiences bear no resemblance to the personal experience of others *(personal fable)*. The influence of these two forms of adolescent egocentricity can be seen in adolescents who don't want to take their medication at school because 'everybody will notice', and in sexually active adolescents who refuse to use condoms because they truly believe that 'other people get HIV, but not me'. Egocentrism usually diminishes as adolescents approach about 16 years of age. Despite adolescent egocentrism, adolescents can understand the points of view of other people and they can see how the thoughts or actions of one person can influence those of others. As their 'perspective-understanding skills' increase, adolescents develop the capacity to learn from others (Thom et al., 1998).

## Emotional development

Adolescents experience certain emotional changes as a result of their physical, cognitive, personality and social development. They often experience negative emotions, mood swings and emotional outbursts. The fact that adolescents tend to focus on themselves could also contribute to the fact that they are more inclined to experience feelings of anxiety, guilt, shame and embarrassment. On the other hand, because of their ability to think in a more abstract and complex way, they are more likely to show insight into their own and other people's feelings.

## Moral development

One of the most important developmental tasks of adolescents is to develop a personal value system or a clear view about what is right and what is wrong. In order to develop a personal value system, adolescents have to question existing values, decide which values are acceptable to them, and then incorporate these values into their personal value systems. Once they have achieved an ability to think in abstract terms and once they are able to see that other people's perspectives and opinions may differ from their own, adolescents also develop the ability to approach moral issues in a more mature way. Although many adolescents are still at a *conventional level* of moral reasoning (a law and order approach), they begin to accept rules because they can identify with them and perceive them as essential for preserving the coherence of society (Kohlberg, 1978). Once adolescents develop some capacity for *principled moral reasoning*, they begin to see that absolutes and rules may be questioned because such rules may be based on someone else's subjective point of view — a point of view that is open to various interpretations and (therefore) disagreement. They will only adhere to rules that are useful, that support individual and social rights and that promote the common good.

## Social development

### Importance of the peer group

Because adolescents have an intense desire 'to belong', their social development is characterised by an increasing interest in and involvement with the peer group. The peer group plays an important role in the adolescent's psychosocial development. Interaction with friends satisfies the adolescent's emotional needs. The peer group serves as an important source of information and it also provides adolescents with opportunities for socialisation.

### Conformity

A characteristic of adolescent peer-group relationships is an increase in conformity. *Conformity* refers to the tendency to give in to social pressure (in this case, peer

## Moral development of adolescents

Thom et al. (1998, pp. 466–467) mention the following factors as factors that could influence an adolescent's moral development:

- Cognition: The adolescent's value system is influenced by his or her ability to formulate hypotheses, to investigate and test them, to make certain deductions, and to think in an abstract manner.
- Parental attitudes and actions: The relationship between the adolescent and his or her parents plays an important role in whether or not the adolescent will internalise moral values. Parents who are warm and loving, who are consistent models of commendable moral behaviour and who apply disciplinary techniques which promote calm discussion of the effects of misbehaviour and the importance of upholding certain values with their children, undoubtedly promote the development of moral maturity in their children.
- Peer interaction: Interaction among peers who confront one another with different viewpoints, promotes moral development. Adolescents often advance to higher levels of moral development when they have opportunities to discuss moral issues with their friends.
- Religion: Some studies indicate that adolescents' attitudes to religion affect their moral development and behaviour. Hauser (1981) found that religious youths show greater moral responsibility than non-religious youths. They also identified more with their parents' attitudes, values and behaviour than youths who were not religious. Hauser also found less premarital sexual intercourse, alcohol abuse and drug abuse amongst religious adolescents.

Not all individuals reach moral maturity. Moral immaturity always contains the following two characteristics:

- Egocentrism: This is the inability to see matters from another person's point of view. Egocentric individuals consider only what is important to themselves when they are confronted with a moral dilemma. For example, sexually active adolescents who do not regard the use of condoms as a shared responsibility, are reasoning in an egocentric moral fashion.
- Heteronomous acceptance of others' value systems: This means that the individual is under the authority of the values of others (such as, for example, his or her parents). Such an individual has not formed an independent and autonomous value system which they can truly call their own.

pressure). Young adolescents tend to conform more than older adolescents because younger adolescents are very sensitive about the approval of the peer group and they conform in order to be accepted. They have also not yet developed sufficient self-confidence and independence to make their own choices. Conforming to the peer group also provides them with the guidelines they need to make their choices. While conforming to the peer group might benefit the adolescent to a certain extent, an excessive degree of conformity could exert a negative influence on an adolescent's identity development and on his or her development towards autonomy. Excessive conformity could also cause an adolescent to become involved in high-risk behaviours such as early sexual activity, smoking, alcohol and drug abuse, and antisocial behaviour. Peer group pressure is, of course, not the only cause of such negative behaviour. One usually finds that the adolescent has been influenced by a complex interaction of personality characteristics, family pressures, cultural expectations, and educational and socioeconomic factors.

## Sexual development

Because of accelerated physical development during puberty, adolescents become increasingly aware of their sexuality, and their newly developed sexuality begins to play a large role in their interpersonal relationships. It is during this phase that adolescents also discover their sexual orientation (i.e. whether they have a sexual preference for people of their own sex, the opposite sex or both). They are often confused and worried if they experience homosexual feelings. Adolescents may also worry about the changes in their bodies. Although they may have many questions about sex, adolescents are often unwilling to ask these questions because they don't wish to be shamed by appearing to be uninformed (Davidson, 1988). The period during early adolescence may be the best time for conveying information about sex, for instilling values and for encouraging critical thinking because young adolescents don't feel the strong emotions (such as shame, fear and embarrassment) about sex and sexuality that many adults do (Pies, 1988). Even though older adolescents sometimes tend to think (or pretend) that they 'know it all', they often still remain open to information provided by trusted adults.

An important developmental task that adolescents face is to satisfy their sexual needs in a socially acceptable way so that their sexual experience will contribute positively to the development of their identities. There is widespread evidence that adolescents are more and more sexually active and that they are becoming sexually active at a younger and younger age than adolescents previously did. Perhaps these changes can be attributed to earlier sexual maturation, peer-group pressure, changed values and attitudes in society, and the powerful influence that mass media exert on young people. Although adolescents are able to understand that behaviour has consequences, they often do not believe that the consequences may happen to them (personal fable). Adolescents also tend to be unconsciously under the spell of an illusion of personal immortality — and this dangerous illusion might well make them more willing to engage in unsafe practices.

### Masturbation

Parents are often concerned about their children masturbating (the self-stimulation of the genitals). Masturbation occurs at any age, and, if not excessive, it is normal and healthy behaviour which causes no physical harm. Masturbation is most common at four years of age and during adolescence. For preschoolers it forms a part of sexual curiosity and exploration. It may however be an expression of anxiety, boredom or unresolved conflicts if it is repeated too often and too openly (examples are a young boy who repeatedly touches his penis, and children who masturbate openly and publicly). Masturbation, like other forms of sex play, is a private act, and parents should emphasise this to children when teaching them socially acceptable behaviour (Wong et al., 1999, p. 711). For adolescents, masturbation is seen as an opportunity to discover their own sexuality and to satisfy their sexual needs — especially if they are not ready for a sexual relationship. Masturbation nowadays is regarded as a safe sex practice and a way of satisfying one's sexual needs while avoiding HIV infection. Masturbation is only regarded as a problem or as abnormal when it replaces social and other activities to such an extent that it hinders the adolescent's development or social interactions (Thom et al., 1998).

## Identity development and self-concept

According to Erikson (1968), one of the main psychosocial tasks of the adolescent years is identity formation — to ask and answer the questions: 'Who am I?' and 'What do I want from life?' Steinberg (in Wong et al., 1999, p. 898) describes identity development during adolescence in the following way: 'Before adolescence the child's identity is like pieces of a puzzle scattered about the table. Both cognitive development and social situations encountered during adolescence push individuals to combine puzzle pieces — to reflect on their place in society, on the way others view them, and on their options for the future.' Social forces play an important role in the adolescent's sense of self. The people with whom the adolescent interacts serve as mirrors that reflect information back to the adolescent about who he or she is and who he or she ought to be.

As their identities develop, adolescents' views of themselves (self-concepts) also change. Adolescents' self-descriptions become less concrete and more abstract; they include less physical and more psychological components; they illustrate a greater awareness of themselves, and they include descriptions of themselves in terms of their social competencies (such as, for example, whether they are friendly, helpful or kind) (Thom et al., 1998).

We can divide HIV/AIDS education in the adolescent years into two categories if we base it on the developmental characteristics mentioned earlier:

- The *junior secondary school phase* for learners in grade 7 to grade 9 (approximately 13 to 15 years old). HIV/AIDS education in this phase is discussed in section 9.8 below.
- The *senior secondary school phase* for learners in grade 10 to grade 12 (approximately 16 to 19 years old). HIV/AIDS education in this phase is discussed in section 9.9 on page 191.

## 9.8   HIV/AIDS EDUCATION AND LIFESKILLS TRAINING IN THE JUNIOR SECONDARY SCHOOL PHASE (GRADES 7 TO 9)

### The young adolescent's perceptions of illness, HIV and AIDS

The young adolescent in grades 7 to 9 (approximately 13 to 15 years old) has a much better understanding of illness in general and HIV and AIDS in particular than the child in the middle childhood years.

### Definition and causes of illness, HIV and AIDS

The young adolescent is able to locate a specific disease in the context of a broader class of illnesses to which it belongs. They understand the concept of a *syndrome*, and do not see illness merely as a collection of symptoms without any causative link between them. They realise that an illness can result in external as well as internal symptoms. They can understand the causes of illness in more complex ways and can explain the interaction between multiple causes and the dysfunctions of internal body parts or processes.

While the young adolescent understands that HIV/AIDS can be caused by sex and drugs, they also appreciate the fact that the presence of the causal factor (sex or drugs) does *not always* lead to HIV/AIDS, but that infection will depend on the presence or absence of other important components (the most important being the presence of the HI virus). Younger children (in the middle childhood years) tend to think that sex and drugs *per se* cause AIDS.

Young adolescents can also appreciate the *relative* susceptibility or vulnerability of all people. Although they still see some groups as being more susceptible than others, they realise that *anybody* can become infected under certain circumstances. They do not restrict HIV/AIDS any longer to individuals or groups that they perceive as different from themselves; they are able to distinguish similarities and differences between groups, and they are able to perceive themselves as members of these groups.

## A complex understanding of the consequences of HIV/AIDS

Apart from understanding the definition and causes of HIV/AIDS, young adolescents also have a more complex understanding of the effect or consequences of HIV/AIDS. Where the young child in the junior primary school phase sees death as *immediate* with no time lapse between the onset of infection and death, and the child in the senior primary school phase sees only *time* as the variable factor between infection and death, the young adolescent is able to appreciate that there are *many variables* that are significant between the onset of infection and death. They understand that medication, care and a healthy lifestyle may prolong the life of the HIV-infected person. They know that HIV-infected people will eventually die of AIDS, but that some will live longer than others.

## Fear of HIV/AIDS

Young adolescents have a more realistic fear of HIV/AIDS than their younger friends. Their understanding of the biological mechanisms underlying the causes and prevention of HIV/AIDS makes them more realistic. They realise that, although anybody can become infected with HIV, certain forms of behaviour can prevent infection. Their fear is thus mitigated because they know that they have control over what choices they will make. While this knowledge unfortunately does not eliminate the irrational fear of AIDS completely, it allows the adolescent to cope more effectively with these fears and it allows him or her to develop a more realistic and reasonable fear of HIV/AIDS. The young adolescent's anxiety to be socially acceptable may however put him or her at risk of being infected by HIV if he or she is pressurised into making the wrong decisions. Some adolescents are afraid because they were already sexually active *before* they knew how to prevent HIV. Other adolescents are filled with anxiety because they have been the victims of sexual abuse or rape.

## Prevention of HIV/AIDS

The emphasis of HIV/AIDS education programmes in the junior secondary school phase should be on *prevention strategies*. At this stage the young adolescent knows how HIV is transmitted and how it is not transmitted. They also usually have a good grasp of the complex workings of the human body and they possess a more sophisticated knowledge of sexuality. The emphasis during this stage of the education should also be on the acquisition of lifeskills so that young adolescents will have the opportunity to acquire whatever skills are necessary to prevent themselves from becoming infected with HIV.

## Implications for HIV/AIDS education and lifeskills training in the junior secondary school phase

- As you repeat the basic information that was given to the children in the senior primary school phase about disease, sound health practices, basic human biology, attitudes, values and skills, present this same information together with examples that are relevant to the *adolescent's* current worldview.

- Because young adolescents often experience high levels of confusion and stress (the result of their rapid emotional, physical and social development and the constant onslaught of new experiences), it is very important to present them with exercises that will develop their self-concept in a positive way. A positive self-concept will instil self-awareness, self-confidence and personal pride.

- Because young adolescents are just *beginning* to develop the skills of abstract thinking, the facts and information they are given about HIV/AIDS must be direct, specific, frank and concrete (Pies, 1988).

- What young adolescents need is a general and basic overview on HIV/AIDS which includes a clear description of how HIV is transmitted, how HIV is not transmitted and how they can protect themselves from the virus. It is vital to discuss all aspects of the disease with young adolescents — and not only modes of transmission and prevention.

- Although young adolescents believe that nothing bad can happen to them, they do understand the concept of risk. The reduction of risk can be explained to the younger adolescent by using the metaphor of a seatbelt that one uses to protect oneself from a serious accident. It is important for adolescents to be able to identify the kind of risk behaviours in which they and their friends are involved (these may not all necessarily be sexual behaviours) and to have a clear idea of how they can reduce the risks inherent in such behaviour.

- Young adolescents must have an absolutely clear understanding of what sexually risky behaviour is, and they should be equally clear about the risks of needle sharing. They should also be well informed about risk reduction techniques.

- Help adolescents to understand that it is perfectly acceptable to postpone sexual activity until they themselves really want to engage in it. They should be encouraged to understand that they do not need to engage in sexual activity because of peer pressure or the relentless pressure of modern media such as television, films, radio and magazines. Promote abstinence or advise adolescents at least to postpone engaging in forms of adult sexuality (such as intercourse). Stress the importance of having only one loyal sex partner in a stable relationship (preferably within the marriage relationship). Tell adolescents that if they are already sexually active (or using drugs), they *can* stop if they want to, they *can* seek help, and they *can* protect themselves effectively from infection.

- Be *specific* when you use terminology. Make sure that adolescents know what you are talking about. If you use the phrase 'sexual behaviour', adolescents may think that it also includes kissing and hugging somebody. Rather use the phrase 'sexual intercourse' if that is what you are referring to.

- The importance of reinforcing lifeskills cannot be sufficiently emphasised. These include decision-making skills, communication skills, assertiveness, a positive self-concept, self-efficacy, self-confidence, the handling of peer pressure and care for oneself and others. Use role play so that adolescents can have opportunities to practise these skills in safe circumstances. (A good scenario for role play might be (for example): What would you say to a boy who says 'If you really love me, you will do it'?)

- Remember that the peer group is important for the social development of the adolescent and that participation in peer group activities should not be discouraged (unless such activities are harmful to the child). The teacher should rather use the peer group to influence the adolescent's behaviour. Peer education, where a member of the peer group provides the information, often works very well.

- Teach or reinforce the value that men and women are equal and that they should respect each other. Emphasise the value that a man must always ask a woman's permission before having sex with her, that if a woman says 'No' a man should accept and respect her 'No', and that any man who forces a woman to have sex with him when she has said 'No' is a rapist (as indeed he is in South African law).

- Adolescents need to know how HIV/AIDS affects their communities, their country and the world (Pies, 1988). Teach them to do research and to use the library, newspapers, journals and the Internet to get the latest statistics on HIV/AIDS. They should also read about the financial and human cost of HIV/AIDS.

- Adolescents should be given information on where to turn for advice, help and support if they should ever need it. Teach adolescents how to find resource and referral information in the phone book, on the Internet or from local community sources. Display the contact numbers for the AIDS hotline, AIDS Training, Information and Counselling Centres and local clinics in a place where adolescents can have access to them without having to ask for the information. The availability of confidential services is very important for adolescents — especially when they have concerns relating to sensitive issues such as sexual or substance-use behaviours. They will certainly be unwilling to seek help if they think that their parents may find out about the visit.

It is not enough to know *why* and *what* to teach young adolescents about HIV/AIDS. It is also extremely important to know *how* to teach this information. Teachers should be trained to convey the information in a direct but non-threatening and sensitive way. They must have a very good knowledge about all aspects of HIV/AIDS and the complex nature of the epidemic. They must also be given the opportunity to explore their own concerns about sexuality and drugs and to practise effective communication techniques.

Conveying safer sex messages is often a huge problem for teachers in the junior secondary school phase, because — although some adolescents are sexually active — there are also adolescents who are sexually 'naive', and teachers don't want to 'shock' or offend them. This is a real dilemma because — while adolescents' rights 'not to have certain information' have to be taken into account — life-saving information which they will definitely need in the future may not be withheld from them. One solution may be to give all the important 'theoretical' information in the first part of a session and to inform the students that you are going to demonstrate (for instance) condom use, in the second part. Inform the students that although you think it is important for them to have this information, they are welcome to leave the class if they feel uncomfortable with it. It is also preferable to separate boys and girls when demonstrating the use of condoms. Teenage girls often don't mind condom illustrations, but they frequently prefer the teacher not to use dildos (or rubber penises) to demonstrate the use of condoms. Make sure that sexually active adolescents know where to go if they need information, condoms, etc.

## 9.9   HIV/AIDS EDUCATION AND LIFESKILLS TRAINING IN THE SENIOR SECONDARY SCHOOL PHASE (GRADES 10 TO 12)

HIV/AIDS education for adolescents in the senior secondary school phase does not really differ from adult education. It is however important to remember that adolescents respond better to messages that emphasise their *rights* rather than their *responsibilities*. Assure adolescents that it is their right to have information, and it is also their right to protect themselves. The right to information and protection indirectly implies responsibility.

Davidson (1988, pp. 454–455) offers the following guidelines for HIV/AIDS education in the senior secondary school phase:

- Revise the information given in the junior secondary school phase, and make sure that adolescents have correct information about the definition of AIDS, the effect of the virus on the immune system, the transmission of HIV, the symptoms, the management of infection and testing.
- Reinforce the knowledge that adolescents can prevent HIV/AIDS by abstaining from or postponing sex, by having sexual relations within the context of a mutually faithful relationship with an uninfected partner, by always using latex condoms (even in combination with other birth control methods), by not using drugs, and by never sharing needles or syringes.

- While we should make HIV/AIDS issues as real and vivid as possible, we should try not to frighten learners. Movies about HIV-infected people or classroom visits from people with HIV infection often help students to overcome their denial of the disease and give HIV/AIDS a human face.

- The focus should be on *healthy behaviours* rather than on the medical aspects of the disease.

- Help adolescents to examine and affirm their own values.

- The ability to *plan ahead* is often a powerful deterrent to unsafe behaviour. Adolescents who have future plans (e.g. to study, to have a career, to have children) are often less inclined to engage in high-risk behaviour, especially young women when they know what devastating effects HIV can have on babies.

- Students should *rehearse* making responsible decisions about sex, and powerful and definite responses to risky situations.

- Students should know they have a right to abstain from sexual intercourse or to postpone becoming sexually active. They should be helped to develop the skills they need to assert those rights.

- It must not be assumed that all students will choose abstinence.

- Information about HIV/AIDS should be presented in the context of other sexually transmitted diseases.

- It is important to be honest and to provide information in a straightforward manner. Be explicit. Use simple, clear words. Explain in detail. Use examples.

- Sexual vocabulary can be expanded to include the slang expressions or words used by teenagers if that helps to get the message across more effectively.

- It is important to be non-threatening and to work in such a way that one alleviates (rather than creates) anxiety.

- Students should be given the opportunity to ask questions anonymously. Students usually enjoy the idea of a 'question basket' very much. (Put a basket somewhere in the class and invite them to put anonymous questions in this basket. Answer the questions in the group.)

- Discussion of dating relationships can provide opportunities and pretexts for teaching decision-making skills.

- Teaching about HIV/AIDS can often be effectively enhanced by:
  o movies and other visual aids
  o role plays and other participatory exercises
  o same-sex groupings (to encourage more candid discussions) followed by sharing in a mixed-sex group (to increase comfort level in discussing sexual subjects with members of the opposite sex)
  o involvement of students in planning and teaching — let young people (whenever possible) speak the message *to each other*

- The use of adolescent models and peer educators should never be under-estimated. Adolescents learn best when they learn from their peers.
- HIV/AIDS education should also include discussions of critical social issues raised by the epidemic, such as protecting the public health without endangering individual rights, orphan care, etc.
- Teachers should have resources to help students to find answers to detailed medical questions.
- Students should be taught the kind of research skills that will enable them to continue to evaluate the HIV/AIDS crisis.
- Students should know where to go for help if they need it, and they should be taught how to access medical services if they need them.

**Enrichment**

**Educational activities to build knowledge, attitudes, values and skills**

Children and adolescents need a supportive environment in which to practise their decision-making and communication skills. It is not enough to teach young people to 'just say no' to drugs or sex. Young people should be provided with learning opportunities to practise effective and successful behaviours for living healthy lives (Pies, 1988). We can use different methods for instilling the necessary knowledge, attitudes, values, and skills. Such methods include (Edwards & Louw, 1998):
- Graphic activities: the use of puzzles, games, collages, illustrations, cartoons, maps, charts, photographs, posters, transparencies and slides
- Oral activities: panel discussions, short plays, role plays, dialogues, debates, reports, songs, talks and interviews
- Written activities: essays, articles, letters, mock press releases, TV programme reviews, songs, plays, diary entries, poems, interviews and dialogues
- Audio-visual activities: slides with commentary, stories on tape, pictures or photographs with commentary and videos

## 9.10 A SAFE SCHOOL ENVIRONMENT

There are no known cases of HIV transmission in schools or institutions during educational activities. It is however important to apply universal precautions when in contact with blood, open wounds, sores, breaks in the skin, grazes and open skin lesions. All body fluids and excretions (such as tears, saliva, mucus, phlegm, urine, vomit, faeces and pus) containing blood should also be handled with care. Adhere to the following rules:

- Blood, especially in large spills such as blood from nosebleeds, as well as blood stains, should be handled with extreme care. Don't touch blood with your bare hands. Always wear latex gloves. Always flood spilled blood with a hypochlorite solution (household bleach or Jik) before cleaning it. Prepare the solution with one part of Jik to ten parts of water.

- Skin accidentally exposed to blood (or other body fluids containing blood) should be washed immediately with soap and running water.
- All bleeding wounds, sores, breaks in the skin, grazes and open skin lesions should be cleaned immediately with running water and/or antiseptics.
- If there is a biting or scratching incident that results in skin being broken, the wound should be washed thoroughly with running water and disinfectant.
- Blood splashes to the face (mucous membranes of the eyes, nose or mouth) should be flushed with running water for at least three minutes.
- All open wounds, sores, etc., should be covered securely with a non-porous or waterproof dressing or plaster so that there is no risk of exposure to blood.
- Cleansing and washing should always be done with running water and not from containers of water. Where running tap water is not available, containers should be used to *pour* water over the area to be cleansed.
- If blood has contaminated a surface, clean the surface with a freshly made, clean bleach solution. The person cleaning the surface should wear latex gloves.
- Blood-contaminated material should be sealed in double plastic bags and incinerated or sent to an appropriate disposal firm.
- If instruments (for instance, scissors) become contaminated with blood or other body fluids, they should be washed and placed in a strong bleach solution for at least one hour before drying and reuse.
- Latex gloves should be available at every sports event and should also be carried by the playground supervisor. Every teacher should have a pair of latex gloves in his or her classroom. Emergency treatment should not however be delayed because gloves are not available. Bleeding can be managed by compression with material that will absorb the blood (a towel, for example). Unbroken plastic bags can also be used if latex gloves are not available, but extreme care should be taken. People who have skin lesions should not attempt to give first aid when no latex gloves are available.
- All schools should ideally have at least two first-aid kits. These kits should contain disposable latex gloves (two large and two medium pairs); rubber household gloves to wear over the latex gloves when handling blood-soaked material in specific instances (e.g. when broken glass makes the use of only latex gloves inappropriate); absorbent material; waterproof plasters; disinfectant (or household bleach); scissors; cotton wool; gauze tape; tissues; containers for water; and a resuscitation mouthpiece for mouth-to-mouth resuscitation so as to avoid contact with blood or other body fluids from the patient's mouth.
- Although the risk of HIV transmission as a result of contact play and contact sport is generally insignificant, teachers should make sure that no learner who

has an open wound, a sore, a break in the skin, etc. participates in contact play or sports. If bleeding occurs during contact play or contact sport, the player should be taken off the playground or sports field immediately and treated. Clothes soiled with blood must also be changed.

- All educators, sport coaches and other staff members should be given appropriate information and educated about HIV transmission, the application of universal precautions and the importance of adhering to such precautions.

- Learners should be given appropriate information and training in the application of universal precautions. Train learners how to manage their own bleeding or injuries, and teach children, especially those in the pre-primary and primary schools, never to touch blood, open wounds, sores or any other skin lesions. They should be taught to call for assistance from a teacher or other member of staff — and not to handle emergencies such as nosebleeds, or the cuts or scrapes of friends on their own. (See chapter 15 for more information about universal precautions and infection control in hospitals and at home.)

**Enrichment**

### Testing for HIV in schools and disclosure of HIV status

According to the law, nobody (learner, educator, or any employee) may be forced to have an HIV test. Testing for HIV and disclosure of one's HIV status is voluntary. Teachers may under no circumstances force a child to disclose his or her HIV status. Teachers who are given such information must treat the information as confidential and must ensure that no unfair discrimination results from it. Information about a learner's HIV status can only be disclosed by an educator to another person with the written permission of the learner (if more than 14 years) or of his or her parents.

## 9.11 CONCLUSION

The school has a very important role to play in empowering children with the necessary knowledge, attitudes, values and lifeskills to protect themselves against HIV infection and AIDS. The responsibility for protecting our children should however not be placed on the shoulders of schools alone. There are many children, such as school dropouts, orphans and street children, who cannot be reached by the formal educational system. HIV/AIDS prevention and lifeskills training programmes should also be presented by organisations such as churches, civic organisations, youth groups, and by individual volunteers, so that children who do not attend schools can also be reached.

- If you work with children (in a school, a church, an orphanage or in any other capacity), identify the developmental stage in which the children are and then use the information in this chapter to develop an HIV/AIDS education and lifeskills training programme that will be appropriate for your group of children. Identify personal, social or cultural differences that are specific to the group with which you are working, and devise ways to make provision for these differences in your programme.

- Many learners will become orphaned or will lose close family members and will need emotional help and guidance from educators. Orphaned learners may face enormous financial hardship and have great difficulty in paying for school fees, uniforms and books. Others may be forced to remain at home so that they can look after their younger siblings and act as heads of their households. Some of these children may themselves be infected, or be caring for others who are infected and ill. If you are a teacher, develop a policy for your school to assist AIDS orphans. If you are a minister of religion or a religious leader, develop a plan of action for your congregation or religious group to provide assistance to orphans.

# HIV/AIDS Counselling

**Learning outcomes**

**After completing Part 3 you should be able to:**

- apply basic communication skills to interviewing a client
- counsel a client who wants to be tested for HIV (pre-HIV test counselling)
- counsel a client who tested HIV positive
- counsel a client who tested HIV negative
- do basic counselling to help HIV-infected individuals and their significant others to cope with the day-to-day demands of the illness
- recognise serious problems such as severe depression and suicidal tendencies, and refer clients for professional help if necessary
- do emotional, spiritual and bereavement counselling
- develop a programme for caregivers who work in the HIV/AIDS field to care for themselves in such a way that they can prevent burnout

## INTRODUCTION TO PART 3

The need for counselling and for skilled HIV/AIDS counsellors is very great indeed. Professional psychologists, counsellors and psychiatrists often cannot cope with the demand. This situation is aggravated by the fact that not many people have access to professional services. It is therefore of the utmost importance to train every helper working in the HIV/AIDS field with the necessary knowledge and skills so that he or she will be able to give his or her clients basic counselling. Counsellors should also be trained to recognise serious problems and to refer clients if they do not know how to cope with serious problems themselves.

The basic counselling principles and skills needed to be a skilled helper are all discussed in **Chapter 10**. The values underlying the counselling process, as well as basic communication skills, are explained and practical guidelines for cross-cultural counselling are given. The basic principles of pre- and post-HIV test counselling are discussed in **Chapter 11**. Helpful guidelines and hints are given on which questions to ask, what information to provide, and how to handle the important issues of informed consent and confidentiality. Specific issues that HIV-infected individuals and their significant others are dealing with (such as anxiety, depression and feelings of suicide) are discussed in **Chapter 12**, and specific attention is given to counselling children and the very important issue of care for the caregiver. **Chapter 13** reviews the principles of spiritual, emotional and bereavement counselling.

# 10 Basic Counselling Principles and Skills

*Diving deep*

*And Koki swam through the black water*
*or he drifted silently with the sound of cool water in his ears.*
*But sometimes he dived deep down*
*into the cold shadows of the pool.*

The advent of HIV/AIDS in the world has forced all of us to accept a revolutionary paradigm shift. This paradigm shift is a movement from *curing* towards *caring*. Because we have no *cure* for HIV/AIDS, we have no alternative but to focus our interventions on *caring* for the physical as well as the psychological welfare of the HIV-infected individual and his or her significant others. The HIV-infected individual needs to find ways to live a psychologically healthy life after diagnosis. Because people need extensive counselling in order to be able to do this, the need for counselling people with HIV/AIDS and their friends and relatives will soon far exceed the capacity of all the trained counsellors in sub-Saharan Africa. The sad reality in sub-Saharan Africa is that very few HIV-infected people indeed have access to trained counsellors outside of the pre- and post-HIV test counselling context. This makes it vitally urgent to equip everyone in the helping professions with the necessary skills to be effective HIV/AIDS counsellors. According to Johnson (2000, p. 2), 'the single most important requirement to be an HIV/AIDS counsellor, is to have compassion for another person's struggle to *live* beyond the confines of a disease, and the willingness and commitment to walk the walk with this person and his or her significant others'.

This chapter will not review the various theoretical models of counselling. It will focus instead on explaining the basic principles and procedures of the counselling process. It will, in addition, examine the values and skills that all counsellors need for helping their clients. Although the basic counselling principles, values and skills described in this chapter are applicable to *all* clients who seek help (irrespective of culture, age or presenting problem), the counsellor may sometimes adapt his or her approach to take individual or cultural differences into account.

## 10.1 A DEFINITION OF COUNSELLING

Although there are numerous definitions of counselling in existence, the author has chosen the following definition of counselling for the purposes of this book (Johnson, 2000, p. 3):

> Counselling is a structured conversation aimed at facilitating a client's quality of life in the face of adversity.

When one says that counselling is a *structured* conversation, one means that it is not a *social* conversation. *Conversation* implies a dialogue and interaction between two people; conversation does *not* imply a monologue (the kind of situation in which the counsellor drones on and *tells* the client what to do). Counselling is also *facilitative* rather than prescriptive. The intention of counselling is not to 'solve' everything by 'prescribing' treatment, but to *help or assist* clients to review their problems and the options or choices they have for dealing with these problems (Egan, 1998).

## 10.2 THE AIMS OF COUNSELLING

The aims of counselling or helping a client must always be based on the *needs* of the client. The purpose of counselling is twofold: (1) to help clients manage their problems more effectively and develop unused or underused opportunities to cope more fully, and (2) to help and empower clients to become more effective self-helpers in the future (Egan, 1998). Helping is about *constructive change* and making a substantive *difference* to the life of the client.

The counsellor should have a specific focus when he or she counsels HIV-infected clients. This specific focus is the client's response to his or her seroconversion status (i.e. the fact that he or she is HIV positive). The counsellor cannot change the *adversity* inherent in the client's status or the events that caused it. The counsellor's sphere of influence is defined by the aftermath of the disclosure of the HIV-positive status — how the client reacts, how significant others react, and how these reactions might impact upon symptom development, the course of the disease and the quality of the client's life.

'The aim of counselling the HIV-infected individual is therefore to focus on life beyond infection and not to dwell unnecessarily on the constraints of the disease' (Johnson, 2000, p. 3). The counsellor's role is to facilitate the client's quality of life by helping him or her to manage problems, to effect life-enhancing changes and to cope with the kinds of problems that will arise in the future.

## 10.3 THE PROCESS OF HELPING

According to Egan (1998, p. 24), all worthwhile helping models or processes that focus on problem management and change should help clients to ask and answer the following four fundamental questions for themselves:

- Current scenario: *What are the problems (issues, concerns, undeveloped opportunities) I should be working on?* The answers to this question constitute the client's *current state of affairs* or *current scenario*.
- Preferred scenario: *What do I need or want in place of what I have?* Answers to this question constitute the *preferred state of affairs*, or *preferred scenario*.

- **Strategies:** *What do I have to do to get what I need or want?* Answers to this question produce *strategies for goal-accomplishing action.*

- **Action:** *How do I make all this happen?* Answers to this question help clients to move from *planning mode* to *action, getting-it-done,* or *accomplishment mode.*

The purpose of counselling is to help clients to develop answers to these four questions.

## Question 1: 'What are the problems?'

To elicit the *current scenario,* the counsellor must help clients to tell their 'story' in such a way that the counsellor (as well as the client) gets a clearer picture of the problem situation. The counsellor must also help clients to break through 'blind spots' that prevent them from seeing themselves and their problem situations as they really are. Because clients often present with a whole range of problems and issues, it is up to the counsellor to help the client to identify and work on *those issues that will make a difference.*

**(e.g)** *Example*

Let's use the fictitious example of an HIV-positive client called Mary. Don't assume that you as counsellor know what Mary's problem is. If Mary makes an appointment with you, don't assume (for example) that her problem must be her HIV-positive status. Mary may already have accepted her HIV status a long time before. She may be seeking counselling now because she feels uncertain about getting involved in a relationship with a very supportive man who has accepted her HIV status and who has proposed marriage. Allow Mary to tell her 'story'. By 'listening' to herself (as she tells her story), Mary may get a much clearer picture of what is going on in her life. She may, for instance, realise for the first time that she feels very lonely — despite the love of her young daughter and her partner. By listening to her and by asking appropriate questions, you can help her to recognise her blind spots (one of which may, for example, be that although she has accepted her HIV status, she does not accept the fact that she is still worthy of somebody's love). By listening to her story, you can also help Mary to identify the issues which are really bothering her. Such issues may include self-acceptance, an ability to open herself up to receiving love, a fear of rejection and loss, feelings of worthlessness, a fear that she may infect her partner and a deep concern for her daughter's future when she dies.

## Question 2: 'What do I need and want?'

The *preferred scenario* spells out possibilities for a better future and it culminates in an *agenda for change*. The counsellor must help clients to discover and commit themselves to what they need and want for a better future. Gelatt (1989, p. 255) has said that 'the future does not exist and cannot be predicted. It must be imagined and invented'. Help clients to imagine (envision) a better future. Brainstorming possibilities for a better future often helps clients to understand their problems more clearly. By understanding their problems more clearly, they begin to acquire real *hope* for the first time. Help clients to choose realistic and challenging goals so that they can manage their key problems. Realistic and reachable goals focus clients' attention and actions, they mobilise energy and effort, they motivate clients to search for strategies to accomplish the goals, and they increase a client's determination to grasp what he or she wants. When goals are realistic, clients can make a realistic commitment to work towards them.

 *Example*

Encourage Mary to tell you what she wants and needs for her future. She may want the following: to be there for her daughter as long as possible; to be able to accept love again; to feel worthwhile (i.e. to feel that she still has something useful and valuable to offer society). By 'listening' to herself, Mary also realises that she feels lonely because she has nobody with whom she can discuss her health concerns, and that what she therefore needs is to be part of a group with whom she can discuss her problems.

Egan (1998, p. 28) warns that the counsellor should never move from 'What is wrong?' to 'What do I do about it?' without exploring the question 'What do I need and want?' Helping clients to discover what they *really* want has a profound impact on the entire helping process.

## Question 3: 'What do I have to do to get what I need and want?'

Clients now need to discover ways to bridge the gap between their current scenario (what they have) and their preferred scenario (what they need and want). They have to ask themselves what they have to do to get what they need or want. The counsellor must help clients to see that there are many different ways of achieving their goals. They should think (and brainstorm) about these different ways and choose the action strategies that best fit their talents, style, personality, resources and timetable. The counsellor should help clients to organise their actions into a coherent, simple, achievable *plan* that they will be able to execute to accomplish their goals.

According to Egan (1998, p. 30), a plan of action is a *map* the client uses to get to where he or she wants to go.

 *Example*

Following the counsellor's advice, Mary joins a group called 'Positive Women'. She discusses her health concerns in the group, and obtains a lot of useful advice about healthy living. She is also motivated by the group to change her lifestyle (by eating healthily, stopping smoking and starting with an exercise programme) so that she can boost her immune system. At the next counselling session, Mary reports back that she once again feels in charge of her life. She has realised that if she looks after her health (and her immune system in particular), she might prolong her life and so be around for a longer time for the sake of her daughter.

By associating with other women who are also HIV positive, Mary now feels less lonely. Prompted by the group, Mary decides to do volunteer work (something she had never thought of before). Her decision to do volunteer work makes Mary realise that she can be useful to society (this fulfils one of her great needs). She therefore enters the process of deciding which particular kind of volunteer work will suit her personality and style best. As she thinks about it she rules out working in a hospice (she feels it might prove to be too depressing). Because she is a shy person, public speaking will also not suit her. She does however like working with children and may therefore decide to care for AIDS orphans. Although Mary still does not feel ready for marriage, she feels more comfortable about not infecting her partner after discussing safer sex practices with her counsellor, with the adviser at 'Positive Women' and with her partner.

### Question 4: 'How do I make all this happen?'

The client must now move from the planning mode to the *action* mode. Action should however not be the 'last stage' of change. The client needs to act from the very first counselling session, i.e. he or she needs to begin to make the transition from the current to the preferred scenario. The counsellor should therefore encourage clients to act — even if it is in small ways — from the very beginning of the counselling process. In the example above, Mary took the first step by joining a support group of HIV-positive women. Helping is ultimately about getting the client to work towards constructive change. As Egan (1998, p. 31) puts it: 'There is nothing magic about change; it is hard work. If clients do not act in their own behalf, nothing happens.'

*Example*

To fulfil her need to do something productive with her life, Mary decides to look after an AIDS orphan over weekends. The child is the same age as her daughter, and they enjoy each other's company. By giving unconditional love to another person, Mary begins to feel worthy again. And because she then feels good about herself, she is able to accept love and appreciation from others and her relationship with her partner becomes even better than it was.

If the counsellor is to help the client to answer fundamental questions about the current scenario, the preferred scenario, strategies and action, he or she should structure the counselling conversation in such a way that the client's telling of his or her story will enable him or her to identify problems and identify constructive changes. The following division of the counselling process into four phases may offer a helpful framework for the counsellor to use in his or her quest to help the client.

## 10.4 PHASES IN THE COUNSELLING PROCESS

The counselling process occurs in four phases. These are: (1) *defining* the relationship, (2) gathering *information*, (3) *describing* the problem, and (4) making *interventions*. According to Johnson (2000), these phases are generic to most therapeutic models. This means that the phases of the counselling process will always be the same — no matter which theoretical assumptions or model the counsellor uses. Our dividing of the counselling process into four phases is, however, arbitrary. In practice, the phases will often overlap and interact with one another. We offer this differentiation of phases only to provide the counsellor with a framework that might be helpful to keep track of the counselling process. The framework also guides the counsellor when he or she gets stuck in the conversation, when he or she needs to consider the requirements of the current phase (in which he or she and the client find themselves), and when he or she needs guidelines before initiating new and unexplored therapeutic topics of conversation. Every interview or counselling session with clients consists of these four phases.

The phases in counselling and their characteristics can be summarised under the following four headings (Johnson, 2000, pp. 5–12):

### Phase 1: Defining the relationship

The counsellor must clarify the counselling relationship in terms of its objectives, process and parameters. How counsellors define themselves and the counselling context is crucially important for effective and ethical counselling. Defining the relationship usually occurs in the first few minutes of counselling. The following points should be kept in mind when defining the relationship:

- Provide a context that is unambiguously therapeutic. Establish a safe, confidential setting that clearly distinguishes the counselling relationship from social conversation.

- Provide a physical setting that is conducive to enhancing the therapeutic relationship (see 'Attending' on page 214).

- Introduce yourself, the process and the context. Don't assume that your client knows what counselling entails. Brief the client as to the objectives and procedures of counselling, and provide some idea of what is expected of the client, and what he or she may anticipate in return. Share the main features of the helping process (as explained in 'The process of helping' on page 201) with the client so that he or she can become an active collaborator in the process.

- Allow the client to negotiate the definition of the relationship by listening, observing and confirming.

- Be sensitive to *how* and *what* you communicate. Convey the critical message of *trust* (i.e. that you are trustworthy), *acceptance* (by being non-judgemental), and *structure* (i.e. that you are skilled).

- Assure the client that you will maintain absolute confidentiality (see 'Confidentiality' on page 214).

- De-pathologise the client's response to his or her HIV-positive status. For example, if the client refers to his or her 'horrible affliction', reply by referring neutrally to his or her 'HIV-positive status'.

- Do not be judgemental about any significant other in the client's life. Convey your neutral understanding of people's reactions to the disclosure of the client's status.

Counselling skills, which are central to this phase of counselling, are:

- observation skills. Distinguish between observation (what you observe) and inference (the sense that you make of your observations). *Inference* is inevitably the source of labelling and blaming.

- sensitivity to non-verbal behaviour (posture, direction, initiative, eye contact, etc.) — which is achieved through the practice of the communication skill of attentiveness (see 'Attending' on page 214).

- tracking skills. Observe the client's initiatives and connect with the client at that level. Don't follow your own agenda.

- being responsive to the emotional tone of the client's story. Show the client that you have understood him or her by reflecting his/her emotions in your response.

**Summary:** The aim of the first phase of counselling (*defining the relationship*) is to establish an open relationship in which the client will feel safe enough to address personal issues and to disclose information to the counsellor.

## Phase 2: Gathering information

Every conversation with a client involves some form of inquiry. During the initial interview, the counsellor spends a considerable amount of time obtaining information about the client's current and preferred scenario so that both the counsellor and the client can understand the problem(s) and begin to think about planning possible intervention strategies. During follow-up interviews, counsellors routinely request information about attempted interventions and the events that have taken place since the previous counselling session. This phase is very important because it represents the means by which the counsellor constructs his or her understanding of the client's world. How the counsellor goes about gathering information determines what and how much he or she understands of the presenting problem. The counsellor should resist any attempt to give advice or to offer 'quick' solutions.

The gathering of information is facilitated by (1) a supportive, client-centred approach, and (2) an active, benevolent curiosity.

● *Supportive client-centred helping* means that the needs of the client are central, and that the ultimate purpose of the process is to identify and implement actions that will improve the client's situation (Egan, 1998). It is therefore important to allow the client to tell his or her story in his or her own way. Client-centred helping is most clearly evident in counselling techniques such as basic empathy, advanced empathy, self-disclosure and immediacy. (These skills are discussed under the headings 'Basic empathy' on page 218, and 'Advanced communication skills' on page 222.)
● *Active, benevolent curiosity* relies on the counsellor's observation and questioning. By using active listening techniques and communication skills, the counsellor tries to gain an accurate understanding of the client's problems, the way in which he or she is experiencing these problems, and what the client needs for a better future. The counsellor should keep the following points in mind when he or she interviews clients:
  o Learn and adopt the client's 'language'. To speak the client's 'language' is a vital source of understanding and communicates empathy and acceptance.
  o Use facilitative questions (open questions and not closed questions).
  o Be sensitive to feedback about specific content.
  o Be respectful.
  o Be patient and revisit topics if it is necessary to do so.
  o Avoid suggesting solutions and prescriptions. Allow yourself time to develop your understanding of the client's world.

o Deal with multiple levels of understanding (content, emotions, behaviour and cognition).

o Involve context in your enquiry.

o Focus on *process over time*. The counsellor should attempt to understand patterns and trends rather than diagnostic entities (we do not only want to understand *that* the client is depressed, we also want to understand *how* he or she is depressed in terms of context and process).

**Summary:** The primary purpose of the *information gathering phase* is to make the counsellor an 'expert' on the client's context and his or her response to HIV/AIDS. The counsellor needs to listen attentively to what the client says. Coming to premature conclusions about the client and his or her problems leaves the counsellor with a limited (inadequate) understanding of the client's world as the basis for *descriptions* (phase 3) and *interventions* (phase 4).

## Phase 3: Describing the problem dynamic

'Knowledge or understanding is power only through description and application' (Johnson, 2000, p. 9). Once the counsellor has dealt with the information-gathering phase, he or she needs to articulate his or her understanding of the problem dynamic on the basis of that information. The depth of the counsellor's understanding will depend on the nature and comprehensiveness of the information gathering phase, which in turn will determine the efficacy of the interventions (what the client needs to do to get what he or she needs and wants).

The first formal intervention that the counsellor should make in the counselling process is to describe his or her understanding of the problem in its situational context (the problem dynamic). (Keep in mind that a problem is never usefully described as a static entity or as a specific diagnosis.) The client enters counselling with a fairly restricted view of his or her problem, and the counsellor's much wider perspective and understanding benevolently challenges the client's singular experiences. In the example in 'Question 1: "What are the problems?"' on page 202, the counsellor helped Mary to become aware of the complexity of her problem. Although she entered counselling with one problem in mind (her relationship with her partner), she came to realise (through the counsellor's questioning and description of the problem dynamic) that she also had problems about accepting and forgiving herself for her HIV-positive status.

It is important for counsellors to explain their understanding to clients. All clients (but HIV-infected clients in particular) are entitled to know what the counsellor thinks. It is not a characteristic of counselling for the counsellor to gather insights which he or she keeps secret so that he or she can manipulate the client's behaviour. When the counsellor shares what he or she understands with the client, the counsellor conveys congruence, transparency and respect for the client's ability to resolve personal issues autonomously. By *not* describing his or her understanding, the counsellor introduces a power-political dimension into the counselling relationship. This 'power-political dimension' means that the counsellor uses his or her expertise, experience and (secret) superior knowledge to control and manipulate the client. Such an approach obviously constitutes an implicit but serious breach of ethics.

To describe the problem dynamic does not imply that the problems are more important than the solutions. But without a comprehensive understanding of the problems, the interventions or actions may be misguided and useless. If the counsellor in the example given on page 202 had concentrated *only* on the problem with which Mary presented (i.e. whether she should marry her partner or not), he would have missed the point and failed completely to help Mary to improve the quality of her life.

The following guidelines will help the counsellor to describe the problem dynamic:

- Introduce the phase and focus attention on what you are about to say.
- Be concise but comprehensive in your descriptions.
- Use culturally and developmentally appropriate language (the client must above all be able to understand you).
- Never blame and never judge.
- Include significant role players in your description.
- Focus on relationships rather than individual attributes (the latter are more impervious to intervention or change.) If, for example, Mary is a very shy and introverted person who does not share her feelings with her partner, the counsellor should rather focus on how Mary and her partner should handle this shyness in their relationship than on how to change Mary's personality.

**Summary:** *Describing the problem dynamic* is an attempt to articulate aspects of the client's experience in such a way that they are recognisable and confirming, but in a sense novel to the client. This phase focuses on facilitating self-exploration, clarifying feelings and describing the problem in such a way that interventions can be planned.

## Phase 4: Intervention or action

Intervention is not a solution. It is a *process* in which the client becomes involved in order to improve the quality of his or her life. This is the phase in which the client answers the questions 'What do I have to do to solve my problems?' and 'How do I make it happen?' In addition to providing supportive, client-centred counselling, the counsellor also acts as an active agent of change.

The aim of a supportive client-centred stance is to give the client an opportunity to resolve personal issues about his or her HIV-positive status in a safe environment. In this process the counsellor will use a number of *non-directive* counselling techniques such as basic empathy, advanced empathy, self-disclosure, immediacy, reflection and interpretation. (See 'Basic communication skills for counselling' on page 214, and 'Advanced communication skills' on page 222 for a discussion of these skills.) However, a more *directive stance*, in which the counsellor attempts to influence a client's behaviour in a specific context, also has its place in counselling — especially in HIV/AIDS counselling. Directive counselling is often helpful in those cases where the focus should be on practical, accessible aspects of the client's response to HIV/AIDS. Mary's concerns about infecting her partner with HIV (see the example in 'Question 1: "What are the problems?"' on page 202) could only be laid to rest by taking a directive stance and giving her information about safer sex practices.

In order to be directive in HIV/AIDS counselling, the counsellor needs to have the following skills:

● A good working knowledge of HIV infection and AIDS and the ability and interest to keep abreast of developments in this rapidly changing field.

● The ability to communicate information in an accurate, consistent and objective manner.

● Feeling comfortable when speaking to people about sexuality and sex. If the counsellor feels embarrassed to talk about sex, the client will not feel free to discuss sex.

**Summary:** The focus in the *intervention* or *action phase* moves from the identification and description of problems to setting goals which are aimed at resolving the problem, deciding on methods of achieving them, and monitoring and evaluating the results.

**Activity**

Ask a colleague or friend to role play a counselling session (or an interview) with you. Ask the friend to play the role of the client and to think of a specific problem that he or she would like to discuss with you. Ask a third person to listen to the interview and to make notes to indicate (a) whether or not you moved through all four phases of the interview (defining the relationship, gathering information, describing the problem dynamic and planning intervention), and (b) whether you asked all four questions necessary to the counselling process (current scenario, preferred scenario, goals and action).

## 10.5  VALUES UNDERLYING THE COUNSELLING PROCESS

The counsellor's values and attitudes play a critical role in the helping process. The way counsellors see themselves, their clients, the helping process, and the world around them will affect the way in which they counsel.

Counsellors should enter the helping process with a sincere *respect* for their clients, an open and genuine *attitude*, and the *intention* of helping their clients to *empower* themselves and take *responsibility* for their own lives.

### Respect

Respect is an *attitude* which portrays the belief that every person is a worthy being who is competent to decide what he or she really wants, has the potential for growth, and has the abilities to achieve what he or she really wants from life. Respect is fundamental to the helping relationship. 'Without the attitude and belief that every person is worthy of our respect and esteem, the counsellor cannot communicate empathetically or facilitate growth because he or she will not be able to create an atmosphere of acceptance and freedom in which the client can reveal his or her deepest, darkest and most painful experiences without fear of rejection' (Du Toit, Grobler & Schenck, 1998, p. 77).

A counsellor can show his or her respect to clients in the following ways (Du Toit et al., 1998; Egan, 1998; Long, 1996):

- Accept the client by showing *unconditional positive regard*. This means that you as counsellor accept the client as he or she is, irrespective of the client's values or behaviour and of whether you as counsellor approve of those values and behaviour or not. This does not mean that the counsellor has no values or aims of his or her own. It only means that the client's values come first during the counselling process. To be able to give unconditional positive regard is extremely important in the HIV/AIDS field. A judgemental counsellor who condemns clients or who makes clients feel that their sexual behaviour is offensive to the counsellor will only cause harm. Such a counsellor will not be able to facilitate healing.
- Respect the client's *rights*. Individuals have a right to be *who they are* — a right to their own feelings, beliefs, opinions, and choices.
- Respect the *uniqueness* of each client. The counsellor should not apply generalisations. He or she should rather work with the specific characteristics, behaviour and needs that each client manifests in the counselling situation.
- Refrain from *judgement*. Counsellors are there to help their clients, not to judge or to blame them. Since HIV-infected individuals often already feel that they are 'guilty' or 'bad' before counselling even starts, only non-judgemental attitudes on the part of the counsellor will facilitate understanding and growth.

- Remain *serene* and *imperturbable* and never react with embarrassment, shock or disapproval when people discuss painful situations or their sexual practices with you.
- Realise that respect is always both *considerate* and *tough-minded*. Although the counsellor should 'be for the client', this does not mean that the counsellor will always take the client's side or act as the client's advocate. 'Being for' means taking the client's point of view *seriously* — even when it needs to be challenged.
- Inherent in respect is acknowledgment and honouring of individual *diversity* in culture, ethnicity, spirituality, sexual orientation, family, educational and socio-economic status. Avoid stereotyping while respecting people's *traditions* and *customs*.
- When doing group counselling (e.g. in the workplace, or when seeing a family), it is important to accept the values of group members as well as the differences in their values. A counsellor shows respect in a group by carefully listening, understanding and accepting what group members are saying within their context or frame of reference.

**Genuineness or congruence**

Genuineness or congruence refers to a set of attitudes and behaviour that underlies the way in which counsellors relate to clients. A *congruent* person is honest and transparent in the counselling relationship because he or she surrenders all roles and façades (Rogers, 1980). A genuine or congruent counsellor demonstrates the following values or behaviour when he or she has dealings with his or her clients (Egan, 1998; Gladding, 1996; Okun, 1997):

- Be *yourself*. Be real and sincere, honest and clear. Speak and act congruently in the helping relationship or (in other words) practise what you preach.
- Be *honest* with yourself and your clients.
- Don't *overemphasise* the helping role and don't take refuge in the role of counsellor. To help other people should be an integral part of your lifestyle. It is not a role that you should play only when you need to.
- Don't be *patronising* or *condescending*.
- Keep the *client's agenda* in focus. Don't pursue your own agenda or inflict yourself on others.
- Don't be *defensive*. Know your own strengths and weaknesses.
- Strive towards achieving *openness* and *self-acceptance* because these qualities will enable you to accept people whose behaviour conflicts with your own personal values. Remember that it is impossible to hide negative feelings from clients. No matter how hard you try to conceal them, clients will sense your incongruence.

- When a client reacts negatively to you or criticises you, examine the behaviour that might have caused the client to think negatively. Try to understand the client's point of view and continue to work with him or her. Since genuine helpers are at ease with themselves, they should also be able to examine negative criticism calmly, objectively and dispassionately.

## Empowerment and self-responsibility

One of the values underlying counselling should be the desire to empower clients to take responsibility for themselves and to identify, develop and use resources that will make them more effective agents of change in the counselling sessions as well as in their everyday lives. The empowerment of clients should be based on the following values (Egan, 1998, pp. 52–53):

- Believe in your client's pursuit of *growth, self-actualisation* and *self-determination*. View this pursuit in terms of the *client's* frame of reference and accept that you as counsellor cannot decide what the client's goals should be or what would be best for him or her. Accept the principle that the client knows himself or herself better than anyone else, and that he or she is therefore in the best position to explore, expose and understand the self.
- Believe in the clients' *ability to change* if they choose to do so. Clients have more resources for managing problems than they, or sometimes their helpers, assume. The counsellor's basic attitude should be that clients have the resources both to participate in the counselling process and to manage their lives more effectively. Since these resources may be blocked or disabled in a variety of ways, it is the task of the counsellor to help clients to identify, free and utilise these resources.
- Refrain from *rescuing* the client. Rescuing refers to the voluntary, *unnecessary* assumption of responsibility for another person's feelings, choices, or actions. Rescuing is implicitly disrespectful of the other person's ability to take responsibility for himself or herself. Rescuing reflects the *rescuer's* needs. It is typically motivated by needs such as lack of confidence in the capability of the person being rescued, a need to feel important, or a need to be needed (Long, 1996).
- *Share* the helping process with clients. Clients have the right to know what they are getting into. Explain to them exactly what the helping process entails, what they can expect from you, and vice versa.
- Help clients to see counselling sessions as *work sessions*. Only the client can make change happen. The counsellor can merely make suggestions about how the client might change.
- Help clients to become *better problem solvers* in their daily lives. Help them to apply problem-solving techniques to their current problem situation and help them to adopt more effective approaches to future problems that they will encounter in their lives.

## Confidentiality

Confidentiality in the counselling context is non-negotiable. A counsellor may under no circumstances disclose the HIV status *or any other information* to anybody without the express permission of the client. Confidentiality is an expression of the counsellor's respect for the client.

Confidentiality in the HIV/AIDS field is a controversial issue. Counsellors often become involved in endless debates about the rights of HIV-infected individuals as opposed to the rights of their partners and the rights of the community in general — HIV/AIDS is, after all, a very serious and life-threatening condition. It is, however, not the task or responsibility of the counsellor alone to solve these moral dilemmas. Counselling is a *partnership* and a relationship of *shared* responsibility between the counsellor and client (Du Toit et al., 1998).

Whenever the counsellor feels overwhelmed by moral demands, or by his or her own sense of responsibility, he or she should fall back on this partnership, and decide on a course of action together with the client. If a counsellor feels that it is necessary to disclose a client's HIV-positive status to a third party (e.g. for referral purposes or to protect a sex partner if the client refuses to use condoms), the reasons for the disclosure must be explained to the client. The counsellor must convince the client that the disclosure will be in everybody's best interest. However, the information may only be disclosed with the express permission of the client. If the client still refuses, the counsellor has to respect this decision.

## 10.6 BASIC COMMUNICATION SKILLS FOR COUNSELLING

Since counselling is a *conversation* or *dialogue* between the counsellor and client, the counsellor needs certain communication skills in order to facilitate change. Communication skills such as attending, listening, basic empathy, probing and summarising, are all essential tools for both relationship-building and constructive change (Egan, 1998).

## Attending

*Attending* refers to the ways in which counsellors can be 'with' their clients, both physically and psychologically (Egan, 1998, p. 62). Effective attending (the way you orient yourself physically and psychologically to clients) tells clients that you are with them and that they can share their world with you. Effective attending also puts you in a position to listen carefully to what your clients are saying.

There are certain microskills that counsellors can use when attending to their clients. Egan (1998, pp. 63–64) summarises these skills under the acronym *SOLER*. The counsellor should, however, be sensitive to the individual and cultural differences that manifest in the way people show and react to attentiveness (see the attending skills in cross-cultural counselling on page 231). These microskills are only external *guidelines* that can help you to show your inner attitudes and values of respect and genuineness. There are also other ways to show respect and genuineness. It is important for both the counsellor and the client to feel comfortable with the way in which attentiveness is expressed.

- **S:** Face the client *Squarely*: Adopt a posture that indicates involvement. The word *squarely* may be taken literally or metaphorically to mean that the bodily orientation you adopt should convey the message that you are involved with the client. If facing a person squarely is threatening to that person, a more angled position may be preferable — as long as you pay attention to the client. A desk between you and your client may, for instance, create a psychological barrier between you.

- **O:** Adopt an *Open* posture: Ask yourself to what degree your posture communicates openness and availability to the client. Crossed legs and crossed arms may be interpreted as diminished involvement with the client or even unavailability or remoteness, while an open posture can be a sign that you are open to the client and to what he or she has to say. The word *open* can also be taken literally or metaphorically. This means that you can still be attentive — even if you cross your legs.

- **L:** *Lean* towards the client (when appropriate) to show your involvement. A slight inclination towards the client might be a way of signalling that you agree (or are at least sympathetic), while leaning back can convey the opposite message. Egan (1998) warns that leaning too far forward, or doing it too soon after meeting a client for the first time, may frighten the client because the client may interpret it as a demand for some kind of (premature) closeness or intimacy. If you read the client's body language, you can prevent yourself from making mistakes.

- **E:** Maintain good *Eye* contact, but don't stare. Eye contact with a client conveys the message that you are interested in what the client has to say. If you catch yourself looking away frequently, ask yourself why you are reluctant to get involved with this person or why you feel so uncomfortable in his or her presence. Be aware of the fact that direct eye contact is not regarded as acceptable in all cultures (see 'Attending skills' on page 231).

- **R:** Try to be *Relaxed* or natural with the client. Don't fidget nervously or engage in distracting facial expressions. The client may begin to wonder what it is in himself or herself that makes you so nervous! Being relaxed means that you are comfortable with using your body as a vehicle of personal contact and expression and for putting the client at ease.

Effective attending puts counsellors in a position to listen carefully to what their clients are saying or not saying.

**Activity**

> Watch two people in a coffee shop or at an eating place who are intimately engaged in conversation. How many of the microskills of attending (SOLER) do they show? Can you see that the skills of attending are natural skills, and that all people who really care for others display them?

## Listening

Listening refers to the ability of counsellors to capture and understand the messages clients communicate as they tell their stories, whether those messages are transmitted verbally or non-verbally, clearly or vaguely (Egan, 1998, p. 62). Clients want more than the physical presence of the counsellor: they want the counsellor to be present psychologically, socially and emotionally.

According to Egan, active listening involves the following four skills:

- Listening to and understanding the client's *verbal* messages. When a client tells you his or her story, it usually comprises a mixture of experiences (what happened to him or her), behaviours (what the client did or failed to do), and affect (the feelings or emotions associated with the experiences and behaviour). The counsellor's first task is to listen carefully to what the client has to say. Listen to the mix of experiences, behaviour and feelings the client uses to describe his or her problem situation. Also 'hear' what the client is *not* saying.
- Listening to and interpreting the client's *non-verbal* messages. Counsellors should learn how to listen to and read non-verbal messages such as *bodily behaviour* (posture, body movement and gestures), *facial expressions* (smiles, frowns, raised eyebrows, twisted lips), *voice-related behaviour* (tone, pitch, voice level, intensity, inflection, spacing of words, emphases, pauses, silences and fluency), *observable physiological responses* (quickened breathing, a temporary rash, blushing, paleness, pupil dilation), *general appearance* (grooming and dress), and *physical appearance* (fitness, height, weight, complexion). Counsellors need to learn how to 'read' these messages without distorting or over-interpreting them. They also need to learn to listen to the whole context of the helping conversation — to verbal and non-verbal messages — without becoming fixated on specific details.
- Listening to and understanding the client in *context*. 'People are more than the sum of their verbal and non-verbal messages' (Egan, 1998, p. 72). The counsellor should listen to the whole person in the context of his or her social settings.
- Listening with *empathy*. Empathic listening involves attending, observing and listening ('being with' the client) in such a way that the counsellor develops an understanding of the client and his or her world. Empathic counselling is *selfless* because it requires helpers to put their own concerns aside to be fully 'with' their

clients. Skilled helpers also listen to any 'slant' or 'spin' that clients may give their story. While clients' feelings about themselves, others and the world are real, their *perceptions* are often distorted. 'Tough-minded' listening is needed to detect the gaps and distortions that are part of the clients' experienced reality (so that it can be challenged at a later, more appropriate stage, if necessary). According to Egan (p. 75), 'to be client-centred, helpers must first be reality-centred.

Active listening is unfortunately not an easy skill to acquire. Counsellors should be aware of the following hindrances to effective listening (Egan, 1998, pp. 75–78):

- **Inadequate listening:** It is easy to be distracted from what other people are saying if one allows oneself to get lost in one's own thoughts or if one begins to think about what one intends to say in reply. Counsellors are also often distracted because they have problems of their own, feel ill, or because they become distracted by social and cultural differences between themselves and their clients. All these factors make it difficult to listen to and understand their clients.

- **Evaluative listening:** Most people listen evaluatively to others. This means that they are judging and labelling what the other person is saying as either right/wrong, good/bad, acceptable/unacceptable, relevant/irrelevant, etc. They then tend to respond evaluatively as well.

- **Filtered listening:** We tend to listen to ourselves, other people and the world around us through biased (often prejudiced) filters. Filtered listening distorts our understanding of our clients.

- **Labels as filters:** Diagnostic labels can prevent you from really listening to your client. If you see a client as 'that women with AIDS', your ability to listen empathetically to her problems will be severely distorted and diminished.

- **Fact-centred rather than person-centred listening:** Asking only informational or factual questions won't solve the client's problems. Listen to the client's whole context and focus on themes and core messages.

- **Rehearsing:** If you mentally rehearse your answers, you are also not listening attentively. Counsellors who listen carefully to the themes and core messages in a client's story always know how to respond. The response may not be a fluent, eloquent or 'practised' one, but it will at least be sincere and appropriate.

- **Sympathetic listening:** Although sympathy has its place in human transactions, Egan (1998) warns that the 'use' of sympathy is limited in the helping relationship because it can distort the counsellor's listening to the client's story. To sympathise with someone is to become that person's 'accomplice'. Sympathy conveys pity and even complicity, and pity for the client can diminish the extent to which you can help the client.

## Basic empathy

According to Egan (1998, p. 81), basic empathy involves *listening* to clients, *understanding* them and their concerns as best as we can, and *communicating* this understanding to them in such a way that they might *understand themselves* more fully and *act* on their understanding. In order to do this, the counsellor must temporarily forget about his or her own frame of reference and try to see the client's world and the way the client sees himself or herself as though he or she were seeing it through the eyes of the client. Empathy is thus the ability to *recognise* and *acknowledge* the feelings of another person without *experiencing* those same emotions — it is an attempt to understand the world of the client by temporarily 'stepping into his or her shoes'. This understanding of the client's world must then be shared with the client in either a verbal or non-verbal way.

### The key elements of basic empathy

Egan (1998, pp. 84–95) helps us to understand the fundamentals of empathy when he dissects the concept in order to identify and describe its key components. In what follows below, we present a very simplistic but clear description of what empathy is.

- **Formula for basic empathy:** Basic empathy can be expressed in the following 'formula':

  You *feel* . . . [name the relevant emotion expressed by the client] . . .

  *because* (or *when*) . . . [indicate the relevant experiences and behaviours that gave rise to the feelings] . . .

  Example: 'You *feel* furious *because* he didn't tell you that he was HIV positive.' While the counsellor does not 'solve' the client's problem with this response, he or she demonstrates an understanding of the client's problem that will prompt the client to share more of her feelings or experiences.

- **Experiences, behaviours and feelings as elements of empathy:** An empathic response has the same key elements as the client's story, namely experiences, behaviour and feelings. The counsellor should respond to the client's feelings by referring to the correct *family* of emotions and by referring to the correct *intensity* of emotions. Egan named four main families of emotions, namely *sad*, *mad*, *bad*, and *glad*. *Fear* can also be included. These feelings can be experienced in different degrees of intensity. Thus, for example, the client can feel *sad*, *very sad*, or *extremely sad*. Keep the following in mind about the expression of feelings or emotions:

  o Clients don't always name their feelings and emotions verbally. While they often express feelings non-verbally, these non-verbal expressions still convey a vital part of the message and the counsellor should try to understand what is being conveyed.

- o Be cautious. Some clients feel threatened if the counsellor names and discusses their *feelings*. If this is the case, concentrate on *experiences* and *behaviours* and then *gradually* introduce actual named feelings into the
discussions.

- o Some clients can talk about some feelings (e.g. anger), while avoiding others
(e.g. hurt). The empathic counsellor will be able to pick this up and deal with
it accordingly.

- o Don't either overemphasise or underemphasise feelings or emotions. Remember that emotions go hand in hand with experiences and behaviours.

- o Use your own words, phrases or statements to express empathy. Be true to
yourself. Egan warns that your responses to your clients should come from
*you*. They should not be canned responses from a textbook (1998, p. 87).

- **Principles to guide the use of basic empathy:** The counsellor should use the
following principles to guide him or her in the use of basic empathy:

  - o Empathy should be used in *all the phases* of the counselling process (see
'Phases in the counselling process' on page 205) to help the client to answer
the four fundamental questions about current and preferred scenarios, strategies and action (see 'The process of helping' on page 201). Empathy offers
support, builds trust, paves the way to more effective participation from the
client, and creates the atmosphere for stronger interventions on the part of
the counsellor.

  - o Respond to the *core messages* in a client's conversation. Because it is impossible to respond with empathy to everything a client says, it is necessary to
identify and respond to the core messages.

  - o Respond to the *context* of what is said, and not only to the words or non-
verbal behaviour of the client. The context of what is said includes everything
that surrounds the client's words, such as his or her socioeconomic background.

  - o Use empathy to stimulate *movement* in the helping process. For example, a
client moves forward when empathy helps him or her to explore a problem situation in more detail or to investigate possible interventions or actions. Em-
pathetic statements that accurately reflect how a client feels put pressure on
the client to move forward.

  - o Empathy is also a tool to *check* if you understood the client correctly. Allow
the client to correct you. Remember that the client understands his or her
world far better than you do. If your response is correct, the client will usually
acknowledge it verbally or non-verbally, for example, by nodding, by using an
affirmative word or phrase, or by moving forward in the helping process. If
your response to your client's story is wrong, he or she will either say so, fum-

ble, stop dead, or change the conversation. Be alert to the client's cues and get back on track.

o *Don't pretend* to understand. Admit if you have 'lost' the client, and work to get back on track. Counsellors sometimes lose their clients, either because the client is too confused and emotional to express himself or herself clearly, or because the counsellor gets distracted.

## The DON'Ts of empathy

Some of the stumbling blocks to effective empathy are the following:

- *No response*: Although clients differ in how they deal with silence, they may think that what they have just said does not deserve a response from the counsellor. A brief response is better than silence most of the time. Even a somewhat inaccurate, tentative response is better than no response, questions or clichés.
- *Distracting questions:* Counsellors often ask questions to get more information from the client in order to pursue their own agendas. They do this at the expense of the client, i.e. they ignore the feelings that the client expressed about his or her experiences.
- *Clichés*: Avoid using clichés. Clichés are hollow, and they communicate the message to the client that his or her problems are not serious. Avoid saying 'I know how you feel' because you don't.
- *Interpretations:* Empathy is not interpreting. The counsellor should respond to the client's feelings and should not distort the content of what the client is telling the counsellor.
- *Advice*: Although giving advice has its place in counselling, it should be used sparingly to honour the value of self-responsibility (see 'Empowerment and self-responsibility' on page 213).
- *Parroting*: To merely repeat what the client has said is not empathy but parroting. Counsellors who 'parrot' what the client said, do not understand the client, are not 'with' the client, and show no respect for the client. Empathy should always *add* something to the conversation.
- *Sympathy and agreement*: Empathy is not the same as sympathy. According to Du Toit et al. (1998), sympathy stems from the facilitator's own experiential world rather than that of the client. To sympathise with a client is to show pity, condolence and compassion — all well-intentioned traits but not very helpful in counselling. According to Egan (1998, p. 97), 'sympathy denotes agreement, whereas empathy denotes understanding and acceptance of the person of the client'. For example: If Mary is cross with her previous partner who infected her with HIV, an *empathic* counsellor will be able to understand Mary's feelings towards her ex-partner. A *sympathetic* counsellor will experience emotions of anger towards Mary's ex-partner.

- *Confrontation and arguments*: Avoid confrontation and arguments with the client. Counsellors who argue with their clients are not showing empathy, they are approaching the client from their own (i.e. the counsellor's) frame of reference. This may cause the client to become defensive (Du Toit et al., 1998).

## Hints for communicating empathy

Egan (1998, p. 97) suggests the following ways for the novice counsellor to improve his or her empathic responses:

- *Give yourself time to think*. Assimilate and reflect on what the client has said in order to identify the core message that the client is communicating.
- *Use short responses*. Don't make speeches. Keep your responses short, concrete and accurate and base them on the core message that the client has been giving you.
- *Gear your response to the client, but remain yourself*. Part of being empathic is to share in your client's emotional tone (e.g. tone of voice). If a client speaks excitedly about his or her successes, it is not very empathic if the counsellor responds with a dull, flat tone of voice. It is however important for the counsellor to be true to his or her own nature. A counsellor who says and does things just to be on the client's wavelength will not come over as empathic, but as 'phoney'.

## Probing or questioning

Probing involves *statements* and *questions* from the counsellor that enable clients to *explore more fully* any relevant issue of their lives (Egan, 1998, p. 81). Probes can take the form of statements, questions, requests, single words or phrases and non-verbal prompts. Egan (p. 112) gives the following advice about probes:

- Keep in mind that probes serve the following purposes:
  - to encourage non-assertive or reluctant clients to tell their stories
  - to help clients to remain focused on relevant and important issues
  - to help clients to identify experiences, behaviours and feelings that give a fuller picture to their story, in other words, to fill in the missing pieces of the picture
  - to help clients to move forward in the helping process
  - to help clients understand themselves and their problem situations more fully
- Use a mixture of probing statements, questions and interjections.
- Use questions with caution. Don't ask too many questions. They make clients feel 'grilled', and they often serve as fillers when counsellors don't know what else to do. Don't ask a question if you don't really want to know the answer! If you ask two questions in a row, it is probably one question too much.
- Avoid close-ended questions that begin with 'does', 'did', or 'is'. Ask open-ended questions — that is, questions that require more than a simple *yes* or *no* answer.

Start sentences with 'how', 'tell me about', or 'what'. Open-ended questions are non-threatening and they encourage description.

- If a probe helps a client to reveal relevant information, follow it up with basic empathy rather than another probe.
- Use a mixture of empathy and probing to help clients to clarify problems, identify blind spots, develop new scenarios, search for action strategies, formulate plans, and review outcomes of actions.

### Summarising

It is sometimes useful for the counsellor to summarise what was said in a session so as to provide a focus to what was previously discussed, and so as to challenge the client to move forward. Summaries are particularly helpful under the following circumstances:

- *At the beginning of a new session.* A summary at this point can give direction to clients who do not know where to start; it can prevent clients from merely repeating what they have already said; and it can pressure a client to move forwards.
- *When a session seems to be going nowhere.* In such circumstances, a summary may help to focus the client.
- *When a client gets stuck.* In such a situation, a summary may help to move the client forward so that he or she can investigate other parts of his or her story.

The counsellor can also help the client to summarise the major points of what has already been said. This helps the client to 'own' the process and to move on (Egan, 1998).

### Integrating communication skills

Communication skills should be integrated in a natural way in the counselling process. Skilled counsellors continually attend and listen, and use a mix of empathy and probes to help the client to come to grips with their problems. Which communication skills will be used and how they will be used depend on the client, the needs of the client, the problem situation, the phase of counselling (e.g. defining the relationship, gathering information, describing the problem dynamic or planning interventions) and the questions the client needs to ask himself or herself (e.g. current scenario, preferred scenario, strategies and action).

### 10.7 ADVANCED COMMUNICATION SKILLS

Basic communication skills are needed to observe and hear clients, to understand them and to communicate this understanding to them. Advanced communication

**Activity**

Role play a counselling session, but concentrate on your communication skills this time. Ask a third person to listen to the interview and to make comments on your attending, listening, basic empathy and probing skills. Did you move through all four phases of the interview (defining the relationship, gathering information, describing the problem dynamic and planning intervention)?

skills require a different kind of understanding. In such a situation, the client is challenged to tell that part of his or her story which was hidden, distorted or repressed (Du Toit et al., 1998). Advanced communication skills that could be used to challenge clients to develop new perspectives and to change their behaviour are: advanced empathy, immediacy, helper self-disclosure and information sharing, suggestions and recommendations.

## Advanced empathy

Advanced empathy is the process whereby a counsellor helps the client to explore themes, issues and emotions that are new to his or her awareness (Johnson, 2000). Advanced empathy involves the 'message behind the message' or the 'story behind the story'. Although advanced empathy is still empathy, it challenges the client to explore deeper feelings.

The following questions can help counsellors to probe a bit deeper as they listen to their clients (Egan, 1998, p. 170):

- What is the client only half-saying?
- What is the client saying in a confused way?
- What is the client hinting at?
- What covert message is hiding behind the explicit message?

For example, if you say to a client who is furious because her partner did not tell her that he was HIV positive: 'You feel angry because he did not tell you, but perhaps you also feel a bit hurt' — this may bring a new dimension to the fore. This client was prepared to talk about the anger, while the *hurt* — although a very real problem — was lurking in the background.

Egan (1998, p. 171) warns that advanced empathic listening deals with what the client is actually trying to say, and not with the counsellor's *interpretation* of what the client is saying. 'Advanced therapy is not an attempt to *psych the client out.*'

Advanced empathy can be used in the following ways (Du Toit et al., 1998, pp. 169–185; Egan, 1998, pp. 172–175):

- **Help clients to make the implied explicit:** There is usually more than one intended message encoded in the explicit message. The counsellor must search for those deeper messages embedded in something the client said earlier, or in non-verbal behaviour such as tone of voice or facial expression.

- **Help clients to identify themes in their stories:** Stories usually consist of many themes which might refer to feelings (such as themes of anxiety or depression), behaviour (such as themes of avoiding intimacy), or experiences (such as themes of being a victim). These themes are usually *implicit* in the story of the client, and the counsellor has to listen very carefully to identify the themes. Clients are often unaware of these themes. If they are pointed out to them, the client may begin to understand his or her story in a completely new light. Egan (1998, p. 173) warns counsellors, however, 'to make sure that the themes they discover are based on the client's story and are not just the artifacts of some psychological theory. Advanced empathy works because clients recognise themselves in what you say'.

- **Avoid negativity and blaming:** Themes should be pointed out to clients without blaming anyone and without making value judgements about anyone's behaviour. The *way* in which the theme is communicated to the client is very important. Du Toit et al. (1998, p. 175) give the following example: A counsellor can for instance say the following: 'Correct me if I have misheard, but what I seem to be hearing is that you've been experiencing a need for closeness.' Don't say: 'What I hear is your need for closeness, but I sense that your husband maintains his distance.' Du Toit et al. go further to say that 'such a statement implies a reproach against the husband. If the theme of closeness is identified, the client will make the connection herself'.

- **Help clients to make connections:** Clients often tell various stories without seeing the connections between them. Egan calls these various stories 'islands' and the counsellor should try to see how these 'islands' (stories, statements, experiences, problems and contexts) can be connected. The counsellor should try to determine which of the things that occur on island A might also be on islands B, C and D. It is the task of the counsellor to give feedback to the client and to help him or her to build a bridge between these islands. This bridge is built with empathy, and it is not merely an interpretation by the counsellor.

- **Share hunches with clients:** Advanced empathy means sharing educated guesses or hunches about clients and their overt and covert experiences, behaviour and feelings with them in the hope that this will help them to see their problems more clearly. The counsellor can, of course, only form hunches if he or she uses the communication skills of active listening, understanding, empathy and probing effectively. Hunches can help clients to see the bigger picture, to see what they were merely implying or hinting at, to see things they overlooked and to identify themes.

## Immediacy

Immediacy is a skill used by the counsellor to communicate what is happening between him or her and the client in the counselling relationship while it is happening. Immediacy improves the working alliance in counselling, and it will also influence the parallel processes or relationships occurring in the client's life outside the counselling relationship. For example, some of the difficulties clients experience in their day-to-day relationships may also be reflected in their relationships with counsellors. If a client tends to be dependent and indecisive in his or her relationships with other people, he or she will also be dependent and indecisive in the counselling relationship. By using immediacy, the counsellor can help the client to move beyond this problem — in the counselling sessions as well as in his or her everyday life.

According to Du Toit et al. (1998, p. 190), there is one golden rule of immediacy that the counsellor should never forget: The 'I rule'. The counsellor must always comment in the first person, such as: 'I sense that . . .', or 'I'm wondering whether . . .', or 'I am a bit confused . . .'. When using the 'I rule', the counsellor includes himself or herself in the situation, and it is therefore more difficult to blame the client. Never start a sentence with 'You are' when using immediacy.

According to Egan (1998, p. 183), the skill of immediacy can be useful in the following situations:

- When a session is *directionless* and no progress is being made. For example: 'I feel that we are stuck here. Perhaps we should stop a moment and take a look at what we are doing.'
- When there is *tension* between client and counsellor: 'I have the feeling that we seem to be getting on each other's nerves. It might be helpful to stop for a moment and clear the air.'
- When *trust* seems to be a problem: 'I see your hesitancy to talk to me . . .'
- When *diversity* or some kind of *social distance* between the client and counsellor gets in the way: 'I get the feeling that the fact that I am black and you are white . . .'
- When *dependency* interferes with the helping process: 'I feel as if I must give my permission every time before you are willing to . . .'
- When *counterdependency* blocks the relationship: 'It seems that we are letting this session turn into a struggle between you and me . . .'
- When *attraction* between the counsellor and client is sidetracking the helping relationship: 'I think we like each other. . . . This might be getting in the way of the work we are doing.'

Immediacy is a complex skill because it demands competence in a variety of skills such as empathy, self-awareness and advanced empathy. It should be used with care by more experienced helpers.

**Helper self-disclosure**

Self-disclosure literally means 'to disclose yourself to another person'. A certain amount of indirect self-disclosure automatically happens in counselling when a client experiences some of the characteristics of the counsellor (such as warmth, congruence, etc.). Direct self-disclosure is the purposeful sharing of information about yourself that the client wouldn't otherwise know (Long, 1996). Self-disclosure therefore involves the ability of the counsellor to share information about his or her own feelings, experiences or behaviour with the client in an appropriate and constructive manner. If used correctly, self-disclosure can enhance the helping relationship and aid in problem solving. In a sense, the counsellor becomes a positive role model who indirectly challenges the client with 'If I could do it, you can do it too'.

However, self-disclosure is a controversial issue and it should only be used by experienced counsellors, and only if it will help a client to reach a treatment goal. Okun (1997, p. 274) sets the following guiding principle for self-disclosure: 'The helper's self-disclosure should be for the client's benefit. This means the helper does not burden the client with his or her problems but instead regulates the quality and timing of self-disclosure to help the client focus more on his or her concerns and to encourage exploration and understanding.' Clients are not interested in rambling stories about the counsellor's own life, and these can make them very uncomfortable. They may start wondering who the client is!

Self-disclosure is often used very effectively in the HIV/AIDS context where HIV-positive co-helpers are used to tell their stories. Clients often appreciate this because it brings them into contact with HIV-positive individuals who have worked through many of the problems they are still struggling with.

**Information sharing, suggestions and recommendations**

Sometimes clients are unable to explore their problems fully and take action because of a lack of information (Egan, 1998). It is therefore often necessary for counsellors to provide their clients with the necessary information, or to help them search for it, in order to move forward in the helping relationship. Information sharing is especially important in the HIV/AIDS field. Although information often does not 'solve' the client's problem, it can give them new perspectives on how to handle their problems. Information sharing includes both giving information and correcting misinformation. Egan (p. 177) warns that counsellors should observe caution when giving information:

● When information is challenging or shocking (e.g. an HIV-positive result), be tactful and know how to help the client handle the news. (See 'Counselling after a positive HIV test result' on page 247.)
● Do not overwhelm the client with information.

- Make sure that the information you give is clear and relevant to the client's problem situation.
- Don't let the client go away with a misunderstanding of the information.
- Be sure not to confuse giving information with giving advice. Giving advice is seldom useful.
- Be supportive and help the client to process the information.

Don't tell clients what to do, and don't try to take over their lives. The values of respect and empowerment should always be kept in mind, and clients should be supported to make their own decisions. Suggestions and recommendations do however have a place in counselling (especially HIV/AIDS counselling) because they identify ways in which clients can more effectively manage their problems. Suggestions and recommendations should however be given in such a way that they do not rob clients of their autonomy.

## 10.8 COUNSELLING IN A TRADITIONAL AFRICAN SOCIETY

For a century or more, indigenous or traditional African healing and modern Western forms of counselling and psychotherapy operated side-by-side — in almost mutual isolation. Although traditional healing and Western counselling are based on different philosophical assumptions, there are certain similarities that are universal to counselling. There are however also many differences which should be taken into account if Western counsellors* want to render a helpful service to clients coming from traditional African backgrounds. To ignore a client's cultural background not only leads to misunderstanding, it can also be anti-therapeutic and harmful (Beuster, 1997). The following are some of the philosophical differences of which the Western counsellor should take note.

### Differences between traditional African and Western beliefs and assumptions

One of the most important differences between the traditional African approach and Western thinking is the degree to which traditional African thought is characterised by a holistic outlook. The traditional African approach is truly holistic in its integration of the biological, psychosocial and transpersonal aspects of illness. Traditional African people do not distinguish between physical and mental illness. They see illness as affecting the whole human being — including a person's relationship with his or her ancestors and the community. They believe that physical, mental and

*The concept 'Western counsellor' does not necessarily refer to a white counsellor, but to any counsellor who has been trained in the Western-European philosophical or psychological tradition.

social systems are interconnected and that changes in one system inevitably effect changes in the others.

The traditional African approach does not regard the individual as being more important than the group (African philosophy has no tradition of the kind of individualism that is so highly valued in the West), and it recognises the important role that social factors play in the causation, maintenance and cure of illness. As we noted in chapter 7, Africans believe that whatever affects the individual also affects the whole group, and vice versa. Collective societies stress a joint 'we' consciousness, emotional dependence, collective identity and group solidarity (Bodibe & Sodi, 1997). In the African tradition, people do not generate knowledge by introspectively examining their own feelings, their own thinking or their own intelligence (the ancient Western tradition of self-analysis). Africans acquire knowledge from their relationships with the sky, the land, their families, their communities and their ancestors (Beuster, 1997; Bührman, 1986; Hammond-Tooke, 1989; Mbiti, 1969).

In contrast to the importance that Africans accord to group identity, Western societies are saturated in the tradition of individualism and the rights of the individual. This tradition emphasises personal autonomy and individual initiative: an 'I' rather than 'we' sense or mode of self-consciousness. To focus on the *self* is however seen as irrelevant and even as deviant in many African cultures. Skilled helpers should take the following quotation to heart and remember it when helping people from traditional African cultures that differ from their own:

> A trend that has swept the Western world in recent years has been the idea that individuals should be self-sufficient, autonomous, independent, self-directed and governed principally by what is best for them as individuals. Such qualities are often equated with mental health, but an African with such qualities would be regarded as extremely unhealthy (Durie & Hermannson in Bodibe, 1992, p. 151).

There is also a tendency for Western counsellors to overemphasise the rational, logical and intellectual while neglecting the unconscious, intuitive and transpersonal sides of the psyche (Beuster, 1997; Bodibe, 1992; Bodibe & Sodi, 1997).

### Similarities and differences between traditional African healing and Western counselling

Bodibe (1992, p. 155) discusses the following similarities and differences between traditional healing and Western psychotherapy or counselling:

Traditional healing and Western counselling display the following *similarities*:

● Both approaches emphasise the importance of building a relationship that is based on *trust*.

- Both aim at personality *integration* (wholeness) and *positive growth*.
- Both approaches emphasise the expression of *feelings* (although the ways of expressing feelings differ).
- Both rely on the *communication skills* of observation, active listening and probing to establish the problem dynamic. The traditional healer usually bases his or her diagnosis (problem dynamic) on careful *observation* of physical symptoms or strange behaviour, on *listening* to the client's story as told by the client and his or her family members, on the asking of *questions* (probing) which relate to ancestral influences, marital harmony or discord, sexual functioning, the nature, content and frequency of dreams, financial matters, the situation at work and relationships with superiors, and on *exploring* these areas carefully. An African diagnostic tool their Western counterparts don't use is *divination* — which can be done by bone-throwing (*impamba*), the involvement of ancestral spirits through psychic abilities, and the interpretation of dreams and visions as a form of divination (Bodibe, 1992; Felhaber, 1997).

There are, however, also many *differences* between traditional healing and Western psychotherapy:

- The African approach is symbolic, intuitive and integrally part of traditional African beliefs and cosmology, while Western counselling is based largely on scientific and logical principles which have no direct link with symbolism.
- The traditional diviner is directive in his approach. He or she gives advice to his or her client by functioning as the mouthpiece of the ancestors who possess superior wisdom. Western counselling is based on the principle that the client has to take responsibility for his or her own actions and decisions. It is therefore mainly non-directive.
- The African tradition emphasises the unity of body and mind, and tends to be more holistic in its approach to diagnosis and treatment. In Western counselling, the *psychological domain* is given preference (i.e. the person's feelings, thoughts and experiences). While traditional African people often don't *talk* (or want to talk) about their feelings in the same way that Western people do, they often give strong *expression* to their feelings through songs and dancing.
- Traditional healers emphasise the unity of the person and the community, but Western counselling usually emphasises the individual and the self.
- Traditional African healing, with its vibrant dance and the accompanying songs, involves an emotive and active experience of participation — as opposed to the more cerebral, abstract, sedentary and sedate forms of Western counselling.
- While the main tools of the traditional healer are divination, dream interpretations and the use of rituals, music, dance, and drumming, the main tools of the Western therapist are the psychotherapeutic interview, testing (both assessment/diagnostic and projective) and (in some cases) hypnosis.

- The traditional healer explores the client's relationship with his ancestors and neighbours because human conspiracies with witches and sorcerers can cause problems (see 'Witches and sorcerers as causal agents of illness' on page 113). Western counsellors often concentrate on the exploration of feelings, the promotion of insight and reconstruction of reality.

- While the main disposition of traditional healers is to sort things out between the client and the ancestors, the main purpose of Western counselling is to develop inner resources to deal effectively with external factors and intrapsychic conflict.

### The person-centred approach in Africa

The person-centred approach of Carl Rogers has had a tremendous influence on counselling in the Western world. Although most of the values and principles of the person-centred approach, such as empathy, warmth, caring, respect, congruence, unconditional acceptance and growth, are universal to people of all cultures, the person-centred approach should be adapted to take cultural and philosophical differences into account when it is used in Africa. Change in Africa is not directed by the self (what the 'self' wants), or by an *internal locus of control*, but by the group or an *external locus of control*. To create change in traditional Africa, the focus should shift from the individual to the group.

Du Toit et al. (1998, pp. 199–200) suggest that the following implications of a person-centred approach should be taken into account when therapists work cross-culturally:

- The counsellor should respect the client and his or her own culture and allow himself or herself to be led into the client's frame of reference.

- Cross-cultural counselling is a learning process for both the counsellor and the client. It is a process of finding common ground and understanding.

- To *assume* is to *stereotype*. Admission of one's own ignorance is the only way in which one can begin to understand and appreciate the wisdom and subtleties of a culture that is alien to one's own.

- If we listen, ask, explore, and learn, clients will show us the appropriate ways in which we can collaborate with them in their endeavour to grow and develop.

### Practical guidelines in cross-cultural counselling

The following practical guidelines may be helpful in cross-cultural counselling (based on material from Du Toit et al., 1998, pp. 201–207; Gillis, 1994, pp. 177–179; Nefale in Van Dyk et al., 2000; Seepamore, 2000; Sue & Sue, 1999):

### The counselling process

- Although the *four phases of counselling* (defining the relationship, gathering information, describing the problem dynamic, and intervention) stay the same in cross-cultural counselling, the ways in which they are presented may differ slightly to accommodate the client.

- The *four questions* that you want your client to answer during the counselling process (current scenario, preferred scenario, what do I need to do, and action) may also vary if you keep in mind that traditional Africans don't always think in terms of what 'I' prefer (preferred scenario), or that they don't always make decisions as individuals (what 'I' need and want). Clients often have to go back to the group or the family to decide what will be the best for them as a group. Seepamore (2000) said the following in this regard: 'The counsellor may think bad of me — think that I can't make up my mind because I cannot answer him. What he doesn't understand is that I cannot make these decisions on my own. I have to discuss them with my family first.' A solution may be to send the client home with 'homework' to discuss the questions of current scenario, preferred scenario, and possible interventions with his or her significant others. Some clients even prefer to bring their family with them for counselling.

- *Insight* into their feelings or emotions is not valued much in cultures that believe in a group orientation. Insight is often believed to be a symptom of the kind of individualism that only benefits the individual — as opposed to the group.

- If you (or the client) feel uncomfortable because you come from different ethnic groups, bring it up in the first session. You can, for example, use a statement like: 'Sometimes clients feel uncomfortable working with a counsellor of a different race. Would this be a problem for you?'

- Identify the client's expectations and worldview. Find out what the client believes counselling is, and explore his or her feelings about counselling.

- Strive to work within the client's cultural frame of reference, and encourage the client to correct 'cultural' misunderstandings on your part.

- In the *intervention* or action phase, it may be necessary for the counsellor (at least in the beginning) to take a more *directive role* than usual, particularly in instances where the client's traditional helpers are normally directive (giving advice). The counsellor should however gradually involve the client in goal-setting and empower him or her to make his or her own choices (often with the approval of the group or significant others).

### Attending skills

- Make sure that the way you orient yourself to be with your client (*attending*) does not affront your client instead of making him or her feel at home. Read your client's body language and be guided by it.

- Familiarise yourself with traditional forms of greeting, and make sure you are able to pronounce and spell the client's name correctly. Don't make judgements based on stereotypes such as the client's hairstyle or dress.

- Bear in mind that people from different cultures may have different attitudes towards matters such as personal communication distance, punctuality and time schedules.

- If you are much younger than your client (or from a different sex), it may pose a problem. Elderly people (in African culture) customarily don't discuss their problems with younger people because 'they are children'. Discuss this potential problem with your client.

- Respect the client's customs and ways of communicating. These may include making or avoiding of eye contact, who should sit, stand or walk first, how a man should act towards a woman and a woman towards a man, and how adults and children should behave towards each other in the specific culture.

- Be aware of the fact that direct eye contact is not an admired form of behaviour in all cultures. In many cultures, it is regarded as rude, a challenge, or even as confrontational. In some cultures, it would be regarded as ill-mannered if a young person were to look directly at an older person. Let the client be your guide — observe him or her and be sensitive to what is comfortable for him or her.

- Many counsellors have the habit of touching their clients as a way of showing empathy. However, touching another person is not appropriate in all cultures. It may be seen as degrading (you touch a child out of sympathy, not an adult) or, if the touching involves a person of the opposite sex, it may be seen as an expression of sexual attention.

- Bodily distance may also be important to the client. Use your client's body language and do not offend your client by sitting too close or too far away. It is a good idea to invite the client (and his or her family) to choose where they would like to sit or stand. Allow *them* to select a comfortable distance.

- Don't close the door when other clients are sitting in a waiting room — especially when you are counselling somebody of the opposite sex. 'If the counsellor closes the door, it makes the other people very uncomfortable. They will ask each other: "What are those two doing in there?"' (Seepamore, 2000).

- Using first names may be regarded as an expression of over-familiarity, especially if the client is an older person. In African culture, first names are reserved for close friends, and clients will often say — or think (without any malice) — 'You are not my friend'.

## Listening and probing skills

- The skill of *active listening* is extremely important in cross-cultural counselling. The counsellor can only really become part of the client's world if he or she listens carefully to what the client says and doesn't say.

- Cross-cultural work sometimes offers the advantage that counsellors know that they will be at a disadvantage if they do not *listen* and *describe the problem dynamic* correctly. If the counsellor is aware that he or she does not know what meanings the client attaches to particular situations, he or she will put a lot of effort into exploring meanings with the client. The counsellor shouldn't assume (as he or she tends to do with people of the same culture) that he or she knows which meanings clients attach to situations.

- Try to use the client's own words and expressions whenever possible. Emphasise to your client that if he or she does not understand anything clearly, he or she must ask for clarification. Alternatively, if you have misunderstood something, the client must feel free to correct you.

- Be careful how and what you ask during the *information gathering phase*. An older client (older than you) will not discuss his or her sexual life with a younger counsellor because that is not an acceptable practice in African culture. The counsellor should accept that this is not a question of trust, but of custom.

- Where appropriate, enquire about the client's traditional family structures and support systems, as these may differ from culture to culture.

## Empathy

- *Empathy* can be used to bridge diversity gaps. According to Egan (1998), it is impossible for a counsellor really to understand the world of clients who differ from him or her in significant ways. Empathy based on effective attending and listening is one of the most important tools the counsellor has in order to get as close to understanding the client's world as possible.

- Although the counsellor should be sensitive to differences, he or she should be careful not to assume differences where there may be none. When working cross-culturally, the basic theory, values and communication skills are exactly the same as with people from the counsellor's own cultural group. Empathy is empathy in any culture or language — it is a way of being, regardless of the people we are in contact with. We simply might have to adapt the phrasing or our method of expressing feelings.

- Metaphors and stories work very well in a traditional African context to communicate empathy. Wildervanck (in Du Toit et al., 1998, p. 203) mentions that the following metaphors were very effectively used by counsellors to convey empathy in the African context:

o To empathise with somebody who missed a wonderful opportunity: 'The steenbok jumps out of the cooking pot.'
o To convey the understanding that a child takes after her mother: 'She comes from the breast milk.'
o To empathise with a person who has many problems and frustrations: 'You have grabbed the clay cooking pot by its hot side.'

- Be true to yourself. Don't do or say things that you feel uncomfortable with. If you talk to a client from the heart, on a person-to-person basis, using the skills of attending, listening and empathy to demonstrate your openness, honesty and genuine desire to help, trust and rapport will develop between you and the client.
- Keep in mind that traditional African people may find it difficult to talk about their *feelings*. They often don't even have words in their own language to describe feelings. Counsellors should be creative and allow clients to express their feelings in traditional ways such as singing, dancing, miming ('*Show* me how you feel') and writing poetry.
- Some cultures associate maturity and wisdom with one's ability to control emotions and feelings, and they will not feel comfortable with expressing their emotions in a counselling setting. Counsellors who are not aware of this might misinterpret their behaviour.
- Be cautious in allowing periods of *silence* to develop. In a counselling environment where feelings of acceptance and trust are paramount, nothing undermines the helping relationship more quickly than enforced silences. A short, emphatic response is better than silence.

*Self-disclosure*

- Use *self-disclosure* (you disclosing to the client) at appropriate times. This is often an important means of establishing trust because it may be seen as a sign that the counsellor accepts the client.
- Keep in mind that clients from other cultures may find it difficult to disclose their intimate details to you in a counselling context. Cultures that do not believe in the appropriateness of intimate revelations of personal or social problems often see disclosure as not only exposing the *individual* in counselling, but also as exposing the *whole family* because the individual is regarded as an integral part of the family system.

*General cultural considerations*

- When counselling cross-culturally, the counsellor should take great care to avoid being perceived as being in any way condescending or patronising.
- Explore, actively challenge and acknowledge your prejudices, stereotypes and cultural assumptions about other groups.

- Recognise the limitations that cross-cultural counselling imposes on helpers. If you find it difficult to be genuinely accepting and non-judgemental, or if it becomes clear that further progress is impossible because of perceived or real cultural differences, suggest another helper with whom the client may feel more comfortable.

When working cross-culturally, the counsellor (and the client) has to (dialogically) cross certain borders. By crossing borders we do not mean either invading the physical territory or the personal space of others, but rather going beyond our own mental and social borders and reaching out to others' worlds in a gentle and non-threatening way. Borders are not seen as obstacles, but as a learning experience (Du Toit et al., 1998, p. 204).

### Language barriers — the use of a translator or interpreter

Language barriers between counsellors and clients pose problems, especially in South Africa with its 11 official languages! There are unfortunately not enough trained counsellors always to address clients in their own language. Counsellors often have no other choice than to use translators or interpreters to rephrase what they have said in a way that is understandable to the client. This is far from ideal, and counsellors should be aware of the problems of using the services of a third person in the counselling process. Translators often translate according to their own personal frame of reference; they may add their own experiences, interpretations, prejudices, and comments in the message to the client, confidentiality may be violated, and the relationship between the counsellor and the client may be jeopardised in favour of a relationship between the translator and the client. Keep the following precautions in mind when using the services of an interpreter or translator (Wong et al., 1999, p. 208):

- Using a child as an interpreter is considered an insult to adults in some cultures because children are expected to show respect by not questioning their elders.
- In some cultures class differences between the interpreter and client may cause the client to feel intimidated and less inclined to offer information. Choose the translator or interpreter carefully and provide time for the interpreter and client to establish rapport.
- If informed consent is obtained through an interpreter, make sure that the client is fully informed of all the aspects of the procedure (e.g. testing) to which he or she is consenting.
- Communicate directly with the client when asking questions to reinforce interest in the client. Observe his or her non-verbal responses but don't ignore the interpreter.
- Ask one question at a time.

- Don't interrupt the client or interpreter while they are conversing.
- Don't make comments to the interpreter about the client because they may understand at least some of the language in which you are conversing.
- Be aware that some words (e.g. medical words) may have no equivalent word in another language. Avoid medical jargon if possible.
- Allow time after the interview for the interpreter to share something that he or she felt could not be said earlier and ask the interpreter about his or her impressions of non-verbal messages.
- Arrange for the client (if possible) to speak to the same interpreter on subsequent visits.

## 10.9 CONCLUSION

HIV/AIDS forces all of us in the helping professions to be counsellors. It is no longer only the task of the psychologist to counsel. The task may be daunting, but if you keep the definition of *counselling* in mind, namely that counselling *is a structured conversation aimed at facilitating a client's quality of life in the face of adversity*, and if you use the qualities that drew you to the helping professions in the first place, you can render a very important service to those in need. To further assist you in your task, the counselling skills that you have encountered in this chapter will be applied to specific contexts in the following chapters. Chapter 11 will give you guidelines on pre- and post-HIV test counselling, chapter 12 will deal with specific considerations in counselling the HIV-infected client and his or her significant others, while bereavement and spiritual counselling will be discussed in chapter 13.

# 11 Pre- and Post-HIV Test Counselling

. . . . . . . . . . . . . . . . . . . . . . . . . . . . . . . . . . . . . . . . . . . . . . . . . . . . . .

*Worrying about the beast*

*That night the fires burnt high*
*and glimmered through the poles,*
*separating them from the bush . . .*
*and nobody slept because of the darkness*
*that threatened to engulf them.*

. . . . . . . . . . . . . . . . . . . . . . . . . . . . . . . . . . . . . . . . . . . . . . . . . . . . . .


The HIV test is different from all other tests. It has phenomenal emotional, psycho-logical, practical and social implications for the client. HIV testing should therefore **never** be done without thorough pre-test counselling. Pre-test counselling that is done in a proper and comprehensive way prepares the client and counsellor for more effective post-test counselling. Because clients are often too relieved or shocked to take in much information during post-test counselling, the health care professional should make use of the educational opportunities offered by pre-test counselling.

The basic principles of counselling, values and communication skills that are discussed in chapter 10 should form the basis for pre- and post-HIV test counselling. Pre- and post-HIV test counselling are specific counselling contexts where these principles and skills should be applied.


## 11.1 PRE-HIV TEST COUNSELLING

The purpose of pre-test counselling is to provide individuals who are considering being tested with information on the technical aspects of testing and the possible personal, medical, social, psychological, legal and ethical implications of being diagnosed as either HIV positive or HIV negative. The purpose of pre-test counsel-ling is further to find out why individuals want to be tested, the nature and extent of their previous and present high-risk behaviour, and the steps that need to be taken to prevent them from becoming infected or from transmitting HIV infection.

The following guidelines should be used for HIV pre-test counselling.


### Reasons for testing

Explore why clients want to be tested. Is it for insurance purposes, because of anxiety about lifestyle, or because the person has been forced by somebody else to take the test? What particular behaviour or symptoms are causing concern to the client? Has the client sought testing before and, if so, when? From whom? For what reason? And with what result? These questions provide the counsellor with an opportunity to ascertain individuals' perceptions of their own high-risk behaviour, and with an opportunity to assess whether they intend to be tested and whether their fears are realistic or if they are unnecessarily concerned. If you as a counsellor have suggested to the client that he or she be tested for HIV, explain to the client the reason why you think a test would be advisable. The following are some of the reasons that clients who want to be tested often adduce:

- Their partner has requested it.
- They want to determine their HIV status before starting a new relationship.
- They want to be tested prior to getting married.
- They feel guilty and concerned about having had multiple sex partners.
- They have had recent sexual encounters in which they did not use condoms.
- They are manifesting symptoms that are giving them cause for concern.
- They have been referred by an STD or TB clinic because they have tuberculosis or a sexually transmitted disease.
- They have come to reconfirm a positive HIV test.
- Their current partner is HIV positive, or they were once involved with a partner who was HIV positive.
- They plan to become pregnant and want to check their HIV status before they do.
- They have been raped or assaulted.
- They need to be tested after an occupational exposure (e.g. a needlestick).
- They are simply curious.

The reason why a client wants to be tested is important because it sets the scene for the rest of the pre-test counselling session.

**Activity**

Frances comes to you for an HIV test. She works as a nanny in a private household and her employer wants her to be tested for HIV. Frances is afraid of the test, she does not really know what to expect, and she is uncertain if she really wants to be tested or not. How would you advise Frances?

## Assessment of risk

Assess the likelihood of whether the person has been exposed to HIV by considering how much and how frequently he or she has been exposed to the following risk factors and lifestyle indicators:

- What is the client's sexual risk history in terms of frequency and type of sexual behaviour? Has the client been involved in high-risk sexual practices such as vaginal or anal intercourse with more than one sex partner without the use of condoms? In the case of anal sex, was it anal-receptive or anal-insertive sex? Did the client have sex with a sex worker (or prostitute)? Or is the client's sex partner HIV positive?

- Are there any other risks involved? Is the client an injecting drug user, a prisoner, a migrant worker, a refugee or a sex worker? Did the client at any time receive money, gifts or drugs for sex? Has the client ever been raped or coerced to have sex with another person? Does the client have another sexually transmitted disease or tuberculosis?
- Has the client received a blood transfusion, an organ transplant or blood or body products? (Testing transfusion blood for HIV may not take place in some developing countries.)
- Has the client been exposed to possibly non-sterile invasive procedures such as tattooing, piercing or traditional invasive procedures such as male or female circumcision and scarification?
- Has the client been exposed to HIV-infected blood in the work situation?

**Activity**

> What questions will you ask Frances so that you will be in a position to assess the likelihood of whether she has been exposed to HIV or not?

### Beliefs and knowledge about HIV infection and safer sex

Determine exactly what your client believes and knows about HIV infection and AIDS and correct errors by providing accurate information about transmission and prevention. Ask your client questions about his or her past and present sexual behaviour and provide information about safer sex practices and a healthier lifestyle. Find out if the client knows how to practise safer sex, how to use a condom correctly, and where to get hold of condoms. Give them condoms if necessary.

### Information about the test

It is important to ensure that your clients know what the HIV test entails (see 'HIV testing as diagnostic tool' on page 57). Explain the following points to clients:

- There is a difference between being sero-positive and having AIDS. The HIV antibody test is not a 'test for AIDS'. It indicates that a person has HIV antibodies in the blood and that the person is infected with HIV. It does not say when or how the infection occurred, or in what phase of infection the person is.
- The presence of HIV *antibodies* in the blood does not mean that the person is now immune to HIV. On the contrary, it means that he or she has been infected with HIV and that he or she can pass the virus on to others.
- The meaning of a positive and a negative test result (see Questions on page 60 to 62).

- The meaning of the concept of the 'window period' (see 'The window period' on page 59). Stress the need for further testing if the person practises high-risk sexual behaviour and tests negative.
- The reliability of the testing procedures. A positive HIV antibody test result is always confirmed with a second test and the reliability of test results is usually high. False-positive or false-negative results may however occasionally occur despite the general reliability of HIV tests (e.g. a false negative test result because the person is in the window period).
- The testing procedure. Explain how blood is drawn for the test, where it is sent, when the results will be available and how the person will be informed of the outcome.

**Activity**

You don't want to overload your clients with information during the pre-test counselling session, and you want to send them home with something to read. Design a pamphlet in which you explain everything they need to know about the HIV antibody test.

## The implications of an HIV test result

The possible personal, medical, social, psychological, ethical and legal implications of a positive test result should be discussed with clients prior to testing. Inform clients about all the advantages and disadvantages of testing. The following advantages can accrue from taking the test:

- Knowing the result may reduce the stress associated with uncertainty.
- One may begin to make rational plans for preparing oneself emotionally and spiritually to live with HIV.
- Symptoms can be confirmed, alleviated or treated.
- Prophylactic (preventative) treatment can be considered.
- Anti-retroviral treatment can be considered.
- Adjustments to one's lifestyle and sex life can protect oneself and one's sex partners from infection.
- One can make decisions about family planning and new sexual relationships.
- One can plan for future care and orphan care.

The disadvantages that might accrue from taking an HIV test (especially if its result is positive) include:

- Possible limitations on life insurance and mortgages
- Having to endure the social stigma associated with the disease
- Problems in maintaining relationships and in making new friends

- A possible refusal on the part of uninformed medical and dental personnel to treat an HIV-positive person. (A refusal to treat HIV-infected individuals of course goes against the provisions of the South African Constitution.)
- Possible dismissal from work (although it is illegal to dismiss people because they are HIV-positive)
- Possible rejection and discrimination by friends, family and colleagues
- Emotional problems and a disintegration of one's life
- Increased stress levels and uncertainty about the future
- The stress and negative effects of maintaining a secret if the person decides not to disclose his or her test results

Assure the client (if he or she is HIV positive) that medical treatments which can help to keep him or her healthier for longer are available.

### Anticipate the results

It is important for the counsellor to anticipate a positive HIV antibody result and to talk about how the client will deal with a positive test outcome. Anticipating a positive result helps the counsellor to ascertain the client's ability to deal with, and adjust to, a positive result. The counsellor also gains insight into some of the potential problems associated with a positive test outcome. To prepare the client for the possibility of a positive test result paves the way for more effective post-test counselling. Albers (1990) suggests that in order to prepare the client for the test result, the following questions should be asked:

- How would you feel if you tested negative? How would you feel if the test were negative but you were advised to be tested again in three or six months' time because you may still be in the window period?
- What would your reactions and feelings be to a positive test? Would a positive test change your life? How? What negative changes would you anticipate? What positive changes can you imagine?
- Do you intend to tell others if you test positive? Who would you tell? Why that person? How would you tell them? Why would you tell them? Clients must be warned about people's possible reactions. Often those closest to the client cannot cope with such news. The counsellor must help clients to think not only of themselves but also of those who are to be told. (For example, if the client says to you: 'The news will surely kill my old and frail mother,' you may ask: 'Why do you want your mother to know?') Clients must also be warned that some people may not keep the information to themselves, and that this might have harmful effects for the client.
- How would you tell your sex partner? If the test result is positive, the sex partner also needs to be tested.

- How would a positive test result change the circumstances of your job, your family, your relationships? Would your relationships be improved or hindered by telling people you are HIV positive? What do you believe their reactions would be?

- Where would you seek medical help? How do you feel about a disease that requires a lot of care, lifestyle changes, commitment and discipline? Do you have members of your family or friends who could help you to be disciplined about your health? Could you take medication every four hours if necessary?

- Who could provide (and is currently providing) emotional and social support (family, friends, others)?

The choice to be tested remains the client's prerogative. The advantages of testing can be explained to clients, but clients should not be forced to be tested if they feel that they will not be able to deal with the results. The mere *knowledge* of people's HIV status will not necessarily protect them, or their loved ones, from infection. People who prefer not to be tested should however live as if they are infected and practise safer sex at all times. People who suspect they are HIV-infected should also refrain from donating blood.

**Activity**

After discussing her extra-marital affairs with you, Frances decided that she should be tested. She is however extremely worried about what and how she is going to tell her husband if her test result comes back positive. You decide to do a role play with Frances. Simulate the role play situation by asking a friend to play the role of Frances's husband, while you take the part of Frances.

## Confidentiality of test results

The counsellor should stress the confidentiality of test results. Assure clients that their right to confidentiality will be respected at all times. If individuals choose not to disclose their status, they must be reassured that no information will be communicated without their prior permission to anyone. The client's consent must be obtained before anyone can pass on any information about his or her HIV status to any other health care professional who also treats the client. If the counsellor explains why other health care professionals need to know about the client's HIV status, most clients will consent to this information being given out.

## Informed consent

The decision to be tested can only be made by the client and their informed consent must be obtained prior to testing. Consenting to medical testing or treatment has two elements: *information* and *permission*. Before an HIV test can be done, the client must understand the nature of the test, and he or she must also give verbal or written permission to be tested. A client may never be misled or deceived into consenting to an HIV test.

**Confidentiality**

Health care professionals are ethically and legally required to keep all information about their clients confidential. Any information about a patient's illness or treatment can only be given to another person with the patient's consent. The right of HIV-infected people to be treated fairly and confidentially should be recognised and accepted. If clients do not have the assurance that health care professionals will keep their diagnosis confidential, they might be too scared to go for treatment. Because people living with HIV infection often face discrimination and prejudice, it is even more important to keep the information about their infection confidential.

**Informed consent**

According to the law, health care professionals may not do an HIV test on a person unless he or she clearly understands what the purpose of the test is, what advantages or disadvantages testing may hold for him or her as client, why the health care professional wants this information, what influence the result of such a test will have on his or her treatment, and how his or her medical protocol will be altered by this information. The psychosocial impact of a positive test result should also be discussed with the client (Fine, Heywood & Strode, 1997).

### Information about giving the results and ongoing support

Explain to the client when, how and by whom the results of the test will be given to him or her. Assure the client of personal attention, privacy, confidentiality and ongoing support and advice if needed. Arrange the follow-up interview where the results will be made available. Take note of the fact that some traditional black people bring family members with them when they come back for the results. One should accommodate such preferences when patients require them.

### The waiting period

Waiting for the results of an HIV antibody test can be an extremely stressful period for the client. This waiting period can last from 2 to 14 days, depending on where the test is done (whether by a private practice, a governmental health service or a rural clinic). The results of rapid HIV antibody tests are, of course, available within 10 to 30 minutes (see 'Rapid HIV antibody tests' on page 58). However, if the client has to wait for the test results, the counsellor should anticipate this difficult waiting period by discussing the following points with the client:

- Find out the names of people whom the client might contact for moral support while he or she waits for the results.
- Encourage him or her to contact you or a colleague if they have any questions.
- Counsel the client on how to protect sex partners (e.g. to use condoms) in the interim period.
- Encourage the client to do something enjoyable to keep himself or herself occupied while waiting for the results (e.g. hiking, going to the movies or playing soccer with friends).

**Activity**

As a lawyer, you are asked by a friend to act on his behalf. While he was in the hospital, blood was drawn and an HIV test was done without his consent. The superintendent of the hospital insists that your friend did give his consent for the HIV test by signing the form below. What is your opinion?

---

**Consent to blood tests**

I, the undersigned, agree to the drawing of a blood specimen to be tested for the presence of blood transmissible pathogens.

Name of patient: . . . . . . . . . . . . . .

Signed: . . . . . . . . . . . . . . . . . . . . . .

Date:  . . . . . . . . . . . . . . . . . . . . . . .

---

Devise a legally acceptable consent form for an HIV test for this hospital.

## Conclusion

Pre-HIV test counselling is extremely important. It should not only be seen as a preparation for the HIV test, but as a golden opportunity to educate people about HIV/AIDS and safer sex. Remember that this may be the one and only time that you will see the client because he or she might decide not to be tested, or not to come back for the test results after all.

How would you handle the following phone call? 'Hello, my name is Mrs Johnson. I sent my nanny, Frances, to you a week ago for an AIDS test. I am just phoning to get her results.'

**Note:** Don't be abusive or angry. Use this as an educational opportunity for Mrs Johnson.

## 11.2 POST-HIV TEST COUNSELLING

Not many things in life could be as stressful as going back for HIV test results. For many clients it feels as if the counsellor holds the key to the future in his or her hands.

Although the post-HIV test counselling interview is separate from the pre-test counselling interview, it is inextricably linked to it. The pre-test counselling interview should have given the client a glimpse of what to expect in post-test counselling. Pre- and post-test counselling should preferably be done by the same person because the established relationship between the client and counsellor provides a sense of continuity for the client. The counsellor will also have a better idea of how to approach the post-test counselling because of what he or she experienced in the pre-test counselling.

Counselling after testing will depend on the outcome of the test — which may be a negative result, a positive result or an inconclusive result.

### Counselling after a negative HIV test result

For both the client and the counsellor, a negative HIV result is a tremendous relief. A negative test result could however give someone who is frequently involved in high-risk behaviour a false sense of security. It is therefore extremely important for the counsellor to counsel HIV-negative clients in order to reduce the chances of future infection. Advice about risk reduction and safer sex must be emphasised (see chapter 8).

Many people who practise high-risk behaviour and test negative believe that they are 'immune' to HIV and that precautions are therefore unnecessary. This dangerous assumption must be rectified. Explain to clients that nobody is immune to HIV and that they risk being infected if they do not change their behaviour. The metaphor of playing Russian roulette is apt here: the more times you pull the trigger, the greater your chances of being killed.

The possibility that the client is in the 'window period' or that the negative test result may be *false negative* should also be pointed out. If there is concern about the

HIV status of the person, he or she should return for a repeat test after 3 to 6 months and ensure that he or she takes appropriate precautions in the meanwhile.

> Don't underestimate the extreme importance of counselling a client who tested HIV negative. This may be your only chance to talk to this person about his or her sexual practices, potential drug abuse and other risk behaviours, and to educate him or her about safer sex practices. Free condoms can be given out at this session together with advice on how to use them and where to get more when needed. Use this counselling session to prevent a future situation where somebody else has to give the client a positive HIV test result.

## Counselling after a positive HIV test result

The health care professional needs to be tremendously responsible about the way in which he or she communicates a positive test result to a client. The way people react to test results depends to a large extent on how thoroughly the counsellor has educated and prepared them both before and after the test. Although it is good to encourage the client to ask questions, one should not bombard a client with information that he or she is unable to absorb at that moment. Learn to be comfortable with silence. Counsellors don't always have to say something.

When a test is positive, the following guidelines for counselling may prove useful (Albers, 1990; Eastaugh, 1997; Van Dyk, 1999):

### Sharing the news with the client

Positive (as well as negative) test results should be given to the client personally. Feedback should take place in a quiet, private environment and enough time should be allowed for discussion. The news of a positive result ought to be communicated openly, honestly and without fuss. Simple and straightforward language should be used. Do not give the individual false hopes and (alternatively) do not paint a hopeless scenario. Choose neutral words when conveying a positive HIV test result. Don't attach value to the news by saying 'I have **bad** news for you' — because such an attitude reflects a hopelessness in the mind of the counsellor. Rather say: 'Mr Peterson, the results of your HIV test came back, and you are HIV positive.' A positive result does not have to be a death sentence and the counsellor's task is to convey optimism and hope.

There are a few DON'Ts that we need to observe when sharing a positive HIV test result with a client.

- Don't lie or dodge the issue.
- Don't beat about the bush or use delaying tactics. Come to the point.
- Don't break the news in a corridor or any other public place.
- Don't give the impression of being rushed, distracted or distant.

- Don't interrupt or argue.
- Don't say that 'Nothing can be done' because something can always be done to ease suffering.
- Don't react to anger with anger.
- Don't say 'I know how you feel' because you don't.
- Don't be afraid to admit ignorance if you don't know something.

**Enrichment**

**Sensitivity to the client's needs**

The counsellor should be sensitive to the individual and the cultural needs of each client. Nomsa, a black woman, relayed her experience as follows: 'The counsellor looked very nervous, made small talk, and offered me some tea. I thought: "Now why is she offering me tea? What is wrong?" I got cross with her because I'm not here for tea. I'm here for my test results.'

On the other hand, Maria, a white Afrikaans-speaking woman, would have loved a cup of tea. She said: 'Everything was so correct and clinical. I would have loved a cup of tea to calm my nerves. My mother always made us some tea when things in life went wrong.'

It is very stressful for health care professionals to share positive HIV test results with their clients. What makes it worse is the traditional medical dictum that one should 'not get involved' — which encourages the kind of emotional repression that prevents a health care professional from showing any kind of distress or human emotions. The following words of Eastaugh (1997, p. 92) should be kept in mind by all health care professionals who have to share a positive HIV test result with their clients: 'Never has a client complained because the health care professional shed a tear with him; indeed, it seems that clients gain support in dealing with bad news when they perceive their informant is also distressed. It is cold, professional detachment that causes greater offence.'

### Client reaction to a positive HIV test result

It is never easy to tell people that they are HIV positive. Counsellors have to work through their own feelings about the results before they counsel. Clients' responses to the news usually vary from one person to another, and may include shock, crying, agitation, stress, guilt, withdrawal, anger and outrage. Some may even respond with relief. The counsellor should not take these reactions personally and he or she should show empathy, warmth and caring. Allow clients to deal with the news in their own way and give them the opportunity to express their feelings. Maintain neutrality and respond professionally to outbursts. Don't show surprise or make value-laden comments such as 'There is no need to be upset with me!' Because the loss of health is a bereavement, it manifests with all the components of denial, anger, bargaining, depression and acceptance. The counsellor must respect the personal nature of an individual's feelings.

## Responding to client needs

People's needs, when they receive an HIV-positive test result, vary, and the counsellor has to determine what those needs are and deal with them accordingly. Fear of pain and death are often the most serious and immediate problems and these can be dealt with in various ways. Talking to clients about their fears for the future is one of the most important therapeutic interventions that the counsellor can make. Often it is enough for the counsellor just to be 'there' for the client and to listen to him or her.

Some clients want information about anti-retroviral medication. Convey hope by explaining to clients that anti-retroviral therapy may reduce the viral load in the blood, but also be honest and tell them that it is unfortunately not a cure for HIV infection. Explain that opportunistic infections can be successfully treated and prevented with medication.

One of the major concerns for HIV-positive people is whom to tell about their condition and how to break the news. It is often helpful at this point to use role-play situations in which the client can practise communicating the news to others. (See 'Disclosure of HIV-positive status' on page 270.) The client may also ask the counsellor to convey the news to loved ones. (See 'Confidentiality and privacy' on page 408 for the legal implications of confidentiality and conveying the news to sex partners.)

In responding to a client's needs, an attitude of non-judgemental empathic attentiveness is more important than doing or saying specific things. Listening is more important than talking, *being with* more important than *doing to* (Macfie, 1997).

## Crisis intervention

Crisis intervention is often necessary after an HIV-positive test result is given (see 'Crisis intervention' on page 281). Make sure that the person has support after he or she leaves your office. A person in crisis should never be left alone: he or she should have somebody with whom to share the burden. Ask the client where he or she is going after leaving your office. Let the person think about and verbalise his or her plans for the next few hours. Although it is better for the client not to be alone, personal needs should be taken into consideration: some people *prefer* to be alone and to work through a crisis all by themselves.

Be sensitive to the possibility of suicide. The possibility of suicide can usually already be identified in the pre-test counselling session. If the client shows any suicidal tendencies, emergency hospitalisation should be arranged if a friend or family

### Shared confidentiality as opposed to secrecy

HIV-positive individuals often battle with the question of 'whom to tell'. While some individuals decide to share the information with a selected few who will keep the information confidential, others decide to keep their HIV-positive status a secret. Shared confidentiality is encouraged where clients share the information (on a confidential basis) with family members, loved ones, caregivers and trusted friends who are willing to support them. The obverse of this is that clients should be encouraged to withhold the information from people who do not have their best interests at heart. Yet other clients prefer to keep their HIV-positive status a total secret — or they share it only with very close family members. Although it remains the client's choice whether to share the information or not, secrecy may have very negative consequences. It may isolate and alienate the client from a support system that he or she may desperately need. The kind of social support that is generally provided to families with terminally ill members cannot be openly given to families who keep the HIV diagnosis a secret. Bereavement may ultimately also be very difficult to handle in these families because the bereavement will be the culmination of a long process of denial.

member cannot be with the client. Make sure that your client does not leave your office without support to help him or her through the first few days. Don't ever give an HIV-positive result on a Friday because there are often no support systems available over weekends.

### Follow-up visits

When people hear that they are HIV positive, they usually experience so much stress that they absorb very little information. Follow-up visits are therefore necessary to give clients the opportunity to ask questions, talk about their fears and the various problems they encounter. Significant others, such as a lover, spouse or other members of the family, may be included in the session. During follow-up visits, clients should be offered a choice concerning their treatment.

If health care professionals are not in a position to do follow-up counselling, information about relevant health services should be given. If there is a concern that the person might not return for follow-up counselling, information about available medical treatments such as anti-retroviral therapy, treatment of opportunistic infections, and social services for financial and ongoing emotional support should be given. Give the client a handout with whatever relevant information he or she may need (such as the telephone numbers and addresses of AIDS centres and other social services).

Create a user-friendly pamphlet or booklet for HIV/AIDS counsellors to use as a handout after post-HIV test counselling. The pamphlet should include information for people who test HIV negative as well as HIV positive. Include information (names, telephone numbers and addresses) of available resources, support services and AIDS centres. Please note that a handout should never take the place of personal pre- and post-HIV test counselling!

## Support systems

Find out what support systems are available to clients. Refer them to support systems where people meet on a regular basis to talk about their difficulties or simply to relax and enjoy each other's company. Information about support systems such as the buddy system is usually available at the nearest AIDS centre or from the offices of NGOs (non-governmental organisations) who work in the community.

## Advice about health and sexuality

HIV-infected individuals may live a relatively healthy life for many years. It is therefore important to convey information about safer sex, infection control and health care in general. It is very important to advise HIV-infected individuals to change their sexual behaviour — not only to protect their sex partners, but also to protect themselves against re-infection with other strains of the virus. (For a detailed discussion, see 'The promotion of health and the strengthening of the immune system' on page 366.)

## Medical check-ups

Encourage clients to go to their family doctor or health clinic for regular medical check-ups. Infections and opportunistic diseases can be prevented if they are treated in time.

If you really want to know what your clients are going through while waiting for their HIV test results, go for testing yourself. Make notes of your feelings and emotions while going through the process and ask yourself the following questions: Was the pre- and post-test counselling properly done? How did it make you feel? How would you do the counselling differently? How did you feel while waiting for the results? What did you do while waiting? Who did you tell? Who supported you while you were waiting for the results? Will your own testing experience influence your counselling of a client? How?

### Counselling after an inconclusive HIV test result

If a test result is inconclusive, the counsellor must explain to the client what such a test result means. It means that the result is ambiguous or indeterminate, and it is not possible at that stage to say if a person is HIV positive or not. The test result may be inconclusive because the test is cross-reacting with a non-HIV protein or because there has been insufficient time for full sero-conversion to occur after exposure to HIV.

When a test result is inconclusive, other methods may be used to try to achieve a reliable result. The test can also be repeated after 2 weeks. If it is still inconclusive, it should be repeated at 3, 6 and 12 months. If it is still inconclusive after 1 year, it should be accepted that the person is not infected with HIV.

Waiting for further tests to be done after inconclusive results can induce acute and severe psychological effects in people. Clients should be supported while waiting for the results. They should also be encouraged to use safer sex practices while waiting.

## 11.3 CONCLUSION

An HIV-positive test result makes a tremendous and irreversible impact on a person's life. Important decisions and changes have to be made by the client and his or her loved ones to live within the constraints that are imposed by the presence of the virus. The counsellor must therefore undertake the very important task of helping the client to live a healthy and happy life after diagnosis. Chapter 12 discusses the specific counselling needs of HIV-infected individuals and their affected loved ones.

Activity

- Ask a friend to role play a post-HIV test counselling session with you. Counsel the friend on the results of his or her HIV test if the test result is positive. Remember that role play can be very draining and disturbing and that it is always necessary to debrief afterwards. Say to your friend: 'Thank you Peter for doing the role play with me. Fortunately this was only a make-believe situation. I am not really a counsellor and you are not my client.'
- Ask a friend to play the role of a sex worker who tested HIV negative. Counsel her on the results of her HIV test.
- You are a social worker working in an AIDS unit established by the Department of Social Services. You have a very heavy daily case load. Some mornings when you arrive at your office, 30 people are already waiting — either to be tested or to get their results. You feel dispirited because it is almost impossible to do proper pre- and post-test counselling if you don't have time to do them. Organise a workshop with colleagues who experience the same problem and try to find solutions for this problem.
- What do you do if a client does not want pre-test counselling before taking an HIV test?

# Counselling the Infected and Affected

················································

*Listening to the fear*

*And then the listening women saw the fear
embedded deep in the words of the men.
Hidden among the reeds,
below the smooth surface of the water.*

················································

'AIDS is the stuff of all our nightmares, triggering many of our deepest fears' (Watts, 1988). These words — spoken by an HIV-infected client — aptly express why AIDS is different from any other life-threatening disease. The diagnosis of HIV infection or AIDS evokes severe emotional reactions — not only in the *infected* person, but also in his or her *affected* significant others. The counsellor can only help those who are infected and affected by HIV/AIDS to *live beyond* the diagnosis if he or she has an understanding of what the infected person and his or her loved ones are going through. But it is also important for the counsellor to realise that to be an HIV/AIDS counsellor is to be an *affected other oneself*. The counsellor should therefore also be aware of his or her own feelings and work through them if he or she wants to be able to counsel effectively.

## 12.1 THE EXPERIENCES OF AN HIV-INFECTED INDIVIDUAL

The following case study describes the psychosocial experiences of a person with AIDS after he was diagnosed with the illness in 1986 (Palermino, 1988, p. 63):

 ·····················································

*One person's experience of AIDS*

My doctor gave me the news. My first reaction was one of relief. The years of uncertainty had ended. The myriad of symptoms could all be explained. No more worries about if I would develop AIDS. I now had it.

The next day, I lay in bed exhausted and began to realise the full meaning of the diagnosis. What may lie ahead? I had moments of denying it was really happening; I wanted to believe I would be well in a few days. I phoned my supervisor at work and told her I would be back in two days. I only briefly wondered if there had been some mistake. Maybe I had been misdiagnosed. My mind was racing. I could not concentrate on anything for more than a few seconds. Ninety percent of my thoughts were death-related or reflections on what life choices I had made. Mistakes, broken dreams . . . What would my funeral be like? My obituaries? What infection would finally kill me?

Suffering and grief were what I felt. Imagine losing your job, your love relationship, your home, and all of your friends. On top of that you feel you have no future, you will not feel the wind against your skin, or watch snow fall. You will not hear music or go sailing with friends. And you will not love or be loved.

I had crossed the line. The line between the living and the dead. I feared being alone and yet needed to be alone. In my 20s I grew to believe in God, or my higher power, as I prefer to call him. Had he betrayed me? I felt ripped off. Yet I also had a sense of universal truths, of my own connection with all that I feared losing. And I do believe that on some level I have always been a part of this world and always will be.

Through the first week, my biggest concern was telling my parents. They are both in their 70s. One cannot know for sure the reactions of friends and loved ones. I didn't expect it, but my oldest brother Paul has become one of my main sources of support since my diagnosis. One friend sent a card with the following note: 'I know there is nothing I can say or do to change your diagnosis. My heart is with you. I love you. If you need anything, call. I am here for you if and when you're ready. Take things slowly, be gentle with yourself, meditate, scream, cry, laugh. Be yourself.' In the height of the crisis of being diagnosed her words were of great comfort.

The early weeks of my diagnosis were the most challenging so far. The week after I was diagnosed with Pneumocystis, the doctor found a Kaposi's sarcoma lesion in my mouth. I was afraid to see my doctor. What else might he find? I was terrified I would die if he did not keep a close watch, and yet I feared he would continue to find other infections. He and his staff were excellent when I needed them the most. He is a model doctor because when I need things explained, he always takes the time to do so. One day his office staff needed to take several tubes of blood. One drew blood while another massaged my belly. A personal touch is so important when you are being assaulted by so many needles and so much machinery.

Second to facing death, I believe financial concerns are the major issue for most people with AIDS. The bureaucracy and intricacies of disability and medical coverage are astounding and infuriating. Loss of career status has also been a difficult transition.

I have experienced varying periods of depression, grandiosity, rage, and gratefulness. I had thoughts of suicide several times during the first weeks. Looking back, I see it as an attempt to control what was happening to me.

If I am going to die, I want to say when and how. I had seen all the horrible possibilities of the disease and wondered what would befall me. I started to bargain: I can accept weight loss and chills, but not fevers. Skin lesions? Yes, but not constant vomiting or diarrhoea. And I was most terrified about going insane due to neurological infections.

One friend who had been diagnosed the year before told me: 'Things will fall into place, it gets easier.' He was right. Eight months have passed since my diagnosis. I continue to experience the roller coaster effects of having a life-threatening illness, but the peaks and valleys are less dramatic. For now my health is relatively good and I can go on with living. I have grown to accept what I can and cannot do each day, to enjoy that which I can do and appreciate the mere fact that I am alive today. I try to do something joyous every day.

. . . . . . . . . . . . . . . . . . . . . . . . . . . . . . . . . . . . . . . . . . . . . . . . . . . . . . . . . . . . . . . . . .

**Activity**

Read the above case study and answer the following questions:
- List the psychosocial experiences, feelings and concerns that the client had.
- What were the client's concerns about his significant others?
- What positive experiences or feelings did the client have after his diagnosis?

The above case study shows that HIV-infected people often experience the following psychosocial, spiritual and socioeconomic experiences and needs:

## Fear

HIV-infected people have many fears. They are particularly fearful about being isolated, stigmatised and rejected. They fear the uncertainty of the future: will there be pain or disfigurement, and who will look after them? They are afraid of dying — and particularly of dying alone and in pain. Many HIV-infected people have experienced the pain and death of loved ones and friends who have already died of AIDS and they know and fear what awaits them. Fear may also be caused by not knowing enough about what is involved in HIV infections and how the problems can be handled.

## Loss

HIV-infected people often feel that they have lost everything that is most important and beautiful to them. They experience loss of control, loss of autonomy, loss of their ambitions, their physical attractiveness, sexual relationships, status and respect in the community, financial stability and independence. They fear the loss of their ability to care for themselves and their families and they fear the loss of their jobs, their friends and family. They mourn the loss of life itself. HIV-infected people also feel that they have lost their privacy and their control over their lives once they begin to need constant care. But perhaps the most commonly experienced loss is the loss of confidence and self-worth occasioned by the rejection of people who are important to them — people who were once friends but who now reject them because of the physical impact of HIV-related diseases that cause, for example, facial disfigurement, physical wasting and loss of strength or bodily control.

## Grief

People with HIV infection often have profound feelings of grief about the losses they have experienced or are anticipating. They grieve for their friends who die from AIDS, and they grieve with and for their loved ones — those who must stay behind and try to cope with life without them.

## Guilt

Guilt and self-reproach for having contracted HIV and for having also possibly infected others are frequently expressed by HIV-infected individuals. They often feel guilty about the behaviour that may have caused the infection. Feelings of guilt may be associated with a person's unresolved conflicts about homosexuality or about sexuality in general. Having to tell family members and friends that one is HIV positive often means that one also has to tell them for the first time about one's sexual preferences or sexual behaviour. There is also guilt about the sadness that the illness will inflict on loved ones and families — especially children. Previous events that may have caused others pain or sadness but which still remain unresolved will often now be remembered and be the cause of even greater feelings of guilt and anguish.

## Denial

Most HIV-positive people go through a phase of *denial*. Denial is an important and protective defence mechanism because it temporarily reduces emotional stress. Clients should be allowed to cling to their denial if they are not yet ready to accept their diagnosis because denial often gives them a breathing space in which to rest and gather their strength. The counsellor should however confront this denial if it causes destructive behaviour such as refusing appropriate medical care or continued indulgence in unrestrained high-risk behaviour.

## Anger

HIV-infected people are often very angry with themselves and others, and this anger is sometimes directed at the people who are closest to them. They are angry because there is no cure for AIDS and because of the uncertainty of their future. They are often also angry with those who infected them and with society's reaction of hostility and indifference.

## Anxiety

The chronic uncertainty associated with the progress of HIV infection often aggravates feelings of anxiety. HIV-infected people often experience anxiety because of the prognosis of the illness, the risk of infection with other diseases, the risk of infecting loved ones with HIV, social, occupational, domestic, and sexual hostility and rejection, abandonment, isolation, and physical pain, fear of dying in pain or without dignity, inability to alter circumstances and consequences of HIV infection, uncertainty about how to keep as healthy as possible in the future, fears about the ability of loved ones and family to cope, worries about the availability (or unavailability) of appropriate medical treatment, a loss of privacy and concerns about confidentiality, future social and sexual unacceptability, their declining ability to function efficiently, and their loss of physical and financial independence. One can see the raw anxiety in this client's moving plea ('An open letter', 1988):

> A telephone call is not contagious and no one will die from visiting me occasionally. I'm not going to infect anyone if they hug me once in a while. I'm not asking for miracles, or approval, or sympathy. But this is only the beginning of the nightmare. What will happen when I get seriously ill? When I am in hospital, too weak to help myself, emaciated, fighting for life, and scared? I'm going to need friends. Please, don't let me die alone!

### Low self-esteem

The self-esteem of HIV-infected people is often severely threatened. Rejection by colleagues, friends and loved ones can cause one to lose confidence and a sense of one's social identity — and thus to experience reduced feelings of self-worth. The inability to continue in a career or to participate in social, sexual and loving relationships also diminishes the client's self-esteem. The physical consequences of HIV infection such as physical wasting and the loss of strength and bodily control contribute even more to a lowering of self-esteem.

### Depression

HIV-infected individuals often experience depression because they feel that they have lost so much in life — and that they themselves are to blame for it. The following factors all serve to increase depression: the absence of any cure and the resulting feeling of powerlessness, knowing others who have died of AIDS, the loss of personal control over their lives, self-blame and feelings of guilt. It is important for counsellors to recognise signs of depression and to refer their clients to a professional psychologist if necessary. (See 'Depression' on page 276 for a more complete discussion.)

### Suicidal behaviour or thinking

Inwardly directed anger may manifest as self-blame, self-destructive behaviour or (in its most intense form) suicidal impulses or intention. Suicide may be construed as a way of avoiding pain and discomfort, of lessening the shame and grief of loved ones, and of trying to obtain a measure of control over one's illness. Suicide may be either *active* (deliberate self-injury resulting in death) or *passive* (concealing or disregarding the onset of the possibly fatal complications of HIV infection or disease). The counsellor should be aware of the fact that there is a significantly higher risk of suicide among HIV-infected individuals. (See 'Suicide' on page 278 for a more complete discussion.)

## Obsessive conditions and hypochondria

Some HIV-infected individuals become so preoccupied with their health that even the smallest physical changes or sensations can cause obsessive behaviour or hypochondria. This may be temporary and limited to the time immediately after diagnosis, or it may persist in people who find it difficult to adjust to or accept the disease.

## Spiritual concerns

HIV-infected people who are confronted with death, loneliness, and loss of control often ask questions about spiritual matters in their search for religious support. They may want to discuss the concepts of sin, guilt, forgiveness, reconciliation, and acceptance. (See 'Spiritual and emotional counselling' on page 310.)

## Socioeconomical issues

Socioeconomical and environmental problems, such as loss of an occupation and income, discrimination, social stigma (if the client's diagnosis becomes commonly known), relationship changes, and changing requirements for sexual expression, may contribute to psychosocial problems after the diagnosis of HIV infection. Because many HIV-infected people also have to cope with financial problems, they often cannot afford to *buy* the anti-retroviral therapy that might give them a longer lease on life.

The client's perception of the level and adequacy of social support is also a very important factor because it may become a source of pressure or frustration when it is most needed.

## 12.2 THE IMPACT OF HIV INFECTION ON AFFECTED SIGNIFICANT OTHERS

The significant others in an infected person's life play an important role in the person's physical and psychological care. But these people often themselves need help to come to terms with (1) their own fears and prejudices and (2) the implications and consequences of their loved one's sickness and ultimate death. The counsellor can play a tremendous role in counselling the lovers, friends and family of the HIV-infected person in the practicalities of physical and emotional care.

Counsellors should be open-minded about what might constitute a 'family' in these circumstances. 'Family members' may include families of choice (lovers and friends — especially when the infected person is either gay or lesbian) as well as families that are related by birth or marriage. Sometimes the 'real' family of an infected person will reject him or her completely. In such circumstances it is often only the family of choice (the lover and friends) who will care for the loved one until the end (and beyond). It is important for the counsellor to respect these extra-legal relationships.

Affected significant others experience more or less the same psychosocial feelings as do their HIV-positive loved ones — the same feelings of depression, loneliness, fear, uncertainty, anxiety, anger, emotional numbness and, at times, hope. The impact of HIV infection on affected others can be summarised as follows (Johnson in Van Dyk et al., 2000, p. 12):

- Affected others often experience fear and anxiety about their own risk of infection as a function of their relationship with the HIV-positive person. They scrutinise the relationship or contact for possible risk situations in the past and this places a huge strain on the relationship.

- Affected others (especially the partner of the HIV-infected person) are often furious with the infected person for 'bringing this onto them'.

- Affected others begin to anticipate the loss of the HIV-positive person and issues of loss, bereavement and uncertainty are introduced into the relationship at a time when this may not be appropriate.

- Affected others, especially if they are very close to the infected person, often feel unable to cope with the new demands that the infection places on them. They feel incompetent, unqualified and powerless in their interaction with the HIV-positive significant other. These feelings contribute to a need to distance themselves from the disease process as well as the person. '*Denial* of the illness becomes a negation of the person, accounting for much of the isolation experienced by the HIV-positive person' (Johnson in Van Dyk et al., 2000, p. 12).

- The HIV-positive status of a significant other sadly often acquires a certain *relational currency*. This means that friends, relatives and colleagues tend to 'use' the infected person's sero-positive status as an issue in their ongoing relationships with each other. Old scores are settled, new ones are initiated, and relationships are redefined around the issue of the HIV-positive person's illness. Interactions often take place around — rather than *with* — the HIV-infected person.

- Disclosure of a loved one's sero-positive status is always a shock, and no two people react in the same way to the news. Affected others' responses can range from involvement, caring and support on the one hand, to abandonment, indifference, and antagonism on the other. Sadly, HIV-infected people are often rejected by their significant others because of the stigma that still surrounds this disease in many societies — including our own.

- Affected others suffer in many ways as a result of untimely deaths. People who die of AIDS are usually young (between 20 and 35 years old), and this leads to the 'unnatural' situation where parents outlive their children. Grandparents who are preparing themselves for a quiet and contented old age now often find themselves forced to nurse and care for sick and dying children as well as grandchildren.

- Children suffer tremendously when their parents are infected, and the needs of children with infected parents are often neglected. There is no tradition of talking to children as equals and on an intimate basis in many African societies, and caregivers often report seeing 'the suffering of children, who are too often hovering in the shadows of a sick room, seeing and hearing everything but never addressed directly' (UNAIDS, 2000a, p. 33). Children are largely excluded from the counselling process in Africa because (among other reasons) caregivers often simply do not know how to talk to children.

- Significant others often have to fulfil a role for which they are not trained, namely that of *caregiver*. They have to look after seriously ill loved ones. This can be an arduous, disconcerting and all-consuming task that utterly drains all the caregiver's physical, emotional and (often) financial resources. If there are unresolved relationship issues in such circumstances, they can quickly become acutely aggravated.

- Neurological complications and deterioration in mental functioning in the client can be extremely disturbing to significant others. They may feel that they are already losing their loved ones and this can precipitate an early grieving process.

- The *needs* of affected significant others are similar to those experienced by the HIV-infected person. These needs are acceptance, respect, certainty, affiliation, support, love and caring.

## 12.3 HELPING THE INFECTED PERSON AND AFFECTED SIGNIFICANT OTHERS

The main function of the HIV/AIDS counsellor is to be supportive of his of her infected and affected clients, to listen to their problems and to empower them to solve their problems and better their lives.

## Support and empowerment

Counsellors must allow their clients to verbalise their fear, anxiety, anger, sorrow, guilt or shame because this will give counsellors the opportunity to identify possible problem areas that will need to be addressed and processed (Carbello, 1988; Miller, 1988; Miller & Bor, 1988).

Counsellors must empower HIV-infected people to make decisions for themselves. They should in fact be encouraged to continue to make decisions for as long as possible. The individual's control over everyday life situations should be reinforced, facilitated and encouraged. Counsellors should assure their clients that they can still be productive in economic, intellectual and social spheres for many years. Clients should therefore be encouraged to go back to their work and resume normal lives as quickly as possible. The contentions that infected people are unemployable, that they should not be given educational opportunities and that they should not be allowed to remain socially active could very well cause the collapse of a whole society because treating all HIV-infected people as passive invalids (when they can still make a useful and active contribution) would place intolerable and unsustainable economic, medical and psychological burdens on the community.

What follows below are various practical suggestions about how counsellors might support people living with HIV infection (Miller & Bor, 1988):

- Compile, with each client, a list of their problems (their current scenario), and let them reflect on what they want (their preferred scenario).
- Assist the client to identify possible solutions to these problems. Encourage clients to come up with their own solutions because clients will be more likely to implement solutions that they find feasible and practical.
- Ask the client to make a list of his or her good qualities and possible limitations. He or she should, for instance, list his or her coping skills, describe the level of his or her self-esteem, analyse his or her personality style, communication style, sense of humour — and any other strengths and weaknesses that may be important.
- Examine and discuss possible solutions to whatever problems the client may have identified. Assess each solution in terms of the client's actual capabilities and capacity. Refrain from giving advice and suggesting solutions.
- Ask the client to write down the answer to the following question: 'Why must I go on living?' Once this has been done, encourage him or her to work towards those goals and to make new and longer-term goals along the way. Clients should set goals that will give them a sense of purpose and pride (goals such as 'I want to see my children growing up').
- Identify the ways in which clients have dealt successfully with their problems in the past and help them (if necessary) to develop new coping skills.

- Empower clients to make their own decisions and to take control over their lives wherever and whenever possible.
- Make a note of any relationship problems between the client and his or her loved ones, friends and family, and other health providers.
- Encourage the client to call on peer support (buddy systems) or self-help groups. The counsellor may also be able to put clients in touch with each other on an individual basis. This should however not happen without the discretion of the counsellor and the consent of the individuals involved.

## Peer support (buddy system)

Peer support (buddy systems) or self-help groups are part of a growing network of non-governmental AIDS service organisations which provide personal care and peer-based psychosocial support for HIV-infected people and their affected significant others. Clients should be encouraged to become involved in these groups or to form their own groups if none exist in their communities. The following issues are usually dealt with in peer support groups (WHO, 1990b, pp. 32–33):

- Learning to live with HIV infection. Many of the people involved in the peer support group may have considerable experience of the implications of living with HIV. They can describe the medical and psychological problems they have experienced and the interventions they found most useful.
- Helping caregivers and loved ones to handle the pressure of living with sick or distressed people on a daily basis. Practical advice about the management of health problems (such as bleeding, vomiting, incontinence and the disposal of dressings) can be exchanged.
- Reducing stress and avoiding conflict. Buddies can exchange practical advice on how to overcome anxiety, depression and other psychological problems that can cause stress and conflict.
- Deciding how best to talk about HIV/AIDS to loved ones, friends and colleagues. Disclosing a diagnosis of HIV can be particularly stressful, and buddies can share ideas on what to say, to whom, when and how.
- Dealing with feelings of loneliness, depression, powerlessness and suicide. The peer support group can provide help and mutual support. Advice from people who have actually experienced those feelings personally and who have coped with them successfully is more valuable than theoretical information.
- Advice about sexual relations and the implications of safer sex behaviour. Peer support groups can discuss all aspects of these problems and opportunities and give each other good advice about safer sex practices. Peer commitment to safer sex also helps to make these practices socially acceptable, attractive and sustainable.

## Medical management

Counselling is often influenced by the infected and affected person's experiences with other forms of health care related to the HIV infection. Clients and their families often feel that medical management of their illness has been insensitive or handled without sufficient regard for privacy. In cases like these, it is the task of the counsellor to persuade the client to comply with recommended treatment programmes.

It is often the task of the counsellor to help the client to gain access to appropriate medical care and to participate in the decision-making process about treatment. If any special needs arise, such as evidence of neurological disease or dementia, the counsellor should be prepared to communicate with and counsel the family, loved ones and caregivers on the day-to-day management of the client (see 'Alteration of mental status: confusion and dementia' on page 394). The counsellor should also be able to coordinate a range of health and social services when needed. Many people with HIV infection also seek care from traditional or complementary healers, and the counsellor should encourage their clients to talk about these services and to incorporate them into their health care plan.

Enrichment

**How medical and psychological symptoms may affect the counselling process**

The medical and psychological symptoms of HIV and AIDS can often affect the counselling process in a number of ways (Johnson, 2000):
• The symptoms of opportunistic infections and the side effects of medication may increase levels of pain and discomfort to such an extent that the continuity and progress of the counselling process may be adversely affected.
• In advanced stages of AIDS, cognitive disorders like dementia may develop. Dementia may make it difficult or impossible for the client to participate in counselling.
• Psychological symptoms such as feelings of hopelessness, anger, suspicion, depression and isolation may negatively influence the client's attitude to counselling.
• Frequent hospitalisation may disrupt counselling.

## The ecological or systems approach in counselling

No one lives in a vacuum. An individual's sero-positive status has a tremendous influence on the systems in which he or she exists, and the infected person is simultaneously affected by these systems. The response of the affected others should therefore be seen by the counsellor as part of a relational process between the infected client and the affected significant others. This *relationship*, rather than the individual person, should become the focus of the counselling process (Johnson, 2000).

The *ecological* or *systems* approach is often used by counsellors to improve observation, communication skills and the relationships within the system (e.g. the family). Techniques used may include the following (Okun, 1997; Sue, Sue & Sue, 2000):

- Rearranging the system by *reframing* the problem from a systems perspective (when, for example, the family is using the infected person's HIV status to defer the resolution of other underlying problems in the family)
- Teaching verbal and non-verbal communication and problem-solving skills by providing feedback, new information and coaching (e.g. family members are trained to attend, to listen and to show empathy, and they are given opportunities to practise problem-solving skills)
- Assigning direct and indirect behavioural tasks to different family members so that they can help to enhance the functioning of the family system
- Providing the family with the guidance, support and practical information they need to help each other (e.g. by providing information about how to handle the infection in the family or cope with a family member who is depressed)
- Using bibliotherapy. This means giving reading material that teaches family members how to think positively and to overcome negative thinking.

According to Egan (1998), the same counselling principles that apply to individual counselling (see chapter 10) also apply to the family or systems approach. The only difference is that the *family* becomes the client. The counsellor should help the family to identify their problems, concerns and issues about the virus in their system (*the current scenario*), to verbalise what they as a family want or need within the limits imposed by the virus (*the preferred scenario*), to identify what they as a family need to do (*strategies*), and to implement strategies that will improve communication within the family and so enable them to live more effectively with the problems created by the virus (*action*).

Counsellors must have enough self-knowledge to know when they are not able to help clients because of inadequate training in family therapy or because the problems being experienced by families are too serious (i.e. beyond the helping capacity of the counsellor). In such cases, HIV/AIDS counsellors should never hesitate to refer clients for appropriate help. (Readers interested in family therapy may find the following source helpful: Goldenberg, I. & Goldenberg, H. (1985). *Family therapy: an overview* (2nd ed.). Belmont: Wadsworth.)

## Counselling HIV-infected and -affected children

Children are affected by HIV/AIDS in different ways. They may be infected with HIV themselves, they may have one or two parents who are HIV-infected or they may be orphaned because of the AIDS-related deaths of their parents. The counsellor should keep the following points in mind when he or she counsels children (Johnson, 2000; Wong et al., 1999, pp. 209–211):

- Parental or custodian consent should always be obtained before counselling children.
- Use the same phases of the counselling process as you do with adults (see 'Phases in the counselling process' on page 205) but take special care to make sure that the child *understands* what you are saying.
- Use the child's language, but never 'talk down' to the child. To adopt the child's language is a vital source of understanding and it communicates empathy and acceptance. Assume a position that is at eye level with the child, speak clearly in a quiet, unhurried and confident voice, be specific, and use simple words and short sentences — especially with younger children.
- Be honest with children and allow them to express their concerns and fears.
- Children are very alert to non-verbal messages and they attach meaning to every gesture and move that is made. Children will *sense* your personal feelings, attitudes, and anxieties. Make sure that your non-verbal messages are consistent with your spoken words (or else the child will pick up the discrepancy).
- Keep the *child's* understanding of death and dying in mind when counselling children. (See 'Children and bereavement' on page 308.)
- Keep a child's age and developmental phase in mind when counselling him or her. (See enrichment box 'The child in counselling' on page 267.)
- Clarify the counselling process and your role in relationship to the child. Explain the reason, aim, and method of counselling.
- Provide a considerate counselling context and use a few age-appropriate props rather than an overwhelming 'toyshop atmosphere'.
- Allow children time to feel comfortable and develop the relationship in a patient, caring manner. Avoid sudden or rapid advances, broad smiles, extended eye contact or other gestures that may be construed as threatening. Talk to the parent if a young child is initially shy, or communicate through objects such as dolls, puppets or stuffed animals before questioning a young child directly. Give older children the opportunity to talk without the parents being present.
- Be patient and revisit topics if necessary. Reflect the child's feelings and confirm your understandings with the child.
- Do not be discouraged by apparent inattentiveness when you talk about sensitive issues. This is often a child's way of coping with stressful issues.
- Use a variety of communication skills (see enrichment box 'Creative ways to communicate with children' on page 268).
- Be sensitive to ethical issues (obtain parental consent, maintain confidentiality, clarify liaison with other professionals with the parents as well as with the child, and avoid potentially ambiguous situations).

**Enrichment**

## The child in counselling

The counsellor should keep the child's age and developmental phase in mind when counselling him or her.

- Because children under 5 years are egocentric (in developmental terms), they see things only in relation to themselves. Counsellors should therefore focus communication on them. Young children think concretely and interpret words directly. Counsellors should therefore avoid phrases which might be misinterpreted by a small child. Small children will, for instance, take your explanation of an injection as a 'little stick in the arm' literally to mean — a stick or branch in their arm.

- Younger school-age children want a reason and explanation for everything that the counsellor does, but they want no verification beyond that. School-age children are very concerned about bodily integrity and they are often worried that something may harm or injure them (or their possessions). The counsellor should help children to voice their concerns and should introduce activities to reduce their anxiety.

- Because adolescents often fluctuate between child-like and adult thinking and behaviour, they often tend to seek the security of the more familiar and comfortable expectations of childhood when they become anxious. The counsellor should anticipate these shifts in identity and adjust the course of interaction to meet the needs of the moment. In their communication with adolescents, counsellors should be supportive, attentive and try not to interrupt or to ask prying and embarrassing questions. They should also avoid comments or expressions that convey surprise or disapproval. Resist any impulse to give advice, and listen very carefully to everything the adolescent says. Confidentiality is of great importance when interviewing adolescents. Explain to parents and adolescents the limits of confidentiality — specifically the fact that the young person's disclosures will not be shared unless they indicate a need for intervention (as in the case of suicidal behaviour).

- Do not blame or discredit *any* of the adults in the child's world. Although these relationships may be painful to the child, adults are and remain significant people in the child's life.

- Do not enter into alliances with other people in the counselling process. Remain neutral.

- Be sensitive to the potentially 'abusive' aspects of counselling children. (You are an adult in a position of authority, and the child has limited say in what happens.)

- Avoid mindless, extended therapy. Focus on the presenting problem, and *work*. Children should not remain in counselling any longer than is necessary. Be aware of the fact that children often feel that being in counselling means that there is something wrong with them.

- Be sensitive to cultural issues in counselling children. Be prepared to learn from children from other cultures.

## Creative ways to communicate with children

- **Storytelling:** Ask children to tell a story about an event (e.g. being in hospital). Show them a picture and ask them to tell a story. Cut out comic strips, remove the words and ask children to add words to the pictures.
- **Mutual storytelling:** Ask the child to tell a story. Tell your own story. Base it on the child's story but change the negative events of the child's story to a positive outcome in your story.
- **Bibliotherapy:** Give the child a book to read (or read it to the child) and explore the meaning of the book with the child. Ask the child to retell the story, to draw a picture based on the story, to talk about the characters, or to summarise the moral or meaning of the story.
- **Dreams:** Ask the child to talk about a dream or nightmare, and explore the meaning that the dream might have with the child. Dreams often reveal unconscious and repressed thoughts and feelings.
- **'What if' questions:** Encourage children to explore potential situations and to consider different problem-solving options by asking 'what if . . .' questions. Children's responses indicate what they already know, what they don't know, what they are curious about, and this gives them the opportunity to practise coping skills.
- **Three wishes:** Ask the child: 'If you could have any three things in the world, what would they be?'
- **Rating game:** Use some type of rating scale (sad and happy faces, or numbers) to rate the child's feelings about an event.
- **Word association game:** Recite certain key words, and ask children to say the first word that comes into their minds when they hear this key word.
- **Sentence completion:** Present a partial statement and ask the child to finish it. For example: 'The thing in the world I like best is . . .'
- **Pros and cons:** Select a topic and ask the child to list five good things and five bad things about it. According to Wong et al. (1999), it is a very useful technique to use when focusing on relationships because it enables people to list things they like and dislike about each other.
- **Non-verbal techniques:** You may suggest to older children (and adults) that they keep a journal or diary. Ask them to write letters that are never posted, to draw and to play.

(Based on Wong et al., 1999, pp. 212–213)

## Ethical concerns in counselling

Keep the following ethical concerns in mind when counselling HIV-positive clients (Johnson, 2000, p. 17):

- It is preferable not to make notes during counselling sessions. If the counsellor prefers to make notes, he or she should do this discreetly and with the consent of the client.
- As was pointed out in chapter 10, confidentiality is non-negotiable.

- Referrals, reports and liaison with other people who are involved should be dealt with in a transparent manner.
- Avoid being drawn into alliances with specific individuals or factions.
- Never disqualify other counsellors or professionals or agencies.
- Guard against stereotyping.
- To be an HIV/AIDS counsellor is to be an activist (whether you like it or not). HIV-positive people still experience a lot of rejection and discrimination in society, and it is often necessary for the counsellor to assume the role of an activist in fighting such problems in society.
- Find a competent supervisor for your counselling activities. Such supervision will ensure that you are on the right track. Proper supervision will also be a source of new ideas for you and it will prevent burnout.

## Referral skills

It is sometimes necessary to refer clients to another professional for specialised help. Referral should be done with great sensitivity towards the client. A special relationship usually develops between the counsellor and the client, and HIV-infected people who are confronted by many losses may experience the referral as a termination of the counselling relationship — in other words, just another loss that has to be coped with. The client may also experience the referral as a rejection.

Referral should never be seen as 'passing the buck'. Rather than terminating the counselling relationship by referring the client, referral should involve the co-opting of *additional* helpers into the counselling process (Johnson, 2000, p. 18). If, for instance, the client has specific spiritual needs in counselling, a spiritual counsellor or minister can be co-opted into the counselling process. According to Johnson, the 'family of caring professionals is thus extended, rather than having the client migrate from one counsellor to another'.

The different counsellors involved in a client's care should define their separate involvements so as to prevent duplication or contradiction of the counselling activities.

## 12.4 SPECIFIC THEMES IN HIV/AIDS COUNSELLING

HIV/AIDS brings very specific and unique themes out into the open, and counsellors should spend time exploring these issues with their clients. The following prominent themes tend to emerge repeatedly in HIV/AIDS counselling (Johnson, 2000):

- uncertainty about the progress of the disease, especially as current treatment options lengthen life expectancy
- relationship problems with significant others
- issues surrounding the disclosure of HIV-positive status

- dealing with the fear, stigma and stereotypes associated with HIV infection
- career and financial concerns
- sexual relationships
- stress and anxiety
- depression and suicidal thinking
- spiritual and existential matters
- issues about death and dying

Some of these themes are discussed in other parts of the book. We will however deal in more detail in this chapter with disclosure, fear, stigma and stereotypes, stress, anxiety, depression, suicide, and crisis intervention.

### Disclosure of HIV-positive status

Whether or not to disclose their HIV-positive status is a difficult decision for HIV-infected individuals to make because disclosure (or non-disclosure) is often followed by major and life-changing consequences. Counsellors should help their clients carefully to consider the benefits as well as the negative consequences disclosure may have for them as individuals. Because disclosure is a very personal and individual decision, all relevant personal circumstances should be taken into account. Clients should also decide if they want *full disclosure* (i.e. publicly revealing their HIV status) or *partial disclosure* (i.e. telling only certain people, such as a spouse, relative or friend). Disclosure can be accompanied by the following benefits (Southern African AIDS Training [SAT] Programme, 2000):

- Disclosure can help people to accept their HIV-positive status and reduce the stress of coping on their own.
- Disclosure can help a person to access the medical services, care and support that they need.
- Disclosure can help people to protect themselves and others. Openness about their HIV-positive status may help women to negotiate safer sex practices.
- Disclosure may help to reduce the stigma, discrimination and denial that surround HIV/AIDS.
- Disclosure promotes responsibility. It may encourage the person's loved ones to plan for the future.

Disclosure can also be accompanied by negative consequences such as problems in relationships (e.g. with sexual partners, family, friends, community members, employer or colleagues), rejection, and the conviction that people are constantly judging one. The following case studies illustrate the various kinds of experiences that people had after disclosing their HIV-positive status.

*Case studies on disclosure*

**Testimony 1 — Disclosure and a new lease of life:** 'I was tested unknowingly in 1988 and the result was disclosed in the ward where everybody heard. I was shocked and felt humiliated. When I got home, I only told my husband. I hoped he would support me but he accused me and after a short while he abandoned me. I suffered alone for the next five years without telling anybody. I wasted away because there was nobody to advise me on what to do. I did not tell my parents and sisters about my HIV status because they were very negative on the issue of HIV. The miraculous change came in 1993 when I got my first counselling at The Centre in Harare. It was like I started living again. I stopped mourning for myself and started getting confident. I now knew the right foods to eat and how to avoid stress. I became a happy person and started gaining back my weight. I was introduced to other people living with HIV and AIDS and started feeling comfortable talking about the illness.' (SAT Programme, 2000, p. 5.)

**Testimony 2 — Fear, love and support:** 'I tested HIV-positive in July 1990. What made me disclose? I believe it was fear. Fear of illness. Fear of the unknown. I felt so alone and needed to talk to someone. I just could not handle it on my own. Love and support from everyone around me made it easier. Their acceptance gave me strength and courage to keep telling more people. I wouldn't have told so many if the first people had rejected me. If I had to do it again, I wouldn't do it differently. My friends have always given me support, so I guess I'd still tell them first.' (SAT Programme, 2000, p. 3.)

**Testimony 3 — Life needs courage:** 'I decided to come out publicly because a lot of Swazis are dying and they think HIV is a problem in other countries but not ours. I have had problems with my wife's family. They accuse me of being unfeeling and insensitive — to them it was humiliating that everyone knows my status. But my wife stood by me and we are still together. In the long run I feel good about my choice. Just talking about my situation has helped a lot of HIV-positive people and their relatives. My advice is to remember that life needs courage.' (SAT Programme, 2000, p. 7.)

Clients should think through all the pros and cons very carefully and plan ahead before they disclose their HIV-positive status. The counsellor can support the client by using the following guidelines (SAT Programme, 2000, pp. 6–7):

- Help the client to take time to think things through. 'Disclosure is a process, not an event.' Discuss the implications of disclosure fully so that the person has an opportunity to consider in advance what the reaction of family, friends, colleagues and others might be. Make sure it is what the client *wants* to do and assist him or her to plan how he or she is going to do it.

- Be practical. Help the client to develop a 'plan' for disclosure. Such plan will include preparations that need to be made before disclosure, who the client will inform first, how and where the disclosure will take place, and what the level of disclosure will be.
- Identify sources of support, such as groups for people living with HIV and AIDS, church members and counselling organisations.
- Role play to help the client prepare for disclosure.
- Provide support and reassurance to the client and help them to accept themselves.
- Prepare the client for a shocked and even hostile reaction from other people. Reassure clients that people close to them will probably learn to accept their HIV status over time.
- Help clients to realise that once a decision to disclose has been made, it may be easier to begin with those nearest to them: relatives, family, friends, or someone to whom they are very close and whom they trust.
- Assist the client to think about the likely response of the person to whom he or she has decided to disclose. Help the client to assess how much the person he or she plans to disclose to knows and understands about HIV and AIDS. This will help the client to decide what they need to tell the person and how to tell them. Such preparation will make disclosure less traumatic for both of them.
- It is important for a client to be strong enough to allow others to express their feelings and concerns after their disclosure. Assist the client to work on these issues over time.
- Provide the client with information and support to 'live positively' and give information on safer sex practices to protect sex partners.
- Counsellors should protect their clients against undue pressure to disclose.
- The counsellor should be willing to mediate the disclosure process if the need arises (e.g. if the client asks the counsellor to be present when he or she discloses his or her HIV-positive status).
- Disclosure can be particularly difficult for gay and lesbian people. They may find it difficult to discuss their sexuality with a support group of non-gays or non-lesbians — who may be prejudiced or who may simply not understand the issues involved. The counsellor should refer the client to support groups that are sensitive to the needs of gay and lesbian people (there are many non-governmental gay and lesbian organisations that focus on the needs of gay and lesbian people).

## Dealing with fear, stigma and stereotypes

Because HIV/AIDS continues to generate fear, misunderstanding, misinformation and discrimination, it is important that counsellors and other health care professionals do everything in their power to counter these negative attitudes. People infected and affected by HIV need society's support — and not rejection.

It is however only possible for health care professionals to become advocates for acceptance and care if they *look inward* and first examine their own beliefs, values, assumptions and attitudes towards HIV/AIDS. This can be done individually or in groups by asking the following questions (WHO, 2000a, p. 6-5):

- What fears or misunderstandings do I have?
- How might these fears or misunderstandings affect my work?
- Where do these fears or misunderstandings come from?
- How can I overcome these fears or misunderstandings in order to provide care, support, counselling, education, and advice in the prevention and care of HIV/AIDS?
- What influence do I have on others who care for people infected and affected by HIV/AIDS?
- What is my role in providing and promoting safe, moral and ethical care to people living with HIV and their significant others, caregivers and communities?

The irrational and often exaggerated fears associated with HIV/AIDS can be directly addressed through *educational programmes* based on sound medical, social and psychological knowledge. To be successful, such programmes must be sustained and supported over time. *Prevention* strategies will continue to be compromised if fear, ignorance, intolerance and discrimination against HIV-infected people persist. Health care professionals have a responsibility to help 'normalise' HIV in the communities where they work so that modes of transmission and prevention can be addressed without the emotional and attitudinal values which are currently hindering open dialogue.

Counsellors and other health care professionals should not only 'advocate for Universal Precautions, but also for universal tolerance and knowledge about HIV/AIDS' (WHO, 2000a, p. 6-4).

## Stress

All of us experience some stress and anxiety in our day-to-day encounters with stressful situations at work, financial concerns, family demands and social interactions. Moderate amounts of stress are usually not harmful, and can even be stimulating. Excessive stress however can be detrimental to one's health.

Researchers believe that many diseases are caused or aggravated by an interaction of social, psychological and biological factors. Chronic stress was, for example, found to create greater susceptibility to many diseases such as flu, dermatitis and the recurrence of herpes symptoms (Sue et al., 2000). Research also found that psychological factors such as stress, emotional inhibition (e.g. keeping the fact that you are gay a secret), a negative self-concept ('I am responsible for the bad things that happen to me'), and a lack of social support contributed to a more rapid progression from HIV infection to AIDS (Cole, Kemeny & Taylor, 1997). Self-efficacy and an ability to cope with stressors were, on the other hand, associated with a slower deterioration of the immune system in HIV-infected individuals. It was also found that psychological and social stressors, such as looking after a partner with dementia — especially without social support — as well as the loss of a partner (bereavement), weakened the immune system of the affected other significantly.

There are also indirect links between stress and immune depression. People who experience a lot of stress or who are depressed also tend to sleep less, eat less nutritiously, consume more alcohol, and give less attention to their physical care. All these factors can decrease immune functioning.

**Enrichment**

### Stress and the immune system

While stress itself does not cause infection or diseases directly, it may decrease the immune system's efficiency and thereby increase a person's susceptibility to disease. Stress produces physiological changes in the body. For example, part of the stress response involves the release of several neurohormones, such as corticosteroids and endorphins, which impair immune functioning. Endorphins, for instance, decrease the natural ability of killer-T cells to fight tumour development. A deficient immune system may further fail to detect invaders or to produce antibodies to protect the body against these invaders (Sue et al., 2000).

**Treatment** for stress can include medication for the physical symptoms of stress, stress management or facilitation of lifestyle changes to actively reduce stress. Relaxation training is an important component of stress management and clients should be taught the ability to relax the muscles of the body in any stressful situation. The relaxation technique is based on tensing and relaxing muscles. Clients are taught to contract (tense) and then relax specific muscle groups (e.g. first the hands, then the arms, the legs, etc) for several minutes at a time until they learn to monitor their own relaxation. Relaxation exercises can be combined with mental imagery which enables clients to imagine being in peaceful, beautiful and calm places.

Counsellors should also help people to change their lifestyles to prevent illness and to enhance the quality of their lives. Clients should, for instance, be encouraged to avoid or change stressful situations, establish priorities, postpone low-priority tasks without feeling guilty, take time out for themselves, engage in relaxing and enjoyable activities, exercise regularly, eat nutritious foods, share their lives and problems with friends, meditate or do whatever helps them to be relaxed (Sue et al., 2000; Van Dyk, 1999).

## Adjustment disorder

People often find it difficult to adjust to common life stressors such as the loss of a job, bereavement, divorce or separation. A person can be said to have an adjustment disorder if his or her response to a stressor is *maladaptive*: this means that the person experiences excessive distress and is unable to function as usual in his or her social, occupational, or academic life (Carson, Butcher & Mineka, 1998; Sue et al., 2000).

Adjustment disorders usually develop within 3 months after the stressful event and they usually disappear within 6 months. They are characterised by diverse symptoms such as anxiety, depression, a combination of anxiety and depression, and behavioural and/or emotional disturbances. Adjustment disorders are usually not very serious, and they usually decrease in severity or disappear when the stressor has subsided or when the individual learns to adapt to the stressor or to the new situation. Adjustment disorders can however become chronic and last for longer than 6 months in cases where the stressor is chronic (e.g. a medical condition such as HIV infection).

Bereavement often causes adjustment disorders. Complicated or prolonged bereavement is often found in situations where there has been an untimely or unexpected death — as is very often the case with AIDS-related deaths. People who feel resentment, hostility, or intense guilt towards the deceased also often experience extreme adjustment disorders (Carson et al., 1998).

## Acute stress disorder and post-traumatic stress disorder

Some people experience **acute stress disorder** after an HIV-positive diagnosis, or after the death of a significant other. An acute stress disorder is an anxiety disorder that develops in response to an extreme psychological or physical trauma. The overwhelming anxiety that the person usually experiences can seriously disrupt a person's social or occupational functioning (Sue et al., 2000).

Acute stress disorder is accompanied by the following symptoms (Carson et al., 1998; Sue et al., 2000):

- Severe feelings of anxiety and helplessness
- Feelings of dissociation, emotional unresponsiveness, numbness, and withdrawal from social contact
- Persistent reliving or re-experiencing of the traumatic event through intrusive, recurring thoughts, repetitive dreams about the event, illusions, and flashbacks
- Sleep disturbance, irritability, finding it difficult to concentrate or remember things, and restlessness
- Avoidance of interpersonal involvement and loss of sexual interest

A condition can be diagnosed as *an acute stress disorder* if the symptoms occur within 4 weeks of the traumatic event and last for a minimum of 2 days and a maximum of 4 weeks.

If the symptoms last for longer than 4 weeks, a diagnosis of **post-traumatic stress disorder** should be considered. While the symptoms of post-traumatic stress disorder are similar to those of acute stress disorder, they differ primarily in *onset* and *duration*. Post-traumatic stress disorder can occur at any time after the stressful event (acute stress disorder occurs within 4 weeks), and post-traumatic stress disorder always lasts for longer than 1 month (acute stress disorder lasts only from 2 to 28 days). If the symptoms of post-traumatic stress disorder begin within 6 months after the stressful event, the reaction is considered to be acute. If symptoms begin more than 6 months after the event, the reaction is considered to be delayed.

Not all people who experience a traumatic event develop acute or post-traumatic stress disorder. Factors such as the person's individual characteristics, his or her perception of the event, and the existence of support groups also influence whether an acute or a post-traumatic stress disorder will develop (Sue et al., 2000).

**Treatment** for anxiety symptoms often includes anti-anxiety medications, crisis-intervention approaches, debriefing, and cognitive behavioural approaches such as systematic desensitisation.

Systematic desensitisation relies on the principle that it is impossible to be both anxious and relaxed at the same time (Okun, 1997). Clients are first trained to relax (by tensing and then relaxing the muscles). If they are in a relaxed state, desensitisation follows by introducing the issue that usually arouses anxiety. Say, for example, that an HIV-positive person who has to visit the hospital frequently is absolutely terrified of hospitals. After teaching the client how to relax, the counsellor should introduce the anxiety-provoking (but not harmful) issues by starting with the least anxiety-provoking object or circumstance, and then work gradually up to the most anxiety-provoking stimuli. The counsellor could, for example, begin by showing the client a video of a hospital, then drive the client past the hospital in a car, then walk past the hospital with the client, then let him or her walk alone, then enter the hospital, and so on.

Debriefing sessions with peer support groups in which clients can express and release their anxious emotions are also beneficial in helping them cope with anxiety and stress. Discussion and support groups are very helpful in assisting clients in the adaptation process after a traumatic experience.

## Depression

While depression is a common problem in our society, it is frequently experienced by HIV-infected individuals. Anybody working in the HIV/AIDS field should at least be able to recognise the symptoms of major (or serious) depression and refer clients for treatment and therapy if they are not able to assist clients themselves.

The symptoms of depression may be categorised as follows (Sue et al., 2000):

- *Affective symptoms:* The most striking symptom of depression is a depressed mood characterised by feelings of sadness, unhappiness, worthlessness, anxiety, and apathy. Depressed clients often say that they have lost the joy of living.
- *Cognitive symptoms:* Clients report feelings of futility, emptiness and hopelessness. They often have profoundly pessimistic beliefs about the future; they find it difficult to cope with daily life because of a loss of motivation, interest and energy. Suicidal thoughts, guilt, negative thinking and concentration problems are also common among depressed people.
- *Behavioural symptoms:* Low energy levels are one of the most common behavioural symptoms of depression. Other symptoms include neglect of personal appearance (dirty clothing, unkempt hair, lack of personal hygiene), crying, agitation, social withdrawal, slow or reduced speech, and passivity. Depressed people often have dull, mask-like facial expressions. They move slowly and they do not initiate new activities. These symptoms are called *psychomotor retardation*. Although psychomotor retardation is common in people with depression, some depressed people (paradoxically) report states of agitation and restlessness.
- *Physiological symptoms:* Depressed clients often complain of a loss of appetite and weight (some clients however have an increased appetite and experience weight gains), sleep disturbance (difficulty in falling asleep, waking up early, waking up during the night, insomnia, nightmares), loss of libido or aversion to sexual activity, disrupted menstrual cycle in women (lengthening of the cycle, 'skipped' periods, decrease of menstrual flow), and constipation.

In order for a condition to be diagnosed as a **major depressive disorder**, the symptoms of depression should be present for at least 2 weeks and they should represent a radical change from the individual's previous levels of functioning. Counsellors should take note of cultural differences in the expression of depression — especially when these concern the duration of mourning after the loss of a significant other. Counsellors should also be aware of the fact that depression in children and adolescents often presents in 'disguised' forms such as boredom, restlessness, and feelings of worthlessness or even belligerency.

Depression can be **treated** with a combination of *biomedical* intervention (antidepressant drugs and electroconvulsive therapy) and *psychotherapy*. Psychotherapy focuses on the cognitive (cognitive-behavioural therapy) and interpersonal (systemic therapy) aspects of depression. Interpersonal psychotherapy targets the client's interpersonal relationships and focuses on the conflicts and problems that occur in these relationships. The identification of role conflicts and improvements in the ability to communicate and use social skills should help clients to find relationships more satisfying.

Cognitive-behavioural therapy teaches the client to identify negative, self-critical thoughts, to note the connection between negative thoughts and depression, to examine each negative thought, and to try to replace these thoughts with realistic interpretations of each situation. Clients are asked to list their negative thoughts and to think of rational alternatives, and to do pleasant and rewarding things.

The treatment of depression will to a large extent depend on the client's symptoms. It is also important to remember that it is easier to influence a depressed client's behaviour and cognition than it is to change his or her feelings. It is therefore a good idea to focus on behaviour or cognition. Encourage depressed clients to join support groups and try to involve the client's significant others. Don't ever ignore suicide threats!

## Suicide

The belief that people who threaten to commit suicide are not serious about it, or will not actually make such an attempt, does not accord with the facts. According to Sue et al. (2000), at least 80 % of suicides are preceded by either verbal or non-verbal behaviour cues that indicate the suicidal person's intentions. More than two-thirds of the people who commit suicide communicate their intent to do so within the 3 months preceding the act.

### Mood indicators of suicide

Factors that are closely linked with suicide are hopelessness or negative expectations about the future, and depression. Although one cannot make the assumption that depression *causes* suicide, the correlation between depression and suicide is very high — in adults as well as children and adolescents. Oddly enough, people very seldom commit suicide while they are severely depressed. Because severely depressed people have very low energy levels and their motor functioning is slowed down or retarded, they are unable to reach the levels of activity required for suicide. The danger period often occurs after some treatment when the depression begins to lift and when the person's energy and motivation levels begin to increase again. Researchers have found that most suicide attempts occur when depressed hospitalised patients go home for weekend leave, or soon after discharge (Sue et al., 2000, p. 370).

Other mood indicators of suicide are sadness, heightened feelings of anxiety, anger, guilt and shame. Long-term stress and the consumption of alcohol and drugs are also associated with suicide.

## HIV/AIDS and suicide

HIV infection and AIDS are associated with an increased likelihood of suicide (Sherr, 1995). Some studies report the risk of suicide as being 36 times greater in HIV-infected individuals. It seems that suicidal thoughts and acts in association with HIV/AIDS tend to concentrate around the time of *diagnosis* and again at the *end stage of disease*.

According to Sherr (1995, p. 22), the reasons for suicide may differ for the two 'peak periods' in the life of the HIV-infected individual. Suicide ideation (fantasising about suicide) or suicidal acts at the time of diagnosis may be triggered by factors such as the way in which testing was carried out, a lack of social support at the time, the individual's inability to cope, and inadequate emotional resources. Suicide at the later phase of AIDS is usually associated with deterioration of health, physical illness associated with pain, disability or disfigurement, a decrease in the quality of life, and a feeling that people at least want to control the way they die (Pugh, 1995). Those whose loved ones die as a result of suicide are particularly vulnerable to commiting suicide themselves, especially if they themselves are HIV positive.

There is also a disturbing correlation between HIV testing (before the results are known) and thinking about suicide. Different studies have found that anxiety and suicidal thoughts, which were very high at the time of HIV testing, dropped 10 weeks later — regardless of the results of the HIV test (Pugh, 1995, p. 48). It seems that the negativity and suicidal thinking are related to the stress and uncertainty of HIV testing, rather than to serostatus when asymptomatic. The importance of proper, conscientious and thorough pre- and post-HIV test counselling can therefore not be sufficiently emphasised.

## Children, depression and suicide

Because suicide is on the increase in children and adolescents, it is important to know the warning signs of depression and suicidal thinking in young people. Parents and teachers should be on the lookout for warning signs such as depression, previous suicide attempts, significant changes in behaviour or extremes in mood and behavioural patterns (such as signs of increased anxiety or withdrawal, a decline in school attendance and achievement, inability to concentrate, lack of interest in hobbies and usual social activities, preoccupation with death or suicide, impulsive risk taking, marked changes in everyday living habits such as eating, sleeping and hygiene, and repeated running away from school) (Gillis, 1994).

Van den Boom (1995) reported a study done by Weller and colleagues on the impact of bereavement on children. They evaluated a group of children between the ages of 5 and 12 years who had recently lost a parent. One-third (37 %) of the children displayed symptoms of major depression while 47 % of the depressed children reported morbid and suicidal ideation. They came to the conclusion that physical and emotional support, an environment in which the child feels able to express distressing or conflicting thoughts, feelings and fantasies about the loss, and stability and consistency in the child's environment are all extremely important in helping the child to work through the experienced loss.

## Prevention of suicide

According to Sue et al. (2000), the successful prevention of suicide is a three-phase process: (1) knowledge and identification of the risk factors and warning signs of suicide, (2) evaluation of the probability (high, moderate or low) that the person will commit suicide, and (3) implementation of action to prevent suicide. Prevention can be based on crisis-intervention, psychotherapy and hospitalisation. The following aspects of suicide prevention should be borne in mind:

- Counsellors should feel comfortable about discussing suicide with their clients. To discuss suicide with clients will not encourage a suicidal attempt — as is wrongly believed by some people. Clients are often relieved to be able to openly discuss suicide with their counsellor. Direct questions (such as the following) should be asked if they are appropriate or necessary (Sue et al., 2000, p. 382):
  - o 'Are you feeling unhappy and down most of the time?' If the answer is 'Yes', then ask:
  - o 'Do you feel so unhappy that you sometimes wish you were dead?' If the answer is 'Yes', then ask:
  - o 'Have you ever thought about taking your own life?' If the answer is 'Yes', then ask:
  - o 'What methods have you thought about using to kill yourself?' If the client specifies a particular method, then ask:
  - o 'When do you plan to do this?'
- The amount of detail involved in a suicide threat can indicate the level of its seriousness. A person who provides specific details such as method, time and place is at much greater risk than the person who describes such factors vaguely.
- Suicidal potential increases if the person has direct access to a means of suicide such as a loaded pistol.
- If you believe that the risk of suicide is very high, take action to influence the client's immediate environment. Don't let the client leave your office without a clear treatment plan and the involvement of significant others. Don't hesitate to involve other health care professionals in the prevention plan.
- Some counsellors use a 'contract' as a means of preventing suicide. This means that they ask the client to agree or promise — verbally or in writing — not to commit suicide within, for instance, the following week. Such an agreement can be a very powerful means of blocking suicidal attempts.

- The prevention of suicide depends on the counsellor's ability to recognise the signs and precipitating events. In almost every case of suicide, there are certain hints that the person is about to commit suicide. Suicide is also often preceded by a precipitating event such as the loss of a loved one, family discord, or a chronic or terminal illness such as AIDS.

- A person may verbally communicate his or her intention to commit suicide. These communications can be direct ('I want to die'; 'I'm going to kill myself') or indirect ('You will be better off without me'; 'I won't see you again')

- Behavioural clues can be communicated directly or indirectly. The most direct clue is an actual suicide attempt. Even if the act was incomplete, it should be taken as demonstrating a very serious intent to commit suicide. Indirect behavioural clues include actions such as putting one's affairs in order, giving away one's possessions, buying a casket, saying goodbye to people, and making a will. The counsellor should however be able to distinguish between (1) this behaviour as an indicator or sign of suicide, and (2) the normal and rational behaviour of someone who knows that he or she is about to die from a fatal condition such as AIDS. (In the second case, it is only natural that someone who has a fatal illness should wish to get their affairs in order because they know that their death is impending.) If the situation appears to be strange or unusual, the counsellor should keep the possibility of suicide in mind.

- Detect and treat depression immediately.

**Activity**

If you work in the HIV/AIDS field, it is almost inevitable that you will have to cope with a suicide threat at one or other time. Do you know how to handle it? There are many crisis management centres that also offer suicide prevention services. Make a list of the services (such as Lifeline, the AIDS helpline, FAMSA, Telefriend, or Depression and Anxiety Support Group) offered in your community. Contact one or more of these centres and find out what type of services they offer, how they handle suicide threats, who offers the services, and what type of training their counsellors have received. If you have the time, and want to do something for your community, why don't you volunteer to work for one of the services in your community?

## Crisis intervention

Crisis intervention is a form of emotional 'first aid' or a short-term helping process designed to provide immediate relief in an emergency situation (Gillis, 1994). Crisis intervention is active, direct and brief, and occurs shortly after a crisis has happened. The same phases of the counselling process (discussed in chapter 10) apply in these situations, and empathic listening is vitally important.

The crucial issue is not the actual crisis situation itself, but a client's *emotional reaction* to the situation and his or her *ability to deal with it.* Clients in crisis experience apathy, depression, guilt, and loss of self-esteem. They find that the ways they used to solve problems in the past no longer work for them any more, and they find this very upsetting and frightening.

The major goal of short-term crisis intervention is to provide individuals and their families with as much support and assistance as possible. This will help clients to regain their psychological balance as quickly as possible (Okun, 1997). Keep the following points in mind when you are engaged in crisis intervention:

- Ascertain who and where to call for support in an emergency. Have the telephone numbers of crisis clinics, hot lines and suicide prevention centres ready at hand — as well as telephone numbers for referrals to professionals. You should not have to *begin* to fumble around for telephone numbers at the very height of a crisis.
- Crisis intervention is directive. The client is usually in no state to think straight, and he or she needs your advice and direction immediately.
- Immediate hospitalisation (voluntary or involuntary) for medical treatment, evaluation, and therapy by a psychiatric team every day until the crisis has passed are often necessary. Make sure that you know what hospitals and facilities are available.
- Enlist relatives and friends to help monitor the client when he or she leaves the hospital. Provide the family (and client) with telephone numbers where they can reach 24-hour help if necessary. There are various organisations in the community (such as Lifeline and the AIDS helpline) that offer suicide prevention services and counselling.
- Ensure ongoing therapy.

## 12.5 CARE FOR THE CAREGIVER

NOTHING can be more stressful and draining on the caregiver's resources than caring for or counselling patients or clients with HIV infection or AIDS. Caregivers as well as patients are faced with nightmarish existential issues such as the vulnerability of youth, continuous physical and psychological deterioration, their own mortality, the fear of contagion and death. If caregivers do not also learn how to care for *themselves, they* will not survive the onslaught of the AIDS pandemic.

### Who are the caregivers?

Africa has so many AIDS patients that hospitalisation is not always an option. The enormous need for care leaves the community with no other choice than that they should care for their own sick. A UNAIDS (2000a) study carried out in Uganda and in South Africa found that the caregivers who battle with HIV/AIDS in their communities comprise the following groups and individuals:

- At the family level, the burden of care is predominantly borne by *women and girls*. Men are also increasingly willing (or forced) to care for sick partners. However, the least acknowledged caregivers within the home are *children*. When one parent dies, there is often no one else to look after the other parent when he or she falls ill.
- The backbone of community care programmes for people with AIDS are *volunteers*. Some are 'informal' volunteers such as friends, neighbours and church members. The majority of volunteers who work for AIDS care programmes are 'formal' volunteers who are recruited, trained and supervised by the organisations for whom they work.
- *Health care professionals* (mostly nurses and welfare workers) work with AIDS patients in hospitals, clinics and on a home-based care basis. One of their responsibilities is to recruit, train and support volunteer caregivers in the community.
- *Traditional healers* are widely consulted throughout Africa and — because their importance within communities is often not officially recognised — they care for people with HIV/AIDS without training or support from the formal health services sector.

Caregivers are often not trained to care for patients with AIDS, and those who are trained carry a very heavy load. Because society cannot afford to lose its caregivers to stress and burnout, it is therefore important for us to take good care of our caregivers.

## Stress and burnout

Burnout or role-stress may be defined as 'a syndrome of physical and emotional exhaustion, involving the development of a negative self-concept, negative job attitudes, and loss of concern and feelings for clients' (Pines & Maslach, 1978, p. 233).

Stress among caregivers manifests itself in a wide variety of signs and symptoms such as:

- Loss of interest in and commitment to work and a lack of job satisfaction
- Failure to observe punctuality and neglect of duties
- Feelings of inadequacy, helplessness and guilt
- A loss of confidence and diminished self-esteem
- A tendency to withdraw both from clients and from colleagues
- A loss of sensitivity in dealing with clients or patients; referring to clients in a dehumanised or purely impersonal way (which may include sick humour)

- Avoidance of clients or limiting the time spent with them, and frequent and earlier-than-necessary referral of clients to other health care professionals
- Indifference to the suffering of others; experiencing boredom with clients, and seeing all clients as being alike
- A loss of quality in performance of work. Caregivers often work harder, but accomplish less.
- Irritability, tension, tearfulness, loss of concentration, sleeplessness, chronic exhaustion, depression and feelings of distress
- Vulnerability to all kinds of illnesses and psychosomatic symptoms
- Deteriorating relationships with colleagues and friends, tensions and distress in personal life; difficulties in getting on with people
- An increased use of alcohol or drugs in order to cope at home or at work
- A decision to leave the job or profession

### Causes of stress and burnout

Much of the stress experienced by caregivers is inherent in the nature of the work itself — the fact that they are dealing with an incurable and extremely cruel disease that mostly kills young people and that causes terrible suffering. The following causes of stress and burnout among health care professionals and volunteers caring for AIDS patients in Africa are listed in the UNAIDS report (2000a):

- *Financial hardship*. AIDS in Africa is often concentrated among the very poor. A training officer in Uganda said the following: 'The messages about living positively, eating well, looking after your health, can seem cruel when people are struggling to bring in *any* food to the home' (UNAIDS, 2000a, p. 28). The caregivers themselves are often in a similar position. 'We go to see hungry people and we are hungry too,' said a volunteer in KwaZulu-Natal.
- *Stigma associated with HIV and AIDS*. HIV/AIDS stigmatises both infected individuals *and* uninfected people working in the field. This 'secondary stigma' can have a powerful effect on the caregiver's status with family, friends and the public at large. Being avoided because he or she works with people with AIDS can be very stressful for a caregiver. Ostracism of this kind can deprive the caregiver of much needed support.
- *Secrecy and fear of disclosure* among people with AIDS make the task of caring for AIDS patients very difficult. If they are supposed to keep the HIV-positive diagnosis a secret, family caregivers often find it difficult or impossible to seek help from outside. Caregivers from outside cannot easily pass on knowledge or health care skills to the family members if the family members do not know that the patient has AIDS. The caregiver must thus carry the responsibility alone. It is also impossible for the caregiver to prepare the family for death if the AIDS diagnosis is a secret.

- *Over-involvement with people with AIDS and their families.* Caregivers often experience stress because they are unable to be there for their clients when they need them, because they are unable to meet needs such as the need for food, because they experience feelings of inadequacy and guilt when they can do no more to help a person, because of feelings of loss and sadness after the death of a client, and because of a lasting anxiety about the family members who are left behind — especially if these are children. Setting professional boundaries is often difficult in African communities since the extended family system means that a person is rarely a stranger in a village or community. 'From your name people can see what clan you are from, and there is always someone to whom you are related by clan.'

- *Personal identification with the suffering of people with AIDS.* Because many caregivers are HIV-infected themselves, they observe at first hand while caring for people with AIDS how they too will become sick and die.

- *Difficult patients.* Many caregivers who look after sick family members experience stress because the sick family member may often be moody, uncooperative, and hostile. Patients, on the other hand, often feel hurt, angry, dependent, and vulnerable because AIDS has put them in this vulnerable position.

- *The terrible plight of children.* Caregivers often do not know how to care for or talk to the children who stay behind.

- The *workload* may be very demanding, and caregivers often experience stress because of a lack of 'space' and privacy in their work.

- Many health care professionals and volunteers are frustrated because:
  o they do not get the *necessary support from superiors*
  o they feel that they work in isolation
  o they don't have a voice in decisions that affect them and their work
  o finances for volunteer workers and important prevention projects are often drastically cut
  o creativity is discouraged because innovative ideas and suggestions are not implemented
  o they have too little autonomy and responsibility
  o the necessary supportive infrastructures and supervision are not always in place
  o training, skills and preparation for the work are often inadequate
  o there is often a lack of medication and health care material
  o referral mechanisms are not available
  o valuable workers resign out of frustration

- *Family caregivers* also suffer from isolation, the effect of HIV and AIDS on their personal relationships and family dynamics, insecurity and fear about the future, difficulty in disclosing to or in communicating with children, and difficulty in facing bereavement.

## Managing stress and burnout

It is important for the self-preservation of caregivers and for their emotional survival, that they should take care of themselves. Employers should also do everything possible to support their employees in the fulfilment of their duties. According to the UNAIDS (2000a) report on caregivers in Africa, a first requirement in supporting caregivers is to formally acknowledge the fact that their work is inherently stressful, and that feelings of distress are a legitimate reaction to their experiences rather than signs of personal weakness or lack of professionalism. Bottled-up feelings almost inevitably lead to burnout, and caregivers need to feel confident and free to express doubts and distress and to seek timely help. The following skills may help caregivers and counsellors to cope with the pressure of working with HIV-infected people (UNAIDS, 2000a; Van Dyk, 1999):

- *Re-evaluation of expectations and performance goals*: It is important for professional caregivers and counsellors to know themselves. They should take time to think about what they realistically can expect from themselves and their clients and, in the light of this, they should be encouraged to re-evaluate their performance goals. If they feel that they do not reach these goals, they should establish new, more obtainable goals. Caregivers should, for example, accept that the emphasis in caring for AIDS patients is on *caring* and not on *curing*. Caregivers should learn not to take responsibility for things they cannot help or alter. They should know that they can only do their best, and nothing more, and that they are not perfect. The message that 'bad things happen and it is not your fault' is very important.

- *Care for yourself:* The caregiver is responsible for his or her own physical and mental health, and it is therefore important for the caregiver to look after himself or herself. A healthy diet and enough exercise, rest and sleep are important. Caregivers should nurture themselves and take time out to do things that they enjoy, like walking, listening to music, or reading. They should actively search for ways to cope with stress that work for them, and use these methods of coping. Relaxation exercises, breathing exercises, visualisation, and meditation work very well in coping with stress. It is also very important for caregivers to create strict boundaries between their professional and personal lives. They must force themselves to forget the suffering of their patients when they close the door to go home. Caregivers should maintain a balance between *identification* with a patient and *over-identification*: they should empathise but not lose objectivity. This is of course a luxury not enjoyed by family caregivers who look after their own sick loved ones, or who close the door after a patient only to go to somebody at home who is also HIV positive.

- *Using support systems:* Caregivers cannot cope with the tremendous burden of HIV/AIDS without support on a personal as well as an organisational level. Caregivers should create and use their personal support systems — which may be someone like a spouse or partner to whom they can talk. Caregivers should also be encouraged to talk and listen to each other. Group support can be very powerful, and allow colleagues to share their concerns, problems and fears. A social support system relieves stress, loneliness, depression and anxiety, and it strengthens our sense of self-worth, trust and life direction. If support groups do not exist, caregivers should take the initiative and form their own groups. Support systems should be put in place for caregivers who look after their own families — a task which is impossible if secrecy and non-disclosure is the norm in a community.

- *Organisational support:* Volunteer and home-based care organisations, hospitals and clinics cannot afford to lose the caregivers who are the mainstay of care for people with AIDS. For the sake of their morale and self-confidence, caregivers at every level need to know that their work is recognised and valued. Words of praise and thanks from superiors are therefore important. Frequent meetings between caregivers and supervisors are important to discuss policy and to share problems. Management should involve caregivers in decisions, and ask their opinions — they are after all the people working in the field. Caregivers should also be allowed flexibility and scope to use their own initiative in caring for patients. It is however important that caregivers have a clear understanding of their duties and the limits of their responsibilities for any client. Managers should create a supportive environment for the caregiver to work in by assuring that a good network system is in place. Caregivers should know when and where to refer a client to at all times, and where to go for help themselves. The appointment of mentors with counselling skills (e.g. volunteer psychologists) to look after the caregivers working in the front line is very helpful. These mentors should however be responsible for the *welfare* of the caregivers, and not for the quality or style of their work. Managers of HIV/AIDS programmes should further ensure that their caregivers receive good salaries, and that their weekends and annual leave are respected. In regions where caregivers and their clients are poor, income-generating activities (such as food gardens) should be financed and supported to ensure that caregivers and their clients have food.

- *Knowledge is empowering:* Knowledge gives people confidence, control, and choices in life, and it has lasting value. Training plays a central role in the management of stress and burnout among caregivers. Refresher courses for caregivers and upgrading of skills are therefore very important. Issues of stress, burnout and coping skills should be directly addressed in training sessions. The training needs of caregivers should be identified.

- *Working in a team:* Working in a multidisciplinary team is an effective way of protecting staff from undue stress because it spreads the burden of care and responsibility. For example, it is very helpful to disperse the emotional burden when a patient is dying by extending the team or caregivers who sit with the patient. Family, extended family and volunteers from the church can, for example, take turns to sit with the dying patient and to comfort him or her.

- *Expression of grief:* One of the most difficult times emotionally for caregivers is when patients or clients die. The death of a patient evokes a sense of personal loss in the caregiver. It is therefore very important for caregivers to grieve and to cry without shame if they need to do so. The caregiver should explore his or her own personal and cultural mechanisms and rituals in dealing with death, and use them.

## 12.6 CONCLUSION

It is important for caregivers — nurses, social workers, psychologists, counsellors, volunteer workers and family caregivers — to know themselves, to understand the tremendous burden that HIV/AIDS places on them, to recognise the signs when they are in psychological trouble, and to know where to find help and how to care for themselves. Only when they are able to care for themselves will caregivers be able to give quality time to those in their care.

# Spiritual, Emotional and Bereavement Counselling

**by Peet van Dyk**

*Faculty of Theology and Religious Studies, Unisa*

*Who will save us?*

*And she kept her song soft,*
*her mourning for lost humanity.*
*Who will save them from the beast?*
*Who will prevent him from coming in to rule?*

AIDS has to some degree shattered our whole worldview. It has exposed and under-mined our facile optimistic assumptions about knowledge, science and technology and brought us face to face with our neglect of the emotional and spiritual aspects of life. It has exposed the spiritual poverty underlying the ideals of rampant materialism and exploitative expansionism — ideals that characterise modern Western culture (Van Arkel, 1991). One may therefore realistically claim that HIV/AIDS challenges all aspects of modern life. It is for this reason that HIV/AIDS counselling needs to adopt a holistic approach that takes all aspects of modern life into account. While clients need the necessary information and knowledge to be able to cope with the disease (cognitive information), they also need to be equipped to cope emotionally and spiritually with the ravages of the disease. Because one counsellor cannot realistically deal with all the ways in which the pandemic affects both individuals and society, it is preferable to have teams of experts, each of whom is skilled in one particular aspect of coping with the pandemic, to counsel those who are affected. In this chapter we will explore:

- how counsellors can facilitate the process of bereavement (i.e. of both the HIV-infected client and his or her significant others)
- possible emotional coping strategies
- ethical and religious problems and dilemmas engendered by the disease

## 13.1 WHY SPIRITUAL COUNSELLING OF HIV-INFECTED PEOPLE IS SO DIFFICULT

To counsel HIV-infected clients is often extraordinarily difficult — especially when one has to counsel them about the emotional and religious issues that have arisen in their lives as a result of the disease. One of the most obvious reasons for this difficulty (often noted by previous researchers) is the fact that HIV/AIDS is to a large extent a *sexually transmitted* disease. Rational understanding of its origins, progress and ultimate effects is therefore often clouded by sexual taboos, denial, superstitions, stigmatisation and the irrational fears that are evoked in many people by sexuality and sexually transmitted diseases (Sunderland & Shelp, 1987; Van Arkel, 1991). For this reason, and for many others, many HIV-infected people tend to avoid any kind of counselling that addresses the religious or spiritual issues provoked by the disease (Van Arkel, 1991). This understandable but ironic situation means that many of the most urgent and troubling spiritual and existential questions that confront HIV-infected people often remain unanswered at a time when their need for spiritual comfort, consolation and understanding is more acute than it has ever been at any other time in their lives. Those who seek spiritual counselling are often deeply disappointed because many members of the clergy (from whatever religion they might come) find it difficult to deal with people who are infected with the HI virus and who live in the expectation that they will die sooner rather than later. In addition, HIV-infected people are understandably reluctant to expose their true feelings and experiences in counselling sessions because of their expectation of being condemned and judged (Sunderland & Shelp, 1987).

Another revolutionary feature of the HIV/AIDS pandemic is that it has undermined and eroded the most basic traditional features of spiritual counselling. The basic task of the spiritual counsellor has always been to deliver a message of *hope* to the person who is ill (both in a spiritual and physical sense). Even in the case of terminally ill cancer patients, the spiritual counsellor could always offer some kind of consolation: he or she could always keep alive the hope 'that a miracle might still happen' — the hope that the disease might go into remission and that the patient might be healed (Goss, 1989). Although this ray of hope naturally diminishes in intensity as patients approach death, it is never totally absent from spiritual counselling. Even when there seemed to be little hope of recovery, a 'silent agreement' or complicity always existed between the patient and spiritual counsellor. This agreement was that the counsellor would continue to express *hope* — a hope that became a shared form of denial that bound the counsellor and the sick person together.

Another feature of most spiritual and religious counselling (especially within the Christian faith) is that as hope for *physical* recovery gradually diminishes, the spiritual counsellor often counteracts the patient's approaching death by focusing increasingly on *eternal* hope — the hope that the person will continue to enjoy a spiritual life in another world after death has intervened.

The peculiar nature of HIV/AIDS has drastically undermined all these features of the traditional counselling process. These undermining factors include the relative 'impossibility' of maintaining hope of physical recovery, the length and erratic progress of the illness and its accompanying opportunistic infections, the stigma (the moral disgrace) that is frequently attached to HIV infection, the lack of social support (manifested as avoidance behaviour by loved ones and members of the community), untimely and multiple losses, protracted illness and disfigurements, and neurological complications (Sunderland & Shelp, 1987).

Counselling of people with HIV/AIDS focuses on three major topics. These are bereavement counselling (i.e. counselling of both the HIV-infected person and the significant others), and spiritual and emotional counselling. We shall first deal with bereavement counselling before discussing spiritual and emotional counselling.

## 13.2 BEREAVEMENT COUNSELLING

The bereavement experienced by a person who has lost a loved one and the bereavement experienced by a terminally ill or dying person are very similar. Both people experience a grievous sense of loss: in the first case, one experiences the loss of a loved one, and in the second case, one experiences the loss of one's future, one's hopes, one's loved ones, one's health, self-esteem, well-being and one's dignity as a human being. In either case, people are confronted with their own mortality. Terminally ill people are *directly* confronted by their own imminent death — the imminence of which becomes more pressing as the disease progresses — while people who have lost loved ones are *indirectly* confronted with the possibility and spectacle of their own *future* death through the death of the loved one. It is therefore understandable that the process of bereavement is often very similar for both those who are dying and those who are forced to witness death. In all cases where HIV-infected people are still leading relatively normal and healthy lives for extended periods, the counsellor needs to facilitate a process of *reinvestment* in life. This is also an important element in the counselling of a person who has lost or is in the process of losing a loved one.

In the HIV/AIDS scenario, the counsellor is therefore confronted with the dual process of bereavement, that is, counselling the HIV-infected person as well as the bereavement of the significant others who will be left behind when the client dies. It is important to realise that in the case of a lengthy terminal disease (such as HIV infection), bereavement already begins with the loss of some or all of the following features of normal, healthy human life: health, shared pleasurable activities (such as sex), relationships, family, the sense of the future, certainty, an understanding of the meaning of life, hope, energy, enthusiasm, employment (which confers the sense of identity) and personal independence (Perelli, 1991; Sherr, 1995). The significant others of the infected person also begin the process of bereavement as they are forced to witness how their loved one gradually loses all the features of normal health and active human existence. In the case of the sex partners of HIV-infected people, the partners may also have the added agony of worrying about whether they will become infected by their infected partners.

## Attachment theory

Bereavement is triggered primarily by the sense of loss that occurs when one loses something or someone to which one has become attached. Humans (and animals) have a strong tendency to make strong affectional bonds with others and react strongly when those bonds are threatened or broken (Worden, 1982). According to Bowlby's (1977) theory, we do not form these attachments to satisfy our biological drives — but rather to fulfil our needs for security and safety. Forming attachments with significant others is normal behaviour for both children and adults.

Separation or loss initiates a process of grief. Grief is a very basic (and to a large extent an automatic and instinctive) biological reaction that causes aggressive behaviour and stimulates attempts to regain the lost object (Bowlby, 1977). The extent to which human beings grieve a loss depends on how attached or close they were to the person or object of their loss. Grief is not always triggered by an *actual* loss. The mere anticipation of loss (as when a person is diagnosed with a life-threatening disease such as HIV/AIDS) may be sufficient to initiate the grief process (Sheir, 1995). Although human mourning processes may be based on 'primitive biological processes', it is important for us to realise that human grieving also displays many unique features. Among human beings, for example, one finds an almost universal belief in an afterlife in which one can rejoin one's loved ones (Worden, 1982).

## Tasks of mourning

Many counsellors regard the process of mourning as being similar to the process of healing from an illness: mourning occurs until normal functions once more become predominant in the bereaved person's life. Among such functions, emotional and physical equilibrium are the most important. The process of restoration requires the bereaved person to perform some of the 'tasks of mourning' before equilibrium can be re-established and the process of mourning can be completed. Since these tasks form part of a process, they require effort — an effort which Freud called 'grief work'. The tasks of mourning frequently overlap one another and do not necessarily follow in any specific serial sequence. The grieving person may therefore complete some tasks simultaneously — although in other cases the finalisation of one task may depend on the prior completion of a previous one. Thus, for example, one cannot process the emotional impact of a loss until one has accepted the *reality* of the loss (i.e. the fact that it has actually happened).

After Elizabeth Kübler-Ross published her well-known work, many counsellors over-simplified her work by describing her stages of bereavement (i.e. denial, anger, negotiation, depression and acceptance) as *discrete* (or separate) phases that follow each other in strict order. They believed that it is impossible for the bereaved person to progress to a subsequent stage before the previous one has been adequately dealt with. This (mistaken) idea often caused counsellors to 'force' their clients through consecutive stages of bereavement without taking individual differences and the individuality of grieving into account (De Villiers, 1988) and without appreciating the fact that most people tend to work through several phases simultaneously. Worden (1982) tries to obviate the idea of discrete stages (stages that follow one another) by avoiding the term 'stages'. By preferring the active term 'bereavement tasks' he also emphasises the fact that the process of bereavement is not a process that 'flows over' or overwhelms the person, i.e. it is not a process that has to be passively accepted by the bereaved person. Bereaved people should actively *work through* their grief *in their own time*. Bereavement is not a process that can be rushed or artificially expedited. We will also therefore talk about 'tasks of bereavement' in order to emphasise that dealing with loss is an *active* process.

### Task 1: To accept the reality of the loss

When a loss occurs, the first reaction is always a sense that it has not happened. This is often accompanied by a feeling of numbness, shock or unreality. This reaction is typical when a loved one dies (even when it was expected) *and* when a person hears for the first time that he or she is infected with HIV or is terminally ill. The first task of grieving is to face the reality of the death or the loss of health which will eventually end in death. For the person who has lost a loved one, this requires an acceptance of the belief that reunion is impossible — at least in this life. Part of this process involves typical searching behaviour — looking for the person, momentarily forgetting that the person is not there any more, and misidentifying people as the lost one. The equivalent behaviour for people diagnosed with a life-threatening disease (e.g. HIV/AIDS) is to momentarily forget about the HIV-positive status and/or to live as though they were not infected.

Denial of the loss may vary from slight distortions of the reality of the situation to severe delusions. Delusions may range from the bizarre to the more 'natural'. They may, for example, take the form of 'mummification' — the process that occurs when the bereaved person lovingly preserves all the possessions of the deceased loved one. Some people with a life-threatening disease may be reluctant to let go of a risky lifestyle and — in the terminal phases of the disease — they may begin to cling tenaciously to possessions that they will never need again — just in case they do need them again! This is one of the primary reasons why people often die after a long illness without having taken care of their estate and without having made proper arrangements to distribute their possessions.

In the case of HIV-infected people (especially when they have been diagnosed as HIV positive at a relatively early stage of the infection), the process of accepting the reality of their status may be an extremely difficult and drawn-out process. Because infected people initially show no symptoms (or only very mild ones) and because they may continue to remain healthy for many years after infection, their tendency towards denial of their illness is encouraged, and they may continue to carry on living as though nothing has happened.

When denial takes the form of mild distortions of reality, these may serve the temporary role of buffering the intensity of the loss. Even so, it is important that the distortions do not hinder the eventual acceptance of the reality of the disease and approaching death (Worden, 1982). It is also common for people to deny loss by min-imising the importance of the loss or by removing all objects or people from their life which may remind them of the loss. Selective forgetfulness and denying the irrevers-ibility of the death or of the disease are also common. In the case of HIV-infected people it is especially difficult to distinguish between a healthy sense of hope (e.g. that a cure or effective treatment for AIDS may be found) and a systematic denial or refusal to accept that they will eventually die.

Unfortunately, certain unrealistic religious attitudes may sometimes transgress the boundary of offering reasonable comfort and hope to the individual and so become complicit in denying reality. Such unrealistic attitudes may either take the form of refusing to accept that God is not going to heal the sick person, or (by denying the importance of this life) to focus entirely on the life after death. When hope thus becomes denial, it may complicate the process of bereavement and make it more difficult to complete the bereavement process.

Worden (1982, p. 12) evaluates this tendency as follows:

> It should be emphasised that after a death it is very normal to hope for a reunion or to assume that the deceased is not gone. However, for most people this illusion is short-lived, at least for this life, and this enables them to move through to Task II (i.e. to experience the pain of grief).

Most counsellors nowadays agree that accepting death is at best only partial (Irion, 1985). Complete acceptance is an ideal which can probably never be reached com-pletely. The degree of partial acceptance varies from person to person and will also depend on how close the deceased was to the bereaved person and how complic-ated their relationship may have been. To fully accept one's own death is also not really possible — especially when one is still relatively young, as is often the case with HIV-infected people. Some degree of denial will therefore always remain and may sometimes serve the important function of lessening the pain.

### Task 2: To experience the pain of grief

Grief makes people experience emotional pain and this may sometimes also man-ifest itself as physical pain. Because nobody likes to experience pain, most people will consciously or unconsciously try to avoid pain as far as possible. Although some forms of denial and avoidance may be necessary to protect the person against the kind of pain that threatens to overwhelm the person, people who have experienced a loss must eventually permit themselves to experience the pain. Parkes (1972, p. 173) describes the necessity of experiencing and going beyond the pain by saying that 'anything that continually allows the person to avoid or suppress this pain can be expected to prolong the course of mourning'.

The intensity of pain depends on the personality of the bereaved person and on how precious the lost person or thing was to the bereaved person. The threat of losing (within the foreseeable future) one's health and everything that one has accumulated in one's life will necessarily cause most people to feel a severe degree of pain. Confronting the reality of HIV/AIDS may generate a variety of *fears* that may cause severe emotional strain. These fears may include the following (Sunderland & Shelp, 1987):

- Fear of *impairment*. To admit illness is to arouse a feeling that one is somehow inferior to the general (healthy) community. It also arouses the spectre of one's own mortality. Illness generally also causes some degree of social isolation (the illness prevents one from enjoying the normal pleasures of social life).

- Fear of *uncertainty* may be very acute. It may spur people to take various measures to reacquire their earlier undisturbed state of mind or equilibrium. To test HIV-positive initiates a major health crisis that severely threatens all one's stabilities, hopes, certainties, life plans, ambitions and ordinary day-to-day capacities. This kind of crisis always causes profound emotional stress and is accompanied by associated changes in outlook and adaptive changes in the client's personality. While such changes may be occasions for growth, they may also stimulate psychological and spiritual regression and deterioration.

- Fear of *stigmatisation and ostracism* are very real factors when one has been diagnosed with HIV/AIDS. It is the fear of *rejection and isolation* that causes AIDS patients the greatest pain. Diseases such as venereal diseases and AIDS evoke self-righteous judgements in some onlookers — who may not hesitate to judge and blame the sick person for his or her condition. The fear, self-righteousness and herd instinct in some communities are sometimes so great that they regard the person with AIDS as having committed a 'crime'. Stigmatised people may therefore be denied the ordinary privileges of social life. If infected people are perceived as being 'guilty' (for example, because they are known to be homosexual or promiscuous), members of a community may sometimes hold such people responsible for the consequences of their disease and deny them their sympathy or (worse) even seek to punish them. These acts of hostility may include acts such as termination of employment, denial of access to medical schemes, and various other measures of exclusion which are sometimes concealed as 'reasonable' attempts to protect others. In Africa racism may also play a role in hostile and indifferent attitudes towards infected people.

- Fear of *sexuality*. Because sexual transmission is the primary way in which people become infected with HIV, infection with HIV is surrounded by an aura of superstition, mystery, taboos, fear and the double standards that many people have with regard to all matters relating to sex. Because of all these accompanying negative conditions, it may be very difficult to talk openly and rationally about the disease and to counsel people living with HIV.

- Fear of *death* is an extension of the fear of infection and impairment — sickness is proximity to death. Often the *anticipation* of dying carries with it the same emotional stress as the reality itself.

The experience of pain in the case of HIV-infected people and their significant others may be complicated by the fact that they may actually deny themselves the right to grieve — whether consciously or unconsciously. For example, by blaming either themselves or the deceased person for the loss, they may make it more difficult to accept the pain of loss or allow themselves to experience the pain. In many cases such an attitude will increase the intensity and continuity of the pain. Counsellors should therefore facilitate this grieving task by assuring people of their right to grieve (even though society may try to deny them the right to engage in this process). Various *forms* of guilt often cause difficulties in the bereavement counselling of the HIV-infected and those affected by HIV-related losses.

Because society in general often stigmatises grieving as morbid, unhealthy and demoralising, a counsellor's work may be regarded by such people as wrongly stimulating a mourner's grief. This is not so. The absolute avoidance of pain (i.e. the negation of the second task) is to feel nothing at all (Worden, 1982). Cutting oneself off from any feelings by implementing thought-stopping procedures to short-circuit unpleasant thoughts or by deliberately stimulating pleasant thoughts are both ways of avoiding legitimate pain. Examples of cutting-off behaviours may include compulsive travelling by bereaved people or an adoption of an artificial, over-stimulated lifestyle that is out of keeping with the bereaved person's previous way of life. Some people utilise such cutting-off behaviours (which may include alcohol and substance abuse) to stop themselves from thinking or getting into touch with their pain.

Eventually the person should allow him- or herself to face the pain and all the emotions which go with it. Of all these emotions, *anger* is probably the most common — *but usually the least expected by the bereaved*. In such circumstances, one should acknowledge one's anger. One may be angry because life is not fair; one may be angry at the person who has infected one, or angry with oneself because one was not more cautious. One may even be angry with the deceased because his or her actions precipitated the loss and therefore caused all the grief with which the bereaved person now has to deal. Even when there is no obvious or rational reason for being angry with the deceased person, it is perfectly natural for a bereaved person to *blame* the dead person for having abandoned him or her. However irrational and illogical such emotions may seem to be, they are very widely experienced by bereaved people and are therefore part of the *reality* of bereavement.

Grieving openly is often difficult for HIV-infected people or for loved ones because of the secrecy and stigma associated with sexually transmitted diseases. Experiencing pain alone or secretly often makes the pain worse. Bereavement counsellors in HIV/AIDS-related cases should therefore make a conscious effort to refer such people to support groups or help them to share their pain with others. If this is not possible or if bereaved people do not want to share their grief with their family and friends, they should at least become members of a support group.

People who deny themselves conscious grieving usually break down at a later stage. Their breakdown may not be obvious or it may manifest itself in the form of acute and chronic depression. One of the aims of grief counselling is to help people to process their painful experience so that they won't carry their pain with them throughout their lives.

In the case of HIV-infected people, the purpose of grief counselling is to prevent them from being so traumatised that they stop living long before AIDS develops or before their health starts to deteriorate. It is only by experiencing the pain that we can allow it to become less acute. It is only by processing pain and undertaking grief work that we can slowly return to normal and begin to get on with the remainder of our lives. In those cases where the task of experiencing the pain has not been properly or adequately completed, we should refer a client to a psychological counsellor so that he or she can work through the process in therapy and so prevent psychological problems such as chronic depression from arising at a later stage.

### Task 3: To adjust to a changed environment

While experiencing a loss means different things to different people, every person who experiences a loss is forced to adjust to the new circumstances and the new environment that have been created by the loss. People have to discover, for example, what it is like to live without the deceased person or what losing one's health, prospects, lifestyle and future actually mean in practice. Complete realisation of what the loss entails usually emerges only a few months after the loss has occurred. One might realise, for example, what it means to live alone, to sleep alone in an empty house or manage household affairs and finances alone. Bereaved people only sometimes discover the exact role that the deceased person played after his or her death. Those who are left behind often appreciate the full implications of their loss by being forced to adjust to new circumstances, to learn new skills or even just to do things which they never had to do before. Many people resent this process of adjustment and become deeply frustrated by small and irritating things that have to be attended to and that seem to take up a lot of their time.

While the manner in which HIV-infected people experience loss when their positive diagnosis first becomes known is not very well defined, it is nonetheless an extremely painful experience because it ultimately means that one will lose what is most precious to one — one's own life. What makes it even worse is the realisation that the HIV-positive diagnosis is merely the first stage in a long and painful process of loss — which will inevitably culminate in one's death. This long and painful process may include losing one's partners, one's close friends, the support of one's family, one's work, one's financial security, one's previous (normal and healthy) lifestyle, one's health and even one's dignity. This series of unimaginably painful, frightening and humiliating losses — to which the person *must* adapt — are even more stressful because they are often unanticipated and unpredictable.

One can illustrate this process by contemplating a typical example. The majority of HIV-infected people have been accustomed to leading very active lives and many have never been in hospital, undergone any extensive medical treatment or been required to take medication on a regular basis. Then suddenly, as AIDS begins to manifest and opportunistic diseases begin to appear, they have to subject themselves to constant and expensive courses of treatment — which may make them feel very ill (due to the side effects) and which may also quickly deplete and drain their financial resources. AIDS patients may receive chemotherapy, radiation treatment or begin to take anti-retroviral drugs. The taking of anti-retroviral medication entails a strict regimen: some drugs have to be taken before meals and some after meals — and often the only way to get the timing right is by setting alarm clocks and rearranging one's whole daily schedule. This may be extremely difficult or even impossible for people with only a basic education or no formal education at all (such as, for example, people living in traditional communities in rural Africa). But even people with higher education, high incomes and privileged lifestyles are very often disturbed and disorientated by the daunting demands that HIV/AIDS treatment imposes on them. Either way, HIV/AIDS can easily disrupt all the accustomed patterns, habits, assumptions and rhythms of one's life — and this disruption and disorientation can increase one's anxiety levels exponentially.

Successful adjustment to the task of adaptation requires people to redefine their loss in such a way that *the positive aspects of the loss* can also be appreciated. Thus, for example, if one begins to live a far less selfish life by helping other HIV-infected people in need, one may become a far more mature person. Bowlby (1977) describes the task of adaptation to loss as a person's recognition of their changed circumstances, a revision of their representational models, and a redefinition of their goals in life. In many cases the HIV-infected person may successfully learn to live life each day to its fullest and begin to enjoy the beauties of nature and creation ever more acutely — beauties that he or she might previously have taken for granted (Perelli, 1991).

What is certain is that adaptation to difficult situations will become even more difficult if people allow themselves to sink into a swamp of self-pity and if they intensify their helplessness by not developing the necessary coping skills or by withdrawing from the world (Worden, 1982).

The task of adapting to changed circumstances is probably an area in which bereaved people can be most pro-active if they deliberately develop and train themselves in those practical skills that will enable them to cope successfully with those practical problems that have been created (or are being created) by their loss. Thus, for example, if HIV-infected people become involved in hospice programmes or become involved in informing other people about the practical aspects of handling the disease, they may become extremely well trained in the very skills that they may later need in handling their own worsening health situation.

### Task 4: Withdrawing emotional energy and reinvesting it in another person or field of life

One can only *reinvest* one's emotional energy once one has withdrawn one's focus from the deceased person. Mourning therefore entails the psychological task of detaching one's memories and hopes. If one is the survivor, one has to deliberately loosen oneself from the pervasive influence of the dead person. But this may be extremely difficult because it may be perceived as a dishonouring of the deceased person (Worden, 1982).

To the HIV-infected person, this shifting of focus or acquisition of emotional detachment is more subtle and difficult to express. It may entail, for example, becoming less focused on one's eventual death and more focused on one's remaining life — a life that may last for over a decade or more. Redirecting one's emotional energy towards living one's life to the fullest is vitally important and it is the only way to improve the quality of one's remaining life. As long as one focuses exclusively on the negative aspects of the disease and one's impending death, one will have no emotional energy left to invest in living.

Failure to complete this task is described by Worden (1982, p. 16) as 'the failure to love again'. As long as one remains obsessed by the past (whether that past may be a person or one's previous healthy life), one chooses not to love. And choosing not to love makes happiness impossible. It is vital for people infected by HIV to rediscover *the ability to choose life* (even though life may have disappointed one and even though one sometimes feels that life (or God) is 'unfair'). This choosing of life requires one not to sink down into depression and psychological deterioration long before physical death intervenes. The HIV-infected person therefore ultimately has to choose between two options: he or she must either choose (1) immediate death-in-life (even though this may not be physical death), or (2) a life lived to the fullest

— which means a purposive and deliberate investment of all one's emotional and psychic energy in one's life.

The task of reinvesting emotional energy is a very difficult task to accomplish and many bereaved people get stuck at this point (sadly only realising later (at the very moment of loss) that they allowed their life to prematurely 'stop'). Grief counsellors should therefore pay special attention to investigating all the possible ways and means in which clients can reinvest their emotional energy.

**Principles and procedures of bereavement counselling**

Once we have understood all the tasks of bereavement, we still need to appreciate how a counsellor can help a bereaved person to *work through* these tasks. Because there is no fixed formula for doing this, counsellors will have to adapt their procedures to each specific case and person. The grief counsellor may find the following principles and procedures useful (Worden, 1982):

*Ways to actualise the loss*

One of the best ways of helping people to come to terms with their loss is by letting them talk about it. In the case of survivors this may include talking about the following points:

● Where did the death occur?
● How did it happen?
● Where were you when you heard about it?
● Who told you about it?
● What were the funeral and service like?

In the case of an HIV-infected person, the above questions can be adapted as follows:

● Why and when did you go for HIV testing?
● How and by whom was the news revealed to you?
● How did you react to the news and what did you do immediately after receiving the news?

In addition to talking about the loss, many people need to 'process' the loss by reviewing the events in their minds and by (ritually) visiting the grave of the deceased or other places associated with the loss. Going through these processes will help the bereaved person to actualise the loss and to accept the reality of it.

*Assist the person to identify and express feelings*

Grief is frequently such an unpleasant and painful experience that it sometimes compels mourning people to avoid or suppress their feelings. But this avoidance can make it difficult for them to recognise and adequately express their feelings. The most common of these feelings are:

## Anger

Anger is a very common emotional reaction, but because it is not considered 'proper' or appropriate to direct it at a deceased person, it is often redirected to other people such as a doctor, a social worker or a counsellor. Because people often find it difficult to express anger towards themselves or towards close partners, they may deny (suppress) any such feelings. It then becomes the task of the counsellor to help grieving people to identify their anger and vent their feelings *by using indirect techniques*. You might, for example, use the following questions to help grieving people to get in touch with their feelings: *What do you miss most about the deceased?* or *What do you miss most from the time before you knew that you were HIV positive?* or *What don't you miss about the deceased person?* or *What don't you miss about the time before you received the news?*

## Guilt

There are many real and imaginary (irrational) reasons why people feel guilty. It is the task of the counsellor to challenge unnecessary feelings of guilt by asking pertinent questions until the client comes to the recognition that their feelings (of guilt) are unfounded and groundless. If however the feelings are based on real (i.e. justifiable) guilt, it is important to emphasise to clients that nobody is perfect and that everybody makes mistakes. In these circumstances it is best to identify possible mitigating circumstances and also to emphasise the necessity for forgiveness (of self or others), when HIV-infected people, for example, feel guilty because they have also infected their partners. In such circumstances, the counsellor may want to ask the following questions: Did you *deliberately* or *unknowingly* infect your partner? Have you asked forgiveness from your partner? Is it possible to forgive yourself? (If the person holds religious convictions, it may also be helpful to encourage them to go to confession or/and ask God's forgiveness in whatever way is appropriate.)

## Anxiety and helplessness

Anxiety and feelings of helplessness are very common among both people who have lost a loved one and people who have a life-threatening disease. Fear of death and a feeling that they can do nothing about their fate often overwhelm AIDS patients. Similar feelings usually occur after the death of a loved one: when we witness the death of another person, we are unavoidably reminded of our own eventual mortality. Bereaved people often have visions and dreams about the body of the deceased person enclosed by the dark and cold earth. Bereaved people are also prone to feel that life has no purpose and that human beings have no control over their destiny. All such feelings may give rise to severe anxiety attacks and bouts of depression. Helplessness is also expressed in feelings that one cannot continue to survive without the departed person and one cannot keep on living because the terrible sword of death hangs over one's head.

Counsellors should take great care to explore such fears and anxieties with their clients and identify the ways in which the person coped *before* the loss occurred. Discuss with them how they can regain their sense of purpose in life and, even more importantly, encourage them to engage in some new activities that will help them to find a new purpose in life. If one can get clients to realise *and experience* that they can do a lot of things to change their own lives and the lives of others for the better, one will have provided them with one of the best antidotes to anxiety and feelings of helplessness. Although HIV-infected people cannot change their HIV-positive status, they can (with the right attitudes and actions) begin to live in an optimistic, altruistic and healthy way. If they do manage to become more altruistic, caring, self-sacrificing and optimistic, HIV-infected people can add many healthy and creative years to their lives. Some clients may also find it helpful to see their HIV-positive status as a timely warning that they should begin to make the most of their lives. At least this disease gives people ample opportunities to prepare themselves for closure, change things and (in many cases) do the things that they always wanted to do but never had the chance of doing.

*Sadness*

Sadness and accompanying crying (weeping) are an integral part of mourning and should not be avoided. They can even to a certain extent be encouraged with the proviso that crying and feelings of sadness should not be allowed to deteriorate into a self-defeating long-term self-pity. Crying should always be 'purposeful' and the counsellor should explore the changing meaning of crying and sadness during the mourning process with the bereaved person. Crying and sadness perform the function of acknowledging the pain of the loss. Other people often expect bereaved people to be sad and to grieve over the lost person or their lost opportunities, health, prospects and life expectancy (as in the case of HIV-infected people). Bereaved people themselves often feel compelled to be sad and to grieve. To deny themselves the opportunity of crying or sadness because of social pressure, anger or any other reason, may unnecessarily complicate and lengthen the grieving process. Counsellors should therefore always emphasise that people who have suffered a loss have the right to cry and to feel sad about their losses — and that it is important and right that they should express these feelings (by crying — but also in other ways).

But the mere *expression* of emotions is not enough. Emotions should always be *focused*. Sadness (for example) should be accompanied by an awareness of exactly what was lost. Anger (for example) should not merely express rage and indignation. The reasons for the anger should be carefully identified and focused upon. Guilt (for example) should be evaluated and resolved, and anxiety should be acknowledged, clarified and managed.

## Help clients to live with their loss

Bereaved people have to deal with practical problems that have evolved because of their loss. The counsellor should use a problem-solving approach and encourage clients to work out their own solutions to problems. It may be necessary for the counsellor to equip the client with decision-making and coping skills so that he or she can cope effectively with the difficult times and pressing problems (problems that will vary from one person to another). Counsellors may collaborate with their clients in the exploration of practical ways and means to solve their problems and cope with the anxieties they are experiencing in their everyday lives. In general however clients should be discouraged from making major life-changing decisions while they are in the middle of the grieving process. Overhasty decisions that involve (for example) changing or resigning from jobs, selling property, moving to another neighbourhood or city/town, and so on, should preferably be delayed. Such changes are frequently unnecessary or may give rise to new (and serious) problems. If one moves from an old neighbourhood, one may become separated from all one's friends and other support systems and this may seriously exacerbate one's feelings of loneliness. While it is admittedly difficult to exercise good judgement during periods of acute grief (and while people are often forced to make some important decisions), it is generally a good rule for bereaved people to postpone important decisions until after they have worked through all the tasks of the grieving process.

## Facilitate new relationships and redefine existing ones

Clients should be encouraged to relocate emotionally. One should emphasise to survivors that it is acceptable and desirable for them to find new friends and/or partners and explain to them that the deceased person would have expected them to keep on living and be happy. Happy memories of the deceased should not prevent the person from developing new friendships — although bereaved people should be equally careful not to jump overhastily into new and ill-advised relationships (the 'rebound' effect). In the case of HIV-infected people, the loss (or potential loss) of sexual partners may be a source of severe emotional and physical stress.

Infected people should be counselled about safer sexual practices with a spouse. But if their uninfected partners or spouses feel uncomfortable about having sex, they should explore together other kind of intimacies (e.g. hugging, caressing and mutual masturbation) — all of which may also be pleasurable and fulfil the emotional needs of both parties.

### Provide time to grieve and expect it to take time

Mourning takes time. It is therefore important that people should expect to go through a gradual process of cutting ties and of making time in their life to grieve. It is also important for both the client and the counsellor to take cognisance of critical times in the grieving process and for the counsellor to prepare the client for this. The first 3 months after the loss and the first anniversary of the event are especially critical — the counsellor and client should prepare properly for these periods by ensuring that the bereaved will have adequate support during these times. But since all people are unique, some people may experience a totally different timetable of mourning which is characterised by different critical times. Variant timetables may be predicated on dates and times that are special or significant to the surviving person (e.g. a wedding anniversary, Valentine's Day, Christmas, New Year's Eve, the birthday of the survivor or the dead person, or the traditional period during which the affected people took their annual holiday). There are many different dates and times which different individuals find significant, and it is important for the counsellor to identify these and make sure that the client is adequately supported at those times.

### Interpretation of 'normal' behaviour

Both the counsellor and the bereaved person should have a clear knowledge of what 'normal' grieving behaviour entails. It is important for the bereaved person to know that they are not 'going crazy', and that they may often have new experiences, feel strange feelings and find themselves behaving in certain ways that may be weird or frightening to them. Typical manifestations of grief may include some of the following behaviours, feelings, physical sensations and cognitions:

- *Behaviours:* Sleep and appetite disturbances, a tendency towards absent-mindedness, social withdrawal, dreams of the deceased, avoidance patterns that prevent one from being reminded of the loss, searching and calling out, sighing, restlessness, crying, an urge to visit significant places which may remind the person of the loss or deceased person, treasuring significant objects. Children may regress to behaviour that is typical of a younger child (e.g. thumb sucking or bed wetting). They may also become very active and excitable or (the reverse) withdrawn and clinging or they may cry and seek attention in various other ways. Other children may become extremely well behaved (they may try to become 'the perfect child') while older children may begin to indulge in various forms of (uncharacteristic) reckless behaviour (Norton & Dawson, 2000).

- *Feelings:* Sadness, anxiety, numbness, guilt, shock, loneliness, fatigue, helplessness, yearning, anger, emancipation, relief. Children may blame themselves for their loss and feel guilty about it. They often feel extremely anxious and afraid of what may happen next and who will look after them. Shock may in some cases trigger a feeling of numbness which may manifest itself as the showing of no emotions at all (Norton & Dawson, 2000).

- **Physical sensations:** Hollowness in the stomach, tightness in the chest and throat, shortness of breath, weakness of muscles and lack of energy, dry throat, over-sensitivity and a sense of depersonalisation. Children at school will find it difficult to concentrate, they may become ill more often and get severe head-aches. Children may also have nightmares and bad dreams (Norton & Dawson, 2000).
- **Cognitions:** Disbelief, confusion, preoccupation, hallucinations and mistaking (wrongly perceiving) objects and people. Children may manifest decreased levels of self-esteem with resultant problems. They may also begin to think in a way that is 'magical' and fantastical — especially when such thinking is related to matters concerning death (Norton & Dawson, 2000).

If any of the above manifestations persist for too long (e.g. if debilitating depression lasts much longer than 3 months, and if the acute part of the bereavement process stretches over a period longer than 12 to 18 months), or if their grief does not diminish in acuteness over time, these may be indications of complicated grief processing *or* pathology. Counsellors should be aware of the fact that unresolved grief can often manifest itself as either medical or psychiatric problems and that these may need psychological therapy or psychiatric treatment.

### Take individual and cultural differences into account

Although many emotional experiences are common to all people who mourn, people may exhibit enormous variations in their manifestations of grief, in the extent to which they demonstrate certain forms of behaviours and in the ways in which they express their grief. Thus, for example, while some people prefer to talk at length about their grief, others may prefer to remain relatively silent while they work very hard at the tasks of processing their grief. The counsellor also needs to be sensitive to the cultural differences because while it is customary in some cultures to be extremely emotional, people from other cultures may behave aggressively while yet others may have a taboo about expressing public grief. In traditional African cultures people often share their grief much more with their community. In these communities consulting the ancestors through traditional healers may be essential for closure of the grieving process. The following case study of a black mother's feelings after her son had died of AIDS emphasises the importance of sensitivity and respect for other culture's customs (Cochrane, Mays & Roberts, 1988, p. 17):

> She watched as her son retreated in coma into a fetal position in the hours before his death. As a mother, she knew that what he needed (and what she needed also) was for her to crawl into bed with him and hold him as he died. But she was deterred by her fears that [the] nursing personnel would not find this behaviour

acceptable and would reprimand her. To this day, she berates herself for sacrificing her son's dying needs in order to maintain their family's ethnic dignity in the face of the predominantly non-black world of the hospital.

*Ensure continuing support and address different defences and coping styles*

Support to the bereaved should be continuous and not offered only for the first few days. Sometimes survivors and people with life-threatening diseases need a lot of persuasion not to withdraw from life but rather to share their grief with others and accept support. The support may come from family and friends, organised support groups and regular counselling sessions. The counsellor and client should discuss all possible support systems and together ensure that they are available and that they serve their purpose.

Different styles of coping with mourning and the ways in which people defend themselves against unbearable pain should be discussed within the confidential and caring counsellor-client milieu. Counsellor and client should together evaluate different practical strategies and their effectiveness in diminishing distress and solving problems. In some cases, the temporary use of prescribed medication such as anti-depressants may also be necessary.

## Ways of facilitating the bereavement process

In their facilitation of the mourning process, counsellors may use various techniques. These may include some of the following (Worden, 1982; Nefale, 2000):

- *Use of objects and memorabilia:* The counsellor can help a client to focus more clearly by using photographs and letters of the deceased or of people who were associated with the loss. Audio and video tapes, jewellery, pieces of clothing and other objects with which the client is comfortable can be used to facilitate talking and bringing the mourning process to closure.
- *Making use of imagery:* Imagining the deceased or visualising certain situations can be very useful for coming to terms with difficult emotions and circumstances. These images should be clearly focused (the images used should not be vague, arbitrary or erratic). If clients direct these images towards a specific person or process, they may begin to understand their emotions and reactions better.
- *Writing:* Writing letters to the deceased or to people who are involved in the loss may also be helpful. The main purpose of these letters is to focus the client. If the person addressed in the letter is still living, the letter need not actually be posted. One may also ask the bereaved person to write a counselling letter to himself or herself — a letter that emphasises the need for a more optimistic and active engagement with life. Or one may suggest that clients write a letter to ask for forgiveness from former partners or somebody whom clients may have infected

with the HI virus (or otherwise negatively influenced because of their illness). Some people may also find it helpful to write fiction or poetry that expresses and identifies feelings and blockages.

- *Drawing:* One may suggest to children (or to adults who prefer to express themselves visually) that they draw a picture about some aspect of the disease or the death of the loved one. These pictures may reveal to the client and the counsellor some aspects of the grieving process that were opaque — or they may express feelings that were difficult to reveal.

- *Role playing:* Playing out certain situations from the past or rehearsing certain difficult situations with which the bereaved person still has to deal may help the client successfully to complete these tasks in future, or else it may bring closure to various processes. Role playing may also be used in a positive way to facilitate the modelling of new life-enhancing behaviour patterns.

- *Cognitive restructuring:* The assumption behind cognitive restructuring is that your emotions and feelings will be influenced by whatever you constantly think about. The counsellor should therefore try to help the client to relinquish various negative or destructive thoughts and adopt healthier and life-affirming thoughts. If one constantly denigrates and criticises oneself by repeating negative things about oneself, such statements will only increase negativity, depression, hopelessness and anger. By helping the client to test the reality status of over-generalisations, expose distortions and reveal irrational thoughts, counsellors can help clients to restructure their thoughts and in so doing change their negative feelings.

- *Memory books:* Memory books may be extremely important ways of handling the grieving process in the context of AIDS losses and death (Nefale, 2000). If the client engages in compiling books that contain photos, mementoes, poems and stories about the family or deceased person, this will help him or her to come to terms with the magnitude of the loss and bring closure — thereby ensuring that the bereaved person is in a position to focus once again on the realities of life without forgetting the lost loved one. In some parts of Africa this technique is often used by HIV-infected parents to make the process of dying easier for themselves and life more bearable for the children who will remain behind after their death (see 'Orphan care' on page 334).

## Children and bereavement

Children only gradually come to a full understanding of death and dying. It is therefore important when counselling children to take their cognitive stage of development into account:

- The pre-school child (3 to 5 years) generally thinks of death in terms of separation and he or she regards it as temporary in nature — something akin to sleep (Gillis,

1994; Johnson, 2000). In the child's view, death is therefore a reversible phenomenon and the child expects the deceased person (or someone similar) to return.

- A young child (6 to 9 years) can already grasp the reality and finality of death, but does not see death as universal (affecting all people) or as personal (applying to him or her).
- Children older than 10 years understand that death is final, personal and universal (Johnson, 2000). It is therefore at this stage that children start to realise that death may also apply to them and that it is a concrete fact of life that nobody can avoid.

When counselling children about loved ones who have died one should appreciate such limitations in children's understanding of death. It is therefore futile to try and explain to a pre-school child that his or her deceased father is never going to return. Although it is not a good idea to deliberately mislead the child by saying (for example), 'Father is only sleeping', or by avoidance of the term 'death' altogether, one should realise that the child will only fully appreciate the finality of death when he or she is older. It is equally futile to force a pre-school HIV-infected child to understand what death really implies.

It is unwise to try to soften the reality or irreversibility of death by avoiding the subject or by using euphemisms that the child may misunderstand. This will prevent the child from confronting his or her own grief and dealing with it (Gillis, 1994). Death should therefore be openly discussed and presented as a normal part of the cycle of life. The physical and emotional comfort of the child and the realisation that there is an adult (or more people) who is prepared to share the child's grief with him or her are of vital importance. Memories about the deceased should be encouraged — the bereaved need to look back before they can once again look forward (Gillis, 1994).

It is also important for children to be allowed to participate in mourning rites and rituals. A good balance should be struck between shocking children with the gruesome details of death and totally excluding them from the funeral arrangements or barring them from the actual funeral. It is important for children to participate in the rituals of death so that they can experience the concreteness of death and feel that they are not alone in their grieving (Gillis, 1994). Although some disruption is inevitable, the daily routine of children should be disrupted as little as possible by death in the family.

**The counsellor's own grief**

If they are to prevent burnout and be able to deal effectively with bereaved people, counsellors should also be able to look after themselves (see 'Care for the caregiver' on page 282). If they are going to participate in bereavement counselling, counsellors should have come to terms with their own mortality and have accepted it in such a way that they can confront the realities of death and talk openly about it to their clients.

It may also be very painful to counsellors to witness and experience the pain and grief of others. Counsellors in the HIV/AIDS field often find that they are constantly attending funerals and are being exposed to a variety of painful experiences. This may eventually become difficult for them to handle. By counselling HIV-infected people and their significant others, counsellors also become more aware of their own losses because they are regularly being confronted by the spectacle of the losses and bereavement of others. This relentless exposure may increase their own anxiety and stress levels and if they are not properly debriefed or counselled themselves, they may eventually suffer from burnout. By deliberately taking regular breaks, attending debriefing sessions and by ensuring that they have adequate support systems to cope with their own grieving process, counsellors can avoid emotional burnout.

**Activity**

Counsellors should perform the following exercise in order to explore their own grief. Ask yourself the following questions and try to answer them by exploring your own experiences and emotions (Van Dyk et al., 2000):
- What was the first death that you can remember? What was your age at the time? When did you attend your first funeral?
- What are the impressions that you remember best from the above experience(s) and events?
- When were you last bereaved and how did you cope with that loss?
- What was the most difficult death that you have ever experienced — and why was it so?
- Whose death from among your present family or friends would be the most difficult for you to handle? Why is this so?
- What is your primary style of coping with loss?
- How do you know when your own grief has been resolved?
- Under what conditions do you think it is appropriate for you to share your own experiences of grief with clients?

## 13.3 SPIRITUAL AND EMOTIONAL COUNSELLING

While researchers often refer to the importance of dealing with the spiritual and emotional needs of HIV-infected clients and their loved ones, this process probably remains one of the most neglected aspects of counselling — especially within the HIV/AIDS context. Although it is important for counsellors not to force their own religious views onto their clients, it is probably more common for counsellors to either totally ignore the religious needs of clients or merely to refer clients to their rabbi, priest, minister or imam.

Unfortunately many clergy cannot counsel HIV-infected people properly because they are themselves ignorant about the disease and all its ramifications. In any event, most infected people would probably avoid approaching their church, synagogue, temple or mosque leaders for advice or consolation because (in their perception) their religious communities would probably be condemnatory rather than supportive. While such negative perceptions about organised religion are unfortunately sometimes true, in many other cases they may be totally unfounded. The fact remains that religious organisations and churches will need to speak much more openly about all aspects of HIV/AIDS and facilitate an open and supportive milieu before HIV-infected individuals will trust them sufficiently to handle their religious needs.

HIV/AIDS counsellors should identify clergy who are willing to become part of the counselling team or equip themselves to also handle the religious and emotional needs of their clients. In the section that follows some guidelines for the spiritual counselling of HIV-infected people, their loved ones and the community at large will be provided. While spiritual counselling will focus on emotional support, it will also attempt to deal with the 'big' theological issues evoked by the HIV/AIDS pandemic. Spiritual counsellors cannot avoid coming to grips with the questions that follow.

## Why does God cause/allow AIDS?

One of the most difficult but nonetheless urgent and immediate questions of life is why God allows suffering to exist on earth. Would it not have been advisable for God to have excluded all suffering (such as illness, pain and death) from this earth? An associated question is: *Is illness caused directly by sin or some kind of transgression?* Although a person may accept that some agent (i.e. a germ or virus) may be the direct cause of disease, such an explanation is not adequate within a religious framework. Ultimately the question still remains: *Why did it happen to me? Why did this agent choose to attack me — and not somebody else?* Possible answers to such difficult questions are reviewed from different points of view or frames of reference below. (It is important to accept that a secular (i.e. an agnostic or atheistic) worldview is essentially also (in a certain sense) a 'religious' belief system and it should therefore also be considered along with all the other possibilities.)

### A secular frame of reference

The above question can be answered quite easily from the perspective of a secular (non-religious) worldview: *there is no ultimate cause*. The agent attacked a specific person either because he or she was accidentally exposed to it (and his or her immune system was vulnerable or unable to fight the organism) — or else certain behaviours (or behaviour patterns) caused the person to expose himself or herself to the organism. For example, the person visited a malaria area without taking precautions and therefore increased his or her chances of getting the malaria parasite into his or her body.

In contemporary Westernised cultures this secular view of disease is very common. The advantage of this point of view is that it generates no guilt because it does not hypothesise about an ultimate cause (such as God) behind a disease like AIDS. With such a worldview, a person doesn't have to feel guilty about contracting the disease and God cannot be blamed for it. The disadvantage of this worldview is that one must accept that one is often exposed to random processes of nature (e.g. disease-causing agents). All that one can do is to try to avoid certain dangerous situations or high-risk environments and take all the necessary precautions to prevent infection. If one then still contracts a disease, one can only accept it in a fatalistic way — 'Bad things sometimes happen to good people.'

From the secular point of view, the question about why a person got infected may therefore express anger rather than represent a quest for a higher causative agent (such as God). From the HIV-infected person's point of view, one simply lived a high-risk lifestyle and did not take sensible precautions.

If the counsellor comes to the conclusion that the client sees life in terms of this framework, he or she should deal with it by addressing the anger and frustration in an appropriate way. This may be done by emphasising *inter alia* the following points:

- People are not machines. Nobody is perfect and therefore people sometimes do take risks or act ill-advisedly.
- One can choose to stay angry with other people (or with oneself) and thereby spoil the rest of one's life, but one cannot change what has happened to one by doing that. It is however possible to choose how one is going to live the rest of one's life by, for example, being positive and by helping others.
- One should be consistent and honest with oneself. If one believes that there is no higher power that directs events on earth, there is no sense in being angry with life in general or in feeling guilty. Anger and guilt can then only be directed at other people or at oneself — and that is not a productive or helpful way of living.

### A Judeo-Christian framework

Within a Judeo-Christian framework one may extend the above questions (e.g. *Why does God allow AIDS?*) to the following:

- Is HIV/AIDS God's punishment?
- Am I a bad person? Did I deserve to get ill because I sinned?

Four basic answers can be given to these two questions:

1. Sickness and death came into the world because of sin (Genesis 6:3). However, this does not mean that one can attribute specific illnesses to specific sins.

Unfortunately this is exactly what is often done by Jews and Christians. For those who think in terms of so-called 'rigid wisdom' (against which the book of Job protests), sin and illness are closely connected because sin always causes sorrow (e.g. disease). In some cases the argument is even reversed. That is, if people get ill, they must have sinned and they should therefore confess and ask for forgiveness. This is, for example, the view of Job's friends — a view that is rejected by the book of Job (Job 4:7) — and that of the Jews who questioned Jesus in John 9:3. Although the view that illness is caused by sin is still very common among Jews and Christians, it is nonetheless unbiblical and causes much unnecessary guilt and pain in people with life-threatening diseases such as HIV/AIDS. This perception should therefore be rejected in the strongest terms: 'bad' people do not become ill more than 'good' people!

2. The purpose of illness (or any suffering) is not to punish us for sins but to test our faith and so make us better people. Suffering sometimes enables us to purify ourselves and grow spiritually.

**Enrichment**

**Disease is 'good'**

People who are suffering often find it unacceptable and frustrating when counsellors offer them the cliché that everything will work out in the end or work out for the good of the faithful. An unqualified statement like this is problematic in many ways. The fact that it may be for the good of the sick person may not be immediately demonstrable and this fact may encourage counsellors to tie themselves in knots in their attempts to prove just how beneficial suffering is for the suffering person. This answer also still does not answer the question: Why is it necessary for God to use suffering and pain to chastise (punish) his children? This question is especially relevant in cases when the person is suffering from a serious disease such as AIDS or cancer — or when it is a baby that is suffering from an incurable disease. It is therefore better to emphasise the fact that on earth we have less than perfect insight into God's plans and dealings in the world rather than merely to state in an unqualified manner that a disease is ultimately for our good.

3. Because of our limited insight and knowledge as human beings, we cannot on the whole make any sense of suffering. Although we accept that suffering may not be intended as punishment, we might believe that it fits into God's plans in some mysterious way — although we often do not know exactly what God's purposes and intentions may be. It is therefore problematic for any religious person (including counsellors) to try and 'play God' by explaining the purpose of suffering or disease.

4. A fourth answer may be an alternative to the three lines of argument presented here. Although it is related to the secularised worldview, it is not necessarily

agnostic or atheistic. The view emphasises the fact that it was God's intention to give humans full freedom and that God therefore created a cosmos which is essentially and basically neutral. Life is therefore a challenge that is presented to humans. The challenge is that human beings should try to make the best of their lives without too much interference from God (Van Dyk, 2000). (Exactly how much a person may allow for God's intrusion into the course of history will depend on that person's worldview.) When something bad therefore happens to the faithful we should not necessarily attribute it directly to the will of God because in a sense it may only fit into the *broader* framework of God's creation. God is therefore still acknowledged to be a force in human life although God (in such a view) remains much more in the background and acts in much more mysterious ways than most Christians and Jews would usually affirm.

Another question which often plagues HIV-infected individuals is the following: If their infection means that they are bad people, that by extension implies that they will end up in hell. Because HIV-infected people tend to be defensive, they are often reluctant to admit these concerns. Counsellors should therefore treat this issue in a sensitive way and rather deal with it indirectly by, for example, not stating it as a question to the infected client but by characterising it as *an unacceptable and false conviction* of many people within the community.

As noted earlier, sin and sickness have no demonstrable relationship with each other. This means that a person who is HIV positive is not *necessarily* a bad person (i.e. the person's moral status is not a causative factor in the disease). Those who affirm that diseases are caused by sin are reflecting an inappropriate, self-righteous and sanctimonious attitude to those in pain. Sadly, such attitudes are also found in faith communities. The people who hold them often have deep unresolved personal issues about sex, sexuality and sexually transmitted diseases.

Even if the person thinks that he or she has sinned (which is in any case true of all human beings), the spiritual HIV/AIDS counsellor should rather emphasise forgiveness and reconciliation to God and other believers. The Old and New Testaments abound with examples of people who sinned and who were subsequently forgiven by God. These include great heroes of faith like Abraham, Moses and King David. Within a Christian framework the examples of the prostitute (John 8) and the robber whom Jesus pardoned on the cross (Luke 23:43) can be used as helpful examples of God's infinite desire for forgiveness (rather than for punishment and retribution).

### A traditional African religious framework

A large number of Africans (even those who become urbanised) still adhere to traditional African beliefs. It is common for Africans to combine traditional beliefs with other religious systems (such as Christianity). Although (mostly white) religious leaders often tend to be negatively inclined towards these forms of 'syncretism' (i.e. the combining of elements from different religions and belief systems), it is important for counsellors to recognise such systems and include traditional African beliefs among their religious perspectives on HIV/AIDS.

In traditional Africa disease is either attributed to natural agents, witchcraft or the displeasure of the ancestors. But even when Africans attribute a disease to an external agent (e.g. a germ or virus) they will also search for the ultimate cause of the disease — i.e. the person or agent who caused or 'sent' the disease (see 'Witches and sorcerers as causal agents of illness' on page 113). Although many Western-trained counsellors might attempt to persuade traditional African people to change their views about illness and suffering, such an approach would be offensive, insensitive, condescending — and doomed to failure. This know-better attitude would be tantamount to trying to persuade a Christian, Jew or Muslim to abandon their faith. It is essential to work **within** the traditional framework of African beliefs when one is dealing with African clients rather than to try to challenge their worldview. If counsellors have no understanding of the African worldview, they should either quickly become better informed — or else desist from attempting to counsel African clients.

Counsellors should rather advise HIV-infected Africans to consult traditional healers who can identify the ultimate cause of their disease and prescribe the necessary medicines and rituals to appease the ancestors or neutralise the bad effects of witchcraft. It is however important simultaneously to warn the person that HIV/AIDS cannot be cured (even though some traditional healers may claim that this is possible). The cleansing rituals and medicine will therefore only improve the infected person's quality of life and will ensure that the person will have no unresolved issues when he or she dies and enters the spiritual world of the ancestors.

*Other religions*

Forgiveness and ways of cleansing the mind and body are basic to all religions. By encouraging people to engage in purification rituals, to meditate and to restructure the remainder of their lives, one may prepare a person for life after death or for reincarnation. One should emphasise that HIV infection is not a condemnation or the end of the road for infected individuals. It may rather be an opportunity for them to prepare themselves properly for the remainder of their lives and for their transition to another world.

**Death from a religious perspective**

One of the most important functions of religion is to provide coping strategies for accepting the inevitability of death. Death is difficult to accept when young people die (especially when they die from diseases such as HIV/AIDS). In African cultures,

## Children and religion

Religious counsellors should always take the developmental stage of children into account when talking to them about God, illness and death. The following few basic points should be taken into account when one is counselling children (Wong et al., 1999):

- Because toddlers' cognitive processes are undeveloped, they have only a vague (or 'concrete') idea of what God and religious teachings mean. Religious routines and rituals (e.g. prayers) may however be comforting to a sick child or a child who has to deal with a close relative who is sick.

- The older pre-school child begins to develop a capacity to understand religious teachings. At this stage they have a concrete conception of God and begin to imagine Him in terms of physical characteristics (as though God were like an imaginary friend). Although young children enthusiastically participate in religious rituals, they still have a limited grasp of their significance. These routines (e.g. prayers) can nonetheless be very comforting to young children, especially during stressful periods such as illness. Religious teaching such as right and wrong, reward or punishment, heaven or hell are understood and wrong-doing provokes feelings of guilt in children. Because pre-school children often misinterpret illness as punishment — for real or imaginary transgressions — it is therefore important to dismiss this idea and to emphasise the unconditional love of God rather than present God as a judge of good or bad behaviour.

- Because young school-age children picture God as human, they usually describe God in terms such as 'loving' and 'caring'. They are fascinated by the concepts of heaven and hell and are afraid to go to hell. These concepts should therefore be dealt with and children should be assured that God loves children and doesn't expect them to be perfect. Children of this age are preoccupied with rules and regulations and expect to be appropriately punished for misbehaviour. Although they try to structure their lives in a logical and systematic way, they still find it difficult to distinguish between natural and supernatural phenomena. Because their understanding of symbols is limited, it is better to explain religion in more concrete terms to children of this age group. The young school-age child usually perceives illness as punishment. Religious acts such as prayers are important and the younger child expects them to be answered. As they grow older, children start to realise that prayers are not always answered and do not become so anxious when they are not.

- During the adolescent years beliefs become more principled and abstract and less emphasis is placed on rituals and practice. Adolescents therefore emphasise the internal rather than the external aspects of commitment. At this stage children can understand and deal with most religious aspects of disease and illness. It is especially the fairness or unfairness of life that will be of great concern to the adolescent who is HIV-infected or has lost a close relative to the disease.

for example, the death of young people is seen as 'unnatural'. In modern Western societies people are also alienated from death. Part of the reason for this is that our culture is so materialistic that people find it difficult to believe in any kind of existence after death. But dying is not unnatural. It is simply a natural part of life — although anxiety about what may be waiting after death is very real, even in the case of religious people. One can therefore expect people to engage in some kind of search for certainty, or attempt to contact the spiritual world — either in an attempt to link up with a loved one or to gain some certainty about life after death. A belief in an existence after death can make an approaching death more meaningful and bearable.

One finds that there are two extremes when it comes to belief in life after death. At the one pole is a total denial of any life after death (i.e. the a-religious view) while at the other extreme people may despise their earthly life and yearn only for the life hereafter. The latter view originated from Plato's philosophy which stated that the fleshly life represents all that is low and unacceptable, and that one's spirit should be relieved to get rid of its imprisoning body. Although this view is also very common among Christians, it is (in its more extreme forms) more Platonic than biblical. The positive aspect of this eschatological worldview is that it may be a big comfort to a person who is suffering and who needs to have some hope for a better future — albeit after death. The negative aspects of this worldview are that it is escapist (although some escapism should not necessarily be denied to an HIV-infected person) and that it sometimes fails to prepare a person adequately to cope with the remainder of his or her life. Why should he or she invest so much energy in the present life if it is so disappointing? Why not wait in anticipation for a better life to come? Such an attitude may cause a person to give up long before death intervenes.

Most people would rather opt for some middle position between totally denying a life hereafter or living only for a life after death. The religious counsellor should therefore emphasise the importance of ensuring the quality of whatever life remains to the HIV-infected person — without denying the potential importance of life after death. Often a balanced view which emphasises the importance of both 'worlds' can offer much comfort to a person with religious beliefs and enhance the quality of their remaining life.

It is important for religious counsellors and their clients to talk about death and for counsellors to attempt to strip the image of death of some of its horror and ugliness. The bereaved person is often comforted if one emphasises that death is a natural process and that it is not necessarily the end — it may in fact be the beginning of something new and wonderful. It should also be emphasised that it is only natural for a person to be uncertain about death. Nobody knows exactly *what* death will be like and everyone ultimately has to face death on their own.

## Ethical considerations

Ethical considerations are of the utmost importance when one counsels HIV-infected people within the family or community. Although one would expect religious communities and churches to be generally supportive and accepting of HIV-infected people, primitive fears and unresolved complexes often override compassion and theological principles and bring out 'unexpected' negative reactions. In their mildest form such negative attitudes may cause indifference when members of the community deliberately or unconsciously ignore the problems of HIV/AIDS sufferers. In their more extreme form, one encounters condemnation, stigmatisation, the labelling of people and a 'laager' mentality.

There are no uniform responses to HIV/AIDS within religious communities. Instead one encounters a whole spectrum of responses. On the one extreme one finds the view that the only effective way of stopping the spread of the disease is for people to strictly adhere to religious teachings about human sexuality and substance abuse (i.e. everyone should avoid sexual intercourse outside marriage, never be promiscuous and always abstain from drug abuse). At the other extreme one finds religious leaders who believe that while religious teachings are very important, these should be supplemented with explicit information about methods that are known to be effective in reducing the risks of transmitting HIV (e.g. condom use) (Lyons, 1988). Experience has shown that the first type of (idealistic) view is not effective and that the more realistic second option is probably a more honest and compassionate way of dealing with HIV/AIDS within a religious context.

The ethical principle of 'saving and sustaining of life' should also be emphasised within a religious context. In Jewish thought the saving of life takes precedence over all other considerations (Rose, 1988). *Reverence for life* plays an equally important role in Christianity and in religions such as Hinduism and Buddhism and this principle should be emphasised as the basis for HIV/AIDS prevention education.

In Christianity (but also to some degree in other religions) believers tend to judge people much more severely for their sexual transgressions — often such judgements are based on double standards and a great deal of hypocrisy and self-righteousness (Sunderland & Shelp, 1987). Such attitudes have no intrinsic connection with any religious principles (and in fact contradict widely held religious principles of acceptance, compassionate care and forgiveness). These negative attitudes should therefore be exposed by religious counsellors for what they are — biased and unacceptable expressions of hatred. This should be emphasised not only when counselling HIV-infected clients who may have suffered because of such attitudes and behaviour but also when training counsellors for dealing with members of the community.

For the same reasons it is hypocritical to keep on discussing the *morality* of teaching people safer sex practices while allowing people to die from AIDS. *All human life is precious* and one cannot reject those who suffer because they transgress principles or moral standards that are dear to one's own heart (or religious beliefs). Although it may therefore be important (and wise) within the framework of religious counselling to emphasise the value of sexual morality and promote the ideal of sexual abstinence outside marriage, churches and other religious organisations will be avoiding their responsibility if they do not accept the realities of life — and those realities are that because it is not easy to change behaviour and morals, one should emphasise the importance of safer sex practices (Van Arkel, 1991). Even if a church does not condone the usage of condoms (inside or outside marriage), it should not neglect to teach its members about the need for safer sexual practices (based on the principles of compassion and the reverence for life).

Although HIV/AIDS in Africa *is primarily a heterosexual disease*, it is nonetheless important that religious counsellors should have an accommodating attitude towards gay people. While churches and religious institutions throughout the world differ in their theological attitudes towards homosexuality, many religions in the past few decades have begun to emphasise the importance of accommodating gay people within religious congregations without condemning them. In this regard — as in every other — it is the task of religious counsellors to avoid hypocrisy and refrain from judging other people, especially when it comes to sexual matters.

The labelling of people as *guilty* or *non-guilty* is rooted in a deep psychological need to create as much distance as possible between a person and a threatening disease such as HIV/AIDS. It is therefore not surprising to learn that similar negative attitudes prevailed during the time of the Black Death of the Middle Ages. True believers should never be guilty of such cruelty and lack of compassion. Their behaviour should be based on generally accepted principles of compassion and not on mindless fear, hypocrisy, denial and neurotic superstition.

Two of the most commonly expressed views about the AIDS pandemic are firstly that it is God's punishment for a sinful and promiscuous lifestyle and secondly that it is a 'natural' way of nature to reduce the numbers of the human population. The first question can be answered by referring to the discussion above which outlines the invalid argument that sin directly causes all suffering and illness, and also by pointing out how many children, haemophiliacs and health care professionals (who have accidentally been exposed to HIV) have died as a result of being infected by the virus. To write of these so-called 'innocent' people as *the exception that proves the rule* is hypocritical and heartless in the extreme — and therefore incompatible with all compassionate expressions of religious dogma.

To view the AIDS pandemic as a 'natural' way of 'culling' people may sound like a heartless but reasonable assumption — until one of one's own close family members or friends becomes one of the so-called 'culled'. When confronted by this point of view, we should always ask ourselves the following questions:

- What are the psychological reasons why anyone should express such a view? Is it an unconscious way of trying to deal with the tragedy of life by exposing the so-called ecological reasonableness of plagues? Or is it a way of withdrawing all emotional energy from the universal tragedy that is playing itself out in our midst?
- Is it a way of making the lack of compassion for HIV-infected people more acceptable by stepping outside of any religious framework and resorting to natural and ecological explanations?

## The role of the church and other religious institutions

An important aspect of religious counselling should be directed outwards towards the church or other religious organisations. Expressed hostility (or the more common forms of indifference) should be exposed and condemned as heartlessness and opposed on all terrains. One can counter such views by educating and involving religious leaders and the faithful in the AIDS field.

In the first place religious counsellors should become part of every single HIV/AIDS counselling team. Where possible, these religious counsellors should be members of the local clergy and they should be adequately trained and noted for their compassionate attitude towards suffering.

All religious institutions should also be encouraged to become involved in an organised way in HIV/AIDS care and counselling by, for example, financially and physically supporting existing hospices or (where necessary) by founding such caring facilities. Research has shown that it is much more desirable in the long term to involve *local* agencies and religious institutions than to depend on often undependable foreign support.

All religions emphasise that compassion should be expressed by actual physical help and the relief of pain, illness, hunger, poverty and other forms of suffering. In Africa poverty has had a severe impact on the spreading of HIV/AIDS and there can be no doubt that it also negatively affects the treatment and care of AIDS patients. AIDS patients often barely have enough food to keep them alive and expensive drugs and healthy food are nearly always beyond their grasp (UNAIDS, 2000a). Care-givers and volunteers themselves are often also hungry and needy. This makes it very difficult for them to care for others because they are often too weak to tend to their own physical needs.

In such circumstances churches, synagogues, temples, mosques and other religious organisations cannot sit back and remain unmoved by the tremendous suffering and dereliction of infected people. In the face of the HIV/AIDS pandemic, religious institutions will have to redefine their usual way of 'caring for the poor'.

They will have to engage in prevention and education programmes and also pay attention to the spiritual and physical needs of people who are suffering from illnesses or who experience desperate poverty because of the loss of breadwinners and parents to AIDS (in the case of the vast numbers of AIDS orphans).

## 13.4 CONCLUSION

The AIDS pandemic can only be countered if it is fought on all fronts, that is, if the church and all other religious institutions are willing publicly to preach about behaviour change and become actively involved in caring for sick and orphaned people. If they fail to do this, their failure will probably become one of the greatest failures by organised religion ever witnessed in the history of humankind on this earth. If religious institutions fail humanity in this crisis, they will forever compromise the credibility of all organised religious institutions and bring into question their relevance and role in contemporary and future society.

# Care and Support for the Person Living with HIV/AIDS

**After completing Part 4 you should be able to:**

- develop a Community Home-Based Care (CHBC) programme for the community in which you live
- devise a practical model for orphan care that will work in your community
- prepare and present a lecture to primary caregivers (involved in home-based care) about the basic principles of infection control at home
- prepare and present a lecture to professional nurses about universal precautions and infection control in the hospital
- advise HIV-infected individuals about a healthy diet and sound nutritional practices. (Remember to take their personal circumstances into account.)
- advise HIV-infected individuals on how to take care of their immune systems by living a healthy life
- teach volunteers the basic principles of caring for a patient with AIDS in his or her home
- apply basic (or advanced) nursing principles in caring for HIV-infected people who present with fever, diarrhoea, skin infections, problems with the mucous membranes (mouth and throat), respiratory problems, nausea and vomiting, genital problems, pain, weakness and mental confusion
- understand the principles of palliative care

## INTRODUCTION TO PART 4

The main theme of Part 4 is the care and support of individuals with HIV infection and AIDS. HIV/AIDS makes demands on the local community and society at large that cannot be met by hospitals alone. Families, loved ones and the community all have an indispensable role to play in the support and care of individuals with HIV/AIDS. Part 4 concentrates on how to care for people with HIV infection and AIDS in different health care settings such as hospitals, hospices, clinics – and in the patient's own home. Practical advice and solutions are offered about how to care for patients in health care settings with very limited resources, facilities and finances – such as we find in many rural clinics and homes.

The importance of family and community involvement in the care and support of HIV-infected individuals is discussed in **Chapter 14**. The basic principles of Community Home-Based Care (CHBC) programmes are presented, as well as guidelines and advice about how to start such programmes in your communities. The plight of Africa's AIDS orphans and strategies or models for the care of orphaned children are also discussed in Chapter 14.

The application of universal precautions to prevent HIV infection in different health care settings is discussed in **Chapter 15**. This chapter offers guidelines about infection control in hospitals, clinics, hospices and homes in which family members have to care for a patient or patients with AIDS.

**Chapter 16** focuses on strengthening of the immune system, the promotion of general health, nutrition, and on the nursing care of general health problems and opportunistic infections. The principles of palliative (terminal) care are also discussed in Chapter 16. In the section entitled **What to do at home**, the author offers practical advice about how to care for a patient with HIV/AIDS with the minimal resources available in many homes.

# 14 Family and Community Involvement

*A pool of light*

*In the silver morning,*
*when the land was still cool and windy,*
*only the village was a pool of light.*

The magnitude of the HIV/AIDS crisis has inevitably meant that both the family and the community have had to become involved in most care programmes. Before the AIDS pandemic became a reality in modern human society, it was not unreasonable to regard pandemics of this kind (such as the Black Death — the bubonic plague pandemic that killed over 50 million people in Europe and Asia in the 14th century) as tragic episodes from the distant past. We were complacent because we had become accustomed to the wonders of medical science and technology. Cures and treatments have been discovered (or are in the process of discovery) for most problems, illnesses and syndromes, and even death itself was considered an enemy that could be defeated or at least delayed. More and more hospitals and clinics were built, and wherever possible medical services such as vaccinations were extended to the majority of the population. And so we continued to be lulled into complacency by the advances and promise of modern medical science and scientific research.

But then HIV and AIDS erupted onto the scene and everything changed. People are dying in their millions and medical science has no cure. Hospitals are inundated and overflowing with very sick and dying AIDS patients while people with curable diseases and conditions are being turned away. Many health care professionals find themselves unable to cope with the demands of the pandemic and begin to suffer from burnout because they can no longer actualise the healing and alleviation of suffering to which they are professionally committed. Because we are a society in crisis, our only hope for coping effectively with HIV/AIDS is to look beyond the crisis and to use the rich resources and strengths that have always resided in our family and community life.

HIV and AIDS make tremendous new demands on health services that cannot be met by hospitals alone. Because HIV infection (and all its accompanying complications) can last for months or years, a person with HIV infection or AIDS may move from the home to the hospital and back again several times. Because hospital care is very expensive, families can often not afford multiple admissions to hospitals. Hospitals themselves do not have the personnel and resources to cope with the huge demands that AIDS makes of them. The only practical and humane solutions are (1) that patients be cared for in their own homes and communities for as long as possible, (2) that we utilise clinics and other health care support systems in the community for advice and support, and (3) that we use hospitals as a last resort when a patient's condition has deteriorated and when professional help is needed.

But the demands on families and the community do not end with the death of the patient. The AIDS epidemic has left behind millions of orphans in Africa and the conditions in which these children live are appalling. If communities do not reach out to help these children, AIDS will also kill our future.

> Because every community has to become involved in the fight against AIDS they must be empowered to do so. It is only through an enormous commitment of resources — within communities and between communities at an international, national and local scale — that the world can hope to contain the HIV/AIDS pandemic and care for those who are ill (WHO, 1993).

Community home-based care (CHBC) will be discussed in the first part of this chapter, and the community care of orphans in the second part. The basic principles of community home-based care that are discussed in this chapter are based on the guidelines that were compiled by Fröhlich (1999) and the WHO (2000a).

## 14.1 COMMUNITY HOME-BASED CARE

### Definition of community home-based care

*Community home-based care* is the care given to individuals in their own homes when they are supported by their families, their extended families or those of their choice. These home-based caregivers are supported by a multidisciplinary team and complementary caregivers who are able to meet the specific needs of the individual and family. The team consists of all the people who are involved in care and support and may include a medical practitioner, nursing supervisor, social worker, health educator, physiotherapist, occupational therapist, AIDS health promotion workers, volunteers, traditional healers, religious healers and religious leaders (Fröhlich, 1999, p. 4).

### The goals and objectives of community home-based care programmes

The main goal of community home-based care programmes is to provide the organisational structures, resources and framework that will enable the family to look after its own sick members. Important functions of CHBC programmes are to *empower* the community and the family to cope effectively with the physical, psychosocial and spiritual needs of those living with HIV infection and AIDS, to *educate* the community about the prevention of HIV transmission, to *support* family members in their care-giving roles, and to reduce the social and personal impact that living with HIV infection and AIDS makes on all those concerned. A very important function of CHBC programmes is to establish a well-functioning *referral system* to hospitals, hospices, clinics and other health care facilities in the community.

## Advantages of community home-based care

Home-based care is often the best way to look after someone with AIDS. The following reasons explain why home-based care is preferable to hospital care (Fröhlich, 1999; WHO, 1993):

● Good basic care can be successfully provided in the home.

● People who are very sick or dying often prefer to stay at home so that they can spend their last days in familiar surroundings — especially when they know they cannot be cured in a hospital.

● Sick people are comforted by being in their own homes and communities with family and friends all around them. The ambience of home prevents the patient from feeling isolated and rejected.

● Home-based care promotes a holistic approach to care. This means that the physical, social, cultural, psychological, emotional, religious and spiritual needs of a patient can all be fulfilled by the family and the health team.

● Home-based care can be comprehensive if it includes rehabilitative, preventative, promotive, curative and palliative care.

● It is usually less expensive for families to care for someone at home. The cost of hospitalisation and transportation to and from a hospital can be financially crippling.

● If the sick person is at home, family members can attend to their *other* responsibilities more easily. It can become very difficult to cope with one's own life if a loved one is in hospital and if the caregiver has to make frequent trips to a hospital to take food to the sick person and to assist in the tasks of physically caring for the sick person.

● Because the pressure on hospitals is reduced by home care, doctors, nurses and other health care professionals can use their time more effectively to care for other critically ill patients in hospitals.

● Home care reduces the enormous pressure on provincial and national health care budgets (which are already strained to breaking point).

● The network of health services available in the CHBC programme enables family members to gain access to counselling support for themselves.

● Families and community involvement in the care of their own patients creates general AIDS awareness in the community and this helps to break down fear, ignorance, prejudice and negative attitudes towards people with AIDS.

● Community home-based care is sensitive to the culture and value systems of the local community — a sensitivity that is often missing in cold, neutral hospital settings.

● The intervention in community home-based care is pro-active rather than reactive.

- Community home-based care puts AIDS care providers in touch with potential orphans and people who really need help desperately.
- Community home-based care is empowering. This means that people take responsibility for and control of their *own* lives and communities.

**Potential problems associated with community home-based care**

The following potential problems associated with community home-based care should be considered:

- Patients often feel isolated — especially when they are confined to the home or bed.
- Many people in communities are not ready for home-based care because of ignorance, superstition and (mainly) a fear of being stigmatised by other members of the community. For these reasons people might reject the concept of home-based care. This situation further contributes to the feelings of anguish, desperation and loneliness that often characterise AIDS and its accompanying circumstances. In a certain South African city with a high prevalence of HIV infection, one hospital runs a training programme for providers of home-based care for the dying *in which the word 'AIDS' is never once mentioned* (UNAIDS, 2000c). This bizarre situation expresses more eloquently than any words can indicate the extent of the prejudice, fear and ignorance that imprisons potential caregivers behind walls of silence and denial and so prevents them from rendering to the community the compassionate care and vigorous leadership that they should be providing.
- Non-compliance with treatment often occurs because the patient or caregivers do not know how or when to administer medication (because they are illiterate and uneducated) or because the medication they require is far too expensive and they do not know where to go for financial aid.
- A lack of knowledge about the disease, treatment, emergency situations and community resources often hampers home-based care, and many caregivers are afraid lest they themselves become infected with HIV.
- One of the greatest dangers that besets community home-based care is that the caregiver might sometimes retire from the care-giving process because of exhaustion and burnout occasioned by the extreme demands of caring for a terminally ill patient. It is absolutely vital for caregivers to have support systems and to know how to care for themselves as well if they want to prevent themselves from being overwhelmed by burnout (see 'Care for the caregiver' on page 282 for more information about this phenomenon). Community home-based care can only be successful if caregivers are well trained and if ongoing support and advice are available.

## The community of caregivers

The community home-based care team consists of the following people:

- The individual with HIV/AIDS
- The family and/or significant others (in the home)
- The programme coordinator who is usually a professional person such as a nurse or social worker
- Professional medically directed services including professional nurses, community health or TB workers, social workers, medical doctors, psychologists or counsellors, pharmacists, physiotherapists, and occupational therapists
- Those trained volunteers and others who offer supportive services such as residential care, respite services, pastoral care, legal aid and advice, transport services, as well as the staff of various NGOs (non-governmental organisations) and CBOs (community-based organisations)
- Complementary services such as those of traditional healers and herbalists
- Community support such as community leaders, traditional leaders, village committees, religious and spiritual leaders, teachers and youth groups

A well-functioning network and referral system should connect the CHBC team with hospitals, hospices, clinics and other community-based health care institutions. Government support in terms of recognition, education, financial support, supplies and staff is indispensable. (See Figure 14.1 for an integrated CHBC system.)

### The role of volunteers in a CHBC programme

Local community volunteers play a very important role in CHBC programmes. According to Fröhlich (1999), many of the perceived disadvantages of using volunteers can be overcome if the volunteers are recognised as key workers in the programme, if they are chosen by members of the community and if they are properly trained in basic home care. A number of factors to be considered when selecting volunteers are age, gender, accessibility (Do they live near the patient?), willingness, commitment, dedication, time (Are they in full-time employment?), an understanding of the problems involved, reliability, honesty, the ability to relate well to people, and the necessary integrity to respect confidentiality and people's basic rights.

Volunteers should be used wherever they fit best in terms of their personalities, qualities, expertise and interest. Volunteers directly involved in patient care should, for instance, be able to speak the language of the patient and his or her family, be able to read, write and calculate, have an interest (and preferably previous experience) in basic nursing care, and they should possess good interpersonal and communication skills. There are also many tasks that need to be performed by other volunteers who are not interested in basic nursing care — tasks such as reading to patients, shopping, cooking and looking after children.

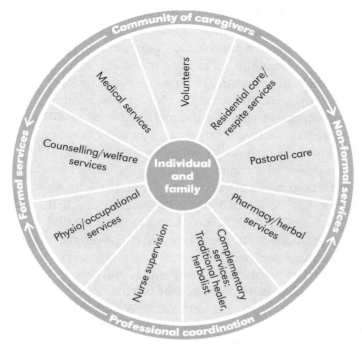

**Figure 14.1**
*Integrated community home-based care services*
(Source: Adapted from Fröhlich, 1999, p. 9)

Enrichment

**The use of children in home-based care — a warning!**

Children can be very helpful in the home when there is a sick person and they can do all sorts of little things like making tea or running errands. The family and the community should however be very careful not to misuse and exploit the children. Tlou (2000) investigated the impact on rural girls (aged between 11 and 16 years) in Botswana who were helping to care for a relative with AIDS. The girls were mostly used for respite care after school hours to allow the primary caregiver a rest. Tlou found that this created potentially disastrous consequences. The girls expressed a lack of knowledge about HIV/AIDS, emotions of fear, helplessness, anticipation of the worst, and they suffered from fatigue and lack of sleep because of caring at night. The schooling of the girls was also affected because they were forced to neglect their homework and skip extra-curricular activities. The consequences of this were that the girls dropped out of the school and therefore missed opportunities for tertiary education. Tlou concluded her research by appealing for close collaboration between the community health team and primary caregivers in families so that home-based care would not become a process of merely 'dumping' patients on women and girls.

## Development of a CHBC programme: where to start

If we want to develop and implement a CHBC programme, we must first compile a community profile in order to establish the extent of the need, resources and networks in a specific community. It is very important to talk to, listen to and collaborate with community leaders (because they are the key role players in any community), and with the HIV-infected people and their families (because they are the people directly affected by the programme) if we want our CHBC programme to be a success. A programme that is developed by outsiders without close consultation with the people in the community will most certainly fail.

After we have compiled a community profile, we should establish programme objectives that meet the needs of the community and appoint a programme coordinator. We then have to recruit staff and volunteers for the CHBC programme and train them thoroughly. An HIV/AIDS awareness programme that runs concurrently with the CHBC programme in the community has to be devised that can obtain the understanding, appreciation and support of the community for the CHBC programme. We also need to collaborate closely with health care professionals, community and religious leaders as we put together the multidisciplinary team that will offer comprehensive care to patients with AIDS. We also need to establish a care network and referral system — and make sure that all health-providing services in the community know about the CHBC programme. Fundamental CHBC practices involve raising funds, instituting a reliable accounting system and monitoring how well the CHBC programme operates by keeping a record of all its activities.

## Implementation of the CHBC programme: what the client needs

Before we can provide a comprehensive service that meets the physical, psychosocial, emotional, spiritual and cultural needs of those living with HIV/AIDS, it is obviously necessary for us to find out exactly what these needs are. It is only when we are fully acquainted with the needs, problems and difficulties of HIV-infected people and their families and caregivers that we can begin to make decisions about what to offer them, who we need to meet their needs, and what kinds of referral we can make (as such needs arise). All the following factors need to be taken into account (Fröhlich, 1999):

- *Medical or nursing needs:* Does the client have any medical or nursing problems that need to be attended to by a nurse or does he or she need to be referred to a clinic or hospital?
- *Basic needs:* Does the client have food, shelter, clothes and blankets, electricity, water and sanitation? If the client lacks these basic requirements, ask the social worker to visit the client.
- *Activities of daily living:* Is the client mobile, or is he or she confined to bed or house-bound? Can the client eat normally or must somebody assist him or her to

eat? Is the client incontinent or is he or she able to use the toilet? Is there a toilet in the home, and if not, can a bedpan or commode be arranged for the client? Who performs the following tasks for the client: collecting water, cooking, bathing, washing clothes, shopping, collecting children from school, caring for pets, maintaining the house and garden? Volunteers can make an invaluable contribution by helping with all these chores.

- *Social needs:* Who is the primary caregiver? How many people live in the house with the client? Do friends, neighbours and family members offer their support?

- *Financial needs:* Does the household have any income? Does the client receive a disability grant or pension? Possible sources of income (e.g. welfare departments, NGOs, help from the church, mosque, temple or other religious organisations) should be investigated and a list compiled.

- *Spiritual needs:* To what religious group does the client belong? Does the client have any spiritual needs that are not being attended to?

- *Hospital, hospice and palliative care:* A time may come when the family is no longer able to cope with a critically ill patient. At this time it is important to refer the patient to a hospital or to ask for help from a hospice. If a patient prefers to die at home, counselling, palliative care and practical support should be available to the patient and the caregivers.

- *Needs of the primary caregiver:* The primary caregiver (who is most often the mother or grandmother of the family) has to carry a huge load. Not only does she often have to look after a sick and dying person, but she also often has to ensure that life goes on for the young ones living in her home. Because this load can sometimes become overwhelming, it is vital for the primary caregiver to get time off from her duties. Volunteers can provide invaluable support by taking over the care of the patient for a few hours while the primary caregiver catches up on lost sleep, goes shopping, visits her friends, or even just goes to see a film.

If the client's needs are to be properly and adequately accommodated, both the client and the family need to be educated in basic health care. This kind of basic health education offers information about how to promote a healthy lifestyle, proper nutrition and the importance of appropriate exercise. Caregivers should be taught how to manage minor illnesses, how to institute universal precautions and prevent accidents from happening in the home (see chapter 15), how to provide basic nursing and palliative care, and when to seek professional help (see chapter 16).

Since a major proportion of caring for AIDS patients consists of counselling, it is necessary for caregivers to be acquainted with the basic principles of counselling (see chapter 10).

## Training of care providers

It is important to train all caregivers who will be involved in community home-based care properly and thoroughly. While the training provided will depend on the level of care offered, it should always include basic nursing care principles, the management of common illnesses, the prevention of HIV infection (through taking the necessary precautions) and basic counselling skills. Home-based caregivers usually benefit from ongoing education, support and supervision. Wherever possible, a home care kit should be made available to all health care personnel who work in the community and in homes. This kit should include disinfectants, soap, utensils for boiling, gloves, protective garments and containers for the safe disposal of equipment and waste (WHO, 2000a).

Activity

- Develop a community home-based care programme for the community in which you live. Make a list of the people in your community who you would like to approach to help you with this programme (professional people as well as volunteers).
- Draw up your own 'Quick Reference Guide' by listing all the resources and services available in your community. Use the following headings in your reference guide: Name; Service provided; Contact person; Address; Telephone number. If possible, visit some of these services and see for yourself what they have to offer. Include the following services and people in your list: hospitals, clinics, hospices, government services, AIDS clinics, NGOs, voluntary counselling and testing (VCT) services, nurses, community leaders, ministers, social workers, physiotherapists, occupational therapists, pharmacists, herbalists, traditional healers.

## 14.2 ORPHAN CARE

The AIDS epidemic has created more than 13 million orphans (children under the age of 15 years who have lost a mother or both parents to AIDS), and 95 % of these children live in sub-Saharan Africa (UNAIDS, 2000c). Because the extended family system (which would have traditionally provided support for orphans) is greatly overextended in those communities most affected by AIDS, it can now no longer take care of its orphaned children. The stigma associated with AIDS deaths in many communities contributes to the fact that many families don't want to look after AIDS orphans. The consequence of this is that these children are often socially isolated and deprived of basic social services such as education.

After their parent's death, children often lose their rights to the family land or house. Relatives move in and often exploit the children by taking possession of their property and by not providing any support for them. Because these children no longer have access to education, and because they lack work skills and family support of any kind, they often end up living on the streets. Since they have no money whatsoever (except what they can raise from begging), they suffer more frequently from malnutrition, illness, abuse and sexual exploitation than children who are orphaned by other causes. AIDS orphans in most cases live without basic human rights and dignity. They don't know how to protect themselves and they have no access to doctors, nurses, and other health care workers and facilities. Some studies have shown that death rates among AIDS orphans are 2.5 to 3.5 times higher than those for non-orphans (HIV Infant Care Programme, 2000).

Some African countries and communities have developed innovative care and support programmes in response to this crisis. There is a general consensus that help for orphans should be targeted at supporting families and improving their capacity to cope rather than setting up institutions (orphanages) for the children (UNAIDS, 2000c; WHO, 2000a).

## Strategies for the care of orphaned children

We now consider the following strategies or models for the care of orphaned children:

### The extended family

Every reasonable attempt should be made to trace relatives. Relatives who cannot afford to look after orphaned children should be helped financially so that they can care for these children. In Zambia, which has the second largest proportion of AIDS orphans in the world after Uganda, non-governmental organisations are providing food, clothing and school fees to orphans and the extended families that take care of them. An organisation in Uganda (UWESO) funds the education of AIDS orphans and also runs a micro-finance scheme to help the caretakers — usually female relatives of the children — to start up small businesses and trading activities.

### Foster care

Foster care means the placement of a child with a non-relative family after careful selection of the family or caregivers. The selection process should take factors such as the traditional cultural background, norms and values of the child and the foster family into account when trying to make a match. Families who foster children usually receive a small foster grant from the government to assist them with some of the costs involved in caring for another child. (See enrichment box 'Adoption is often problematic in Africa' on page 336, which explains why children in Africa are rather *fostered* than *adopted*.)

### Adoption is often problematic in Africa

Adoption is often problematic in traditional African communities in those cases where children (and specifically boys) are not of the same family lineage (clan) as the adopted family. Because ancestors (and the honouring and continuation of their names) are very important in the everyday lives of Africans, it may be problematic to bring 'new' ancestors — those of the orphaned boy — into the family. Adopting a girl is less of a problem because a girl will usually adopt the ancestors of the new family — as happens in marriage (Seepamore, 2000).

### *A community-based foster care model (The 'Alexandra' model)*

Seepamore and Nkgatho (2000) developed an innovative community-based foster care model for orphaned babies and children in Alexandra township in South Africa. (Most of these orphaned babies are HIV- infected.) The Alexandra model is based on the premise that orphans and their foster parents should be actively supported by each other and by the community. Seepamore divided the Alexandra community into three wards. Each ward has its own pool of trained foster mothers, a social worker who is the coordinator, a leader foster parent who networks with the foster mothers in her ward, with the social worker and with other informal community service providers. The foster mothers are trained in home-based care, they are visited each month by the social worker, they attend lectures, they know each other well and they get lots of support and advice. The mothers are supported by a whole team of community workers such as students, volunteers, religious organisations and schools. A supervisor renders supportive services to all the social workers in the team. The Alexandra model has tremendous advantages for the child in terms of improved health, weight gain, psychological well-being and a longer life. The model also helps to promote acceptance of the children by the community and it changes the attitudes of some of the community members. Because they are well trained and supported, foster parents are often willing to look after more than one child, or to repeat the caring experience after a child's death.

### *Group foster care (the 'granny' programme)*

A group foster care model was started in Uganda to accommodate more children in foster care by using group foster care programmes. Older women ('grannies') were appointed and trained as foster parents. The grannies were then allocated different tasks. Some of them tended a food garden while other older, less agile grannies looked after the children. A third group worked in the kitchen where they did the cooking. All the caregivers received food from the kitchen to feed their own families. The granny project resulted in better care and nutrition for the orphans, better nutrition for the whole community (excess food was given to nearby squatters), improved community services (a crèche facility, a toy library and a resource centre were developed), job creation (vendors sold the excess food from the gardens), and a general alleviation of poverty in the community.

## Child-headed households

Households headed by adolescents (sometimes as young as 12 years old) who care for their younger siblings are often seen in our communities. If these children cannot be accommodated in foster care programmes, community (and governmental) support should be offered to help these children to cope with their plight. Religious organisations can play a very important role in providing these children with necessary support. Social workers and nurses should visit the child-headed households at least once a month to check on their social and physical well-being. Students and other youth groups should get involved in supporting, educating and caring for these children.

**Enrichment**

### The memory book project

Children who have lost one or both parents to AIDS are often saddled with a legacy of confusion and grief because many parents remain silent about their HIV status until they die. Although they hope that their silence will protect their children, it only has the effect of leaving the children unprepared to face a future alone. The National Community of Women Living with HIV/AIDS in Uganda is running a highly innovative programme called the Memory Project to counteract this painful situation. The purpose of the Memory Project is to break the silence that exists between infected parents and their children. What happens is that the mother and child often write the memory book together. The memory book takes children on a step-by-step journey through different aspects of their own identity, their family history, their lifestyle, culture and beliefs. These mothers often explain their own HIV status to their children and introduce them to their future caregivers. The memory book consists of photographs, stories, anecdotes about the child and the mother's life, little lessons, and information that a child may need later on in life. 'The memory book embodies a treasure-trove of childhood memories and family history for both parents and children. For the child, it reminds him or her of their roots, gives them a keen sense of belonging when orphaned, and provides answers to questions they would have asked their parents while growing up' ('Memory books', 2000, p. 3). The memory book project in Uganda has stimulated children to take an active interest in the care of their sick parents, to ask questions about their own health and the health of their parents, and to take up the challenge of looking after themselves (as best they can) after their parents have died (Nyamayarwo, 2000). The memory book children will also probably be more careful about thinking about ways to protect themselves from infection when they are older.

*Orphanages*

A last resort (when all other options are inappropriate or unavailable) is orphanages. Orphanages should mainly be utilised to care for abandoned babies or very young children who need care until alternative solutions can be found for them.

## 14.3 CONCLUSION

The orphans of Africa need us as their advocates — advocates who will plead for the recognition of their basic human rights, their dignity and protection. As families and communities we need to get involved. For the sake of our future we cannot afford to look the other way.

> We owe them fathers, and a family
> and loving homes they never knew
> because we know
> deep in our hearts
> that they are all
> our children too.

(From the musical: *Miss Saigon*)

**Activity**

- Devise a practical model for orphan care that will work in your community.
- Read the enrichment box: 'The memory book project' on page 337. What advantages do you think this project holds for the HIV-infected mother?

# 15 Infection Control

. . . . . . . . . . . . . . . . . . . . . . . . . . . . . . . . . . . . . . . . . . . . . . . . . . . . . . . . . . . . . . . . . . . . . . . . . . . .

*Overcoming fear*

*And so he danced . . .*
*until one by one they dropped the blanket of their fear.*

. . . . . . . . . . . . . . . . . . . . . . . . . . . . . . . . . . . . . . . . . . . . . . . . . . . . . . . . . . . . . . . . . . . . . . . . . . . .

The fear of infection should never prevent us from caring for people with HIV infection or AIDS. The risk of contracting HIV while taking care of HIV-infected individuals is very low if caretakers follow a few basic rules to avoid accidental exposure to blood and certain other body fluids. (See 'How great is the risk of HIV transmission when one person has been accidentally exposed to the blood of an infected person?' on page 26 for details about risk of infection.) This chapter will concentrate on the application of universal precautions to prevent HIV infection in all health care settings such as hospitals, clinics, hospices — as well as in the home where family members look after a patient with AIDS.

## 15.1  UNIVERSAL PRECAUTIONS TO PREVENT HIV INFECTION

In 1985, the Centers for Disease Control (or CDC) in the USA developed a strategy of 'universal blood and body fluid precautions' to address concerns about the transmission of HIV in health care settings (CDC, 1989). Universal precautions are based on *risk of exposure to blood* (and other fluids) and **NOT** on a *positive diagnosis of HIV infection*. It is of the utmost importance to keep in mind that *any* patient who enters a hospital or clinic may potentially be infected with HIV. There is no way at all of telling *by merely looking at a person* ('by sight') whether or not individuals are infected with HIV. Believing that precautions should be applied *only* to a person who is known to be HIV positive gives a false sense of security and is a very dangerous attitude. Instead of therefore focusing on *individuals known to be infected with HIV*, it is much safer, more sensible and less prejudiced to concentrate on *all body fluids of all patients* and to observe universal blood and body fluid precautions for *all* patients.

HIV can be transmitted to health care professionals in the health care setting through skin piercing with a needle or any other sharp instrument which has been contaminated with blood or other body fluids from an HIV-infected person, through exposure to broken skin, open cuts or wounds, through exposure to blood or other body fluids from an HIV-infected person, and through splashes from HIV-infected blood or body fluids onto the mucous membranes (eyes or mouth). HIV can be transmitted to patients through contaminated instruments that are re-used without adequate disinfection and sterilisation, transfusion of HIV-infected blood, organ transplants, skin grafts, HIV-infected donated semen, and contact with blood or other body fluids from an HIV-infected health care worker (WHO, 2000a, p. 11-2).

## Blood and body fluids requiring universal precautions

Because the following body fluids can be infectious when they are contaminated with HIV, the universal precautions should be strictly applied whenever there is any possibility of contact with them (these fluids should be considered to be *as likely* to transmit HIV infection as HIV-infected blood, i.e. they carry *the same risk factor* as HIV-infected blood):

- blood (including menstrual blood)
- semen
- vaginal secretions (including menstrual discharge)
- body tissue (or wound secretions)
- amniotic (pregnancy) fluid
- cerebrospinal (brain and backbone) fluid (CSF)
- peritoneal (abdomen) fluid
- pericardial (heart) fluid
- pleural (chest) fluid
- synovial (joint) fluid
- any body fluids containing visible blood, semen, vaginal fluid, or any of the fluids mentioned above

## Body fluids not requiring universal precautions

Owing to the low concentration of the virus in the following body fluids, universal precautions are not required when handling these fluids — **unless visible blood is present**:

- faeces
- urine
- vomit
- nasal secretions
- saliva (spit)
- sputum (lung mucus)
- sweat
- tears

Although universal precautions do not apply to body fluids such as faeces, saliva and urine, health care professionals and other caregivers should always use their common sense when deciding on how to handle these body fluids. Precautions should, for instance, be taken with saliva in a dental setting because such saliva is likely to be contaminated with blood. Care ought to be taken with the sputum of tuberculosis patients that contains blood. Nappies of HIV-infected babies with diarrhoea should also be handled with care when they contain blood. Caregivers in the home care situation will find that they seldom come into contact with body fluids that require universal precautions.

Think back to a time when you had to care for a very sick adult or baby in your home. Make a list of all the body fluids that you came into contact with while caring for this person (direct or indirect contact). Now compare your list of fluids with the list of body fluids requiring universal precautions (see 'Blood and body fluids requiring universal precautions' on page 341) and indicate which of the fluids on your list required universal precautions. How great is the risk to which caregivers are subjected when they look after patients with AIDS in their homes? Do ordinary caregivers actually handle dangerous fluids (requiring universal precautions) on a regular basis?

Enrichment

**Pregnant caregivers and HIV**

Pregnant health care professionals are often very concerned about the possibility of a higher risk of contracting HIV in the health care situation. There is no known increased risk that pregnant health care professionals or caregivers will contract HIV infection. A pregnant health care professional, for example, need not use any special precautions beyond those used by other health care professionals. Should a pregnant health care professional become infected, her risk of transmitting the virus to her baby before, during or after birth is substantially increased (exactly as in the case of any other woman who becomes infected during pregnancy). Since AIDS patients often excrete CMV (cytomegalovirus) — a virus which is found in the urine, saliva, semen, cervical secretions, faeces, or breast milk of immune-depressed patients — a pregnant health care professional should wash her hands frequently and always wear gloves when in contact with any patient's body secretions. CMV infection often leads to stillbirths in pregnant women.

## 15.2 INFECTION CONTROL IN HOSPITALS, CLINICS, HOSPICES AND IN HOME-BASED CARE

The objective for HIV infection control measures is similar to that of any infection, namely, to prevent transmission of infection from one person to another. Infection control measures will also **protect the patient** against opportunistic infections such as diarrhoea and respiratory infections. It is important to remember that a patient with AIDS is much more vulnerable to infections than the caregiver because of the patient's depressed immune system.

Guidelines will now be given on how to prevent HIV infection in 'formal' as well as 'informal' health care settings. Practical solutions will be offered (where applicable) for infection control in the home and in rural clinics where there may be a lack of resources or modern facilities. These guidelines are based on those drawn up by the CDC (1989), the WHO (1988a, 1988b, 1990a, 1993), the Department of National Health and Population Development (1989), as well as Hauman (1990), Lusby (1988) and Pearse (1997).

# Basic hygienic principles: the first step to infection control

Adhering to basic hygienic principles, such as washing your hands, covering all skin lesions and keeping the environment clean, are the first steps to infection control in any health care setting.

## *Hand washing*

Hand washing is the most basic measure health care professionals can take to prevent the spread of infection. Hands should always be washed before and after contact with patients, especially when contact involves direct and prolonged physical

**What to do in the rural clinic**

**The problem of water shortage and hand washing**

Pearse (1997) believes that health care professionals working in rural areas should be challenged to use the available facilities to the best effect, and to use their imagination and creativity to improve hygienic standards and to create a safe working environment. 'To simply say "We do not have the facilities, therefore we cannot comply with basic standards is a defeatist attitude"' (p. 415).

When working in areas where water is in critically short supply and is therefore reserved only for drinking, a waterless antiseptic hand cleanser, such as an alcoholic hand-rub, could be used (if available) to clean hands. Alcoholic hand-rub is effective; it is easily used between patient contacts; it is transportable and relatively inexpensive (Pearse, 1997). Where there is a water shortage, do not pour water into a basin to wash and rinse your hands in the same water. It will be contaminated by the bacteria that were on the hands in the first place. Rather ask somebody to pour water over your hands while you wash and rinse them. Water in a 2-litre plastic milk bottle with holes in the cap works very well to pour water on hands.

Contaminated water should be decontaminated (cleaned) by using a cloth filter, a permanent sand filter, or by boiling the water for 10 minutes. Water can also be decontaminated by adding 2 to 4 drops of sodium hypochlorite (bleach or Jik) to 1 litre of water. Such solutions should stand for at least 20 minutes before they are used. Milton can also be used to decontaminate water, if available.

If only cake soap is available, it must be kept dry between uses. Keep the soap in a well-drained clean soap dish, or raise it off the surface by using a bottle top. The cake of soap can also be hung from a piece of string (which should be changed daily) or a strip of plastic. Wash the soap after every use, and rather use small cakes of soap. Carbolic soap is an inexpensive antiseptic soap to use. Traditional methods of boiling soap (fat, water and caustic soda or lye) should be used to make homemade soap if soap is not supplied.

Paper cloths for drying hands are usually not available in rural clinics. It is however not acceptable to use cloth towels that are constantly re-used all day long. Rather use small towels (such as face cloths) for each hand wash, and wash and dry them in the sun afterwards. Disposable 'Daylee' cloths or Superwipes are re-useable, provided that they are thoroughly washed and sun-dried.

care. Patient care activities of brief duration which involve no contact with blood or body fluids, such as taking blood pressure or administering medication, do not require hand washing between contacts. Health care professionals should use their common sense when deciding whether or not to wash their hands after any kind of brief contact. If you feel uncomfortable about the contact, or if blood or body fluids were visible, then it is certainly appropriate to wash your hands after the contact.

Hands should always be thoroughly washed:

- before and after prolonged physical contact with a patient
- before eating, preparing food, or feeding patients
- before care of severely immune-depressed patients (this means, for example, a patient with AIDS — the last phase of HIV infection)
- immediately after contact with blood or body fluids
- after contact with surfaces, equipment, linen, or rubbish contaminated with blood or body fluids
- before invasive procedures
- in nurseries or children's wards between touching infants, and after nappy changes
- after gloves are removed — even if the gloves appear to be intact. While gloves do provide a protective barrier, they do not necessarily provide enough protection to keep hands clean. Leakage of bacteria and viruses may in some cases occur. Even if no leakage takes place, the bacteria on the hands multiply rapidly inside the moist, warm environment of the gloves. The CDC has therefore emphasised that wearing gloves must not replace hand washing. Hands should be washed *on every occasion* after we have removed our gloves.

**What should we use for washing our hands: Plain (ordinary commercial) soap or an antimicrobial product?**

The CDC recommends plain (ordinary commercial) soap for most general patient care situations in hospitals, clinics, hospices and in the home. Plain soap is adequate for *removing* dirt and transient organisms from the hands and is therefore sufficient and adequate for most situations. Since plain soap however *does not kill* organisms, it is necessary to use a product that contains an antimicrobial ingredient in care settings where patients are at high risk of infection (such settings include critical care units, emergency departments and those settings where frequent exposure to blood and body fluids is likely) (Larson, 1989). For antimicrobial soap to be effective, it should remain in contact with the skin for at least 10 seconds. In addition, the hands should be thoroughly washed, especially between the fingers and under the fingernails. Antiseptics such as Hibitane and alcohol or Hibiscrub, which is used in many hospitals, are able to kill HIV. Betadine and Savlon can also be used.

It is not sufficient merely to *wash* your hands with soap and water after contact with blood or other body fluids. Hands should be **disinfected** with the above-mentioned disinfectants after contact with blood and body fluids.
. . . . . . . . . . . . . . . . . . . . . . . . . . . . . . . . . . . . . . . . . . . . . . . .

**What to do at home**

## Basic hygienic principles

If certain basic rules are followed, there is no risk of acquiring HIV infection from people with AIDS in the home care situation. HIV is not easily transmitted except through unprotected sexual intercourse or close blood-to-blood contact. The following basic principles of hygiene should be applied in the home to protect the caregiver from HIV, as well as the immune-depressed AIDS patient from opportunistic infections such as diarrhoea and respiratory infections:

- Wash your hands with soap and water before cooking, eating, feeding another person or giving medicine, after using a toilet or changing nappies, after changing soiled bed linen and clothing, and after having contact with body fluids.
- Use soap in a pump dispenser rather than bar soap, if possible, because soap in a dispenser cannot easily be contaminated.
- If soap is not available, boil your own soap or use herbal or traditional alternatives.
- Keep wounds covered with a waterproof bandage or cloth. If these are not available, use a leaf or plastic wrap. Both caregivers and AIDS patients should cover cuts or wounds on their hands or other places that are likely to come into contact with other people, their bedding or their clothing.
- Keep kitchen and bathroom surfaces clean at all times so as to prevent fungal and bacterial growth. Household bleach (e.g. Jik) is an effective and cheap disinfectant to use for cleaning. Mix a quarter of a cup of Jik with 2 cups of water for cleaning purposes (see 'Disinfection' on page 359).
- Keep bedding and clothing clean. This will help to keep sick people comfortable and prevent skin problems.
- Don't share personal items such as make-up (sharing make-up can transmit skin infections) or anything that may pierce the skin, such as toothbrushes, razors, needles, or anything else that can cut or come into contact with blood. If it is necessary to share some of these objects (e.g. a razor), boil it in water for at least 30 minutes before use.
- Use clean water whenever possible and boil drinking water, especially water that is going to be given to young children.
- Store food properly to prevent it from spoiling and causing infection.
- When someone in the family is ill (e.g. with flu), wash drinking cups with water and soap before you share them.
- Cover your mouth and turn your head away when you sneeze or cough.
- Wash eating utensils, including items for babies, with soap and water.
- Wash all raw fruit and vegetables with clean water.
- Wash objects that a child or infant frequently puts in its mouth with soap and clean water.

*Covering of skin lesions*

HIV can enter the bloodstream through broken skin. It is therefore important to ensure that your hands are always in good condition.

- Use hand lotion to prevent skin cracking. Do not however apply lotion right after washing your hands or immediately before giving direct care since the lotion might interfere with the action of the antimicrobial soap, and render it ineffective.
- Cover skin lesions on your hands with waterproof dressings until they are healed.
- Treat oozing lesions, weeping dermatitis (skin infections) or other breaks in the skin properly and cover (seal) them at all times.
- Health care professionals with serious oozing skin lesions *should refrain* from direct patient care and contact with patient care equipment until the condition has improved.

*Ensure a clean and safe working environment*

Ensure that your immediate environment is clean and safe to work in. Keep surfaces clean at all times. Disinfect and clean blood-stained equipment and body fluid spills immediately (see 'Cleaning up blood and other body fluid spills' on page 355 for the relevant procedure). Do not bend or re-sheath (or recap) needles to prevent the risk of needlesticks. Always discard needles in a puncture-proof container for disposal, and never let needles or any other sharp object lie around where other people can be injured (see 'Precautions to be used when giving injections and performing invasive procedures' on page 351 for the proper handling of needles).

**Protective clothing**

What cannot be sufficiently emphasised is that it is advisable to **treat all body fluids** to which universal precautions apply **as potentially infectious** because it is impossible to know the HIV status of all patients. Protective clothing should be worn whenever there is a possibility of contact with blood or body fluids.

What follows is a discussion about the universal infection control practices that apply to the wearing of gloves, eye shields, masks, aprons and footwear. Most of these precautions only apply to hospital settings — although their use in other care settings will be indicated where relevant. It is important to remember that workers such as cleaners must also wear protective clothing when they handle contaminated materials.

*Gloves*

Wearing gloves is not recommended for casual contact with a patient. It is not necessary to wear gloves when touching intact skin (such as when giving a backrub, bathing a patient, taking blood pressure or giving medication). If the administration of medication involves contact with mucous membranes, as is the case with rectal or vaginal suppositories, then gloves should obviously be worn.

Rubber latex gloves should always be worn when touching blood and body fluids (to which universal precautions apply), mucous membranes, body tissue, or any compromised skin areas of all patients. Always wear gloves when handling items or surfaces soiled with blood or body fluids and when performing procedures during which hands are likely to be contaminated with blood. Always wear gloves in the following situations:

- drawing blood
- starting IVs
- changing wound dressings
- changing drainage bags
- performing surgical procedures
- performing finger or heel pricks on babies and children
- in emergency situations where tasks involve exposure to blood
- childbirth
- whenever blood contamination is a possibility, for example, while working with restless patients
- for cleaning spills of blood and body fluids
- when a health care professional has open, weeping lesions or chronic dermatitis on his or her hands

In emergency situations (such as accidents) where large amounts of blood may be present, it is important for your gloves to fit tightly around your wrists so as to prevent blood contamination of your wrists around the cuff. If there are a number of victims involved in an emergency situation, you should change your gloves between patient contacts. If it is not possible to change your gloves, you should wash your gloved hands with an antiseptic product (not containing alcohol) after contact with each patient.

While you are wearing gloves, avoid handling personal items such as pens, watches and scissors that could become soiled or contaminated. Remove gloves that have become contaminated with blood or other body fluids as soon as possible. When putting on or removing your gloves do not use your teeth. Avoid skin contact with the exterior surface of the gloves when removing them: peel the gloves off in such a way that the removed gloves turn inside out, thereby inverting the contaminated part so that it is not exposed. Place the used gloves in a plastic bag which doesn't leak. Reusable gloves should be changed, washed and disinfected after contact with each patient. Do not eat, drink or smoke while wearing gloves and do not touch any area of your face. Health care professionals and other caregivers who use gloves, should always wash their hands immediately after removing their gloves.

Extra-heavy-duty gloves are recommended when there is a possibility of injury from sharp instruments (as, for instance, when sharp instruments are being cleaned).

**Gloves**

If gloves must be re-used, wash them in warm, soapy water, air dry them and re-powder them (with baby powder). Do not clean latex gloves with an alcohol solution because alcohol damages latex gloves. Some gloves can be boiled. While plastic disposable gloves are a poor substitute for latex gloves, they may be used if nothing else is available. Vinyl gloves (which are used in gardens) should not be used. They are more expensive than latex gloves, and they have a larger pore size which allows viruses to penetrate (Pearse, 1997).

When gloves are not available at all, use other methods to prevent direct contact with blood and other body fluids (methods such as, for example, the use of a plastic bag, a towel, gauze, a piece of clothing, or any item that forms a barrier between blood or sharp instruments and the health care professional). If nothing else is available, even a big leaf can be used to remove soiled bandages or to hold a bloodstained needle or syringe (WHO, 1988b).

*Eye shields*

The use of eye covering (e.g. safety glasses or face shields) is recommended only for procedures during which there is a potential threat of blood or fluid splashes into the mucous membranes of the eyes. It is therefore advisable to wear eye-protecting glasses during procedures such as a bronchoscopy and during certain surgical, dental, and obstetrical procedures, such as during childbirth. The CDC recommends for example, that masks and eyewear should be worn together or that a face shield should be used by all personnel prior to any situation where splashes of blood, or other body fluids to which universal precautions apply, are likely to occur.

Eye coverings are not required for fine, invisible, mist exposures, such as those produced by ventilators. Because the number of infective organisms in mists of that kind is low or absent, they do not cause transmission of blood-borne diseases (Lusby, 1988).

**Eye protection**

When they begin their training, most nurses buy a watch and a stethoscope. Pearse (1997) believes that a pair of cheap glasses should be part of every nurse's equipment. A pair of clear glass spectacles will provide some protection against blood or other body fluid splashes.

## Masks

Masks, preferably surgical masks, and protective eye or face shields should be worn during any procedure likely to generate droplets of blood or body fluids. The inexpensive thin paper masks with elastic ear loops are however useless and dangerous because they provide little protection for patients or staff (Pearse, 1997). When caring for tuberculosis patients, a mask which is able to filter particles that are one micron in size, and that have a filtration efficiency of 95 %, should be worn.

Wear masks in the following situations:

- where there is extensive and productive coughing
- when a respiratorily spread disease (such as tuberculosis or meningococcal meningitis) is suspected
- for suctioning an intubated patient
- when a patient undergoes a surgical or other invasive procedure
- when a procedure may splash blood or body fluids into the mucous membranes of the eyes, nose or mouth of the health care professional, for example, during bronchoscopy or deliveries
- when protection of the patient against infections is necessary (especially patients with depressed immune systems)

Containers with masks, as well as containers for the disposal of used masks, should be kept inside the patient's room, near the entrance. This will make it easier to put on a mask when entering, and removing it before leaving, the room. Hands should be washed thoroughly after removing a mask.

**What to do in the rural clinic**

**Masks**

If masks are not provided by the authorities, the health care professional could buy the kind of dust mist mask that is available at any hardware store. These masks are re-usable by the same person and they provide some protection. Dust mist masks do not however fulfil the filter requirements for tuberculosis and will therefore not protect the health care professional from tuberculosis.

## Aprons

Health care professionals do not have to wear aprons or gowns for casual contact with patients or for routine care such as taking blood pressure or temperature or while administering medication. Aprons should however always be worn to protect clothing during procedures in which blood or body fluid splashes are likely to occur. A plastic, moisture-resistant, non-sterile apron is more appropriate and adequate for protection, unless a sterile gown for patient protection is required.

Wear aprons in the following situations:

- whenever there is a threat of blood splashes or blood-contaminated secretions — such as during certain surgical or dental procedures, bronchoscopy, or vaginal deliveries
- whenever splatter or heavy soiling is expected (as, for example, when lifting a patient with draining wounds)
- in reverse-barrier nursing when the patient is very ill so as to protect the patient against further exposure to infections
- in children's wards, especially the gastroenteritis section

Wear long-sleeved gowns in labour wards, theatres, burn units and gynaecological wards — all places where massive splashes of blood can be expected.

If a patient's care requires the frequent use of an apron, it is advisable to keep an apron inside the patient's room on a hook next to the bed. Mark the apron with the date and indicate the outside of the apron with a mark to ensure that you always wear the apron with the same side to your body. Spray the front side of a plastic apron with Hibitane and alcohol (or a similar disinfectant) before removing it from the hook. After every 24 hours aprons should be replaced (Hauman, 1990).

**What to do in the rural clinic**

**Aprons**

Plastic gowns are not expensive and they can be re-used by the same person. If plastic gowns are not available, plastic garbage bags can be cut to form a protective 'gown'.

**What to do at home**

**Protective clothing**

Although it will seldom be necessary to wear protective clothing in the home care situation, care should nonetheless be taken to prevent contact with blood or other body fluids to which universal precautions apply.
- Handle soiled items such as wound dressings or menstrual pads with a piece of plastic, paper, gloves or a big leaf. Don't use your bare hands to touch items that are soiled with body fluids.
- Be particularly careful with large amounts of blood (such as during childbirth). Delivery in the home should not be done without latex gloves and a plastic apron or gown. Ask the nearest clinic for a pair of gloves, and use a plastic garbage bag to cut a gown.

*Footwear*

Wearing over-shoes is only necessary in cases where there is a danger that the health care professional's shoes can become contaminated with blood or other body fluids.

Examples of recommended protective clothing for different procedures in the hospital setting are given in Table 15.1.

**Table 15.1**

*Recommended protective clothing for hospital procedures\**

| Task or activity | Disposable gloves | Plastic apron | Mask | Glasses or goggles |
|---|---|---|---|---|
| Bleeding control with spurting blood | Yes | Yes | Yes | Yes |
| Bleeding control with minimal bleeding | Yes | No | No | No |
| Childbirth (rupturing membranes) | Yes | Yes | Yes, because splashing is likely | Yes, because splashing is likely |
| Blood drawing | Yes | No | No | No |
| Lumbar puncture (CSF fluid) | Yes | No | No | Yes, if splashes |
| Starting an intravenous line | Yes | No | No | No |
| Endotracheal intubation, oral/nasal suctioning, manually cleaning airway | Yes | No | No, unless splashing is likely | No, unless splashing is likely |
| Emptying blood-containing drains and other containers | Yes | No | Yes, in case of splashing | Yes, in case of splashing |
| Handling and cleaning instruments with microbial contamination | Yes | No, unless soiling is likely | No | No |
| Handling dressings and body fluids | Yes | No | No | No |
| Measuring blood pressure, or temperature | No | No | No | No |
| Giving an injection | No | No | No | No |

\*Source: Adapted from CDC guidelines, 1989, p. 35

## Precautions to be used when giving injections and performing invasive procedures

Health care professionals can infect their patients with HIV if they use contaminated needles or other instruments on their patients.

- Never use the same needle or syringe on more than one patient.
- Never use the same immunisation needle on more than one child.
- Only use sterile instruments or equipment for all procedures on patients.

### Needlesticks and other 'sharps' injuries

One of the most important measures a health care professional can take to protect himself or herself against injuries that may cause HIV or HBV (hepatitis B) infections is to learn how to handle needles and other sharp instruments. Although the chance of becoming infected is low, injuries with contaminated needles or other 'sharps' are the most common way in which HIV and HBV are spread from an infected patient to the health care professional. The health care professional cannot afford to be lax or careless *for a single moment* when working with needles, scalpel blades or other sharp instruments during procedures, when cleaning used instruments, during disposal of used needles and when handling sharp instruments after procedures.

Always observe the following guidelines:

- Do not resheath, bend or break needles or other sharp objects.
- Do not remove needles from disposable syringes. Rather discard the needle and syringe together.
- Do not manipulate a needle or other sharp instruments by hand.
- Do not remove scalpel blades by hand. Use artery forceps.
- Do not carry syringes with exposed needles (use receivers or some other protection).
- Do not leave used sharp objects lying around.
- Do not dispose of needles or syringes in the rubbish bin.
- Discard used needles (without resheathing them) and other sharp instruments in puncture-proof containers immediately after use. A container should be available in every room where 'sharps' are used.
- Puncture-proof containers should be located as near as is practically possible to where they are to be used. Make sure that the opening of the container is large enough not to obstruct disposal. Place the container below eye level for good visibility. Cover and discard the container before the fill line is exceeded.
- Health care professionals who provide home care should take puncture-proof containers with them to dispose of needles they might use.
- Do not leave used discarded Jelcos (a Jelco is a needle used to start IVs) lying around on the bed after an unsuccessful attempt to start an IV. Before using a new Jelco, dispose of the discarded Jelco safely.

The World Health Organisation recommends that injections and other skin-piercing procedures should be restricted to situations where they really are necessary. If a drug is equally effective when it is administered orally and the patient is able to take it in this manner, there is no reason at all to inject the medication. Reducing the number of unnecessary injections is important for protecting both the health care professional and the patient. Procedures for handling accidental exposure to blood and body fluids of infected patients are discussed under 'Management of occupational exposure to HIV' on page 73, and 'Management of accidental exposure to blood and other infectious body fluids' on page 418.

**Enrichment**

### The safe use of Vacutainers when drawing blood

When Vacutainer systems are used to draw blood, the needle must, unfortunately, be disconnected because the Vacutainer barrels are re-used. An exception to the DO NOT RESHEATH rule may be made when you remove the needle from the Vacutainer barrel after the procedure. Extreme care should be exercised in the following procedures:

* Do not hold the sheath in your hand when inserting the needle.
* Place the sheath on a flat surface or press it into a small block of polystyrene before introducing the tip of the needle into the sheath.
* Only when the whole needle is covered by the sheath should you handle the sheath to remove the needle from the Vacutainer barrel.
* An alternative technique to the above is to place an impenetrable cover or shield over the sheath so that it can protect your fingers while inserting the needle.

**What to do in the rural clinic**

### Disposal of syringes and needles

Use a rigid-walled container to dispose of used 'sharps' (syringes). A coffee tin with a secure lid, a thick, non-penetrable plastic bottle with a screw cap, or a heavy plastic or cardboard box can be effectively used for disposal. If incineration is not possible, dispose of the container with 'sharps' into a deep pit latrine. Do not dispose of 'sharps' in refuse pits or landfills because children often play around these areas. If incinerated, the equipment should be at a temperature hot enough to melt the needles.

## The 'second person' risk of 'sharps' injuries

Health care professionals should be specifically aware of the 'second person' risk. A breakdown of 'sharps' injuries indicated that between 33 % and 48 % of all reported injuries per annum involved a second person (Cope, 1994). In some of these cases the second person was the patient who moved at a crucial moment — thereby accidentally pushing the needle into the health care professional. Good communication with a patient before a procedure and awareness of the risk when dealing with a child or a confused non-compliant patient will help to reduce the risk. 'Second person' risks often also occur in the theatre or when commencing IV therapy or doing a lumbar puncture in the wards. Health care professionals should concentrate intensely and be alert at all times when working with 'sharps'.

The most avoidable and most disturbing 'second person' injuries are those sustained by domestic staff when emptying waste paper bins, handling soiled linen, or while cleaning patient areas. Health care professionals should make sure that they remove all 'sharps' used in a procedure and that they discard them into the correct container immediately after use.

### Invasive procedures

Strict blood and body fluid precautions should be observed whenever a surgical entry into tissues, cavities or organs is made — whether for an operation or for the repair of an injury. In addition to this, bear the following points in mind (College of Medicine, 1991; WHO, 1988b):

- Wear gloves and a surgical mask for all invasive procedures.
- Wear double gloves or extra-heavy-duty gloves in operations where the risk of tearing gloves is high (as in orthopaedic procedures).
- Wear protective glasses or face shields and an apron if blood splashes are likely.
- Avoid unnecessary personnel, equipment or movement in the theatre during operations.
- Avoid the direct passing of sharp instruments between theatre personnel.
- Avoid if possible the use of unprotected sharp instruments such as, for example, scissors instead of a knife.
- If a glove is torn, or any injury from a used sharp instrument occurs during invasive procedures, replace the glove with a new one as soon as possible. Remove the needle or instrument involved in the incident from the sterile field.
- Use a closed drainage system for wounds which require post-operative drainage, especially if the patient is known to be HIV-infected.

### Precautions during vaginal or caesarean deliveries

Health care professionals who perform or assist in vaginal or caesarean deliveries should wear gloves, aprons, masks and eye protection (if splashing is likely) in the following instances:

- while performing internal vaginal examinations on the mother
- during artificial rupturing of the membranes (always wear eye protection)
- during the birth process and when cutting the umbilical cord
- while handling the placenta during birth as well as during the placenta examination
- while suturing tears and episiotomies
- while handling the baby until all the amnion fluid and blood have been removed from the infant's skin

- until post-delivery care of the umbilical cord is complete
- while caring for the mother and cleaning the environment until all blood and body fluids are removed

If the mother is diagnosed as HIV-infected, health care professionals in the maternity ward should observe the following precautions so as to keep the risk of transmitting the infection to the foetus as low as possible:

- Avoid unnecessary rupture of the membranes.
- As far as possible, avoid intra-uterine catheterisation.
- Avoid invasive monitoring (such as the use of foetal scalp electrodes).
- Avoid an episiotomy whenever possible.
- Use Chlorhexidine 0,25 % for vaginal cleansing after vaginal examinations and during labour and delivery (see 'Pregnancy and childbirth' on page 28).
- If possible, avoid the use of forceps or vacuum delivery. But if you have no alternative, rather use forceps instead of vacuum.
- If possible, avoid suctioning of the baby's nose and throat.
- Wipe blood and maternal secretions off the baby as soon as possible.

### Post-partum care of mother and baby

One applies exactly the same post-partum (after-birth) care to an HIV-infected mother and her baby as one would to other patients. Apply the same universal precaution measures. Wear gloves when handling the baby prior to its first bath, when changing meconium nappies or diarrhoeal nappies and when providing cord care.

If a mother is breastfeeding her baby, make sure that good hygiene always prevails. Bleeding of cracked nipples should be prevented or treated immediately, as should mastitis (breast infections) and breast abscesses as well as any sores or thrush in the baby's mouth.

### Cleaning up blood and other body fluid spills

It is important to remember that HI viruses can sometimes live for many hours outside the body **if they remain inside blood or body fluids**. It is vitally important to be extremely careful when cleaning up spilled blood or body fluids. An experienced person should clean blood and body fluid spills. Such tasks should **not** be given to a cleaning woman who does not know how to apply universal precautions. The following points should be borne in mind when cleaning blood and other body fluid spills:

- Wear latex rubber gloves to avoid direct contact with spilled blood or body fluids.
- If splashes are anticipated, wear protective eyewear, a mask and a watertight apron. Where there is massive blood contamination on floors, wear disposable, impenetrable shoe coverings.

- Flood the spillage area with an appropriate disinfectant (preferably sodium hypochlorite or household bleach diluted 1:10 with water) and clean the mixed body fluid and disinfectant with absorbent, disposable towels or paper cloths. Or cover the spill with a towel or cloth soaked in a hypochlorite solution. Some sources recommend stronger solutions of bleach to clean up blood spills (see 'Disinfection' on page 359).
- Clean from the outside to the inside of the spillage area.
- Discard paper towels into a plastic bag immediately and then burn them in an incinerator (or bury them if incinerator facilities are unavailable).
- After removing the mixed body fluid and disinfectant, wipe the surface clean with more disinfectant — starting from a radius of 1 metre outside the spillage area.
- Remove gloves and place them in a plastic bag.
- Wash your hands *immediately* after you remove your gloves.
- If shoe coverings are worn, always remove them while still wearing gloves.
- If you have been wearing gloves, apron, mask, eye coverings and shoe coverings because of massive blood contamination, always take them off (remove them) in the following order: first the shoe coverings, then the gloves, and finally the apron, mask and eye shield.
- Place reusable items in a container with some disinfectant.

**What to do in the rural clinic**

**Cleaning up blood and body fluid spills**

Household bleach or Jik will kill the HI virus. Mix 1 part of Jik with 10 parts of water (approximately a quarter of a cup of Jik with 2 cups of water), and pour onto the spilled blood or on the area after it is cleaned. If latex gloves are not available, use plastic bags as protection for your hands.

## Precautions concerning resuscitation

### Mouth-to-mouth resuscitation

HIV (or HBV) transmission caused by mouth-to-mouth resuscitation has not been documented. Although HIV has been found in saliva, it is present in such small concentrations that the chance of transmission is extremely low. There is however a theoretical possibility that the health care professional may become infected if he or she has a cut, sore or lesion in the mouth which comes into contact with a patient's infected blood and/or saliva containing infected blood.

Although HIV has rarely been detected in saliva, saliva can spread other infectious diseases such as herpes simplex, respiratory viruses, or bacteria which cause meningitis. It is therefore recommended that a device such as an ambu bag (a manual ventilator) or a mouthpiece be used for mouth-to-mouth resuscitation. The device not only protects the health care professional against infections but also gives him or her the assurance of being as safe as possible. It is important for hospitals to ensure that resuscitation devices are readily available in all patient care areas. Resuscitation equipment and devices should be used once only and then disposed of. If they are reusable, they should be cleaned and disinfected thoroughly after each use.

Health care professionals frequently encounter emergency situations outside the hospital where their help is urgently needed. Even though resuscitation bags are usually not available at accident scenes, resuscitation should not be withheld because of a fear of contracting HIV. If the injured person is bleeding through the mouth, the health care professional should first wipe the blood out of the person's mouth with a clean cloth or handkerchief before proceeding with resuscitation. If it is possible, a thin cloth should be placed over the mouth to avoid any saliva or fluid exchange during mouth-to-mouth contact.

Resuscitation bags in the form of key-rings are available and these are valuable assets that health care professionals can easily carry with them at all times. The mouthpiece has a plastic cover to prevent contact with the patient's face as well as a one-way valve that allows the flow of air into the mouth of the patient while preventing fluids like vomit or blood from getting into the mouth of the helper.

### Bleeding at accident scenes

Bleeding patients at accident scenes usually require immediate attention. If the person is conscious, the health care professional can instruct him or her to apply pressure to the wound himself or herself by using a thick cloth (use a T-shirt if nothing else is available). If the person is not able to help himself or herself, the health care professional should stop the bleeding by applying pressure to the wound. If gloves are not available, use a barrier such as a thick cloth, several dressings or a piece of plastic wrap to prevent skin contact with the blood. Health care professionals should take special care to ensure that blood does not come into direct contact with their mucous membranes or any broken skin that they might have. Helpers should take care not to touch their own eyes or mouth, and they should wash their hands with soap and water as soon as possible after they have administered first aid.

It is always a good idea to keep a pair of gloves in a *cool* place in the car at all times for use in emergencies.

### Precautions that must be taken when handling laboratory specimens

● Health care professionals should always wear gloves when drawing blood and when handling any specimen of body fluid, regardless of the source (blood, cerebrospinal fluid, urine, sputum or faeces).

- Cover all open wounds on hands and arms with a waterproof dressing.
- Place all blood or body fluid specimens in firm, leak-proof, unbreakable, plastic containers with secure lids to prevent leakage during transport.
- Avoid contaminating the outside of the container.
- Clean any contamination on the *outside* of the container with an antimicrobial solution before dispatching the specimen. Make sure that the forms accompanying a specimen are clean.
- No special precautionary labels are required on the container or form.
- Do not dispatch specimens in syringes with exposed needles.
- Hands must always be washed after accidental exposure to specimens.
- Cover working surfaces with a non-penetrative material (such as plastic film) that is easy to clean.
- Disinfect any spillage of blood or body fluid with an appropriate disinfectant before cleaning it. Wear gloves when cleaning up blood or body fluids.
- Dispose of specimens carefully by pouring them down a drain connected to a sewer. If this is not possible, decontaminate blood and body fluids with an appropriate disinfectant before disposal. Wear gloves during disposal.

Signs and labels identifying patients known to have infectious diseases such as HIV are unnecessary. They violate confidentiality and they may encourage a double standard of care. **All** body fluids should be viewed as potentially infected with HIV. Receptacles containing infected waste should however be marked with a **biohazard sign** to warn non-medical personnel (such as cleaners) to be careful.

### Cleaning, sterilisation and disinfection of contaminated equipment

Efficient cleaning with soap and water removes a high proportion of any microorganisms. Wear heavy-duty gloves while cleaning contaminated equipment and if splashing with body fluids is likely, wear additional protective clothing. Dismantle all equipment before cleaning and wipe blood-stained equipment clean with paper towels which should then be discarded. Wipe equipment with a hypochlorite solution before sending it for normal sterilisation. If that is not possible, seal the equipment in a strong, clear and labelled plastic bag.

Since HIV is destroyed much more quickly than other organisms, routine sterilisation methods are appropriate for HIV. Table 15.2 on page 359 gives an indication about which methods to use for decontamination.

### Sterilisation

All forms of sterilisation will destroy HIV. Methods of sterilisation recommended by the WHO (2000a) are steam (or moist heat) that is under pressure (e.g. autoclave or pressure cooker), dry heat (such as an oven) — or gas sterilisation (with ethylene oxide) for non-heat-resistant equipment.

- Moist heat (autoclaving) readily kills the HI virus at 121 °C for 15 minutes, 126 °C for 10 minutes, or 134 °C for 3 to 5 minutes.

- Dry heat at 121 °C for 16 hours, 140 °C for 3 hours, 160 °C for 2 hours or 170 °C for 1 hour is sufficient to kill HIV.

- Exposure to ethylene oxide for between 4 and 16 hours, depending on the object and its volume, will be sufficient. The object must then be left for several days to allow the gas to evaporate.

**Table 15.2**
*Decontamination methods**

| Level of risk | Items | Decontamination method |
| --- | --- | --- |
| High risk | Instruments which penetrate the skin/body | Sterilisation, or single use of disposables |
| Moderate risk | Instruments which come into contact with non-intact skin or mucous membrane | Sterilisation, boiling, or chemical disinfection |
| Low risk | Equipment which comes into contact with intact skin | Thorough washing with soap and hot water |

*Source: Adapted from WHO, 2000a, p. 11-5

## Disinfection

Two commonly used disinfection methods are boiling and chemical disinfection (WHO, 2000a). HIV is easily destroyed by boiling for 20 minutes at sea level, and by boiling for at least 30 minutes at higher altitudes. Equipment should always be cleaned before boiling.

Chemical disinfectants are not as reliable as sterilisation or boiling, but they can be used on heat-sensitive equipment or when other methods of decontamination are not available. Chemicals that are effective in destroying HIV include chlorine-based agents (such as bleach), 2 % glutaraldehyde, 1 % biodecyl, 70 % ethyl alcohol, 70 % isopropanol and 1 % iodine.

Because household bleaches (such as Jik) contain hypochlorite, they may be effectively used for disinfection purposes. The hypochlorite concentrations vary from one product to another and should accordingly be diluted with water. A solution of 1:10 — or approximately a quarter of a cup of bleach mixed with 2 cups of water (for a 3,5 % hypochlorite concentration) — is usually sufficient to kill HIV. Some sources recommend a stronger solution of 1 cup of bleach mixed with 2 cups of water to clean blood spills (Evian, 2000, p. 322). Used bleach solutions should be discarded and should never be reused.

What to do in the rural clinic

**Sterilisation and disinfection of instruments**

Boil instruments for 30 minutes from the time when the water actually begins to boil. Don't add instruments after boiling has commenced. Domestic pressure cookers can also be used for 30 minutes at their highest pressure to sterilise equipment. Household bleach (chlorine) is effective for disinfecting equipment if it is soaked for at least 30 minutes. Because disposable plastic instruments cannot be boiled, they should be soaked in household bleach or Milton for 30 minutes. Needles should **never** be re-used, and under **no** circumstances should they be sterilised with disinfectants such as household bleach (or any other disinfectant) because the disinfectants may not penetrate the bore of the needle.

Enrichment

**The safety of hospital apparatus in everyday use**

- **Blood pressure apparatus** and **stethoscopes** cannot contaminate health care professionals or patients — provided that they are used on skin that is intact. Clean the dome of stethoscopes with a 70 % alcohol swab such as Preptic or Webcol if necessary.
- **Thermometers** that are being used for routine observation rounds should be wiped with a 70 % alcohol swab or placed into an alcohol solution after each use. If a patient's temperature is taken more frequently, wipe the thermometer with a 70 % alcohol swab and keep it inside a dry container in the room.
- **Crockery and cutlery** such as cups, plates, knives, spoons and forks should be handled in a normal way. If the patient has bleeding mucous membranes (in the mouth, for example), disposable or exclusive cutlery is recommended.
- **Suction equipment** and **oxygen masks** should be handled in a normal way — provided that their method of use conforms to the principles of universal precautions.
- **Bedpans or urine bottles** should be cleaned with an appropriate disinfectant.
- The HIV-infected patient may use the **ward bath** and **toilet** unless open bleeding perineal lesions are present.

## Disposal of infected waste, linen and garbage

*Infected waste*

Adhere to the following guidelines of the World Health Organisation (1988b) for disposing of infected waste:

- Place needles and other sharp instruments or materials in a puncture-proof container immediately after use and preferably incinerate them.

- Prominently mark all containers containing infected waste with the word **BIO-HAZARD** — *and* the biohazard logo (if possible).

- Carefully pour liquid wastes such as bulk blood, suction fluids, excretions and secretions down a drain connected to an adequately treated sewer system, and if this is not available, dispose of the waste in a pit latrine.
- Regard solid wastes, such as dressings, laboratory and pathology wastes, as infectious and treat by incineration, burning or autoclaving. Other solid wastes, such as excreta, may be disposed of in a hygienically controlled sanitary landfill or pit latrine.

**What to do in the rural clinic**

**Disposal of infected waste**

If incineration equipment is not available, small amounts of infected waste can be burned in a metal drum or in a refuse pit. Infected waste can also be buried in a refuse pit which is at least 2 metres deep and 10 metres away from a water source. Refuse pits should be fenced off to prevent children, scavengers and animals from gaining access to the site.

## Linen

Although soiled linen may be contaminated with pathogenic micro-organisms, the risk of actual disease transmission is very slim. Hygienic storage of clean linen and the processing of soiled linen are adequate procedures for handling linen. When adhering to the following procedures, it is not even necessary to handle linen from 'known' infected patients separately:

- Sort linen into *used linen* and *soiled linen* at the patient's bedside. While it is not necessary to wear gloves when handling used linen, you should wash your hands afterwards.
- Wear gloves and a protective apron when handling linen soiled with blood and other body fluids.
- Bag soiled linen at the location where it was used.
- Do not rinse soiled linen in hospital wards.
- Place and transport linen soiled with blood or other body fluids in leak-proof (thick plastic) bags to prevent environmental contamination.
- If leak-proof bags are not available, fold the soiled parts of the linen towards the inside.
- Wash linen with detergent and water at a temperature of at least 71 °C for 25 minutes. If using low-temperature laundry cycles (i.e. with temperatures less than 70 °C), use chemicals suitable for low-temperature washing at the appropriate concentration.
- In the laundry, keep a strict separation between the pre-wash sorting area and the clean area.

- Laundry workers in the pre-wash area should wear protective clothes such as gloves, gowns, masks and caps.
- Workers in the 'soiled' laundry area should not work in the 'clean' area on the same day.

Protective clothing contaminated with blood or other body fluids should be handled in the same way as linen. Brush-scrub boots and leather goods with soap and hot water to remove dirt and micro-organisms.

**What to do in the rural clinic**

### Washing used and soiled linen

If washing machines are not available, used and soiled linen should be washed in the following ways:

**Used linen** (not soiled with blood or body fluids) can be washed by hand in a tub. Dissolve detergent in hot water, and add the linen. Soak the linen for one hour in hot water (to reduce the bacterial load). Stir the content occasionally with a long stick to ensure that the water and detergent come into contact with all the linen. After this soaking period, the linen can be washed by hand. Rinse twice in clean water. Bleach can be added to the second-rinse water. Hang linen to dry in the sun as soon as possible. Iron with a hot iron.

**Soiled linen** should be soaked for a longer period than used linen — at least until no staining is visible. Soak linen soiled with blood in cold water. Add sodium hypochlorite (bleach) to the water. Use clean water and detergent after the soaking period. You can boil the linen on a stove or on a grid on the fire for 30 minutes if that is the method that you prefer. Rinse twice. Add bleach to the second-rinse water to reduce the level of microbes. Dry in the sun and iron with a hot iron.

**What to do at home**

### Disposal of infected waste, linen and garbage

Put soiled or dirty waste materials such as nappies, used menstrual pads, soiled dressings and used tissues out of the reach of children and animals until they can be removed from the home. Place them in a container that is hard to open until they can be cleaned or properly disposed of. It is preferable to burn menstrual pads and soiled dressings but if this is not possible, dispose of them in tightly sealed double plastic bags in a domestic or public hygienically controlled sanitary landfill or pit latrine.

Keep sheets, towels and clothes stained with blood, diarrhoea, vomit or other body fluids separate from other household laundry. While holding an unstained part, rinse off any blood or diarrhoea with water. Soak linen soiled with blood in cold water with added bleach. Use a stick to turn the linen in the soaking water. Use clean water and soap after the soaking period, and boil the linen for 30 minutes if preferred. Rinse the linen (with added bleach), hang it in the sun to dry and iron it with a hot iron. It is not necessary to use bleach or to boil linen soiled with body fluids that do not contain blood.

## *Rubbish handling*

Adhere to the following precautions when handling rubbish so that you can maintain a safe work environment and prevent accidents:

- Place all dressings and wet rubbish in plastic bags before placing them in holding containers.
- Place broken glass in separate puncture-proof containers.
- Line rubbish bins with strong plastic bags before disposing of rubbish.
- When plastic bags in bins are about two-thirds full, seal them and dispose of them.
- Use plastic bags instead of paper bags on the patient's bedside table.
- Mark plastic bags containing rubbish of known AIDS patients as **BIOHAZARD**. (Do *not* write 'AIDS' on the bag!)
- If rubbish is not removed by local authorities, it should be burned.

## **Post-mortem procedures**

Health care professionals performing post-mortem procedures should follow the normal local procedures and observe the following guidelines as precautions against infection:

- Keep universal precautions for blood and body fluids in mind at all times. For many hours after death, HI viruses can still be alive and active in the body fluids of a deceased patient.
- Handle bodies that have open wounds or are soiled with blood with gloves and plastic aprons.
- Cover leaking wounds on the body with waterproof dressings.
- If the patient has died of AIDS, place the body in a plastic body-bag and seal it tightly.
- Wipe the outside of the body-bag with Biocide or an appropriate disinfectant before it leaves the room.
- If a body-bag is not available, wrap the body adequately so as to prevent contamination.
- After the death (or discharge) of a patient with AIDS, clean the room in the routine way (there is no known environmental-related transmission route of HIV). Because it is not possible for surfaces such as walls, ceilings or floors to transmit HIV, these may be cleaned in a routine household way.
- The mattress cover and bed can be cleaned with a disinfectant after the death of an AIDS patient.

**What to do at home**

**After the death of an AIDS patient**

Universal precautions should be adhered to after the death of an AIDS patient. Hands should be protected when cleaning and laying out the body, or when performing cultural cleansing rituals, particularly if body fluids such as diarrhoea or blood are present. Hands should be thoroughly washed with soap and water afterwards. Wounds on the hands and arms of the caregiver, as well as wounds on the body of the deceased, should all be covered with a plaster or bandage. Any traditional cleansing rites that may spread the infection should be avoided. No special precautions are necessary during the funeral because the HI virus can only live and reproduce inside a living person.

## 15.3 CONCLUSION

Apart from adhering to the universal precautions discussed in this chapter, each hospital department, ward, speciality unit, or clinic should identify those specific procedures that may increase the risk of exposure to blood or other body fluids in their particular environment. In such cases, appropriate precautions should be developed and incorporated into routine practice. The best rule to remember is that *no rules and regulations can ever replace common sense*! If you feel uncomfortable in any situation, just use your common sense and err on the side of safety. It is easy to be safe without being obsessive.

**Activity**

- Prepare a lecture for hospital cleaners on measures to avoid exposure to HIV in their work.
- Prepare and give a lesson to primary caregivers (working in home-based care situations) about the basic principles of infection control at home. Include explanations of basic hygiene, when to wear gloves, the cleaning of body fluid spills, the handling of soiled linen and the disposal of rubbish.

*Tending of Koki*

*One remained silently seated next to Koki.*
*With hands full of grass she cleansed his body*
*where it had been broken and soiled by Raka.*
*She did not cry but sang softly*
*about the holy, bright circle of birth and death . . .*
*and birth and death.*

Because patients with HIV infection and AIDS need both physical and psychological care, any care programme should be holistic, compassionate and person-centred — and it should always take place in a nurturing environment (Fahrner, 1988). Most of the difficulties that HIV-infected people experience are familiar to health care professionals because the physical and psychological needs of people with AIDS are often similar to those of other terminally ill patients. It is however necessary to adopt a much more holistic approach to HIV-infected people because their immune systems are so depressed that they can contract virtually any disease (especially the so-called 'opportunistic infections'). Because of this unique feature of HIV/AIDS, it is impossible to recommend any *one* model of caring for those who are infected with HIV. Caregivers should pay attention to a patient's physical or psychological needs as they arise.

The current emphasis in the treatment and management of HIV infection and AIDS focuses on: (1) strengthening the immune system so that the infected individual can be kept healthy for as long as possible, (2) treating opportunistic infections and caring for general health problems, and (3) the use of anti-retroviral therapy to reduce the viral load in the patient's blood to the lowest possible levels (see chapter 5). This chapter discusses the promotion of general health, the strengthening of the immune system, and the care and treatment of general health problems and opportunistic infections. Practical advice will be offered about how to take care of HIV-infected individuals in hospitals, hospices, clinics and the home setting.

## 16.1  THE PROMOTION OF HEALTH AND THE STRENGTHENING OF THE IMMUNE SYSTEM

One of the most important health measures that HIV-infected people can take is to do everything in their power to stay as healthy and fit as possible. A healthy lifestyle not only improves the quality of the person's life, it also strengthens the immune system to retain its capacity to combat infections. One should discuss each of the following ways of promoting good health with HIV-infected individuals:

## Rest, exercise and a healthy diet

It is important for HIV-infected people to get enough rest and sleep and to keep fit by doing exercises. Regular exercise has been linked to improved cardiovascular fitness and muscle function, increased CD4 cell counts, weight gain, mood improvement and better coping skills in HIV-positive people (La Perriere et al., 1997). It is very important for HIV-infected individuals to start with a regular exercise programme (sessions at least 3 times a week) that includes a balance between cardiovascular (or aerobic) exercise, strength training and stretching. Patients should however be advised to abstain from heavy exercise when they have symptoms such as fever, cough or diarrhoea. It is also important to eat a healthy, balanced diet in order to keep the immune system healthy. (Nutrition is discussed in 'Nutrition' on page 371.)

## Avoidance of drug and alcohol abuse and smoking

The use of substances such as alcohol, tobacco (cigarettes), amphetamines, nitrites (poppers), morphine, cocaine and heroin has been linked to suppression of the immune system, a lowering of the CD4 cell count, as well as to an increase in secondary infections and illnesses such as pneumocystis carinii pneumonia (Nyamathi & Flaskerud, 1989; Siegel, 1986). HIV-infected people who smoke heavily and who abuse alcohol or other drugs should be encouraged to stop these habits — or at least to smoke or use alcohol only very moderately.

There is no evidence that moderate drinking is harmful and people often find that it may help to relieve stress and anxiety. Heavy drinking may however affect the immune system adversely, delay recovery from opportunistic diseases, negatively influence healthy decision making and may in addition cause hepatitis and liver damage. A person with HIV infection who is also co-infected with hepatitis B or C should rather not take *any* alcohol because even small amounts may have adverse effects on the system. Alcohol may also interact negatively with some of the medications the patient is taking.

## Avoiding people with illnesses or infections

A person with a depressed immune system should avoid the company of people with infections. An HIV-infected person should not visit a friend with flu or children with children's diseases such as measles or mumps. Large gatherings of people should also be avoided as far as possible — especially in the winter months.

## Routine visits to the doctor or clinic

HIV-infected people should visit their doctor, hospital or clinic regularly. It is important that infections and illnesses be treated as soon as possible. Warning signs should not be ignored. Advise the HIV-infected individual to seek professional help if any of the following symptoms appear: skin lesions; lesions of the mucous membranes of the mouth, anus or vagina; swollen lymph nodes; extreme fatigue or tiredness; nausea; vomiting; diarrhoea and weight loss; persistent fever; headaches; forgetfulness or dizziness; persistent coughing and shortness of breath; and unusual bleeding (Ungvarski, 1989).

Since children with HIV infection can become ill very quickly, caregivers should not wait too long to take a sick child to a hospital or clinic, especially if a child presents with symptoms such as fever, vomiting and diarrhoea.

**Infection control in the home**

While there have been no reported cases of HIV being transmitted through casual contact in the home, it is very important to control the possibility of infection in the home because of the already depressed immune system of the HIV-infected person.

Infection control in the home, which is discussed in chapter 15, includes basic hygiene principles such as regular hand washing, keeping the environment clean, and not sharing personal care items such as toothbrushes, razors and make-up.

**Pets in the home**

Owning pets can be very rewarding and pleasurable because they can help people to feel psychologically and physically better. There is no reason why HIV-infected people should not keep pets so long as they refrain from cleaning cat litter boxes, bird cages, dog litter, and fish tanks. Serious infections (such as toxoplasmosis and cryptosporidiosis) can be transmitted through pet excreta. These diseases can cause severe diarrhoea, brain infections and skin lesions in people with depleted immune systems. If HIV-infected people have to care for their own pets, excreta must be handled with rubber gloves or vinyl gloves and hands must be washed after removal of the gloves.

HIV-infected people can further protect themselves from infections by always washing their hands after playing with animals, never handling animals that have diarrhoea, never touching stray animals who might bite or scratch, asking a friend to take a sick animal to the veterinarian, and by never allowing your pet to lick your mouth or any open cuts or wounds you may have. Adults should be extra watchful and always supervise an HIV-infected child's hand washing after he or she has been playing with pets.

## Social and sexual life

HIV-infected people should be assured that social contact with friends and family members is perfectly safe. They can enjoy a normal social life with friends on holiday, in the swimming pool, at parties or at religious and school gatherings. As long as there is no exchange of blood or any other body fluids, friends and family members of infected people cannot become infected.

HIV-infected people should however be advised to change their sexual behaviour to protect sex partners from infection and themselves from re-infection with HIV and other sexually transmitted diseases. Being HIV positive does not necessarily mean the end of a person's sex life. HIV-positive people should be advised to limit sexual intercourse to one absolutely loyal (i.e. faithful and monogamous) partner who is aware of the infection and who willingly consents to having a sexual relationship, to always use condoms for any form of sexual contact, to try and avoid anal sex or at least to use double-strength condoms, to avoid the exchange of any body fluids, and (if possible) to use alternative sex practices such as masturbation or thigh sex (see 'General safer sex rules' on page 142). HIV-positive people should always inform their sexual partners about their HIV status.

Some HIV-positive people mistakenly believe that there is no need to protect themselves against further infection, especially if they live with partners who are also HIV-infected. It is however very important for infected people to protect themselves against re-infection. There are many mutations or strains of HIV and some are more virulent than others. Re-infection with another strain of HIV may augment the illness and cause an earlier onset of AIDS.

## Stress management and positive living

Because stress has a very negative effect on the immune system, increased stress often causes a decrease in the number of CD4 cells. It is therefore very important for HIV-infected individuals to learn how to cope with stress. HIV-infected people should be encouraged to join support groups, to practise relaxation techniques, to visit friends, to talk to people, to obtain factual information about their condition from professional people and to ignore wild rumours and sensationalised anecdotal 'information' about AIDS. HIV-infected individuals should concentrate on positive living to promote health and well-being: they should think positive thoughts, not forget to see the funny side of things (even in their darkest moments), engage in enjoyable and life-affirming activities and enjoy life to the fullest.

## Alternative therapies

Because many HIV-infected people make use of alternative therapies, health care professionals should always keep an open mind about this because some alternative therapies can definitely contribute to the psychological and social well-being of their clients. Health care professionals should therefore encourage HIV-infected individuals to discuss various alternative therapies prior to integrating them into their general health care plan.

Many alternative therapies are based on the belief that a positive mind is the strongest weapon against HIV and AIDS and that the power of the mind can control what happens to the body. Alternative therapies are based on the premise that if one believes strongly in oneself and one's abilities (self-efficacy), and if one makes an active attempt to improve the quality of life by living a less stressful life, one can prolong one's life and improve the quality of one's life. Some of the alternative therapies that people use are psychoneuroimmunology (PNI), meditation, mental imagery or visualisation therapy, positive mental reinforcement, reflexology, body massage, aromatherapy and visits to traditional healers. HIV-infected individuals also often make use of acupuncture, homeopathy and hypnotherapy.

Enrichment

**Psychoneuroimmunology (PNI)**

The field of psychoneuroimmunology (PNI) concerns itself with the influence of psychological factors on the immune system. Research studies in PNI have found that psychological stressors such as anxiety, loneliness, helplessness, hopelessness, distress, rage, anger, depression, tension, tiredness, negativity and interpersonal problems all have an adverse effect on the immune system. Subjects who manifested these negative emotions showed a decline in Killer T cell activity — as well as a lower CD4 cell count. A correlation was also found between different personal coping styles and immunological reactions. Positive coping factors, such as a fighting spirit, a sense of humour, the ability to relax, hope, social contact, social support, mothering and caring behaviour as well as the emotional expression of traumatic experiences, all enhanced the immune system (Ader, Felten & Cohen, 1991; O'Leary, 1990; Van Zyl, 1990). PNI has very important implications for the management of HIV infection. Longo and his colleagues (in Van Zyl, 1990) found that subjects who were trained in relaxation, stress management and imagery techniques reported a significant reduction in the incidence of recurrent genital herpes activity when compared with the control group. PNI therapists believe that interventions to reduce psychological distress (which can take many forms) may improve patients' health by strengthening immune functioning. HIV-infected people who practise PNI believe that self-efficacy, a positive self-image, a relaxed, positive attitude towards life, hope, humour and a healthy social support system enable their immune systems to fight HIV infection more effectively.

If you are a computer expert, design an educational computer game for HIV-infected young people to help them 'strengthen their immune systems'. The player should visualise an image of his or her defender cells (CD4 cells, macrophages, killer T cells, etc.) destroying the virus and the infected cells. The player should be able to gain extra points (or CD4 cells) and thereby strengthen his or her immune system by doing the right things (such as eating nutritious foods, stopping smoking, using condoms, going for a jog, saying 'No!' to drugs, washing hands after playing with the dog, and so on).

## 16.2 NUTRITION

There is a strong correlation between malnutrition and immune depression. Research findings suggest that a healthy diet, vitamin and mineral supplementation and defensive eating may enhance the immune response to HIV infection and enhance resistance to opportunistic infections (Saunders, 1994).

### Dietary recommendations

A healthy diet does not necessarily have to be expensive. Locally available, natural, unrefined and unprocessed foods are sufficient and adequate to protect the immune system and to keep a person healthy. What is really important is the *composition* of the meal. Food can be divided into three groups and everyone should try to eat food from *each one* of these groups at *every meal*. A picture of a plate divided into five sections can be used to explain to clients what to eat at each meal of the day.

### *Energy-giving foods: Carbohydrates or starch foods*

Two fifths (2/5 or 40 %) of a person's plate should consist of carbohydrates or energy-giving foods such as potatoes, yams (a variety of the sweet potato), wheat, samp, brown rice, maize meal (unsifted), maize rice, oats, mabela (ground sorghum), rye and brown or wholewheat bread. Avoid refined starches such as white bread, white rice, white pasta, super maize meal or any foods made from white flour and refined cereals. Because sugar, animal fats and vegetable oils are also energy-giving foods, they are beneficial for patients who are trying to gain weight.

### *Body building foods: Proteins*

Proteins in the diet are important 'building blocks' for the development of muscles, cells, teeth and bones. One fifth (1/5 or 20 %) of a person's plate should consist of proteins such as dry peas or beans, soya, lentils, peanuts (or peanut butter), nuts, eggs, red meat, chicken, fish, cheese and milk. Milk is an important source of protein, calcium and vitamins and one to two glasses of fresh pasteurised or boiled milk (or skimmed milk) should be drunk every day. Since there are a number of good sources of high-grade protein other than meat, it is *not* necessary for people to eat meat every day. One can substitute excellent but far less expensive sources of protein (such as beans) for meat. Mopani worms and flying ants are also good sources of protein.

### Protective foods: Vitamins and minerals

Two fifths (2/5 or 40 %) of a person's plate should consist of vegetables and fruit. Vegetables and fruit contain important vitamins and minerals which are vital for fighting infections and strengthening the immune system. Brightly coloured vegetables and fruit (dark green, dark yellow, orange, and red) are the most nutritious. These include carrots, pumpkin, yellow sweet potatoes, pawpaws, spinach, marogo, cabbage, beetroot tops, oranges, tomatoes, guavas, green beans and lettuce. Dark green leaves such as beetroot leaves and the outer leaves of cabbage and cauliflower are also very nutritious. Vegetables should be cooked or steamed lightly because cooking vegetables for too long can destroy vitamins. It is preferable to eat at least one portion of vegetables raw every day (they should be well washed or peeled). Don't throw nutritious foods away. The cooking water of vegetables can, for example, be re-used as a soup or sauce or as the basis for further cooking.

**Activity**

Teach children how to make and care for a vegetable garden. A patch of ground as big as a door (1 metre by 2metres) can provide a constant supply of fresh vegetables!

Specific dietary advice for sick patients who suffer from problems such as anorexia (loss of appetite), nausea, diarrhoea or fever will be given in 'Care of general health problems and opportunistic infections' on page 375.

### Supplements

Many people with HIV infection prefer to supplement their diet with additional vitamins, minerals, nutrients and herbs in order to protect or strengthen their immune systems and maintain or promote weight. Since the health benefits of dietary supplements are a matter of ongoing controversy in the scientific world, many HIV specialists recommend only a multivitamin supplement and a healthy, balanced diet. If HIV-infected individuals choose to supplement their diets, they should do so with caution and discuss the supplements they intend to take with their doctors. Megadosages (large dosages) of any vitamin supplement are definitely not recommended because they may be toxic and harmful to health. Herbs should also be taken with care, because some herbs (e.g. St John's Wort) are implicated in rendering antiretroviral therapy ineffective (Piscitelli, 2000).

Vitamins and minerals which may enhance the immune system (when taken in moderation) are beta carotene, vitamin A, vitamin E, vitamin B6, vitamin B12, calcium, pyridoxine, vitamin C, selenium, zinc, iron, copper, magnesium, and antioxidants. Studies have shown that there is an association between vitamin A deficiency in pregnant women and the risk of MTCT (transmitting the virus to the baby). While vitamin A supplementation may therefore be beneficial for pregnant HIV-positive women, women should be warned that doses of vitamin A that are too high may have harmful effects on both the baby and the mother.

Moducare (natural plant sterols/sterolins extracted from the African potato plant) seems to be effective as an immune booster in HIV-infected individuals who have recently been infected as well as for those with intact or healthy immune systems. In a study which was done by Bouic, Lamprecht and Freestone (2000), it was found that patients (with a baseline CD4 cell count of more than 500 cells/mm$^3$) who took Moducare showed a significant increase in their CD4 cells and a significant decline in the viral loads. Within this group, 15 % showed undetectable viral loads within 12 months after starting the study.

**Eating defensively**

HIV-infected people are usually more vulnerable to contracting food-borne illnesses because of their weakened immune systems. It is therefore important for people with HIV infection to follow basic food safety guidelines and to eat defensively.

- HIV-infected individuals should eat a low microbial diet to avoid microbial infections (and food poisoning). They should always cook meat, chicken and fish very well (because heat kills bacteria) and should avoid products that contain any raw or undercooked meat or dairy products. They should for the same reason avoid raw or soft-boiled eggs because they can be sources of salmonella — as can 'biltong' (dried meat) and 'droë wors' (dried sausage), raw eggs and unpasteurised dairy products (milk and cheese). They should also avoid products that have passed their 'sell by' or 'best used by' date. 'Raw' cows milk or unpasteurised milk should be boiled and then kept in clean containers.

- Food should be handled and stored hygienically. Keeping shelves, counter tops, refrigerators, towels and utensils clean is one of the best ways of preventing the bacterial contamination of food. To prevent cross contamination (e.g. from raw meat to other foods), the food handler should wash his or her hands regularly and not use *wooden* cutting boards for cutting and chopping raw meat, fish or chicken. Uncooked food should be kept separate from cooked food. Food that is mouldy or about to go off should be avoided, and all previously cooked food should be re-heated at a high temperature for some time before it is eaten (the heating process serves in many cases to kill or neutralise dangerous organisms).

- Raw seafood (shellfish, oysters, clams, sushi and sashimi) poses a serious risk of food poisoning for people with AIDS and should never be eaten. Lightly steamed seafood should also be avoided (Food and Drug Administration [FDA] brochure, 1992).

- Fruits and vegetables should always (if possible) be washed, scrubbed with a stiff brush, or peeled. Avoid fruit and vegetables that have been sprayed with pesticides. Canned fruits and vegetables could be used instead of fresh products if fresh products are contaminated. Raw alfalfa sprouts have been identified as carriers of food-borne diseases in the USA, and it is recommended that people with compromised immune systems should avoid eating raw sprouts (Kurtzweil, 1999).

- Water should be boiled if there is the slightest suspicion that the water source may be contaminated.

- One should eat foods with high-kilojoule, high-protein content and avoid low-kilojoule or zero-kilojoule foods. Instruct people about ways in which they can supplement the nutritional value of their meals. The addition of eggs, butter, margarine and milk to gravies, soups or milkshakes can provide additional kilojoules and protein.

- Avoid too many processed foods because many of their nutrients have been destroyed during preparation. Avoid foods that contain preservatives, artificial flavours and artificial colours. Avoid 'junk foods' as far as possible.

- Avoid raw (unpasteurised or unboiled) cow's milk.

Many popular alternative diets are followed by HIV-infected individuals. Health care professionals must make sure that alternative diets are not harmful to the health of the individual and that such diets (1) provide adequate kilojoules and proteins, (2) include a variety of nutritious foods, (3) are not regarded as a substitute for general health care, (4) do not contain substances in amounts that may be physically harmful to the person, and (5) are not unnecessarily expensive (Pike, 1988).

**Activity**

- Devise a dietary plan for an HIV-infected man who lives alone and has to take care of himself. He is a very busy executive of a company and doesn't have much time to prepare food for himself.
- Devise a dietary plan for an HIV-positive woman with very limited financial means who has to care for her large family in a very poor rural part of the country. Because the kind of diet you devise would obviously be tailored to suit cultural tastes, decide on the woman's cultural group before you begin to draw up the dietary plan.

## 16.3  CARE OF GENERAL HEALTH PROBLEMS AND OPPORTUNISTIC INFECTIONS

What follows is a discussion of the most common health problems that people with HIV infection or AIDS may encounter, as well as general care principles to alleviate the symptoms associated with HIV infection and AIDS. Because this discussion is by no means comprehensive, health care professionals and other caregivers are encouraged to use their own initiative and experience to supplement these care principles. If you don't have the equipment or material described in this chapter, just use your imagination and improvise!

Health care professionals should always remember that (as far as HIV/AIDS is concerned) they are also counsellors and educators. Nursing care principles should not only be applied in hospitals, hospices and clinics. They should also be taught on every possible occasion to patients and to those who care for them at home. Because many health problems are recurrent, it is important for HIV-infected individuals and their caregivers to know how to deal with them. Non-professional caregivers can free professional caregivers to attend to really serious cases of need if they themselves have been educated to perform basic care tasks and to provide palliative care.

This chapter will provide a brief description of the symptoms and possible causes of HIV/AIDS-related illnesses and will describe general care principles that can be applied to alleviate symptoms. In the section entitled *'What to do at home'*, additional practical advice will be given on how to prevent and treat symptoms at home with only the most basic and inexpensive commonly available resources. Caregivers at home will also be warned to look out for certain *changes* in the condition of the patient and to seek professional help in the section entitled *'Danger signs'*. (The information provided here is based on Dickinson, Clark & Swafford, 1988; Evian, 2000; Fahrner, 1988; Reno & Walker, 1988; Ungvarski, 1989 and Van Dyk, 1999. Practical advice for home care is based on the WHO publication for AIDS home care, 1993.) (See enrichment box 'General rules about caring for a child with HIV infection and AIDS' on page 376.)

### Fever

Fever (high body temperature) is usually caused by the HIV infection itself, by diarrhoea and dehydration, by opportunistic infections such as tuberculosis, viral or bacterial infections, or by endemic diseases such as malaria. HIV infection itself can cause a low grade fever (37–38 °C). When fever is 38 °C or higher for a prolonged period, it may be caused by factors other than the HIV infection itself. Care for patients with a high temperature includes the following measures:

● Encourage the patient to drink lots of fluid, especially cool fluids. Provide plenty of water, weak tea, broth or juice.

## General rules about caring for a child with HIV infection and AIDS

Since children mainly experience the same symptoms as adults, they are treated in most cases in the same way as adults. In those cases where children have to be treated differently, this will be emphasised. The following general rules apply when caring for a child with HIV infection and AIDS (WHO, 1993, 2000a):

- **Maintain good nutrition.** In most countries in the developing world, HIV-infected mothers are still breastfeeding their babies. The health care professional should help the HIV-infected mother to make an informed decision about whether to breastfeed or bottle-feed her baby. This advice should be based on facts and on the circumstances of the mother and the availability of resources. (See 'Breastfeeding' on page 29.) The growth of the baby should be regularly monitored (preferably once a month at least) so as to ensure that the baby is being adequately fed.

- **Provide early treatment for infections.** Children should be treated early and vigorously for any infections such as measles, ear infections (otitis media), oral thrush, skin infections, STDs in the newborn, unexplained fever, diarrhoea or vomiting. Because the immune systems of children with HIV infection are often impaired, and because presenting symptoms of these diseases may be more persistent and more severe under the circumstances, these children may respond poorly to treatment, develop severe complications and die.

- **Diagnose and treat tuberculosis early.** Tuberculosis is one of the most common and deadly opportunistic infections and the HIV-positive child is very susceptible to contracting tuberculosis. TB prevention and treatment should be available to all family members.

- **Treat the child as normal and ensure a good quality of life.** Since many HIV-infected children live a relatively symptom-free life for months or even years, they should be treated as normal. Let them play with other kids, go to school and do normal 'kid stuff'. Make sure however that the child always maintains high standards of hygiene. This will help to prevent infections.

- **Hospitalisation of children should be avoided if possible.** The hospital environment exposes children to many harmful pathogens or germs that can be dangerous to children with depressed immune systems. Hospitalisation of HIV-infected children should only be considered if the child is seriously ill and needs special care which cannot be given at home (Evian, 2000).

- **Immunise according to standard schedules.** All children, including those with HIV infection and AIDS, should be given all the standard vaccinations (e.g. DPT, polio, measles and Hib titre). The only exception is that BCG (the tuberculosis vaccine) should be given to all healthy HIV-infected children at birth, and not at all to infants with the clinical symptoms of HIV infection. (See 'Immunisation of children and adults with HIV infection' on page 75.)

- Remove any unnecessary clothing or blankets.
- Give sponge baths or use a fan to keep temperature down.
- Pour water on the skin, or put cloths soaked in water on the forehead or chest and fan the body with wet cloths.
- Keep the room well aerated and cool. Open the windows or doors to allow fresh air or a light breeze to penetrate.
- Use medicines that reduce fever (antipyretics) such as, for example, aspirin or paracetamol.
- Make sure that the patient eats nutritious foods (a high kilojoule, high protein diet).

**What to do at home**

**Fever**

The best way to check whether someone has a fever is to measure his or her temperature with a thermometer. If a thermometer is not available, place the back of your hand on the patient's forehead, and the back of your other hand on your forehead. If the person has a fever, you will be able to feel the difference. If the patient has a temperature, take the steps mentioned above to lower his or her temperature. Keep the skin clean and dry in between bathing and cooling sessions to prevent skin problems such as rashes and sores.

**Danger signs**

Patients and caregivers at home should seek professional help if:
- the fever is very high and continues for a long time
- it is accompanied by coughing and weight loss
- it is accompanied by symptoms such as stiff neck, severe pain, confusion, unconsciousness, a yellow colour in the eyes, sudden severe diarrhoea or convulsions
- the patient is pregnant or if she has recently had a baby
- malaria is common in the area where the patient lives, or if the fever has not gone away after one treatment with antimalarial medicine

Watch children with fever very carefully and take them to a clinic if you are unable to break the fever. Fever convulsions are common (and dangerous) in children with high fever. Use lukewarm water at room temperature to bathe babies or very young children. Never use cold water for this purpose because babies and very young children cannot yet tolerate temperatures that are too cold and may even go into shock when suddenly submersed into cold water.

## Diarrhoea

Diarrhoea is one of the most common problems of HIV infection and AIDS. A person has diarrhoea when he or she has three or more loose or watery stools per day. *Acute diarrhoea* lasts for less than 2 weeks, while *persistent diarrhoea* usually lasts for more than 2 weeks.

The most common causes of diarrhoea in people with HIV infection are gastro-intestinal infections from food and water that is not clean and fresh, opportunistic infections such as Kaposi's sarcoma in the gastro-intestinal tract, inappropriate diet, and the side effects of medication.

Diarrhoea can lead to serious dehydration, electrolyte imbalance, malnutrition, weight loss, fatigue (tiredness), weakness and even death. Because diarrhoea is a common and recurrent problem for HIV-infected patients, they need to learn how to live with diarrhoea and to adjust their fluid and food intake appropriately. The following steps should be taken:

● Encourage the patient to drink lots of fluids (such as unsweetened juices, weak tea and food-based fluids such as gruel, soup or rice water) so that he or she remains well hydrated all the time.

● Encourage the patient to consume a bland but nutritionally balanced low-fat, low-sucrose, low-fibre and lactose-free diet. Include foods such as mashed potatoes (not chips), white rice and maize meal, meat, poultry, and fish, cooked (scrambled) eggs, mashed bananas, apple juice, peeled (and preferably cooked) apples, grape juice or avocados, white bread or crackers made from refined (white) flour, noodles and pasta made from (white) refined flour, cooked vegetables such as carrots, potatoes, and soups *without* whole-grain thickeners such as barley. Marmite or Bovril as a soup (a few teaspoons dissolved in boiling water) or spread very thinly on dry toast also helps to restore electrolytic balance. If the patient can tolerate lactose, include *small* amounts of milk, cottage cheese, cream cheese, and yoghurt in the diet. Try to make food (such as rice or mashed potatoes) more appetising by making gravies from the juice of vegetables and meat and thickening them with Bisto or small amounts of maizena. (Remove excessive fat from meat juice before making the gravy.)

● Avoid all foods that may aggravate diarrhoea — especially all foods that are high in fibre. Such foods include (for example) All Bran Flakes and all other whole-wheat or whole-grain products (such as muesli bars), whole-grain cereals (especially if — like muesli — they contain raw ingredients), wholewheat bread (use white bread instead), brown rice (white rice is ideal), unpeeled or fibrous fruit and vegetables (rather feed the patient with bland fruits such as mashed bananas or very finely grated apple), nuts, seeds, popcorn, fried foods, raw vegetables, green vegetables, raisins, currants, dried fruit, foods that are difficult to digest (this will vary from patient to patient), heavily spiced foods, very rich foods, foods that contain excessive amounts of sugar or oil, alcohol and caffeine. Also avoid foods that increase flatus (gas), coffee, very strong tea (rooibos tea is acceptable), commercial aerated colas and chocolate. Tobacco should also be avoided if possible.

**What to do at home**

## Diarrhoea

Prevent diarrhoea by boiling water from an unsafe water supply (e.g. a dirty well or a dirty container) before it is used to prepare food or drinks. Eat only clean and safe food and make sure that stored food is reheated thoroughly at a high temperature. Avoid raw or uncooked meat and peel fruit or wash it well before eating. Always wash your hands before preparing or eating food.

There are three basic rules for treating diarrhoea:

1. Drink more fluids than usual. Drink something after every stool.
2. Continue to eat, even if you only consume small amounts of nutritious foods at a time.
3. Recognise and treat dehydration early. Watch out for the following signs of dehydration: severe thirst, dry mouth, sunken eyes, sunken fontanelle in young children, rapid pulse and breathing, irritability, lethargy (or lack of vitality), poor urine output and a dry skin (skin going back slowly when pinched). Treat with an oral rehydration solution such as Oral Rehydration Salts mixed with water. Or use the following home-made oral rehydration fluid:

Home-made oral rehydration fluid:

Mix 1 litre (4 big cups) of boiled and cooled water with 8 teaspoons of sugar and half a teaspoon of salt. If available, add fresh orange juice for taste and potassium replacement. Adults should take 1 to 2 cups of this fluid after every diarrhoeal stool. (To make 1 cup of rehydration fluid, mix 1 cup of water with 2 teaspoons of sugar and a pinch of salt.)

### Danger signs

Patients and caregivers should seek professional help if patients have diarrhoea and if they:

- are very thirsty
- have a fever
- cannot eat or drink properly
- do not seem to be getting better
- pass many watery stools
- have blood in the stools
- are vomiting and cannot keep fluids down
- are irritable or lethargic
- have a very dry skin

It is very important to encourage children with diarrhoea to drink. Children under 2 years old should drink about a quarter to a half cup of fluid (e.g. the home-made rehydration fluid given above, rice-water, porridge-water, soup or tea) after each loose stool — while older children should drink a half to one cup of fluid after each loose stool. In the case of breast-fed infants with diarrhoea, the mother should continue to breastfeed and try to do so more often than normal (at least every 3 hours.) Watch children very carefully for signs of dehydration and take them to the nearest hospital or clinic if necessary. Severely dehydrated children can go into shock and a coma very easily.

Since every patient reacts differently to foods, it is always a good idea to question the patient about his or her needs and then experiment cautiously with *small* amounts of desired foods to establish an optimal dietary regimen.

- Small, frequent meals will help to prevent abdominal or stomach distension.
- Make foods easier to digest by mashing or grinding the food.
- Foods at room temperature may be better tolerated than very hot or cold foods.

To prevent secondary infections the skin around the rectal area should be kept very clean and dry. The skin should be washed with mild soap and water after each bowel movement and patted dry. Broken skin can be dried with a cool hair-dryer. A lotion can be applied to relieve discomfort, and the patient can sit in warm water containing a pinch of salt or Savlon three to four times a day.

Observe babies and young children very carefully for signs of dehydration such as a dry mouth, eyes and skin, poor skin elasticity, poor urine output, sunken fontanelle and eyes, and rapid pulse and breathing.

## Fluid and electrolyte imbalance

Fluid and electrolyte status should be monitored on an ongoing basis. Assess the skin for dryness and turgor. Measure fluid intake and output daily. Monitor the patient for decreases in systolic blood pressure or increases in pulse associated with sitting or standing. Be aware of signs and symptoms of electrolyte disturbances such as muscle cramping, weakness, irregular pulse, decreased mental status, nausea and vomiting. Monitor serum electrolyte values and report abnormalities to the physician.

- Assist the patient to select foods that will replenish electrolytes, such as oranges and bananas (potassium), cheese and soups (sodium).
- Encourage a fluid intake of 2 500 ml or more per day (unless contra-indicated) in order to regain fluid lost from diarrhoea or vomiting.
- Initiate measures to control diarrhoea.
- If the patient is hospitalised, administer intravenous fluid and electrolytes as prescribed by a physician if fluid and electrolyte imbalances persist.

## Constipation

If HIV-infected patients become constipated, the following measures can be taken:

- Encourage the intake of fluids such as water and fruit juices, as well as fresh fruits and vegetables.
- Constipation can be prevented by using honey, molasses, stewed prunes and grated beetroot.
- Give the patient high-fibre foods to eat if he or she can tolerate them.
- Encourage mobility and exercise.

- Check stools for blood.
- Certain medications (e.g. codeine) can cause constipation. Check the patient's medications with the doctor or clinic.

## Skin problems

Because the skin is an important barrier against infections, it is important to keep skin intact and to treat any skin problems immediately. The following skin problems occur more often in people with AIDS than in healthy people: rashes, itching skin, increased dryness of the skin, painful sores, boils and abscesses, and slow healing of wounds. These skin problems may be caused by genital or oral herpes (thrush), fungal infections (e.g. ringworm), bacterial infections, shingles (herpes zoster), allergies, Kaposi's sarcoma, poor hygiene, immobility, malnutrition, dehydration or by prolonged pressure (bed sores).

Wear gloves when caring for lesions, rashes or weeping skin. The patient's skin can be protected in the following ways:

- Inspect the patient's skin thoroughly every morning and afternoon for redness, lesions or excessive moisture.
- If lesions are present, assess daily for changes in appearance, location and size of lesions.
- Maintain thorough foot and skin care. Skin breakdown can be prevented by stimulating the circulation by means of frequent massaging with lotions, oils or creams. Pay special attention to areas over bony prominences.
- Advise patients with foot lesions to wear white cotton socks and shoes that do not cause the feet to perspire.
- Keep the skin clean and dry.
- Encourage the use of non-perfumed skin moisturisers on a dry skin.
- Avoid the use of strong soaps on the skin.
- Avoid scratching itchy skin as this may lead to broken skin and infections.
- Encourage mobile patients to change their positions at least every 2 hours and to get out of bed as often as possible. If patients are bedridden, turn them from side to side and position their pillows accordingly every 2 hours.
- Use pressure-relieving devices such as sheep skin, foam heel and elbow protectors. Heel and elbow protectors can be made out of cloth or bandages.
- Kaposi's sarcoma lesions (a purplish skin lesion) usually require no care unless they are open and draining. Always report open, draining lesions to the physician for possible chemotherapy. Open lesions should be thoroughly cleaned and left open to air.
- If an incontinent patient is hospitalised, use a condom catheter and faecal incontinence bags to prevent skin irritation and lesions caused by wet skin. If the

patient is at home, keep the skin and linen dry and clean at all times. Use plastic sheeting, undercovers or nappies (for adults) to keep linen clean.

● Clean the perineal area (between the anus and the scrotum or vulva) after each bowel movement with non-irritating soap and water to prevent breakage of the skin and infection.

● Wash genital or rectal herpes with warm water and non-irritating soap, and pat dry or dry with a cool hair-dryer 2 to 4 times per day.

**What to do at home**

### Skin problems

As a general rule, cleaning the skin frequently with soap and water and keeping it dry between washing will prevent the most common problems. Itching can be reduced by cooling the skin with water, by applying lotions such as calamine, and by using effective traditional remedies that are usually available from local herbalists. A very dry skin can be treated by avoiding soap and by applying Vaseline, glycerine, and vegetable or plant oils (or by applying the more expensive oils and creams available in shops). To prevent babies (and confused adults) from scratching themselves, gloves or socks can be put over their hands, and fingernails can be kept short.

The buttocks area of babies with diarrhoea or yeast infections needs the following special care: leave the baby's bottom exposed to air as much as possible, soak the baby's bottom with warm water between nappy changes, change wet and soiled nappies immediately, avoid wiping the buttocks area (rather squeeze water from a cloth or pour water over the area and pat dry) and apply lotions supplied by the local clinic.

Wash wounds with clean water (cooled boiled water if necessary) mixed with salt (1 teaspoon of salt to 1 litre of clean water) or with a gentian violet solution (1 teaspoon of gentian violet crystals in half a litre of clean water). Protect the wound by covering it with clean gauze bandages or cloths. Don't touch soiled (bloody) bandages or dressings with your bare hands: use gloves, plastic bags, or a big leaf to handle the dressings, and always wash your hands. If the wound is on the feet or legs, raise the affected area as high and as often as possible.

#### Danger signs

Seek professional help at the clinic or hospital when the skin problem is associated with any of the following symptoms:

• pus, redness or fever (indicating infection)
• severe pain, difficulty in sleeping and eye problems such as blurred vision (which is often a symptom of shingles)
• allergic reactions to medication
• a bad smell, oozing of a grey or brown liquid, blackening of the skin around a wound with air bubbles or blisters (an indication of gangrene)

- Discourage patients with genital or rectal abrasions to use toilet paper as this may worsen the condition. Soft disposable cloths such as Wet Ones or cotton wool should be used instead.
- A separate wash cloth should be used to wash areas with infectious lesions.
- Discomfort caused by genital herpes can be relieved by Savlon or salt baths and pain medication.
- Protect skin surfaces from friction and rubbing by keeping bed linen free from wrinkles and by avoiding tight or restrictive clothing.

## Problems of the oral mucous membranes (mouth and throat)

Oral mucous membranes are often dry or painful because of secondary infections such as thrush (with white patches and redness), oral herpes simplex (blisters and sores on the lips), malnutrition (cracks and sores on the mouth), dehydration, inadequate oral hygiene, Kaposi's sarcoma of the mouth or throat, hairy leukoplakia, drug therapy, dental problems, and poor fitting dentures (caused by weight loss). It is important to ensure that a patient's mouth remains in a healthy condition so that he or she can swallow, eat and drink properly.

- Inspect the inside of the mouth (preferably with a light) every day before breakfast.
- Give adequate fluids to prevent dehydration and encourage the patient to eat a healthy diet.
- Treat oral thrush or lesions immediately.
- Thorough mouth hygiene should be observed at all times. Patients should have mouthwashes after every meal. In addition the tongue should be cleaned at least 2 to 3 times per day by gently scrubbing with a soft toothbrush if it is coated.
- If the patient has oral thrush, encourage him or her to suck a lemon if that is not too painful to bear. The acid in the lemon juice slows the rate at which the fungus grows. Follow the 'candida diet', i.e. avoid foods containing yeast and sugar and don't drink beer until the oral thrush has been absent (cleared up) for at least 3 weeks.
- Teeth should be brushed with a soft toothbrush — and non-abrasive toothpaste or sodium bicarbonate (baking soda) should be used to avoid injuries.
- Give soft or pureed bland foods to the patient if he or she experiences difficulty in eating.
- Serve moist foods and avoid spicy and acid foods.
- Use a straw for liquids and soups to prevent the food from touching the sore areas.
- Cold foods, drinks or ice may help to numb the mouth and relieve discomfort.

## Mouth and throat problems

To prevent problems in the mouth and throat, one can rinse the mouth with warm salt water (half a teaspoon of salt in 1 cup of water) or with a mouthwash solution after eating and between meals. (Do not allow the patient to swallow the mouthwash because it may cause diarrhoea and nausea.)

Thrush can be treated by gently scrubbing the tongue and gums with a soft tooth-brush, by rinsing the mouth with a mouthwash, salt water or lemon water, and by applying a gentian violet solution 3 to 4 times a day (1 teaspoon of gentian violet crystals in half a litre of water). The gentian violet solution can also be applied to herpes simplex sores (or blisters) on the lips.

If the patient does not have a toothbrush, they can use a tooth-cleaning stick (a stick with one end sharpened to clean between the teeth, and the other end chewed to use the fibres as a brush) or they can tie a piece of rough towel around the end of a stick and use it as a toothbrush (WHO, 1993). If toothpaste is not available, a tooth-cleaning powder can be made by mixing salt and bicarbonate of soda (or ashes) in equal amounts. Wet the toothbrush before dipping it into the powder so that the powder sticks.

### Danger signs

Seek professional help if:

- the sick person is becoming dehydrated or unable to swallow properly
- there are symptoms of oesophageal thrush such as a burning pain in the chest or a deep pain on swallowing

## Respiratory problems

Respiratory problems such as shortness of breath, difficulty in breathing, chronic coughing, chest pains and an increased production of mucus are the most common problems of HIV-infected people. These problems may be caused by colds and flu, bronchitis, tuberculosis, pneumonia (e.g. PCP), respiratory tract invasions by Kaposi's sarcoma or lymphomas, or by anaemia. The following nursing care principles apply in such situations:

- Administer medication for the cough or control pulmonary secretions as prescribed.
- Ensure that the patient takes medication regularly in the case of tuberculosis. With the help of the patient, identify a family member or friend who will assume the responsibility of ensuring that the patient will complete *the whole course* of tuberculosis medication.
- If the patient is hospitalised, give oxygen when needed.
- Apply nasopharyngeal or tracheal suction if necessary while the patient is hospitalised.

**What to do at home**

## Respiratory problems

Help patients to cough (and to drain the lungs) by massaging or patting the back of the chest over the lungs. Teach patients to hold a pillow or hand tightly over the painful chest or rib area while coughing if they find it painful to cough. Teach people to cover their mouths when coughing because the disease-causing agents can usually be passed on to other people through the air. Soothe an irritating cough with remedies such as tea with sugar or honey, or use safe home-made cough syrups. If a constant cough interferes with a person's rest at night, a cough suppressant can be prescribed. The use of a cough suppressant should however be discouraged during the day because it is important to cough and to get rid of mucus and disease-causing bacteria. When someone is experiencing difficulty in breathing, the following measures might alleviate their distress:

- Lie with pillows under the head, or with the head of the bed raised on blocks.
- Sit leaning forward with the elbows on the knees or on a low table.
- Make sure that there is always someone there with the patient. Difficulty in breathing can be very frightening and distressing.
- If a child finds it difficult to breathe, clean the nose if it is congested.

### Danger signs

Advise people to seek help if the sick person has a cough or difficulty in breathing, and if:

- sudden high fever develops
- the person is in severe pain or discomfort
- the colour of the sputum changes to grey, yellow or green
- the sputum has blood in it
- the person has a cough for more than 3 weeks — especially if the cough is also accompanied by the spitting up of blood, pain in the chest or difficulty in breathing (tuberculosis may be the cause)

In children (particularly children below the age of 5) respiratory infections can be very serious. Children should be brought to a clinic or health care professional immediately if they are:

- breathing with difficulty through the mouth or if they are breathing with an audible wheezing
- breathing faster than usual
- unable to drink because of their problems with breathing

- Encourage patients to drink lots of fluids to dilute secretions.

- Teach patients deep breathing and productive coughing techniques (to drain the lungs of accumulated mucus and bacteria) and encourage them to rest between activities.

- Patients with respiratory problems can breathe more freely in an upright sitting position in the bed (the high or semi-Fowler's position).

- Vaporisers and humidifiers can provide symptomatic relief for coughs and are especially helpful when treating children.
- Alleviate factors that aggravate respiratory problems such as anxiety.
- Discourage smoking. If a patient insists on smoking, discourage smoking before eating and before, during and immediately after performing activities.

**Anorexia, nausea and vomiting**

HIV-infected people often experience anorexia (lack of appetite), nausea and vomiting as a result of gastro-intestinal problems, infections, side effects of medication, Kaposi's sarcoma in the intestines and HIV infection itself. In some people with AIDS, nausea and vomiting are short-lived and usually disappear after treatment. In others, nausea and vomiting may be long-lasting and become a part of daily life. These problems may cause weight loss and a fluid and electrolyte imbalance. In such cases, apply the following care principles:

- Stop the intake of food and fluids for 1 to 2 hours if the patient is vomiting. Gradually then introduce the intake of clear fluids such as water or flat Coke. To maintain or restore the fluid balance, increase the amount of fluids as soon as the patient can tolerate it. Later the patient may eat dry toast or crackers.
- Anti-nausea medicine should be taken 30 to 60 minutes before meal-times (or as prescribed).
- Advise nauseated patients not to take liquids before, during or immediately after meals.
- Foods that are low in fat should be introduced — as well as dry, salty foods. Avoid gas-producing, greasy, spicy foods.
- Present food in an attractive and appetising way. Eliminate food odours which may nauseate the patient by keeping the windows of the room open. Serve food cold or at room temperature. Patients should eat slowly in a relaxed atmosphere.
- Encourage patients to rest after meals with their upper bodies in an elevated position.
- In order to increase appetite, encourage patients to take small, frequent meals high in protein and kilojoules throughout the day rather than three large meals. Kilojoule intake can be increased by using extra peanut butter, sugar, honey, ice cream, milk shakes and sweets. Patients should be encouraged to eat all their favourite foods and to drink lots of fluids.
- Encourage the use of nutritional supplements.
- Teach patients relaxation and breathing techniques and encourage them to use these techniques when they are nauseated.
- Thorough oral care should be encouraged to prevent thrush (because thrush makes eating difficult).

**What to do at home**

## Nausea and vomiting

Apply the principles listed under 'Anorexia, nausea and vomiting' on page 386. In addition, try to avoid cooking smells if possible, watch out for signs of dehydration and begin to give an oral rehydration solution, weak tea or other clear liquids to the patient to drink 1 or 2 hours after severe vomiting has stopped. Start with about 2 tablespoons of liquid an hour for 1 to 3 hours. Then increase the amount of fluids to 4 to 6 tablespoons an hour for the next hour or two. If the patient feels up to it, he or she should begin to eat small quantities of dry, plain foods such as bread or rice. Keep the mouth clean and fresh by rinsing it with water or diluted lemon juice.

### Danger signs

Advise caregivers to seek professional help:

- if vomiting occurs repeatedly and fluids cannot be kept down
- if regular vomiting lasts more than 24 hours, particularly if it is accompanied by pain in the abdomen
- if a person has a fever in addition to the vomiting
- if the sick person is vomiting violently, especially if the vomit is dark green, brown, or smells like faeces
- if the vomit contains blood

Note: Be very careful with vomiting children and watch them carefully for signs of dehydration. Babies can dehydrate and die within hours if vomiting (and diarrhoea) are neglected.

## Circulation impairment

Circulation impairment may be caused by factors such as pressure on body parts or by immobility. Circulation problems can usually be assessed if any of the following signs are visible: oedema or swelling of extremities, ulceration or skin breakdown, weak pulses and a cool skin temperature.

- Stimulate circulation by massaging the skin regularly with lotion.

- Encourage the patient to be active. If the patient is bedridden, passive exercises should be performed and the patient should be turned every 2 hours.

- Elevate extremities (e.g. the legs).

- Avoid pressure from cushions or heavy blankets on extremities, as well as tight-fitting clothes.

- A bedridden child who has a severe chronic illness should be held in someone's lap as often as possible. Not only does this improve circulation and avoid bedsores, it also gives the child the love and attention that he or she needs.

## Oedema (swelling)

HIV-infected people often exhibit the symptoms of oedema because of HIV infection, Kaposi's sarcoma, or other opportunistic infections. Intervention and health teaching should include compliance with the following measures:

- Avoid excessive sodium (salt) intake. Read the labels on canned products and substitute other (non-salt) spices for salt (salt substitutes that do not contain salt are sold in most health shops).
- Keep the swollen areas (e.g. the legs) above the level of the heart but take care not to restrict blood flow by placing pillows at pressure points such as those behind the knees.
- Avoid tight-fitting clothes and discourage the patient from crossing his or her ankles or knees.
- Examine the skin over the swollen areas regularly for circulation and skin discolorations or breakdown.

**What to do at home**

**Swelling**

If a person experiences swelling of the legs, raise his or her legs or other swollen parts on pillows, or raise the foot of the bed on blocks.

## Genital problems

Opportunistic infections of the genital area, including certain sexually transmitted diseases (STDs), are common in both men and women with AIDS. These infections often cause pain and discomfort. Genital problems can present as an unusual discharge (a mucus or pus-like substance) from the vagina, the urethral openings or the penis, open sores or ulcers in the genital, groin or rectal areas (which sometimes start as blisters or a rash in or around the genital area), warts in the genital area or around the anus, and swollen glands in the groin. (For more information on STDs see 'STDs and HIV: the deadly alliance' on page 48.) People with STDs are usually not hospitalised. The caregiver should follow the principles and advice listed below when looking after a patient with an STD at home (WHO, 1993):

- Seek treatment for STDs from a health care professional or clinic immediately. Antibiotics can cure most STDs completely.
- Use a condom for every sexual contact. It is dangerous for someone who is already infected with HIV to be exposed to other sexually transmitted diseases.
- Women with an abnormal vaginal discharge should keep the vulva and anal area clean by washing with water and a mild, non-abrasive soap.

- Women should avoid washing out or flushing the vagina (douche), or putting anything (e.g. antiseptics, leaves, herbs) inside the vagina, unless advised to do so by a health care professional. The practice of 'dry sex' should be avoided.

- Open genital sores should be washed with soap and water and they should be kept dry between washings.

- If herpes is diagnosed, advise the person to bathe the affected area with a salt solution (1 teaspoon of ordinary cooking salt in half a litre of clean water) every 2 to 3 hours. Keep the area dry between bathing, and apply calamine lotion, talcum or starch powder.

- If a person suffers repeatedly from candidiasis (vaginal thrush), apply gentian violet (1 or 2 teaspoons of gentian violet crystals dissolved in 1 litre of clean water) to the affected areas.

- Plain yoghurt is very effective in the treatment of vaginal thrush. Rub plain yoghurt on any red areas or dip a tampon in the yoghurt and insert it in the vagina twice a day.

- Women with vaginal thrush should follow the 'candida diet' and avoid all foods containing yeast (e.g. bread) and sugar.

- Women with vaginal thrush should avoid wearing tights or nylon panties (they should wear only cotton panties).

- A rash on the penis or under the foreskin can be alleviated by soaking the penis in a dilute salt and water solution. (Dissolve a teaspoonful of salt in a glass or jam jar of water, pull back the foreskin, put the penis in the water and soak for 5 minutes. Repeat 2 to 3 times a day.) If this procedure does not work, repeat by using a gentian violet solution. Ask for advice from a health care professional if the condition does not clear up in 3 to 4 days.

- Loss of menstruation and irregular bleeding often occurs in women with AIDS. If a woman misses one or two periods she should go the clinic to be examined in order to establish the cause. Women who have stopped menstruating should be supported emotionally because the loss of menstruation often represents a loss of femininity, of motherhood, of a sense of meaning and of self-esteem. This often causes a woman to feel sad and depressed.

People with HIV infection and their families should seek professional help when they suspect that they may have an STD, if they experience difficulty or pain in passing urine, if they have genital warts, genital ulcers, an unusual vaginal discharge that is foul-smelling, itchy, green, yellow or grey in colour, if a woman develops pain in her lower abdomen (particularly if it is accompanied by a fever), if a woman's periods stop or become irregular, if there is a discharge from the penis, and if there is swelling and/or pain in the scrotum.

## Notes on the use of medication

Health care professionals should make sure that their clients know how to take their medication. It is always a good idea to give clients and their families written instructions on how to take the medication. If they cannot read, someone can always be found to read it for them. Pictures can also be used to remind people who cannot read when to take their medication. The World Health Organisation, for example, recommends the following format (WHO, 1993, pp.134–135):

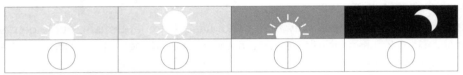

This picture means one tablet four times a day: one at sunrise, one at noon, one at sunset, and one in the middle of the night.

This picture means half a tablet three times a day: one at sunrise, one at noon, and one in the middle of the night.

This picture means one teaspoonful twice a day: one at sunrise and one at sunset.

Advice for giving medication to children:
- Liquid medicines can be squirted slowly into the side of the child's mouth with a dropper or syringe, or poured from a spoon.
- Always praise a child after he or she has taken medicine.
- If the medicine tastes unpleasant, warn the child in advance.
- Coat the child's mouth with peanut butter or use chocolate milk if he or she has to swallow a bitter medication.
- If a pill cannot be swallowed, crush it and mix it with the smallest amount possible of something the child likes to eat. Do not however hide medicine in food because then the child may begin to refuse food.
- If the child vomits immediately after taking a medicine, give the dose again. But if vomiting occurs 20 or more minutes after taking the medicine, do not repeat the dose.

(Evian, 2000; WHO, 1993, p.136)

## Pain

Some people in the later stages of AIDS may experience continuous pain — while others may only experience pain occasionally. There are many factors which cause pain. These include immobility, infections such as herpes zoster (shingles), swelling of the extremities (caused by Kaposi's sarcoma or heart problems), headaches (sometimes associated with encephalitis or meningitis), lesions caused by Kaposi's sarcoma, pain of the oral, rectal or vaginal mucous membranes due to opportunistic infections, muscle aches, chest and abdominal conditions, ulcerations and surgical wounds, and peripheral neuropathy. This last condition is caused when the HI virus infects the nerve cells and causes extreme pain in the lower extremities. Depression and anxiety often accompany a patient's physical pain. Pain should be dealt with in the following ways:

- Encourage the patient to take the medication prescribed by the physician. Pain medicine should be taken on a regular basis as prescribed (e.g. every 4, 6 or 8 hours) because this can help people to feel that they have control over their pain. Patients will feel continuously reassured if they take the medicine before the pain becomes too great.
- Use the 'ladder' approach in the choice of medication. Start with the mildest drugs first (e.g. aspirin or paracetamol) and if that does not help, go up the ladder to moderate medication (e.g. codeine). If the pain persists, morphine can be given, with or without a co-analgesic (Evian, 2000).
- Keep in mind that some pain medications, such as codeine- and morphine-containing drugs, cause constipation. Constipation should be prevented by controlling the patient's diet and by prescribing laxatives.
- Offer comfort measures such as massages and back rubs, warm soaks for painful muscles, joints, feet or legs, ice bags for headaches and soothing music of the patient's choice.
- Encourage relaxation exercises and teach deep and regular breathing techniques.
- Maintain a quiet and restful environment, and limit the number of visitors.
- Listen attentively to the patient and provide verbal support. Remember that pain is influenced by the patient's emotional and psychological state.
- Identify factors that aggravate the patient's pain and try to eliminate them.
- Encourage mental imagery (or the formation of mental pictures). Encourage the patient to imagine or remember a favourite place or event.

## Impaired vision

One of the symptoms of AIDS is impaired vision or blindness due to eye infections caused by the cytomegalovirus (CMV), Kaposi's sarcoma or lymphoma. The fol-

**What to do at home**

## Pain

Keep the environment as calm as possible, talk calmly and in gentle tones to the sick person, avoid bright lights, play soft music, read to the person, apply a cool cloth on the forehead or give a light massage. Ask the patient what you can do to ease the pain. Some patients prefer to be wrapped in a blanket to ease the pain. A child who is in pain should be lifted with the palms of the hands rather than with the fingertips (which may feel like a pinch for a child in pain). Give pain medication regularly. If movement of a limb causes pain, make a home-made splint such as a plank or a rolled newspaper to immobilise the limb.

### Danger signs
Professional advice should be sought:
- if the pain becomes unbearable or if it is associated with new symptoms such as severe headache or weakness
- if there is a sudden or recent occurrence of pain in the hands or feet
- if there is a persistent headache lasting over 2 weeks, a severe headache which is getting rapidly worse and which is not relieved by the usual methods of dealing with pain, a headache associated with vomiting or a headache that affects the sick person's ability to think or move

**Enrichment**

## Aspirin, Reye's syndrome and children

Aspirin has been implicated in Reye's syndrome, a rare but serious illness in children and teenagers with chickenpox and flu. Reye's syndrome is triggered by viral infections (such as flu) and it seems that aspirin (which is taken to alleviate the symptoms of the viral infections) plays a role in turning these viral infections into Reye's syndrome. Reye's syndrome is characterised by symptoms such as encephalitis, headache, fever, nausea, vomiting and convulsions (brain and liver cells are attacked). Children and adolescents should take paracetamol rather than aspirin if they develop symptoms of flu or colds.

lowing principles and procedures should be included in a nursing care plan designed to assist patients with impaired vision:

- Orient patients to their surroundings.
- Do not change the environment.
- Assist patients with feeding, cut their food and describe the various foods on the plate.
- Do not leave hot foods, hot plates or hot liquids unattended with the patient.
- Do not speak more loudly than you normally do because the patient is not deaf.
- Do not leave patients unattended if they are smoking.

- If the patient is in the hospital, keep the bed in the lowest position, make sure that the patient can use the call system and keep a night light on at night for the convenience of patients with impaired vision.
- Apply general safety measures in the home (do not change the position of furniture and remove all loose rugs and exposed sharp objects).
- Promote independence and help the patient to relearn daily activities such as bathing, dressing and feeding.

## General fatigue (tiredness) and weakness

AIDS can often make a person feel very tired and weak, especially in the later stages of the illness. Feelings of fatigue and weakness can be caused by any of the following conditions: chronic HIV infection, opportunistic infections (particularly respiratory illnesses), problems such as diarrhoea, anaemia, prolonged immobility, poor nutrition and depression.

- Help the patient to learn to adjust to his or her limited ability.
- Assist patients with their personal hygiene and movements.
- Encourage regular rest.
- Encourage frequent repositioning and massage the patient's body with lotion to stimulate circulation (this prevents bedsores).
- If necessary, encourage the use of devices such as a cane (walking stick), crutches, a walker or a wheelchair to prevent falling injuries.
- Find ways to make activities easier (these may include sitting down while washing, dressing or preparing food and using a bedpan rather than walking to the toilet or latrine).
- Keep personal items that are frequently used within the patient's reach so that they can be obtained without the patient having to walk to fetch them.
- Measures such as relaxation techniques and guided imagery may decrease the anxiety that contributes to weakness and fatigue.
- Keep the environment safe if the person is weak but moving about, and try not to leave the person alone for long periods.

## The risk of falling

AIDS patients are prone to falling because of factors such as sedation, weakness, mental confusion, severe diarrhoea and hypotension (low blood pressure). Because AIDS patients are usually young and accustomed to independence and self-care, they do not always realise that they currently have to live with unaccustomed limitations. To limit the risk of falling, the caregiver should follow the guidelines listed below:

- Ensure that items used regularly by the patient are within reach.

**Tiredness and weakness**

Involve the whole family in the care of the patient. Make a list of what the sick person can still do alone in the home and of those activities for which the patient needs assistance. Ask family members to help with the things that the patient cannot do. Assist the patient to learn to accept (and ask for) the help of others. Keep the person involved in the activities and decisions of everyday family life (even though the person may be very weak). This will give a patient a sense of belonging and feeling needed.

**Danger signs**

Professional help should be sought if the sick person suddenly becomes very weak (e.g. he or she is unable to walk) — particularly if there are also other symptoms such as high fever, headache or confusion.

- Since severe diarrhoea can considerably weaken patients, persuade them not to walk to the toilet but rather to use a bedpan (or a bedside commode if the patient is in a hospital).
- Encourage the use of devices such as a cane (walking stick), crutches or wheelchair to prevent falling injuries.
- Caregivers and patients should be warned that certain medications (such as IV Pentamidine which is used to treat pneumocystis carinii pneumonia) can cause hypotension (low blood pressure). Low blood pressure can be the precipitating cause of serious falls.
- Use bedside rails to protect delirious or weak patients from falling out of bed in the hospital. If it is impossible to safeguard a patient all the time at home, nurse the patient on a mattress on the floor.

**Activity**

Devise a commode (or portable toilet) for a very weak patient who can get out of bed, but who cannot walk to the outside toilet any more. Use the following materials to construct your portable toilet: an old chair, a piece of wood, a bucket with a lid, a saw, nails and paint.

## Alteration of mental status: confusion and dementia

Some degree of mental confusion (or dementia) is common among people with AIDS because of the effect of HIV on the brain. The mental changes induced by the effects that the HI virus has on the brain may either be scarcely noticeable — or else they may become a serious and obvious disability. The mental changes induced by dementia may include difficulty in one or all of the following areas: (1) an *inability to think clearly* (problems with concentration, memory loss, losing track of conver-

sations or tasks), (2) *behaviour* (irritability and disinterested, confused, disorientated, unpredictable, delusional thinking), (3) *strength or coordination* (patients
start dropping things, they lose their balance and fall, they are slow in their movements, and they exhibit shakiness and difficulty in swallowing) and (4) *personality
changes* (withdrawal and combativeness or irrational aggression). The care and
treatment of a patient with an altered mental status will depend on the specific
manifestations of the problem, and could include any of the following measures:

- Reassure the patient of your presence, *especially at night*, so as to alleviate his
  or her fears.
- Modify the patient's home environment for safety and convenience. Remove
  dangerous objects and medications from their reach.
- Keep the patient orientated to time, place and people by using clocks, a calendar,
  photographs, night lights and written schedules of daily routine, dates of
  appointments and the telephone numbers of friends.
- Keep the environment structured. Avoid unnecessary changes in the patient's
  room or home and only keep familiar objects around the patient.
- Use signs to orientate patients to their surroundings: identify the patient's bed-
  room, bathroom and the kitchen with name plates if necessary.
- Explain the changes in the patient's behaviour or cognitive functioning to the
  patient's family and involve them in the care of the patient.
- Give the patient only one instruction at a time and speak in a slow, simple and
  clear way when you are giving instructions.
- Ask questions that can be answered with either a 'Yes' or a 'No'. Be concrete and
  specific — and give the patient enough time to respond to questions, directions
  or conversations.
- Try to interpret the *feelings* the person is trying to express rather than just the
  words.
- If the person is upset or angry, distract his or her attention by changing the subject, switching on the radio, giving him or her a manual task (such as folding
  clothes) or by removing the person from the upsetting environment.
- Talk about the distant past. Every person should have *some* happy memories of
  things that happened long ago. Help the patient to recall these happy memories
  by skilful questioning. Such memories should give the patient some pleasure.
  (Do *not* allow the patient to dwell on traumatic, upsetting or disconcerting memories from the past.)
- When the patient is hospitalised, encourage the patient's family and friends to
  bring favourite objects from home to the hospital. These objects will make the
  environment more familiar and less threatening.
- Take measures to protect the patient from injury while he or she is hospitalised.
  Place the bell within easy reach, keep side rails up and the bed in a low position,

instruct the patient to wear shoes and slippers with non-skid soles, and monitor any patient who is smoking or shaving.

*Don't*

- expect patients to perform complex or demanding tasks. (Give them one thing at a time to do.)
- argue with patients when they are confused. You will *not* convince the person and he or she will only become even more upset.
- challenge the person's delusions or fantasies. These delusions and fantasies are usually harmless. If you have to cast doubt on a patient's fantasies for some practical reason, then do so in a kind and reassuring way.
- talk to the person as though he or she were a child
- give the person choices because having to make decisions can be very confusing for people in this state

**What to do at home**

**Confusion and dementia**

Take measures to prevent accidents in the home. Pay careful attention to open fires or boiling water, provide canes (walking sticks) or walkers for people who are weak or who tend to become off-balance when they walk, remove loose and potentially dangerous objects in the home, keep walkways clear, do not rearrange the furniture, store poisonous or toxic substances safely out of reach, keep medicines out of reach and only give them according to the prescribed schedule, install handrails or put a securely positioned and stabilised chair in a shower or bath, store sharp objects like knives, scissors, razors and saws safely and out of reach, and try not to leave the sick person unattended for long periods.

**Danger signs**

Pay careful attention to the following danger signs and take appropriate action if:

- there are sudden changes in a person's ability to move or think — especially when these changes are accompanied by a high fever, headache or difficulty in breathing
- the patient begins to manifest serious mental or personality changes
- the patient becomes unmanageable at home

**Activity**

Develop a weekly practical session to teach volunteers who are involved in home-based care to become skilled in performing the following activities:

- bed-bathing a bedridden patient
- bathing a baby
- positioning and lifting a patient in bed

## 16.4 CARE OF PATIENTS WITH A SENSE OF SOCIAL ISOLATION

Patients with HIV infection and AIDS face many problems and stressors which often cause them to withdraw both physically and emotionally from social contact. People with HIV/AIDS are often stigmatised by society. In addition, they are forced to reveal hidden lifestyles to family, friends and co-workers. They are also frequently rejected by loved ones and often have to face and cope with many serious losses. Because of these unfortunate experiences, HIV-infected people often experience emotions such as anxiety, anger, shame, fear, depression, loneliness and a desire to withdraw from social interaction. The infection control measures at home or in the hospital may further contribute to the patient's feelings of isolation. Health care professionals and other caregivers should be sensitive to the HIV-infected person's needs, and they should be able to notice when the person's social interactions deteriorate. The following ways of decreasing the patient's sense of social isolation should be applied whenever possible (Smeltzer & Bare, 1992):

- Assess the patient's usual (currently normal) levels of social interaction as early as possible so as to provide a baseline for monitoring changes in behaviour.
- Obtain an understanding from the patient of how he or she coped with illnesses and major life stressors in the past.
- Encourage patients to *express* their feelings of isolation and aloneness. Assure them that such feelings are not unique or abnormal — and certainly nothing to feel guilty or ashamed about.
- Provide information about how to protect themselves as well as others from HIV infection and re-infection. This may give patients the kind of confidence they need to stop avoiding social contact.
- Assure patients, family and friends that HIV cannot be spread through casual contact.
- Help the patient to explore and identify resources for support and mechanisms for coping.
- Encourage the patient to telephone his or her family and friends — as well as various AIDS support groups.
- If possible, identify and eliminate specific barriers to social contact.
- If possible, encourage social interaction with family, friends or co-workers.
- Encourage patients to keep themselves occupied with their usual day-to-day activities.

## 16.5 PALLIATIVE CARE OF AIDS PATIENTS

Palliative (or terminal) care is active, compassionate and comprehensive care that comforts and supports individuals and families who are living with a life-threatening illness. The purpose of palliative care is to meet the physical, psychological,

## Isolation of the hospitalised AIDS patient

Patients with HIV infection or AIDS should never be isolated in a special room merely because they are HIV positive. There is no way in which an HIV-positive patient can infect other patients if the prescribed universal precautions are observed. Isolation of an HIV-infected person **is** however appropriate if large-scale contamination by blood and body fluids is expected, if the patient is severely immune-depressed and needs to be isolated to protect him or her against secondary infections, if privacy is needed or preferred for one reason or another, and if the patient has another communicable disease such as tuberculosis (so that other patients can be protected). If a patient with HIV infection or AIDS is placed in a room or ward with other patients, the health care professional should ensure that the other patients in the room are not suffering from immune-depression (because this will make them more susceptible to opportunistic infections). They should also ensure that the other patients do not have any infections or diseases that can be transmitted to the patient with AIDS.

social and spiritual needs of the individual and family while remaining sensitive to personal, cultural and religious values, beliefs and practices. Palliative care is planned and delivered by the multidisciplinary team that includes the patient, the family, the caregivers and other health and social service providers — and it should always take into account the needs of the *whole* person. Palliative care includes medical and nursing care, social and emotional support, counselling and spiritual care. It emphasises living, encourages hope, and helps people to make the most of each day. The palliative caregiver must treat the patient with respect and acceptance, acknowledge their right to privacy and confidentiality, and respond caringly to their individual needs. Integral to effective palliative care is the provision of opportunities, encouragement and support for the family and caregivers so that they themselves can work through their own emotions and grief when such emotions are evoked by the care they are providing or by the situation and condition of the patient and the environment (Canadian Palliative Care Association, 1995, p. 12; WHO, 2000a, p. 8-1).

The purpose of palliative care is to:

- affirm the right of the patient and the family to participate in informed discussions and make treatment choices
- affirm life while regarding dying as a normal process
- neither hasten nor postpone death
- provide relief from pain and other distressing symptoms
- integrate the psychological and the spiritual aspects of care
- provide a support system to help patients live as actively and meaningfully as possible until death intervenes

- provide a support system to help the family and loved ones cope during the patient's illness and during their own bereavement
- help the patient to die in comfort, with dignity and in keeping with their expressed wishes (WHO, 2000a, p. 8-2)

It is very difficult for everybody involved to decide when to stop active treatment and to begin to prepare the patient and his or her family for dying. This decision should never be taken by the health care professional alone, but always in collaboration with the patient (if possible), the family and the loved ones. Palliative care usually begins when there is no reasonable chance of improvement, when medical treatment is no longer effective, when the side effects of treatments outweigh the benefits, when the patient with AIDS does not want to continue with treatments, when a child's condition becomes unbearable for both the child or the family, or when the body's vital organs begin to fail.

If possible, the patient should make a choice about where to die. While many people prefer to die at home, others might choose a hospice or terminal care facility. Many hospices also provide trained staff to care for the dying patients as well as their families in their own homes. The support of the local community should be mobilised to help the caregivers (usually the women in the family) to cope with the pressure of caring for a dying patient in the home. (The spiritual, emotional and psychological support of the dying patient and his or her family are discussed in chapter 13.)

## 16.6 CONCLUSION

Tristano Palermino, a patient with AIDS, gave the following advice to health care professionals who care for patients dying with AIDS:

As in life, people facing death have a right to do it their own way. Do not pry or force patients to feel feelings or 'face' death. It's a disservice to force patients to give up their denial or to give cheery false hopes. Sometimes I just want someone to listen. Sometimes I do not want to talk about my medical treatments. Sometimes I do not want to talk at all. If you stay in the moment, contribute what you can, and permit the patient to do the same, you cannot fail. I thank you for your commitment to helping all sick people (Palermino, 1988).

# Legal, Ethical and Policy Issues

**After completing Part 5, you should:**

- understand what basic rights the South African Constitution guarantees to people living with HIV/AIDS
- be in a position to contribute towards the development and evaluation of HIV/AIDS policies in the workplace, hospitals, schools or tertiary institutions
- be able to develop a personal ethical credo that will guide you in your work with people who are infected with HIV or who have AIDS

## INTRODUCTION TO PART 5

The Constitution in South Africa guarantees that people living with HIV and AIDS have the same basic human rights and responsibilities that all the other citizens of this country have. Under no circumstances may employers, health care professionals, teachers or any other person discriminate against people on grounds of their HIV-positive status.

**Chapter 17** discusses the basic rights of people living with HIV/AIDS. It also examines specific applications of the law in the workplace, in medical settings and in schools and tertiary institutions. Advice and recommendations are also made on how to develop effective management and policy plans that take the needs of HIV-positive people into account.

............................................................................

*The law*

*Has he learnt to live under the laws?*
*Those about which our elders sing.*
*Words — finely woven like a net.*

............................................................................

No more complex challenge could ever have been devised to test the moral fibre of the human race than HIV/AIDS. The HIV/AIDS pandemic has given rise to a vast array of ethical, moral and legal issues — many of them unprecedented. Unless we cope adequately with the problems presented by these issues, we stand in danger of collectively slipping back into the ignorance, irrational fear and inhumane conduct that characterised the dark years of the Black Death in late medieval Europe. If that ever happens, history will judge us harshly because it will prove that the *great cruel beast* that was metaphorically alluded to in the beginning of each of these chapters was, after all, not HIV/AIDS — but *us*.

Although we need laws that will guide us to make the right decisions about people living with HIV/AIDS, we should be guided as we attempt to do the right thing, not so much by various laws (however valuable they may be), but by our own common sense, our own ethical and moral values, our compassion and our basic respect for the human rights and dignity of all people.

## 17.1  THE CONSTITUTION AND THE LEGAL FRAMEWORK

The themes discussed in this chapter will be based on South African legislation, policies and proposals. These principles are based on those *basic human rights* which apply to all citizens and which should not be denied to people with HIV infection or AIDS.

The South African Constitution (Act No. 108 of 1996) is the supreme law of the country and all other laws must comply with its provisions. The Bill of Rights (which is part of the Constitution) enunciates a number of basic human rights which apply to all citizens and which therefore also protect people living with HIV/AIDS. According to the Constitution, people have the following rights (based on Van Wyk, 2000):

● the right not to be unfairly discriminated against, either by the state or by another person
● the right to bodily and psychological integrity, which includes the right to security and control over the body
● the right not to be subjected to medical or scientific experiments without the person's own informed consent

- the right of access to health care services, including reproductive health care
- the right not to be refused emergency medical treatment
- the right to information and a basic education
- the right to privacy
- the right not to have the privacy of one's communications infringed

The information given in this chapter on the way in which people with HIV/AIDS should be treated in the workplace, in medical settings as well as in schools and tertiary educational settings is based on the following pieces of legislation, policies, proposals and protections within the common law (Van Wyk, 2000; Whiteside & Sunter, 2000):

- the Employment Equity Act No. 55 of 1998
- the Promotion of Equality and Prevention of Unfair Discrimination Act No. 4 of 2000
- the Labour Relations Act No. 66 of 1995
- the Occupational Health and Safety Act No. 85 of 1993
- the Mines Health and Safety Act No. 29 of 1996
- the Compensation for Occupational Injuries and Diseases Act No. 130 of 1993
- the Basic Conditions of Employment Act No. 75 of 1997
- the National Education Policy Act No. 27 of 1996
- the National Policy on HIV/AIDS for learners and educators in public schools and students and educators in further education and training institutions (Notice 1926 of 1999, *Government Gazette*: Vol. 410, Pretoria, 10 August 1999, No. 20372)
- the Medical Schemes Act No. 131 of 1998
- the proposed notification of AIDS disease and death
- the Department of Health's draft National Policy on Testing for HIV (*Government Gazette*, Vol. 414, Pretoria, 10 December 1999, No. 20710)
- common-law protection of the right to privacy and dignity

## 17.2 THE BASIC RIGHTS OF PEOPLE LIVING WITH HIV/AIDS

People living with HIV infection and AIDS should have the same basic rights and responsibilities as those which apply to all citizens of the country.

### Liberty, autonomy, security of the person and freedom of movement

People with HIV or AIDS have the same rights to liberty and autonomy, security of the person and to freedom of movement as the rest of the population. No restrictions should be placed on the free movement of HIV-infected people, and they may not be segregated, isolated or quarantined in prisons, schools, hospitals or elsewhere merely because of their HIV-positive status. People with HIV infection or AIDS are entitled to maintain *personal autonomy* (i.e. the right to make their *own* decisions) about any matter that affects marriage and child-bearing — although counselling about the consequences of their decisions should be provided (The AIDS and HIV Charter).

### HIV testing

*When may a person be tested for HIV?*

No person may be tested for HIV infection without his or her free and *informed consent* except in the case of *anonymous* epidemiological screening programmes undertaken by authorised agencies such as the national, provincial or local health authorities. In all *other* cases — such as HIV testing for research purposes or when a person's blood will be screened because he or she is a blood donor — the informed consent of the individual is legally required.

Where an existing blood sample is available, and an *emergency situation* necessitates testing the source patient's blood (e.g. when a health care worker has been put at risk because of an accident such as a needlestick injury), HIV testing may be undertaken without informed consent — but only after informing the source patient that the test will be performed and after assuring him or her that privacy and absolute confidentiality will be maintained. While the result of such a test may be disclosed to the health care worker concerned, it must not be disclosed to anyone else (the result of the test must remain confidential). It may only be disclosed to the source patient if he or she asks to be told the result. If an existing blood sample is not available for testing in an emergency situation, the patient must give his or her informed consent for blood to be drawn for the HIV test to be done. Routine testing of a person for HIV infection for the *perceived* purpose of protecting a health care professional from infection is *impermissible* — regardless of consent.

Proxy consent for an HIV test may be given where an individual is unable to give consent. Proxy consent is consent by a person legally entitled to grant consent on behalf of another individual. For example, a parent or guardian of a child below the age of consent to medical treatment may give proxy consent to HIV testing of the child.

*Informed consent, pre- and post-HIV test counselling*

Informed consent, which includes pre-HIV test counselling, is compulsory before HIV testing may be carried out. As was explained in chapter 11, *informed consent* means that the person has been made aware of, and understands, the *implications* of the test. The person should also be free to make his or her own decision about whether to be tested or not, and may in no way be coerced or forced into being tested.

Pre-test counselling should occur before an HIV test is undertaken. It should take the form of a confidential dialogue between the client and a suitable, qualified person where relevant information is given and consent obtained. Post-test counselling should take place as part of the process of informing an individual of an HIV test result.

If a health care facility lacks the capacity to provide a pre- or a post-HIV test counselling service, a referral to a counselling agency or another facility with the capacity to provide counselling should be arranged before an HIV test is performed and when the HIV test result is given. Because this is usually impractical and unfeasible in many countries in Africa, it is advisable for health care facilities to train their **own** personnel to do pre- and post-test counselling.

Anonymous and confidential HIV antibody testing with pre- and post-HIV test counselling should be available to all. People who test HIV positive should have access to continuing support and health services.

*Must a person sign a written consent form before an HIV test?*

According to the law, a person can also consent verbally to an HIV test. It is however advisable to obtain *written* proof that the person has been pre-test counselled and that they agree to have an HIV test.

*Can a hospital test a patient for HIV without his/her consent?*

If a person goes to a hospital for treatment, he/she must still consent to all treatment and testing procedures (including HIV testing). By going to a hospital, people do not give up their rights to privacy and security. They also retain their right to control their own bodies. HIV testing in hospitals may not be done without proper pre-test counselling.

*If a hospital has a wall poster saying that they do HIV testing on all patients, does this mean that all patients automatically give their consent to be tested?*

Wall posters saying a hospital is doing HIV testing on all patients do not constitute consent because (Fine et al., 1997):

● not all patients are literate

● not everyone will see the poster

● reading the poster does not mean that the patient has understood what an HIV test entails and what the results may imply for the patient

If the patient merely reads a wall poster and does not have proper pre-test counselling, he or she will not have the necessary information to make an informed decision about testing. Posters, pamphlets, videos and other media may only be used in making *information* about HIV/AIDS available. None of these media can be regarded as substitutes for pre-test counselling.

 *What if a person refuses pre-HIV test counselling (and HIV testing)?*

The health care professional should accept, after personal consultation, an individual's decision to refuse pre-HIV test counselling and/or HIV testing. Try to find out *why* a person refuses to receive (for instance) pre-HIV test counselling and attempt if possible to rectify (in a friendly and reassuring way) the patient's preconceptions. (Some people refuse counselling because of previous traumatic or negative experiences with inadequate or unsympathetic counsellors.)

 *Are there any exceptions to the rule of informed consent?*

The only exceptions to the rule that a person must give their consent to any treatment, tests or an operation, are when genuine emergencies are involved or when certified mentally ill patients have to be treated.

If a patient needs emergency treatment but is unaware of the treatment (as will be the case if he or she is unconscious), the doctor or hospital does not need consent before carrying out essential treatment that will save the patient's life. *It is however doubtful if an HIV test can ever be necessary before emergency treatment.*

According to The Mental Health Act, consent to treatment or testing of a mentally ill patient should be gained from the person's curator, spouse, parent, child (if the child is 21 or older) or sibling. If the patient is in a mental institution, and none of the above-mentioned people can be found, the medical superintendent can consent on behalf of the patient in serious cases. The patient can however only be tested for HIV *if this information is vital for his/her medical treatment.* In any other cases, such consent could be construed as discriminatory.

## Confidentiality and privacy

People with HIV infection and AIDS have the right to confidentiality and privacy about their health and HIV status. Health care professionals are ethically and legally required to keep all information about clients or patients confidential. Information about a person's HIV status may not be disclosed to anybody without that person's fully informed consent. After death, the HIV status of the deceased person may not be disclosed to anybody without the consent of his or her family or partner — except when required by law.

 *May doctors keep the diagnosis of their patients secret from the nursing staff?*

A health care professional may only disclose a patient's HIV status to other health care professionals with the patient's consent. If the health care professional explains to the patient why it is important for other health care professionals to know the patient's HIV status, most patients will consent to this information being given out. Nurses may, for instance, need to know a patient's HIV status in order to render specialised treatment. It is, for example, of the utmost importance to protect a patient with a depressed immune system from infections and opportunistic diseases. If a patient nevertheless refuses to consent to such information being given out to other health care professionals, the doctor must respect this decision. In such a case the patient should be warned that to keep the diagnosis secret from other health care professionals might very well result in the patient getting unsuitable treatment — and that it might even put the patient's life in danger (Fine et al., 1997).

 *If an HIV-positive client refuses to tell his or her partner about the infection and refuses to protect the sexual partner, may the health care professional disclose the client's HIV-positive status to the partner?*

A client's right to confidentiality and privacy should be respected at all times. Under no circumstances may a client's HIV status be communicated to anyone without prior permission (preferably in writing) from the client. The health care professional or counsellor may therefore not disclose the HIV-positive status of a client to his or her sexual partner/s. The counsellor should rather try to convince the client to disclose his or her status to the sexual partner and to use condoms.

Fine et al. (1997) feel that if a counsellor — against all advice — decides to disclose a client's HIV-positive status to a sex partner, the counsellor should explain this decision to the client first and offer the client the opportunity to inform the sexual partner himself or herself with or without the help of the counsellor. If a health care professional discloses a client's HIV-positive status to anybody without the client's consent, he or she must also be prepared to accept *full responsibility* for the decision, as well as the *possible legal consequences*.

## Health and support services, public benefits, medical schemes and insurance

Because people with HIV or AIDS in South Africa have the right to equal access to public benefits and opportunities, HIV testing should not be required as a precondition for eligibility to such advantages. People with HIV/AIDS have the same rights to housing, food, social security, medical assistance and welfare as all other members of our society. Public measures should be adopted to protect people with HIV or AIDS from discrimination in employment, housing, education, child care and custody and the provision of medical, social and welfare services. *Medical schemes* may not discriminate unfairly — directly or indirectly — against any person on the basis of his or her state of health. People with HIV infection or AIDS (and those suspected of being at risk of having HIV or AIDS) should be protected from arbitrary discrimination in *insurance*. Insurance companies may not unfairly refuse to provide an insurance policy to any person solely on the basis of HIV/AIDS status.

## Education on HIV and AIDS

All people have the right to proper education and full information about HIV and AIDS, as well as the right to full access to and information about prevention methods. Public education with the specific objective of eliminating discrimination against people with HIV or AIDS should also be provided.

## The responsibilities of the media

People with HIV infection or AIDS have the right to fair treatment by the media and to observance of their rights to privacy and confidentiality. The public has the right to informed and balanced coverage and presentation of information and education on HIV and AIDS.

## The right to safer sex

All people have the right to insist that they or their sexual partners take appropriate precautionary measures to prevent the transmission of HIV. The especially vulnerable position of women in this regard should be recognised and addressed — as should the especially vulnerable position of youth and children.

People have a moral obligation to tell their sex partners if they are HIV positive. They must also ensure that their sex practices are as safe as possible (e.g. by using condoms). Disclosing HIV infection to sex partners is a part of one's duty to protect others from potential exposure to the virus. Lawsuits have been filed against HIV-infected people when such people have been suspected of knowingly having placed others at risk through unsafe sex. A person can be held liable for damages if he or she infects sex partners without telling them of their HIV status.

## The rights of prisoners

Prisoners with HIV infection or AIDS should enjoy the same standards of care and treatment as other prisoners. Prisoners with HIV/AIDS should have access to the kind of special care that is equivalent to that enjoyed by other prisoners with other serious illnesses. Prisoners should have the same access to education, information and preventative measures as the general population.

## Duties of people with HIV or AIDS

People with HIV or AIDS have the duty to respect the rights, health and physical integrity of others, and to take appropriate steps to ensure this when necessary.

## 17.3 MANAGEMENT AND POLICY ISSUES

### HIV/AIDS in the workplace

According to The Employment Equity Act of 1998, employers may not discriminate against HIV-positive employees or victimise them in any way. No person may unfairly discriminate directly or indirectly against an employee in any employment policy or practice (e.g. recruitment, appointment, remuneration, training and development, promotion, transfer and dismissal) on the grounds of HIV status. It is however not unfair discrimination to distinguish between applicants or exclude or prefer any particular person on the basis of an *inherent requirement of a job*.

People who are infected with HIV or who are manifesting the symptoms of AIDS must by law receive the same benefits (in all matters affecting sick leave, disability, medical aid, pension funds and death) that are applicable to members who are not infected with HIV. This means that people with AIDS should receive the same benefits (if they are suffering from chronic or terminal diseases or illnesses) that they would have received if they had *not* had AIDS or suffered from any complicating or opportunistic HIV-related infection (Fine et al., 1997; Van Wyk, 2000). No employer is therefore allowed to withhold medical aid or any other benefits from an HIV-infected employee on the grounds of his or her HIV status.

Employers are not allowed to request employees and applicants for employment to go for an HIV test unless an employer can prove that testing is justifiable in the light of medical facts, employment conditions, social policy, the fair distribution of employee benefits or the inherent requirements of a job. If employers believe that testing is justifiable, they must apply for permission from the Labour Court — which will then determine if such testing is permissible in terms of the Employment Equity Act of 1998. If the Labour Court decides that testing is permissible, they will stipulate specific conditions that will regulate matters such as the provision of counselling, the maintenance of confidentiality, the period for which the authorisation applies, and the category of jobs in respect of which such authorisation applies.

No HIV-positive employee has to disclose his/her HIV status to his/her employer. It may however benefit the HIV-infected person if his or her employer knows about the condition so that the employer can make provision for the employee to take time off to visit doctors, receive various kinds of treatment — and even so that the employer can regulate or reduce the HIV-infected person's workload as and when circumstances require.

Employers are not allowed to dismiss, demote or transfer HIV-infected employees on the basis of their HIV status alone — provided that they are otherwise qualified to do the job and provided that they are able to work.

The law requires employers to make reasonable accommodation, such as flexible working hours, rest periods, adapted duties, or extended sick pay with reduced (or no) pay, to help employees who are incapacitated on the grounds of ill health to keep their jobs. However, the law recognises permanent incapacity as a ground on which employment may be terminated only *after all other alternatives have been investigated*.

Information and education on HIV and AIDS, as well as access to counselling and referral, should be provided in the workplace after appropriate consultation with representative employee groups.

 *Are employers legally permitted to dismiss HIV-infected employees if the colleagues of such people refuse to work with them?*

It is unfair labour practice and thus unlawful to dismiss infected employees simply because other employees refuse to work with them (Fine et al., 1997). Employers should take extraordinary measures to persuade unwilling co-workers that they are unreasonable in their attitudes and to assure them that the risk of HIV infection within any normal work situation is extremely limited. The employees who refuse to work with the HIV-infected person should furthermore be made aware that their refusal may be the grounds for disciplinary action against them. It is vitally important to prevent such unpleasant situations from arising by educating all employees about all aspects of HIV infection and AIDS. Health care professionals should also be assured that preventative equipment is available and that everything possible will be done to protect them as employees (Strauss, 1989).

## HIV/AIDS and the medical profession

It is illegal for health care professionals to refuse emergency treatment or life-saving treatment to HIV-infected people on the grounds of their HIV infection. It is also unethical, and in terms of the Constitution, probably illegal for doctors, dentists, nurses and other health care professionals to deny treatment to any person on the grounds of his or her HIV status.

There is no reason at all why a health care professional should refuse to treat a person with HIV infection or AIDS. If the necessary universal precautions are followed and if the health care professional is careful to avoid accidents, there is no way that he or she can contract HIV from an infected patient. Although all medical professionals should be taking precautions against potential HIV transmission, HIV-infected individuals should be *advised* to inform their doctors about their infection because it may impact on their treatment and care.

Medical practitioners are under a legal and ethical duty to ensure that patient information is not revealed to third parties (e.g. other doctors) without the patient's expressed consent. A patient's right to confidentiality and privacy should be respected at all times. Under no circumstances may a patient's HIV status be communicated to anyone without prior permission (preferably in writing) from the person.

The client has the right to bodily and psychological integrity, and must give his or her informed consent to any medical procedures or tests that are about to be carried out. Counsellors should at all times adhere to the law and to the Constitution of South Africa in their handling of HIV/AIDS clients.

 *Should HIV infection and AIDS be made a notifiable disease?*

Regulations on the *notification of AIDS disease and death* were published for public comment by the South African Department of Health in 1999. Because of widespread resistance to such a step and fears for the safety of HIV-infected people, the Government decided in January 2001 to abandon the notification proposal ('Vigs-aanmeldingsplan laat vaar', 2001).

The reasons and implications of classifying a disease as notifiable are to give medical and health care professionals the opportunity to:

● positively identify the disease as soon as possible
● treat patients
● attempt to prevent the disease from spreading to other members of the community

In cases of notifiable diseases such as malaria, tetanus, tuberculosis, typhoid, cholera, viral hepatitis and meningococcal infections, all three of the necessary grounds (justifiable reasons) for notifiability can be achieved. In the case of each of these diseases, (1) positive infection can be diagnosed *as soon as* the first symptoms appear, (2) treatment can start immediately, and (3) the spread of the disease (which is usually transmitted by mosquitoes, through direct contact with urine and faeces, in respiratory droplets and by means of contaminated food) can be prevented if specific preventative measures are taken by those who are at risk.

In the case of HIV infection, none of these necessary grounds (justifiable reasons) for notifiability can really be adduced — even if the infection is made officially notifiable. Swift identification of the infection is impossible because of the long period that elapses between the moment when a person is infected with HIV and the onset of full-blown AIDS and the various serious opportunistic infections that accompany it. During this period people may show no symptoms and are frequently not even aware that they are infected. This long period between infection and visible serious illness and the fact that HIV does not spread through casual contact, renders notification an impractical and unjustifiable procedure.

Notifiability might however be useful because it might give health authorities an opportunity to suggest to infected people that they seek treatment for opportunistic infections and educate themselves about necessary sexual behavioural changes (such as safer sex) as quickly as possible. However, since HIV/AIDS carries such a terrible social stigma and because prejudice against infected people is often very great in many sectors of the community, making the disease notifiable may simply drive people in need of care underground (as they desperately try to escape punishment, stigmatisation and the other negative consequences of having their status known).

 ............................................................

*Should an HIV-infected health care professional be allowed to care for patients?*

The World Health Organisation (1988b) is of the opinion that an HIV-infected health care professional generally does not pose a risk to patients and need not withdraw himself or herself from patient care activities. In addition, it is simply not practical to withdraw nurses, doctors and other health care professionals from active patient care because of the immense shortage of skilled health and medical workers in Africa.

Those health care professionals who are infected should obviously pay careful attention to personal hygiene and safe working practices (such as wearing gloves or covering all cuts and sores with waterproof dressings) and routinely apply universal safety precautions. HIV-infected nurses with oozing lesions or weeping dermatitis should *under no circumstances* be allowed to perform or assist in direct patient care activities until such conditions heal. It is the responsibility of both the employer and the health care professional to make sure that safe procedures are followed at all times and to be aware of any changes in the mental or physical abilities of employees (Expert Advisory Group on AIDS, 1988; WHO, 1988b).

If a patient is infected by an HIV-positive health care professional, both the health care professional and the employer may face civil claims. Liability would depend on proof of either *negligence* or *intent* on the part of the nurse or employer (Strauss, 1989).

HIV-infected health care professionals working in hospitals and similar institutions should be warned that — owing to their impaired immune systems — they have an increased risk of contracting serious infectious diseases from their patients. They should therefore, for self-protection, follow the recommendations for infection control very meticulously and should try to avoid patients with infectious diseases. HIV-positive health care professionals should monitor their physical and emotional health by paying frequent visits to their personal physicians as well as AIDS counsellors.

*Should an HIV-positive health care professional be allowed to perform or assist in invasive procedures?*

Invasive procedures in which possible injury to the health care professional may cause accidental contamination of the patient, may be an area of concern for patient safety. The type of invasive procedure should however be kept in mind before making any decisions. Invasive procedures such as injections and starting of intravenous lines carry very little risk of exposing the patient to the health care professional's blood. It is however recommended that HIV-positive health care professionals such as nurses should seek expert advice if they perform or assist in surgical invasive procedures where blood-to-tissue contact could occur. It may be necessary for them to modify or limit their duties to protect patients.

*Should HIV-infected nurses inform their employers about their HIV-positive status?*

A person is under no legal obligation to reveal his/her HIV status to the employer because HIV is not a highly contagious disease (Fine et al., 1997). In the medical situation however employers are only able to ensure that all reasonable measures are taken to prevent patients from being accidentally infected if they are aware of the nurse's HIV status. It is therefore the ethical (although not legal) duty of nurses to inform their employers if they are diagnosed as HIV positive. The employer must keep this information confidential, and may not inform other people without the infected nurse's expressed consent. The employer may not discriminate *in any way* against the employee who has voluntarily made his or her HIV-positive status known.

## HIV/AIDS in schools and tertiary institutions

Every child has the right to education — whether they are HIV positive or not. HIV-positive children can safely attend the same school as HIV-negative children.

No learner, student or educator with HIV/AIDS may be unfairly discriminated against either directly or indirectly — and they should all be treated in a just, humane and life-affirming way. To prevent discrimination, all learners, students and educators should be educated about the fundamental human rights that are enunciated in the Constitution.

No learner or student may be denied admission to or continued attendance at a school or an institution on account of his or her HIV status. No educator may be denied the right to be appointed in a post, to teach or to be promoted on account of his or her HIV status, and his or her HIV status may also not be a reason for dismissal or for not renewing an educator's employment contract.

There is no medical justification for the routine testing of learners, students or educators for evidence of HIV infection. The testing of learners or students for HIV infection as a prerequisite for admission to, or for continued attendance at, the school or institution is prohibited. The testing of educators for HIV as a prerequisite for an appointment or continued service is also prohibited by law.

No learner, student, parent or educator is *compelled* to disclose his or her (or a child's) HIV status to the school or institution or employer. If they *choose* to do so, any learner or student above the age of 14 years, or his or her parents, is free to disclose an HIV-positive status voluntarily. Any person to whom such information has been disclosed must keep this information confidential.

A continuing, age-appropriate lifeskills and HIV/AIDS education programme must be implemented at all schools and institutions for all learners, students, educators and other staff members. Measures must also be implemented at hostels. Refusal to study with a learner or student, or to work with or be taught by an educator or other staff member with HIV/AIDS, should be pre-empted by providing accurate and understandable information on HIV/AIDS to all educators, staff members, learners, students and their parents.

## 17.4  CREATING A SAFE WORKING ENVIRONMENT

The Occupational Health and Safety Act of 1993 requires that employers (as far as it is reasonably practicable) create a safe working environment. It is also the responsibility of employers to develop policies and programmes to educate and protect their employees. This is not only a legal obligation: it is also an ethical obligation.

### General recommendations

Fine et al. (1997) recommend that employers integrate the following steps, plans and procedures into their management and policy plans:

● Universal precautions should be applied in every workplace.
● Employers should classify activities in terms of the potential risk of exposure to blood and body fluids.

- Employers should make protective equipment and clothes available to all workers who come into contact with blood or body fluids.
- Matters and issues relating to the occupational transmission of HIV/AIDS should be placed on the agenda of companies' Health and Safety Committees so that appropriate control measures can be instituted.
- Employers should ensure that appropriate protective equipment and clothing are used and worn by workers when they perform activities involving blood and body fluids.
- Employers should ensure that appropriate first-aid equipment is always readily available for dealing with spilt blood and body fluids and that staff are trained to institute safety precautions following any accident.
- Employers should develop standard procedures that have to be applied in all activities in which people may be exposed to blood and body fluids.
- Procedures should be instituted for ensuring and monitoring compliance with safety measures.
- If personnel are not complying with safety measures, they should be subjected to appropriate counselling, re-education and training.
- Employers should make certain that workers who might be exposed to infection are well trained and educated in appropriate preventative measures. No health care professional should be allowed to perform a duty which may involve exposure to blood or body fluids without having undergone the necessary training and education.
- All employees should be taught the correct methods of how to clean up accidental blood and body fluid spills.
- If necessary, the workplace should be redesigned so that it becomes a safer place.
- All accidents that result in blood and body fluid exposure should be investigated. Counselling should be made available to all health care professionals who need it. Such counselling should be available to both HIV-positive personnel and all health care professionals who work with HIV-positive patients.
- If employees feel that their work environment is not safe, they have the right to refuse to work and to request an inspector from the Department of Labour to look into the matter. Nurses and doctors may also refuse to carry out certain tasks (such as drawing blood or surgical operations) if proper personal protective equipment is not supplied.

*May health care professionals apply for compensation if they become infected with HIV in their workplace?*

Section 22 (1) of The Compensation for Occupational Injuries and Diseases Act of 1993 provides for compensation for employees who are injured in the course and scope of their employment — provided that such an injury causes disablement or death. Where an employee becomes HIV-infected following an occupational exposure to infected blood or blood products, compensation might become payable if it can be proved that the occupational accident was the direct cause of the person's sero-conversion (i.e. the reason why the person became HIV positive) (Whiteside & Sunter, 2000).

### Management of accidental exposure to blood and other infectious body fluids

It is highly advisable for management to institute strict procedures that govern the accidental exposure of employees to HIV so that they can ensure that their employee's rights will be adequately secured and so that they can protect themselves against unfounded and punitive legal actions.

If a health care professional is exposed to blood and/or other body fluids (through a needlestick or injury with a contaminated sharp instrument), or if infected blood or body fluids come into contact with mouth or eye mucous membranes, open wounds and cuts, the following precautions should immediately be applied (CDC, 1989; Hauman, 1990; WHO, 1988b):

- Immediately rinse blood and body fluid splashes from the skin, eyes and mouth with water or (preferably) with an antimicrobial solution.
- Encourage bleeding in the case of accidental penetrating injuries (such as those resulting from needlesticks) and then wash the area thoroughly with an anti-microbial product (or if that is not available, soap and water).
- Report all accidents through the same channel that you would use to report other on-duty accidents (such reports would usually be made to the medical officer or matron of a hospital). The employer should report the injury to a central committee for possible workman's compensation. The following circumstances applicable to the exposure should be recorded: the nature of the activity the health care professional was engaged in at the time of exposure, a precise description of the injured area, the extent to which appropriate work practices and protective equipment were used, and a description of the source of exposure.
- After exposure has occurred, a blood sample should be drawn from the *source individual* (the patient to whom the health care professional was exposed) as well as from the health care professional. (Note that the source patient must give his or her informed consent for the blood to be drawn and the test to be done.) The blood sample taken from the health care professional at the time of exposure serves as a *baseline specimen* and can be used later to compare future tests.
- If the source individual (the patient) is then found to be HIV positive, or if it is impossible to determine the sero-status of the source individual (e.g. when the

patient refuses to be tested), the test (which was taken from the health care professional at the time of injury) should be repeated after 6 weeks, 12 weeks and again after 6 months. This retesting procedure is essential to make allowance for the so-called window period. If the health care professional can afford it, a PCR test (see 'The PCR technique' on page 60) is preferable because it is capable of proving or disproving HIV infection so much sooner.

- If the health care professional's subsequent test is HIV positive, the baseline specimen taken at the time of the injury should also be tested. If this baseline specimen is HIV positive, it indicates that the health care professional was infected with HIV some time *prior* to the injury. If however the baseline specimen is negative, it is highly probable (provided that one is able to rule out sexual transmission) that the sero-conversion was a direct consequence of this injury with contaminated blood.

- If the source individual is sero-negative, baseline testing of the exposed health care professional as well as follow-up testing after 6 weeks, 12 weeks and 6 months may be performed (if desired) by the health care professional or if recommended by the physician. This procedure takes into consideration the fact that the source individual might have been in the window period at the time of testing.

- If the source individual cannot be identified, testing should still be made available to all health care professionals who are concerned about the possibility of having been infected with HIV because of an occupational exposure.

- The health care professional should report any signs of acute sero-conversion illness that occur within 12 weeks after exposure to blood or body fluids. Illnesses which are characterised by fever, rash or lymphadenopathy (swelling of the glands) may be indicative of recent HIV infection.

- Testing of the source individual (as well as the health care professional) should not be performed without informed consent and thorough pre-test counselling. Post-test counselling and referral for treatment should also (if necessary) be provided.

- In the period after exposure but before the results have been confirmed, health care professionals should modify their sexual behaviour to prevent possible transmission of HIV to sex partners. Safer sex (such as using condoms) should be practised, and health care professionals should refrain from donating blood.

- During all the phases of follow-up testing and counselling it is vital to protect the health care professional's confidentiality.

- Counsel the health care professional about the possibility of post-exposure anti-retroviral treatment. It is important to start anti-retroviral medication as soon as possible after exposure to HIV. (See 'Management of occupational exposure to HIV' on page 73.)

**The ethical and legal implications of HIV/AIDS**

Carry out the following exercise with a group of people, and follow it up with either a lecture or a hand-out about the ethical and legal issues of HIV and AIDS.

Draw three big faces on three separate flipchart papers: (1) a smiling face (with 'agree' written underneath it), (2) an unhappy face (with 'disagree' written underneath and (3) a neutral face (with 'don't know', 'neutral', and 'two sides of the story' written underneath).

Agree

Disagree

Neutral/Don't know/
Two sides to the story

Stick each face up in a different corner of the room. Explain to the group that you will read a statement. The whole group must then get up and walk to either the agree, disagree, or the don't know/neutral/two sides to the story face. Ask two or three participants from each group to explain why they made the choice they did. Then encourage all three groups to debate with each other about the issue. Encourage everyone to listen attentively and respectfully to every opinion that is expressed. (You may have to intervene tactfully but firmly to ensure that this happens.) Allow members to walk over to other groups if they change their minds as a result of the discussion. You should also draw up your own list of ethical and legal issues. Here are a few statements that will stimulate discussion (credit to Ms Emmi Bootha):

- People who are HIV positive should abstain from sexual intercourse.
- Fellow employees have the right to know if someone in their workplace is HIV positive.
- The media has the right to publish the HIV status of any celebrity who has died.
- Pregnant women who are HIV positive should be encouraged to have an abortion.
- Homosexual men should not be allowed to donate blood.
- All domestic workers should be tested for HIV because they are in close contact with children.
- If an HIV-positive person refuses to tell his or her sexual partner about the infection, the counsellor should inform the partner.
- Children who are HIV positive should not be admitted into crèches and pre-school centres.

## 17.5 CONCLUSION

Employers, schools and institutions should have a responsible attitude towards the legal and ethical implications of HIV/AIDS and use the information provided in this chapter to draw up a detailed policy about HIV/AIDS. This policy should (1) include basic principles that acknowledge the rights of all people, (2) create a safe working or school environment, (3) specify detailed procedures for handling and coping with accidents and accidental exposure to blood and body fluids (see 'Management of accidental exposure to blood and other infectious body fluids' on page 418), and (4) provide adequate education about HIV and AIDS. Management should ensure that its HIV/AIDS policy is properly implemented.

# Appendix
## Internet resources in the field of HIV/AIDS

- WHO (World Health Organisation):
  *http://www.who.int/health-topics/hiv.htm*
- CDC (Centers for Disease Control) Division of HIV/AIDS Prevention:
  *http://www.cdc.gov/hiv/dhap.htm*
- Education: Harvard AIDS Institute:
  *http://www.hsph.harvard.edu/organizations/hai*
- Education: Johns Hopkins AIDS Service:
  *http://www.hopkins-aids.edu*
- For the latest statistics on HIV/AIDS: UNAIDS (Joint United Nations Programme on HIV/AIDS):
  *http://www.unaids.org*
- National policy on HIV/AIDS for learners, students and educators in South Africa:
  *http://education.pwv.gov.za*
- South African Department of Health:
  *http://www.health.gov.za*
- AIDS Law Project at the University of the Witwatersrand (South Africa):
  *http://www.hri.ca/partners/alp*
- World Bank — AIDS in Africa:
  *http://www.worldbank.org/afr/aids*
- Beyond Awareness Campaign (South Africa):
  *http://www.aidsinfo.co.za*
- Database:
  The Body: *http://www.thebody.com*
- The HIV Daily Briefing: AEGIS:
  *http://www.aegis.org*
- Important HIV/AIDS Internet Resources (website links):
  *http://www2.wn.apc.org/sahivAids/Aidslink.htm*
- HIV Medication Guide:
  *http://www.jag.on.ca/hiv*
- Guidelines for the use of antiretroviral therapy in Peadiatric HIV infection:
  *http://www.hivatis.org/guidelines/Pediatric/Text/ped_12.pdf*

# Glossary

**AIDS** Acquired Immune Deficiency Syndrome. This acronym emphasises that the disease is *acquired* and **not** inherited. It is caused by a virus that invades the body. This virus then attacks the body's immune system and makes it so weak and ineffectual that it is unable to protect the body from both serious and common infections and pathogens.

**AIDS defining disease** Specific diseases or conditions which indicate the clinical development of full-blown AIDS in a person who is HIV positive.

**Antibodies** Special protein complexes produced by the immune system that attack and neutralise specific disease-causing organisms. The antibodies which the body creates in response to the HI virus are unfortunately powerless to protect the body against the long-term destructive effects of the HI virus on the human body.

**Anti-retroviral therapy** Drugs which suppress or prevent the replication of HIV in cells.

**ART** See Anti-retroviral therapy.

**AZT** The anti-retroviral drug azidothymidine — which is also called zidovudine or Retrovir.

**BCG** The vaccine against tuberculosis.

**CD4 cells** T helper lymphocytes (a type of white blood cell). These cells play an important role in keeping the immune system healthy. The HI virus attaches itself to the CD4 receptors on the outer layer of the CD4 cells. They are also called T4 helper cells.

**CD4 count** The laboratory test most commonly used to estimate the level of immune deficiency in HIV-infected individuals by 'counting' the CD4 cells.

**CHBC** Community home-based care is the care given to individuals in their own homes by their families, their extended families or any other available and concerned helpers, when such home-based caregivers are supported in a systematic and organised way by a multi-disciplinary team, and by complementary caregivers who have the ability to meet the specific needs of the individual and family.

**CMV** The cytomegalovirus. This virus is often excreted in the urine, saliva, semen, cervical secretions, faeces or breast milk of immune-depressed patients. CMV may cause infections of the retinas of the eyes. (Such infections may ultimately cause blindness in the person thus infected.)

**d4T** Stavudine — an anti-retroviral drug.

**ELISA test** ELISA stands for 'enzyme-linked immunosorbent assay'. This is a laboratory test (technique) to detect antibodies in the blood.

**Epidemiology** The study of the determinants, distribution, prevalence and control of disease.

**False negative** A test result that is HIV negative when the person is actually HIV positive.

**False positive** A test result that is HIV positive when the person is actually HIV negative.

**HBV** The hepatitis B virus.

**Herpes zoster (**also known as **shingles)** A condition characterised by an extremely painful skin rash or tiny blisters on the face, limbs or body. Shingles is caused by a virus, and it affects nerve cells.

**HIV** The human immunodeficiency virus — the virus which causes AIDS.

**HIV antibody positive** This phrase means the antibodies to HIV are present in the bloodstream — an indication that the person concerned has been exposed to (and is therefore infected with) the HI virus.

**HIV P24 antigen** A core protein found in the HI virus. The presence of this antigen in the blood is evidence that the HI virus is present in the body. These antigens are usually detectable in the early and very late stages of HIV infection.

**Immune deficiency** A weakening or deficiency in the immune system.

**Informed consent** The kind of consent to medical testing or treatment that is accompanied by *information* and *permission*. Before an HIV test can be done, the client must understand the nature of the test **and** he/she must also give verbal or written permission to be tested. A client may never be misled or deceived into consenting to an HIV test.

**Kaposi's sarcoma** A rare form of skin cancer, characterised by a painless reddish-brown or bluish-purple swelling on the skin and mucous membranes.

**Lymphoid interstitial pneumonia (LIP)** A rare respiratory or lung disease found in HIV-infected children which is characterised by continuous coughing and mild wheezing.

**MTCT** Mother-to-child transmission of the HI virus.

**Nevirapine** An anti-retroviral drug which is often administered to pregnant women to prevent mother-to-child transmission of the HI virus.

**NNRTI** Non-nucleoside reverse transcriptase inhibitor — a class of anti-retroviral medications that include drugs such as nevirapine.

**NRTI** Nucleoside reverse transcriptase inhibitor — a class of anti-retroviral medications that includes drugs such as zidovudine (AZT), lamivudine (3TC) and stavudine (d4T).

**Opportunistic infections** Infections that would not normally cause disease in a healthy body but which exploit the *opportunity* presented by an infected person's weakened immune system to attack the body.

**Oral hairy leucoplakia** Thickened white patches on the side of the tongue.

**Palliative care** is the terminal care of patients dying of AIDS (or any other disease).

**PCP** See pneumocystis carinii pneumonia.

**PCR** Polymerase chain reaction technique is a method of testing for the presence of HIV in the body. The PCR technique does not have to rely on the formation of antibodies in order to diagnose HIV infection — it detects the virus itself in the blood.

**Persistent generalised lymphadenopathy (PGL)** Swollen lymph nodes that are wider than 1 centimetre in diameter in areas such as the groin, the neck and the armpits and that have been present continuously for a period of at least 3 months.

**PI** Protease inhibitor. A class of anti-retroviral drugs which includes drugs such as saquinavir and indinavir.

**Pneumocystis carinii pneumonia (PCP)** A parasitic infection of the lungs caused by a protozoa. PCP is often seen in patients with severe immune deficiency (such as patients in the last stages of AIDS).

**Post-exposure prophylaxis (PEP)** Methods of attempting to prevent HIV infection in a person who has been exposed to infected blood or other body fluids as in the case of, for example, accidental exposure or rape.

**Rapid HIV antibody test** An HIV antibody test that produces rapid or fast results. Rapid HIV tests are relatively easy to use (they involve pricking a finger with a lancet), and the results are usually available within 10 to 30 minutes.

**Retrovirus** A group of viruses, including HIV, which replicate by changing its genetic RNA into DNA by using the host's cells.

**Reverse transcriptase** An enzyme which retroviruses produce and use to transform their viral RNA into viral DNA in the replication process.

**Sero-conversion** The point at which a person's HIV status converts or changes from being HIV negative to HIV positive. This coincides with the time when an HIV antibody test will show that a person is HIV positive. Sero-conversion usually occurs 4 to 8 weeks after an individual has been infected with the HI virus.

**Sero-conversion illness** Some individuals who sero-convert may show flu-like symptoms such as fever, tiredness, rash, sore throat, muscle pains and swollen lymph glands.

**Shingles** See Herpes zoster.

**STD** Sexually transmitted disease. This group of diseases includes (for example) syphilis, gonorrhoea, candidiasis, genital herpes and HIV infection.

**Syndrome** A collection of specific signs, indicators and symptoms that characteristically occur together and that are indicative of the presence of a particular pathological condition.

**T4 cell** See CD4 cells.

**3TC/lamivudine** An anti-retroviral drug.

**T helper cells** See CD4 cells.

**Universal precautions** are a variety of precautions that any person who comes into contact with blood and certain other body fluids or products in a health care setting should always apply so as to prevent himself or herself from being infected by the HI virus (or any other dangerous pathogen such as the highly infectious hepatitis B virus).

**Virus** A microbiological organism which is the smallest and most basic of all known biological organisms.

**Western Blot test** A blood test that detects the antibodies to HIV infection. It is sometimes used to confirm an ELISA test that has produced a (HIV) positive result.

**'Window' period** The time between infection with HIV and the development of detectable HIV antibodies. Any HIV antibody test done during this time will render false negative results (see **False negative** on page 423) — even though the person is actually already infected with HIV.

# Bibliography

Ader, R., Felten, D.L. & Cohen, N. (Eds.). (1991). *Psychoneuroimmunology* (2nd ed.). San Diego: Academic Press.

Adler, M.W. (1988). Development of the epidemic. In L.K. Clarke & M. Potts (Eds.), *The AIDS reader: Documentary history of a modern epidemic* (pp. 84–88). Boston: Branden Publishing Company.

Ahlberg, B.M. (1994). Is there a distinct African sexuality? A critical response to Caldwell. *Africa, 64*(2), 220–241.

Airhihenbuwa, C.O. (1989). Perspectives on AIDS in Africa: Strategies for prevention and control. *AIDS Education and Prevention, 1*(1), 57–69.

Ajzen, I. (1991). The theory of planned behaviour. *Organizational Behavior and Human Decision Processes, 50*, 179–211.

Albers, G.R. (1990). *Counselling and AIDS*. Dallas: Word Publishing.

An open letter from an AIDS patient. (1988, September). *Cosmopolitan*.

Baldwin, J.D. & Baldwin, J.I. (1988). Factors affecting AIDS-related sexual risk-taking behaviour among college students. *The Journal of Sex Research, 25*(2), 181–196.

Bandura, A. (1977). Self-efficacy: Toward a unifying theory of behavioral change. *Psychological Review, 84*(2), 191–215.

Bandura, A. (1989). Perceived self-efficacy in the exercise of control over AIDS infection. In V.M. Mays, G.W. Albee & S.F. Schneider (Eds.), *Primary prevention of AIDS: Psychological approaches* (pp. 128–141). Newbury Park: Sage.

Bandura, A. (1991). Social cognitive theory of self-regulation. *Organizational Behavior and Human Decision Processes, 50*, 248–287.

Baron, R.A. & Byrne, D. (Eds.). (1994). *Social psychology: Understanding human interaction* (7th ed.). Boston: Allyn and Bacon.

Becker, M.H. & Maiman, L.A. (1975). Socio-behavioural determinants of compliance with health and medical care recommendations. *Medical Care, 13*(1), 10–24.

Beuster, J. (1997). Psychopathology from a traditional Southern African perspective. *UNISA Psychologia, 24*(2), 4–16.

Boahene, K. (1996). The IXth International Conference on AIDS and STD in Africa. *AIDS Care, 8*(5), 609–616.

Bodibe, R.C. (1992). Traditional healing: An indigenous approach to mental health problems. In J. Uys (Ed.), *Psychological counselling in the South African context* (pp. 149–165). Cape Town: Maskew Miller Longman.

Bodibe, R.C. & Sodi, T. (1997). Indigenous healing. In D. Foster, M. Freeman & Y. Pillay (Eds.), *Mental health policy issues for South Africa* (pp. 181–192). Pinelands: The Medical Association of South Africa.

Bond, G. (1993). *Death, dysentery and drought: Coping capacities of households in Chiawa*. Paper presented at the Institute of Africa Studies, Lusaka, Zambia.

Botha, A., Van Ede, D.M., Louw, A.E., Louw, D.A. & Ferns, I. (1998). Early childhood. In D.A. Louw, D.M. van Ede & A.E. Louw (Eds.), *Human development* (2nd ed.), (pp. 233–318). Pretoria: Kagiso.

Bouic, P., Lamprecht, J. & Freestone, M. (2000, July). *Use of the plant E-Sitosterol / E-sitosterol glucoside mixture (Moducare) for the management of South African HIV-infected individuals: an open labelled study over 40 months* (Abstract No. WeOrB538). Paper presented at the XIIIth International AIDS Conference, Durban.

Bowlby, J. (1977). The making and breaking of affectional bonds, I and II. *British Journal of Psychiatry, 130*, 201–210.

Brave Gugu hasn't died in vain. (1999, January 2). *The Independent on Saturday*, 3.

Brown, L.K., Nassau, J.H. & Barone, V.J. (1990). Differences in AIDS knowledge and attitudes by grade level. *Journal of School Health, 60*(6), 270–275.

Bührman, M.V. (1986). *Living in two worlds*. Illinois: Chiron.

Caldwell, J.C., Caldwell, P. & Quiggin, P. (1989). The social context of AIDS in sub-Saharan Africa. *Population and Development Review, 15*(2), 185–233.

Campbell, T. & Kelly, M. (1995).Women and AIDS in Zambia: A review of the psychosocial factors implicated in the transmission of HIV. *AIDS Care, 7*(3), 365–373.

Canadian Palliative Care Association. (1995). *Palliative care: Towards a consensus in standardised principle of practice*. Toronto: Palliative Care Association.

Carbello, M. (1988). *Introduction in AIDS prevention and control*. Invited presentations and papers from the World Summit of Ministers of Health on programmes for AIDS prevention (pp. 77–81). Oxford: Pergamon.

Carpenter, C.C.J., Cooper, D.A., Fischl, M.A., Gatell, J.M., Gazzard, B.G., Hammer, S.M., et al. (2000). Antiretroviral therapy in adults: Updated recommendations of the International AIDS Society — USA Panel. *The Journal of the American Medical Association, 283*, 381–390.

Carson, R.C., Butcher, J.N. & Mineka, S. (1998). *Abnormal psychology and modern life* (10th ed.). New York: Longman.

Catania, J., Kegeles, S. & Coates, T. (1990). Towards an understanding of risk behaviour: An AIDS Risk Reduction Model (ARRM). *Health Education Quarterly, 17*, 53–72.

Centers for Disease Control. (1988). Guidelines for effective school health education to prevent the spread of AIDS. *Journal of School Health, 58*(4), 142–148.

Centers for Disease Control. (1989). Guidelines for prevention of transmission of human immunodeficiency virus and Hepatitis B virus to health-care and public-safety workers. *Morbidity and Mortality Weekly Report, 38*, S-6.

Centers for Disease Control. (2000). *HIV/AIDS resources: Frequently asked questions about HIV and AIDS*. Retrieved November 25, 2000, from the World Wide Web: http://www.cdcnpin.org/hiv/faq/prevention.htm

Chipfakacha, V.G. (1997). STD/HIV/AIDS knowledge, beliefs and practices of traditional healers in Botswana. *AIDS Care, 9*(4), 417–425.

Coates, T.J. (1990, June 22). HIV testing only part of the answer. *AIDS Conference Bulletin, 1*.

Coates, T.J. & Collins, C. (1998). Preventing HIV infection. *Scientific American, 279*(1), 76–77.

Cochrane, S.D., Mays, V.M. & Roberts, V. (1988). Ethnic minorities and AIDS. In A. Lewis (Ed.), *Nursing care of the person with AIDS/ARC* (pp. 17–24). Rockville, Maryland: Aspen.

Coker, R. & Miller, R. (1997). HIV associated tuberculosis: A barometer for wider tuberculosis control and prevention. *British Medical Journal, 314*, 1847.

Cole, S.W., Kemeny, M.E. & Taylor, S.E. (1997). Social identity and physical health: Accelerated HIV progression in rejection-sensitive gay men. *Journal of Personality and Social Psychology, 72*, 320–335.

College of Medicine of South Africa. (1991). Management of HIV-positive patients. *South African Medical Journal, 79*, 688–690.

Connor, S. & Kingman, S. (1988). *The search for the virus: The scientific discovery of AIDS and the quest for a cure*. London: Penguin.

Coombe, C. (2000, June). *HIV/AIDS and the education sector: The foundations of a control and management strategy in South Africa*. A briefing paper for the United Nations Economic Commission for Africa (UNECA).

Coopersmith, S. (1967). *The antecedents of self-esteem*. San Francisco: W.H. Freeman.

Cope, F. (1994, June). Sharp management. *Hospital Supplies*, 3–4.

Davidson, D. (1988). National coalition of advocates for students: Guidelines for selecting teaching materials. In M. Quackenbush & M. Nelson (Eds.), *The AIDS challenge: prevention education for young people* (pp. 447–461). Santa Cruz: Network.

Department of National Health and Population Development. (1989). *AIDS information and guidelines for nurses*. Pretoria: Department of National Health and Population Development.

De Villiers, F.M.J. (1988). *Care of the dying. A Christian perspective*. Pretoria: NG Kerkboekhandel.

Dickinson, D., Clark, C.M.F. & Swafford, M.J. (1988). AIDS nursing care in the home. In A. Lewis (Ed.), *Nursing care of the person with AIDS/ARC* (pp. 215–237). Rockville, Maryland: Aspen.

Du Toit, A.S., Grobler, H.D. & Schenck, C.J. (1998). *Person-centred communication: Theory and practice*. Halfway House: Thomson.

Eastaugh, A.N. (1997). Breaking bad news. *Update: The Journal of Continuing Education for General Practitioners, 12*(5), 90–93.

Edhonu-Elyetu, M. (1997). The significance of herpes zoster in HIV/AIDS in Kweneng District, Botswana. *Update: The Journal of Continuing Education for General Practitioners, 12*(5), 116–120.

Edwards, D. & Louw, N. (1998). *Outcomes-based sexuality education*. Pretoria: Kagiso.

Egan, G. (1998). *The skilled helper: A problem-management approach to helping* (6th ed.). Pacific Grove: Brooks/Cole.

Elkind, D. (1978). Understanding the young adolescent. *Adolescence, 13*(49), 127–134.

# Bibliography

Erikson, E.H. (1968). *Identity, youth and crisis.* New York: Norton.

Evian, C. (2000). *Primary AIDS care* (2nd ed.). Houghton: Jacana.

Expert Advisory Group on AIDS. (1988, March). *AIDS: HIV-infected health care workers.* London: Her Majesty's Stationery Office.

Fahrner, R. (1988). Nursing interventions. In A. Lewis (Ed.), *Nursing care of the person with AIDS/ARC* (pp. 115–130). Rockville, Maryland: Aspen.

Feldman, D.A. (1985). AIDS and social change. *Human Organization, 44*(4), 343–348.

Felhaber, T. (Ed.). (1997). *South African traditional healers' primary health care handbook.* Cape Town: Kagiso.

Fine, D., Heywood, M. & Strode, A. (Eds.). (1997). *HIV/AIDS and the law: A resource manual.* Johannesburg: AIDS Law Project.

Fishbein, M. & Ajzen, I. (1975). *Belief, attitude, intention and behaviour: An introduction of theory and research.* Reading, Mass: Addison-Wesley.

Fishbein, M. & Middlestadt, S.E. (1989). Using the theory of reasoned action as a framework for understanding and changing AIDS-related behaviors. In V.M. Mays, G.W. Albee & S.F. Schneider (Eds.), *Primary prevention of AIDS: Psychological approaches* (pp. 93–110). Newbury Park: Sage.

Food and Drug Administration brochure. (1992). *Eating defensively: Food safety advice for persons living with AIDS.* Retrieved October 22, 2000, from the World Wide Web: http://vm.cfsan.fda.gov/~dms/aidseat.html

Franzini, L.R., Sideman, L.M., Dexter, K.E. & Elder, J.P. (1990). Promoting AIDS risk reduction via behavioral training. *AIDS Education and Prevention, 2*(4), 313–321.

Friesen, H., Ekpini, E., Sibailly, T. & De Cock, K. (1997). Diagnosing symptomatic HIV infection and AIDS in adults. *Update: The Journal of Continuing Education for General Practitioners, 12*(3), 102–104.

Fröhlich, J. (1999). *Draft guidelines for community home based care and palliative care for people living with AIDS.* Pretoria: Department of Health — Directorate: STDs and HIV/AIDS.

Garcia, R., Klaskala, W., Pena, Y. & Baum, M.K. (2000, July). *Behavioral change intervention for women at low and high risk for STD/HIV in Columbia* (Abstract No. ThPeC5347). Poster presented at the XIIIth International AIDS Conference, Durban.

Garrett, L. (1995). *The coming plague: Newly emerging diseases in a world out of balance.* New York: Penguin.

Gayton, A.C. (1971). *Textbook of medical physiology* (4th ed.). Philadelphia: W.B. Saunders.

Gelatt, H.B. (1989). Positive uncertainty: A new decision-making framework for counselling. *Journal of Counselling Psychology, 36,* 252–256.

Gillis, H. (1994). *Counselling young people* (2nd ed.). Pretoria: Kagiso.

Gladding, S.T. (1996). *Counselling: A comprehensive profession.* London: Merrill Prentice Hall.

Goss, E. (1989). Living and dying with AIDS. *Journal of Pastoral Care, 43,* 297–308.

Green, E.C. (1988). Can collaborative programs between biomedical and African indigenous health practitioners succeed? *Social Science and Medicine, 27*(11), 1125–1130.

Green, E.C. (1994). *AIDS and STDs in Africa. Bridging the gap between traditional healing and modern medicine.* Pietermaritzburg: University of Natal Press.

Green, E.C., Jurg, A. & Dgedge, A. (1993). Sexually-transmitted diseases, AIDS and traditional healers in Mozambique. *Medical Anthropology, 15,* 261–281.

Green, E.C., Zokwe, B. & Dupree, J.D. (1995). The experience of an AIDS prevention program focused on South African traditional healers. *Social Science and Medicine, 40*(4), 503–515.

Gyeke, K. (1987). *An essay on African philosophical thought: The Akan conceptual scheme.* Cambridge: Cambridge University Press.

Halperin, D. (2000, July). *Neglected risk factors for heterosexual HIV infection and prevention programs: Anal intercourse, male circumcision and dry sex* (Abstract No. TuPeC3477). Poster presented at the XIIIth International AIDS Conference, Durban.

Hammond-Tooke, D. (1989). *Rituals and medicines.* Johannesburg: AD Donker.

Harrison, A., Smit, J.A. & Myer, L. (2000). Prevention of HIV/AIDS in South Africa: A review of behaviour change interventions, evidence and options for the future. *South African Journal of Science, 96*(6), 285–290.

Hauman, L. (1990). *Voorkoming van die oordrag en verspreiding van HBV (Hepatitis B) en HIV (VIGS) in die hospitaal.* Unpublished protocol for nurses, Bloemfontein.

Hauser, J. (1981). Adolescents and religion. *Adolescence, 16,* 309–320.

Heald, S. (1995). The power of sex: Some reflections on the Caldwells' African sexuality thesis. *Africa, 65*(4), 489–505.

Herselman, S. (1997). A multicultural perspective on health care. In M. Bouwer, M. Dreyer, S. Herselman, M. Lock & S. Zeelie (Eds.), *Contemporary trends in community nursing* (pp. 28–53). Johannesburg: Thomson.

Hickson, J. & Mokhobo, D. (1992). Combatting AIDS in Africa: Cultural barriers to effective prevention and treatment. *Journal of Multicultural Counselling and Development, 20*(1), 11–22.

HIV Infant Care Programme. (2000). *The impact of HIV/AIDS on families and children*. Johannesburg: Cotlands.

Holdstock, T.L. (1979). Indigenous healing in South Africa: A neglected potential. *South African Journal of Psychology, 9*, 118–124.

Inhelder, B. & Piaget, J. (1964). *The early growth of logic in the child: Classification and serialization*. London: Routledge & Kegan Paul.

Irion, P.E. (1985). The grief continuum and the alternation of denial and acceptance. In O.S. Margolis et al. (Eds.), *Loss, grief, and bereavement* (pp. 9–15). New York: Praeger.

Janz, N.K. & Becker, M.H. (1984). The health belief model: A decade later. *Health Education Quarterly 11*(1), 1–47.

Jaret, P. (1986, June). Our immune system: The wars within. *National Geographic*, 702–734.

Jeffery, B., Webber, L. & Mokhondo, R. (2000, July). *Determination of the effectiveness on inactivation of HIV in human breast milk by Pretoria pasteurisation* (Abstract No. MoPeB2201). Poster presented at the XIIIth International AIDS Conference, Durban.

Johnson, P. (2000). *Basic counselling skills: Applications in HIV/AIDS counselling*. Unpublished manuscript, Unisa Centre for Applied Psychology, Pretoria.

Kalichman, S.C. (1996). *Answering your questions about AIDS*. Washington: American Psychological Association.

Kohlberg, L. (1978). Revision in the theory and practice of moral development. In W. Damon (Ed.), *Moral development: New directions for child development*. San Francisco: Jossey-Bass.

Kohlberg, L. (1985). *The psychology of moral development*. San Francisco: Harper & Row.

Korber, B. (2000, February). *Timing the origin of the HIV-1 pandemic*. Paper presented at the Seventh Annual Conference on Retroviruses and Opportunistic Infections, San Francisco.

Kurtzweil, P. (1999). *Questions keep sprouting about sprouts*. U.S. Food and Drug Administration. Retrieved October 22, 2000, from the World Wide Web: http://www.fda.gov/fdac/features/1999/199_spr t.html

LaPerriere, A., Klimas, N., Fletcher, M.A., Perry, A., Ironson, G., Perna, F. & Schneiderman, N. (1997). Change in CD4+ cell enumeration following aerobic exercise training in HIV-1 disease: Possible mechanisms and practical applications (Supplement 1). *International Journal of Sports Medicine, 18*, S56–61.

Larson, E. (1989). Handwashing: It's essential — even when you use gloves. *American Journal of Nursing, 89*, 934–939.

Levy, J. (1990, June 21). Levy discusses changing concepts in research. *AIDS Conference Bulletin*, 1.

Lie, G.T. & Biswalo, P.M. (1994). Perceptions of the appropriate HIV/AIDS counsellor in Arusha and Kilimanjaro regions of Tanzania: Implications for hospital counselling. *AIDS Care, 6*(2), 139–151.

Long, V.O. (1996). *Facilitating personal growth in self and others*. Pacific Grove: Brooks/Cole.

Louw, D.A., Van Ede, D.M. & Ferns, I. (1998). Middle childhood. In D.A. Louw, D.M. van Ede & A.E. Louw (Eds.), *Human development* (2nd ed.), (pp. 321–379). Pretoria: Kagiso.

Lowell, W.E. (1980). The development of hierarchical classification skills in science. *Journal of Research in Science Teaching, 17*(5), 425–433.

Lusby, G. (1988). Infection control. In A. Lewis (Ed.), *Nursing care of the person with AIDS/ARC* (pp. 191–202). Rockville, Maryland: Aspen.

Lyons, C. (1988). The religious setting: A natural place for learning. In M. Quackenbush & M. Nelson (Eds.), *The AIDS challenge: Prevention education for young people* (pp. 207–210). Santa Cruz, CA: Network.

Macfie, C. (1997). Loss, grief and mourning. *The Journal of Clinical Medicine: Modern Medicine, 22*(9), 36–41.

Mbiti, J.S. (1969). *African religions and philosophy*. London: Heinemann.

McCall, J.C. (1995). Rethinking ancestors in Africa. *Africa, 65*(2), 256–270.

Memory books. (2000, June 3). *Sukuma Newsletter* (p. 3), XIIIth International AIDS conference, Durban.

Meyer, W.F. (1997). The ego psychological theory of Erik Erikson. In W.F. Meyer, C. Moore & H.G. Viljoen (Eds.), *Personology: From individual to ecosystem* (pp. 203–228). Johannesburg: Heinemann.

Meyer, W.F. (1998). Basic concepts of developmental psychology. In D.A. Louw, D.M. van Ede & A.E. Louw (Eds.), *Human development* (2nd ed.), (pp. 3–38). Pretoria: Kagiso.

Meyer, W.F. & Van Ede, D.M. (1998). Theories of development. In D.A. Louw, D.M. van Ede & A.E. Louw (Eds.), *Human development* (2nd ed.), (pp. 41–96). Pretoria: Kagiso.

Miller, D. (1988). *Counselling of persons with AIDS.* Invited presentations and papers from the World Summit of Ministers of Health on programme for AIDS prevention (pp. 90–94). Oxford: Pergamon.

Miller, R. & Bor, R. (1988). *AIDS: A guide to clinical counselling.* London: Science Press.

Mkaya-Mwamburi, D., Owana, E., Williams, B. & Lurie, M. (2000, July). *HIV status in South Africa: Who wants to know and why?* (Abstract No. MoPeC2376). Poster presented at the XIIIth International AIDS Conference, Durban.

Montauk, S.L. & Scoggin, D.M. (1989). AIDS: Questions from fifth and sixth grade students. *Journal of School Health, 59*(7), 291–295.

Montgomery, S.B., Joseph, J.G., Becker, M.H., Ostrow, D.G., Kessler, R.C. & Kirscht, J.P. (1989). The Health Belief Model in understanding compliance with preventive recommendations for AIDS: How useful? *AIDS Education and Prevention, 1*(4), 303–323.

Moses, S. & Plummer, F.A. (1994). Health education, counselling and the underlying causes of the HIV epidemic in sub-Saharan Africa. *AIDS Care, 6*(2), 123–127.

National Department of Health. (1997). *Protocol for the management of a person with a sexually transmitted disease.* Marshalltown: Gauteng Directorate for AIDS and Communicable Diseases.

Nefale, M. (2000). *Bereavement counselling.* Unpublished manuscript, Unisa Centre for Applied Psychology, Pretoria.

Nel, J.A. (2000). *Facilitation skills.* Unpublished manuscript, Unisa Centre for Applied Psychology, Pretoria.

Ngubane, H.S. (1977). *Body and mind in Zulu medicine.* London: Academic Press.

Norton, J. & Dawson, C. (2000). *Life skills and HIV/AIDS education. A manual and resource guide for intermediate phase school teachers.* Johannesburg: Heinemann.

Nyamathi, A.M. & Flaskerud, J.H. (1989). Risk factors and HIV infection. In J.H. Flaskerud (Ed.), *AIDS/HIV infection: A reference guide for nursing professionals* (pp. 169–197). Philadelphia: W.B. Saunders.

Nyamayarwo, A. (2000, July). *The dilemma of HIV positive parents revealing serostatus to their children* (Abstract No. MoOrD250). Paper presented at the XIIIth International AIDS Conference, Durban.

Okun, B.F. (1997). *Effective helping: Interviewing and counselling techniques* (5th ed.). Pacific Grove: Brooks/Cole.

Okwu, A. (1978, November). *Dying, death, reincarnation and traditional healing in Africa.* Paper presented at the Twenty-first Annual Meeting of the African Studies Association, Baltimore, Maryland.

O'Leary, A. (1990). Stress, emotion and human immune function. *Psychological Bulletin, 108*(3), 363–382.

Osborne, J. (1990, June). Science can provide the light. *AIDS Conference Bulletin,* 3.

Paediatric HIV Working Group. (1997). *Guidelines for the management of HIV positive children.* Marshalltown: Gauteng Directorate for AIDS and Communicable Diseases.

Palermino, T. (1988). Psychosocial issues: One man's experience. In A. Lewis (Ed.), *Nursing care of the person with AIDS/ARC* (pp. 63–69). Rockville, Maryland: Aspen.

Pando, M de Los A., Gianni, S., Salomon, H., Negrete, M., Russell, K.L., Martinez Peralta, L., Carr, J.K. & Avila, M.M. (2000, July). *Risk behavior of HIV-1 infected maternity patients and their sexual partners in Buenos Aires, Argentina* (Abstract No. TuPeC3471). Poster presented at the XIIIth International AIDS Conference, Durban.

Parkes, C.M. (1972). *Bereavement: Studies of grief in adult life.* New York: International Universities Press.

Pasteur, A.B. & Toldson, I.L. (1982). *Roots of soul. The psychology of black expressiveness.* New York: Anchor Press.

Pearse, J. (1997). *Infection control manual. A practical guide for the prevention and control of infection in the health care setting.* Houghton: Jacana.

Perelli, R.J. (1991). *Ministry to persons with AIDS. A family systems approach.* Augsburg: Fortress.

Petty, R.E. (1995). Attitude change. In A. Tesser (Ed.), *Advanced social psychology* (pp. 195–255). New York: McGraw-Hill.

Piaget, J. (1932). *The moral judgement of the child.* London: Routledge & Kegan Paul.

Piaget, J. (1970). *The child's conception of physical causality.* London: Routledge & Kegan Paul.

Piaget, J. (1971). *The psychology of intelligence.* London: Routledge & Kegan Paul.

Piaget, J. (1972). Intellectual evolution from adolescence to adulthood. *Human Development, 15*, 1–12.

Piaget, J. (1973). *The child's conception of the world*. London: Paladin.

Piaget, J. & Inhelder, B. (1969). *The psychology of the child*. London: Routledge & Kegan Paul.

Pies, C. (1988). AIDS education in school settings: Grades 7–9. In M. Quackenbush & M. Nelson (Eds.), *The AIDS challenge: Prevention education for young people* (pp. 185–193). Santa Cruz, CA: Network.

Pike, J.T. (1988). Nutritional support. In A. Lewis (Ed.), *Nursing care of the person with AIDS/ARC* (pp. 159–174). Rockville, Maryland: Aspen.

Pilot Project on Life Skills and HIV/AIDS Education in Primary Schools. (1999, December). *Final report for the Department of Education*, Pretoria.

Pines, A. & Maslach, C. (1978). Characteristics of staff burnout in mental health settings. *Hospital and Community Psychiatry, 29*, 233–237.

Piscitelli, S. (2000). Indinavir concentrations and St John's wort. *Lancet, 355*, 547–548.

Post, J. (1988). AIDS education in school settings: Grades 4–6. In M. Quackenbush & M. Nelson (Eds.), *The AIDS challenge: Prevention education for young people* (pp. 177–183). Santa Cruz: Network.

Prochaska, J.O. & DiClemente, C.C. (1984). *The transtheoretical approach: Crossing traditional boundaries of therapy*. Malabar: Krieger.

Pugh, K. (1995). Suicide in patients with HIV infection and AIDS. In L. Sherr (Ed.), *Grief and AIDS* (pp. 45–58). Chichester: John Wiley.

Quackenbush, M. (1988). AIDS education in school settings: Preschool — Grade 3. In M. Quackenbush & M. Nelson (Eds.), *The AIDS challenge: Prevention education for young people* (pp.169–176). Santa Cruz: Network.

Quackenbush, M. & Villarreal, S. (1988). *Does AIDS hurt? Educating young children about AIDS*. Santa Cruz: Network.

Reno, C.L. & Walker, A.P. (1988). Providing direct nursing care in the adult inpatient setting. In A. Lewis (Ed.), *Nursing care of the person with AIDS/ARC* (pp. 73–94). Rockville, Maryland: Aspen.

Rogers, C.R. (1980). *A way of being*. Boston: Houghton Mifflin.

Rooth, E. (1995). *Lifeskills: A resource book for facilitators*. Manzini: Macmillan Boleswa.

Rose, A. (1988). Educating for life: AIDS and teens in the Jewish community. In M. Quackenbush & M. Nelson (Eds.), *The AIDS challenge:*

*Prevention education for young people* (pp. 219–226). Santa Cruz, CA: Network.

Rosenstock, I.M. (1966). Why people use health services. *Milbank Memorial Fund Quarterly, 44*, 94–127.

Rosenstock, I.M. (1974). The health belief model and preventive health behavior. *Health Education Monographs, 2*(4), 354–386.

Rotter, J.B. (1966). Generalized expectancies for internal versus external control of reinforcement. *Psychological Monographs, 80*(1), 1–28.

Runganga, A.O. & Kasule, J. (1995). The vaginal use of herbs/substances: An HIV transmission facilitatory factor? *AIDS Care, 7*(5), 639–645.

Saunders, L. (1994). *Nutrition in AIDS*. Paper presented at the South African Nutritional Congress, Durban.

Schoepf, B.G. (1992). AIDS, sex and condoms: African healers and the reinvention of tradition in Zaire. *Medical Anthropology, 14*, 225–242.

Schoub, B.D. (1997a). Guidelines to the management of occupational exposure to HIV. *Virus SA, 6*(3), 5–7.

Schoub, B.D. (1997b). Management of HIV in general practice. *Virus SA, 6*(2), 3–7.

Schurink, E. & Schurink, W.J. (1990). *AIDS: Lay perceptions of a group of gay men*. Pretoria: Human Sciences Research Council.

Scott, S.J. & Mercer, M.A. (1994). Understanding cultural obstacles to HIV/AIDS prevention in Africa. *AIDS Education and Prevention, 6*(1), 81–89.

Seeley, J., Wagner, U., Mulemwa, J., Kengeya-Kayondo, J. & Mulder, D. (1991). The development of a community-based HIV/AIDS counselling service in a rural area in Uganda. *AIDS Care, 3*(2), 207–217.

Seepamore, N. (2000, October). *Counselling in the traditional African context*. Paper presented at the Unisa Centre for Applied Psychology, Pretoria.

Seepamore, N. & Nkgatho, E. (2000). *Social work working model for Alexandra township*. Report for the Gauteng Department of Social Services and Population Development, Johannesburg.

Selwyn, P.A. (1986). AIDS: What is now known: history and immuno-virology. *Hospital Practice, 21*(5), 67–82.

Serima, E. & Manyenna, S.B. (2000, July). *VCT a new HIV prevention strategy* (Abstract No. TuPeD3767). Poster presented at the XIIIth International AIDS Conference, Durban.

Sherman, J.B. & Bassett, M.T. (1999). Adolescents and AIDS prevention: A school-based approach in Zimbabwe. *Applied Psychology: An International Review, 48*(2), 109–124.

Sherr, L. (1995). The experience of grief: psychological aspects of grief in AIDS and HIV infection. In L. Sherr (Ed.), *Grief and AIDS* (pp. 1–27). Chichester: John Wiley.

Sidje, G., Foua Bi, K. & Aguirre, M. (2000, July). *The involvement of PLHAs in reducing young women's vulnerability and socio cultural determinants to the HIV/AIDS epidemic in Vavoua (Côte d'Ivoire)* (Abstract No. ThPeD5808). Poster presented at the XIIIth International AIDS Conference, Durban.

Siegel, D., Lazarus, N., Krasnovsky, F., Durbin, M. & Chesney, M. (1991). AIDS knowledge, attitudes, and behavior among inner city, junior high school students. *Journal of School Health, 61*(4), 160–165.

Siegel, L. (1986). AIDS: relationship to alcohol and other drugs. *Journal of Substance Abuse Treatment, 3*, 271–274.

Smeltzer, S.C. & Bare, B.G. (1992). *Medical Surgical Nursing* (7th ed.). Philadelphia: J.B. Lippincott.

Southern African AIDS Training Programme. (2000). *Counselling guidelines on disclosure of HIV status*. Harare: Southern African AIDS Training Programme.

Sow, I. (1980). *Anthropological structures of madness in Black Africa*. New York: International Universities Press.

Strauss, S.A. (1989). *The nurse and AIDS: Legal issues*. Pretoria: SA Nursing Association.

Sue, D., Sue, D.W. & Sue, S. (2000). *Understanding abnormal behavior* (6th ed.). Boston: Houghton Mifflin.

Sue, D.W. & Sue, D. (1999). *Counselling the culturally different: Theory and practice* (3rd ed.). New York: John Wiley.

Sunderland, R.H. & Shelp, E.E. (1987). *AIDS, a manual for pastoral care*. Philadelphia: Westminster Press.

Sy, F.S., Richter, D.L. & Copello, A.G. (1989). Innovative educational strategies and recommendations for AIDS prevention and control. *AIDS Education and Prevention, 1*(1), 53–56.

Taylor, C.C. (1990). Condoms and cosmology: The 'fractal' person and sexual risk in Rwanda. *Social Science and Medicine, 31*(9), 1023–1028.

Thom, D.P., Louw, A.E., Van Ede, D.M. & Ferns, I. (1998). Adolescence. In D.A. Louw, D.M. van Ede & A.E. Louw (Eds.), *Human development* (2nd ed.), (pp. 383–468). Pretoria: Kagiso.

Tlou, S. (2000, July). *The girl child and AIDS: The impact of secondary caregiving in rural girls in Botswana* (Abstract No. ThOrD690). Paper presented at the XIIIth International AIDS Conference, Durban.

True terror of AIDS. (1997). *Update: The Journal of Continuing Education for General Practitioners, 12*(7), 152.

Ulin, P.R. (1992). African women and AIDS: Negotiating behavioural change. *Social Science and Medicine, 34*(1), 63–73.

Ungvarski, P.J. (1989). Nursing management of the adult client. In J.H. Flaskerud (Ed.), *AIDS/HIV infection: A reference guide for nursing professionals* (pp. 74–110). Philadelphia: W.B. Saunders.

United Nations Programme on HIV/AIDS. (1997, October). *Tuberculosis and AIDS*. Geneva: Joint United Nations Programme on HIV/AIDS.

United Nations Programme on HIV/AIDS. (2000a, May). *Caring for carers: Managing stress in those who care for people with HIV and AIDS*. Geneva: Joint United Nations Programme on HIV/AIDS.

United Nations Programme on HIV/AIDS. (2000b, September). *Collaboration with traditional healers in HIV/AIDS prevention and care in sub-Saharan Africa: A literature review*. Geneva: Joint United Nations Programme on HIV/AIDS.

United Nations Programme on HIV/AIDS. (2000c, June). *Report on the global HIV/AIDS epidemic*. Geneva: Joint United Nations Programme on HIV/AIDS.

Update. (1996, June). Provisional public health service recommendations for chemoprophylaxis after occupational exposure to HIV. *Morbidity and Mortality Weekly Report, 45*(22), 463–467.

Van Arkel, J. de J. (Ed.). (1991). *Living in an AIDS culture*. Pretoria: University of South Africa.

Van den Boom, F.M. (1995). The death of a parent. In L. Sherr (Ed.), *Grief and AIDS* (pp. 145–160). Chichester: John Wiley.

Van Dyk, A.C. (1991). *Voorkoming van VIGS: Psigo-sosiale voorspellers van houdings, gedrag en gedragsverandering*. Unpublished doctoral thesis, University of South Africa, Pretoria.

Van Dyk, A.C. (1999). *AIDS care and counselling*. Cape Town: Maskew Miller Longman.

Van Dyk, A.C., Johnson, P., Nefale, M. & Nel, J.A. (2000). *HIV/AIDS Management and counselling: A training manual for the Gauteng Department of Social Services and Population Development*. Pretoria: Unisa Centre for Applied Psychology.

Van Dyk, P.J. (2000). *A brief history of creation*. Pretoria: University of South Africa.

Van Wyk, C. (2000, March). *The legal aspects of AIDS*. Paper presented at the Unisa Centre for Applied Psychology, Pretoria.

Van Zyl, D.A. (1990). Psychoneuroimmunology. In M. Visser (Ed.), *Health psychology in South Africa* (pp. 59–62). Pretoria: HSRC.

Verkragters 'is in ons skole'. (2000, October 7). *Beeld*, 2.

Vigs-aanmeldingsplan laat vaar. (2001, January 12). *Beeld*, 4.

Viljoen, H.G. (1997). Eastern and African perspectives. In W.F. Meyer, C. Moore & H.G. Viljoen. (Eds.), *Personology: From individual to ecosystem* (pp. 591–627). Johannesburg: Heinemann.

Visagie, C.J. (1999). *HIV/AIDS: The complete story of HIV and AIDS*. Pretoria: J.L. van Schaik.

Wainberg, M.A. (2000, July). *Are we closer to a successful microbicide?* Paper presented at the XIIIth International AIDS Conference, Durban.

Wallston, K.A., Wallston, B.S. & De Vellis, R. (1978). Development of the multidimensional health locus of control (MHLC) scales. *Health Education Monographs, 6*(2), 160–170.

Walsh, M.E. & Bibace, R. (1990). Developmentally-based AIDS/HIV education. *Journal of School Health, 60*(6), 256–261.

Walters, J.L., Canady, R. & Stein, T. (1994). Evaluating multicultural approaches in HIV/AIDS education material. *AIDS Education and Prevention, 6*(5), 446–453.

Watts, J. (1988). Breaking the AIDS taboo. *The Illustrated London News, 7082*(276), 26–32.

Weber, J.N. & Weiss, R.A. (1988). HIV infection: The cellular picture. *Scientific American, 259*(4), 81–87.

Whiteside, A. & Sunter, C. (2000). *AIDS: The challenge for South Africa*. Cape Town: Human & Rousseau Tafelberg.

Williams, A.F. (1972). Factors associated with seat belt use in families. *Journal of Safety Research, 4*(3), 133–138.

Wong, D.L., Hockenberry-Eaton, M., Wilson, D., Winkelstein, M.L., Ahmann, E. & DiVito-Thomas, P.A. (1999). *Whaley & Wong's nursing care of infants and children* (6th ed.). St Louis: Mosby.

Worden, J.W. (1982). *Grief counselling and grief therapy*. London: Tavistock Publishers.

World Health Organization. (1988a). *Guidelines on sterilization and high-level disinfection methods effective against human immunodeficiency virus (HIV)* (AIDS Series No. 2). Geneva: World Health Organization.

World Health Organization. (1988b). *Guidelines for nursing management of people infected with human immunodeficiency virus (HIV)* (AIDS Series No. 3). Geneva: World Health Organization.

World Health Organization. (1990a). *Guidelines on AIDS and first aid in the workplace* (AIDS Series No. 7). Geneva: World Health Organization.

World Health Organization. (1990b). *Guidelines for counselling about HIV infection and disease* (AIDS Series No. 8). Geneva: World Health Organization.

World Health Organization. (1993). *AIDS home care handbook*. Geneva: World Health Organization.

World Health Organization. (2000a). *Fact sheets on HIV/AIDS: A desktop reference*. Geneva: World Health Organization.

World Health Organization. (2000b). *Principles on antiretroviral therapy*. Retrieved September 20, 2000, from the World Wide Web: http://www.who.int/HIV_AIDS/WHO_HSI_200 0.04_1.04/001.htm

Wyatt, H.V. (1989). Ambiguities and scares in education material about AIDS. *AIDS education and prevention, 1*(2), 119–125.

Yamba, C.B. (1997). Cosmologies in turmoil: Witchfinding and AIDS in Chiawa, Zambia. *Africa, 67*(2), 200–223.

Zazayokwe, M. (1989). *Some barriers to education about AIDS in the black community*. Paper presented at an AIDS training course of the South African Institute for Medical Research, Johannesburg.

# Index

# Index

# Index

# Index